Social work perspectives on human behaviour

Social work perspectives on human behaviour

Margarete Parrish

Rawat Publications
Jaipur • New Delhi • Bangalore • Hyderabad • Guwahati

ISBN 978-81-316-0552-3

First Indian Reprint, 2012

First published in 2010 by Open University Press, McGraw-Hill Education, McGraw-Hill House, Shoppenhangers Road, Maidenhead, Berkshire, England, SL6 2QL.

Permission for this edition was arranged through Open International Publishing Limited.

Published by
Prem Rawat for **Rawat Publications**
Satyam Apts., Sector 3, Jawahar Nagar, Jaipur - 302 004 (India)
Phone: 0141 265 1748 / 7006 Fax: 0141 265 1748
E-mail : info@rawatbooks.com
Website: www.rawatbooks.com

New Delhi Office
4858/24, Ansari Road, Daryaganj, New Delhi 110 002
Phone: 011-23263290

Also at *Bangalore, Hyderabad* and *Guwahati*

Printed at Chaman Enterprises, New Delhi.

Contents

List of figures xi
List of tables xiii
Acknowledgements xv

Introduction 1
What is behaviour? 1
Relevance for social work 1
A bio-psychosocial perspective 2
Overview of the book 3
Organization of the book 3

1 The role played by theory in understanding behaviour 4
Theories' relevance for social work 4
Necessary components of a theory 7
The functions of theory 8
Implications for practice 9
Criticisms of a theoretical framework to inform practice 12
Questions 12

PART I
Biological Dimensions of Human Behaviour 13

2 Biological and medical influences on behaviour 15
Relevance for social work 15
The bio-psychosocial model 16
The medical model of understanding illness, disease and disability 18
Some basic genetic concepts 18
A bio-psychosocial approach to illness, disease and disability 23
The strengths perspective 24
Variables related to stress 26
The diathesis–stress model 26
Criticisms and shortcomings of the medical model 27
Overview of some specific conditions with which social workers are likely to need familiarity 28
Questions 29

3 Developmental models and considerations 30
Relevance for social work 30
Ante-natal factors 31
Pregnancy 31
The foetal period 33
Prematurity 34
Birth weight 34
Newborns 35
Post-natal depression 35
Infancy 36
Failure to thrive 38
Temperament 38
Fears 39
Toddlers 39
Early childhood 40
Middle childhood 41
Adolescence 42
Sexual orientation 44
Young adulthood 46
Middle and late adulthood 46
Implications for practice 47
Questions 47

PART II
Psychological Dimensions of Human Behaviour 49

4 Freud's psychoanalytic and Erikson's developmental theories of behaviour 51
Relevance for social work 51
Freud's historical background 52
Key psychoanalytic concepts 52
Freud's topographical concept of the mind 55
Freud's structural concept 56
Defence mechanisms 57
The developmental constructs of Sigmund Freud 58
Freud's psychosexual stages 59
Erikson's historical background 62
Key concepts of Erikson's psychosocial theory: the life cycle 63
Erikson's life stages of development 64
Criticisms and debates regarding psychoanalytic and Eriksonian perspectives 71
Implications for practice 72
Questions 73

5 Neo-Freudian or ego psychology perspectives 76
Relevance for social work 76
Historical background 77
Key concepts 77
Object relations theory 82
Transactional analysis 83
Historical contributors 83
Implications for practice 94
Criticisms and debates regarding ego psychology and neo-Freudian perspectives 95
Questions 97

6 Behaviourism 98
Relevance for social work 98
Historical background 99
Key concepts 102
Classical conditioning 103
Operant conditioning 104
Implications for practice 106
Criticisms and debates about behaviourism 107
Questions 107

7 Cognition and theories of learning 110
Relevance for social work 110
Historical background 111
Key concepts of cognition and learning 113
Bandura and the learning of aggression 121
Bandura and self-efficacy 122
Learned helplessness theory 122
Role theory 123
Attribution theory 124
Some basic ideas about intelligence 126
Howard Gardner's theory of multiple intelligences 126
A widening cognitive-behavioural perspective 128
Implications for practice 130
Criticisms and shortcomings of cognitive models 131
Questions 132

8 Humanist and existentialist perspectives on behaviour 134
Relevance for social work 134
Historical background of humanism 135
Key concepts of humanism 136
Historical contributors to existentialism 141
Key concepts of existentialism 143
Implications for practice 145

Criticisms and debates regarding humanism and existentialism 147
Questions 148

9 Influences of trauma on behaviour 150
Relevance for social work 150
Key concepts related to child maltreatment 151
Domestic violence 157
Sexual assault (rape) 160
Traumatic bereavement 162
Implications for practice 163
Questions 167

10 Influences of mental health, alcohol, and other drugs on behaviour 170
Relevance for social work 170
Historical considerations 172
Key concepts regarding mental health 174
Specific types of mental health conditions 177
Suicide 191
Substance misuse and dependence 192
Implications for practice 196
Questions 199

PART III
Social Dimensions of Behaviour 201

11 Systems theory, ecosystems and personal-cultural-social (PCS) perspectives 203
Relevance for social work 203
Historical contributors to systems theory and ecosystems perspectives 204
Key concepts of systems theory 206
Key concepts of ecosystems 209
Key PCS concepts 211
Implications for practice 214
Criticisms and shortcomings of systems, ecosystems and PCS perspectives 216
Questions 217

12 Families and family systems 220
Relevance for social work 220
Historic contributions to social work perspectives on working with families 221
Key concepts about families, family functions, and family systems 223
Family systems 225

Communication 227
Reciprocity, relationships and roles 228
Changing family demographic patterns 232
Divorce and family disruption 232
Lone parenting 235
'Blended' families 236
Fostering and adoptive families 236
Diverse family forms 239
Families with alcohol- and drug-related problems 240
Bereavement 241
Genograms 243
Implications for practice 244
Criticisms and shortcomings of family theory 247
Questions 248

13 Feminist perspectives on behaviour 250
Relevance for social work 250
Historical background 251
Key concepts of feminism 253
Women and poverty 254
Feminism and the family 255
Women and crime 256
Women and domestic violence 257
Feminism and mental health concerns 259
Feminist perspectives on sexual violence 259
Feminist approaches to practice 260
Criticisms and shortcomings of feminist perspectives 261
Questions 262

14 Theories of sociological and socio-economic influences on behaviour 264
Relevance for social work 264
Historical background 265
Key concepts 267
The distribution of resources 270
The role of poverty related to access to resources 271
Criticisms and shortcomings of Marxist theory 272
Implications for practice 273
Questions 273

Bibliography 275
Index 297

List of figures

2.1	The biological, psychological, social model	17
6.1	Basic classical conditioning concepts	103
8.1	Maslow's hierarchy of needs	140
9.1	The power and control wheel of domestic violence	159
10.1	A continuum of mood states	178
10.2	Biological, psychological and social factors relating to depression	179
10.3	An example of a letter written by a woman with paranoid schizophrenia, which she photocopied and distributed by the hundreds throughout a courthouse	188
11.1	A diagram of systems and subsystems	207
11.2	An ecomap for Jim	215
12.1	Commonly used genogram symbols	244
12.2	The Freud family genogram	245

List of tables

2.1 Dominant recessive genetic traits 19
2.2 Continuum between medical model and strengths perspective 25
2.3 Examples of predisposing and protective factors associated with mental health problems 27
3.1 Developmental aspects of responsiveness and expression 37
4.1 Psychoanalytic defence mechanisms 58
4.2 Comparison of Freudian and Eriksonian stages of development 65
4.3 Erikson's later psychosocial stages 67
5.1 Ego functions 78
5.2 Stages in the formation of attachment 80
5.3 Examples of basic responses to infants' distress 81
5.4 Margaret Mahler's stages of separation–individuation 92
6.1 Examples of consequences of reinforcements and punishments 105
7.1 Piaget's stages of cognitive development and moral development 118
7.2 Kohlberg's stages of moral development 120
7.3 Some internal and external attributes associated with causation 125
7.4 Howard Gardner's types of intelligence 127
10.1 Medical, social, and bio-psychosocial perspectives 172
10.2 Drugs, categories and consequences of usage 195
11.1 Acute and chronic dimensions of stress across the PCS framework 213

Acknowledgements

As with most books, this book's author's name alone does not suffice to acknowledge all those who contributed to its coming into existence. To my dear friends Angela Allen, Caroline Burry, and Judi Foster, I wish to express my thanks for your encouragement, enthusiasm, patience and proof reading. To my mentors and role models, Harry Bates, Miriam Dinerman, Jim Gaudin, and the late Eileen Corrigan, Norman Polansky, and Julian Stanley, I wish to express my sincere appreciation for the inspiration you provided me over the years. I am indebted to my stepson and grandson, Nigel and James Warwick, for their invaluable technical support, which far exceeded the 'call of duty'. I wish to express my gratitude to my brave and clever neighbour, Mark Kay, for his combined kindness and computer wizardry in times of crisis.

Most of all, I wish to express my profound gratitude to my dear husband, Malcolm Warwick, for his tremendous support, patience, and good humour throughout two years during which writing this book often took precedence over domestic arrangements, meals, and holidays. I also wish to express my lifelong thankfulness to my beloved parents, whose love and support protected me despite some of my own behaviours. To my extended family, friends, and students, I am grateful for your patience and encouragement. I hope this book lives up to the support all of you have provided me.

Introduction

The ability to observe and understand people's behaviour is an essential component of effective social work practice. For most people choosing to study social work, the subject of human behaviour represents an endlessly fascinating area, because of an innate interest in people and their 'stories'. Thus, while behaviour often entails a great deal of variety and complexity, it remains an intriguing means of understanding people, and a natural source of interest for students of social work.

This book is intended to provide social work students with a wide basis of perspectives on human behaviour on which to build their professional understanding and responses, along with an enhanced appreciation of some of the circumstances that shape behaviour. It stems from over 20 years of teaching social work, both in the US and the UK, which has provided a range of students with and from whom I have had the privilege to learn about behaviour.

What is behaviour?

The discussion of behaviour entails a complex array of patterns and differences. Behaviour has been defined as 'the sum total of the psyche that includes impulses, motivations, wishes, drives, instincts, and cravings, as expressed by a person's behaviour or motor activity' (Sadock & Sadock, 2007: 274). Behaviours range from measurable, observable manifestations of our internal states, to impulsive reactions to fear or pain, to intentional or unintentional responses to an array of factors. Those factors may include age, gender, health, socio-economic circumstances, sexual orientation, and intellectual differences, among others. The following chapters are intended to enhance readers' understanding of various theories and frameworks used by social workers to interpret and assess people's behaviours.

Relevance for social work

By entering a profession that requires high levels of astute observation and listening skills, social work students have undertaken a demanding task. Current social, political and economic factors are contributing to an array of challenges facing social workers; the assessment and intervention skills required of social workers are increasingly complex. To understand people's behaviour, social workers still rely on being able to establish sufficient relationships with them in order to ask the right questions to inform their best practice. Being sufficiently trusted to be told people's personal stories is a great privilege, which is often more earned than given. This book has been written in the hopes of contributing to that process.

Since preparation for entering the profession of social work in the UK now entails studying at a university degree level, the need for social workers to possess an academically sound grasp of human behaviour has become increasingly apparent. This book addresses those concepts from a bio-psychosocial framework. Consequently, this book begins with some of the biological, medical and developmental concerns that relate to the biological dimension of understanding behaviour, before proceeding to the consideration of psychological and social or environmental dimensions.

This book has been written with a genuine hope that its readers find the topic of human behaviour as fascinating as the author does, and that reading this book will contribute to students' effective social work practice when working with people with complex behaviours and difficulties. It has been written as a review of some very broad and complex concepts in the expectation that readers will find their appetites whetted for learning more about those concepts. To do so, readers are urged to explore the original texts cited in the references upon which this book relies.

A bio-psychosocial perspective

This book approaches the study of behaviour from a bio-psychosocial perspective. By using that perspective, the book is intended to address the ways in which multiple dimensions integrate to influence behaviour, through considering the three different dimensions: biological, psychological and social. For the purposes of organization, those dimensions are divided into the larger categories of biological factors (medical, as well as developmental and gender), psychological factors (such as theories that address how and what people think, as well as conditions that influence people's mental health), and social (or environmental) factors. These factors include concepts and theories that provide ways of interpreting behaviour. In the chapter on mental health conditions, readers will note that the criteria from the DSM IV-T-R are used as indicators of distress because of the clinical consistency and objectivity of those criteria.

The chapters all follow the same general format, which includes a discussion of the theory's relevance to social work, historical contributions to the theory's development, key concepts associated with the theory, implications for practice, and some criticisms of and debates about the theory. Each chapter is followed by some questions and exercises for students to consider individually or as discussion exercises with classmates.

Overview of the book

The book is divided into three parts: Part I Biological Dimensions of Behaviour; Part II Psychological Dimensions of Behaviour; and Part III Social Dimensions of Behaviour. The chapters address the following theories, perspectives and concepts:

1 The role played by theory in understanding behaviour

Part I Biological Dimensions of Human Behaviour:

2 Biological and medical influences on behaviour
3 Developmental models and considerations

Part II Psychological Dimensions of Human Behaviour:

4 Freud's psychoanalytic and Erikson's developmental theories of behaviour
5 Neo-Freudian or ego psychology perspectives
6 Behaviourism
7 Cognition and theories of learning
8 Humanist and existentialist perspectives on behaviour
9 Influences of trauma on behaviour
10 Influences of mental health, alcohol, and other drugs on behaviour

Part III Social Dimensions of Behaviour:

11 Systems theory, ecosystems and personal-cultural-social (PCS) perspectives
12 Families and family systems
13 Feminist perspectives on behaviour
14 Theories of sociological and socio-economic influences on behaviour

Organization of the book

Some readers may be puzzled to find chapters about medical and developmental influences preceding those on psychological and social dimensions covered in a social work text book. I hope the logic of the bio-psychosocial framework makes the organization of the chapters self-explanatory. As readers will come to realize from subsequent chapters, the order of the chapters is not chosen out of any deference to the medical model, or to imply any emphasis, so much as to adhere to the logic of the wording of the bio-psychosocial framework. All three dimensions (bio-, psycho-, and social) are considered equally vital, and mutually enhancing. As with visual representations, without all three dimensions, the whole picture would be diminished.

1 The role played by theory in understanding behaviour

Social work practice is increasingly expected to justify itself according to a basis of supportive evidence, which may make the prospect of approaching practice according to theory seem unnecessary, or even frivolous. A sound theoretical base of understanding human behaviour is anything but frivolous, however. This chapter is devoted to considering the role of theory as it applies to the ways in which social workers interpret (and respond to) human behaviour. The premise is that, without a sound theoretical underpinning, social work practice would be based on guesswork, which is a singularly ill-informed way of working with people.

The theories used by social workers are not necessarily unique to the profession. Historically, social workers have used, 'borrowed', and adapted theories that originated in other disciplines, most notably psychology and sociology, along with medicine and biology. The ways in which social workers apply theory, however, are often unique to their practice. That distinction relates to the ways in which social workers apply theories according to how they understand people in the context of their unique circumstances. Thus, social work's contextual emphasis may alter the way in which some theories are applied. So while social workers' application of theories may not be in accordance with some 'purist' approaches, it nonetheless remains theoretically informed and grounded.

Theories' relevance for social work

The terms 'theory' and 'theoretical' have often been used to denote highly abstract, and possibly irrelevant concepts. In some cases, 'theoretical' has an almost derogatory connotation. While some theories rely on fairly abstract concepts, for academic and professional purposes, theories are profoundly relevant because they provide a frame of reference within which to interpret people's behaviour. Theory provides systematic ways of observing, questioning, and interpreting behaviours so that social workers have a conceptual infrastructure of how they conduct assessments and justify their practice. The use of theory reflects a level of rational, systematic thinking that distinguishes social work practice from personal opinion.

Because human behaviour is very complex, the theories used to explain it must be sufficiently complex to be useful. That does not mean that those theories provide absolute, iron-clad explanations that are universally sufficient, but that those theories are reliably applicable. For social workers, the various theories of personality and development provide a means of organizing observations and details of people's behaviour and circumstances in ways that contribute to forming an assessment, which in turn informs what needs to happen next in order to meet people's needs. In doing so, theory can save the practitioner considerable time and energy, which might otherwise be spent 'reinventing the wheel' every time they are called upon to conduct an assessment. As Kurt Lewin is reported to have said, 'There is nothing so practical as a good theory' (Polansky, 1991: 2).

An example of how social workers depend on theory to inform practice can be found in the following scenario:

> 'Eve' (age 21) has a history of learning disabilities, and her first two babies were removed from her care because they were found to be at risk of abuse and neglect. Eve is in a new partnership with a much older man with a history of violence toward women, and who is actively heroin dependent. They have had a baby, who was born prematurely. The baby has respiratory problems, and is on an apnoea monitor. Eve is a heavy drinker. When you arrive at her flat, you find her nearly unconscious from intoxication, with a lit cigarette in her hand. Her partner has taken their baby to the pub, leaving the baby's formula, apnoea monitor, and blanket behind.

Eve's situation poses some difficult and potentially painful decisions for a social worker. Theory would inform a social worker's interpretations of Eve's circumstances in ways that would influence practice. Examples of theoretic approaches include the following:

- Cognitive theories could be applied to explain Eve's capacity to understand consequences of past and present behaviour.

  What can we expect Eve to understand?

- Behavioural theories could be applied to explain how some problematic behaviours come to be repeated.

  What reinforces Eve's involvement with her partner?

- Psychodynamic theory could be applied to interpret ways in which Eve's defence mechanisms may be functioning.

  What role does denial play in her appraisal of her situation?

- Developmental theories could be applied to understanding both Eve's and the baby's life stages and developmental needs.

  Is Eve functioning as a young adult, and is she able to appreciate the developmental needs of her infant?

- Theories regarding substance use/misuse/dependency that address the irrational continuation of usage, despite negative consequences, could be applied.

  Is Eve drinking as a means of self-medication?
  Is Eve genetically predisposed to misuse alcohol?

- Attachment theory could be applied to understand the baby's emotional needs and the potential risks if those needs go unmet.

  Is Eve capable of prioritizing her infant's needs, and of providing a consistent, reliable presence that promotes emotional security?

- Social learning theory that could help explain how Eve's lack of a positive role model has contributed to her current difficulties.

  Has Eve ever experienced sober, reliable, appropriate parenting?

- Learned helplessness theory could be applied to help explain Eve's sense of being destined to be in demeaning, dangerous partnerships.

  Does Eve perceive herself as only deserving abusive treatment?

- Feminist theory could be applied to appreciate the implications of Eve's upbringing and expectations, and her financial dependence on men, regardless of how they exploit her.

  Has Eve ever been empowered to be autonomous, or to feel positive about her role in the world as a woman?

- Systems theory may be applied to understand the role played by Eve's family of origin and social networks, and how they contribute to her frame of reference.

  Does Eve's family of origin, in which she was consistently physically and sexually abused, place her at risk of repeating some of those patterns of raising a family?
  Does living in a neighbourhood in which violence and crime are prevalent make her and her infant more vulnerable?

While the examples of relevant theories clearly do not provide a solution to any of Eve's problems in and of themselves, they can provide the social worker with useful frameworks with which to interpret (and assess) Eve's situation in such a way that the social worker's response can be focused constructively. The use of theory serves to protect Eve from being subjected to a social worker practising without a theoretical framework, which would potentially require having to reinvent an approach to assessment with every service user they meet.

If her social worker relied on a single model or theory to explain Eve's circumstances, the resulting assessment could prove woefully inadequate. Eve's social worker's theoretical perspective (and the breadth of that perspective) will potentially shape everything from how he or she refers to Eve (e.g., as a 'patient' vs. a 'service user', or 'client'), to how the social worker defines Eve's difficulties. The social worker's theoretical perspective will also shape the intervention that occurs in response to their assessment of Eve's difficulties.

Social work's theoretical knowledge base is broadened by its adaptation of theories from other disciplines. Some of those adaptations have been the results of practice wisdom; others have evolved over time. All served the purpose of providing specifically applicable frameworks with which to inform social work practice. To quote Coulshed (1991: 8), 'Theoryless practice does not exist; we cannot avoid looking for explanations to guide our actions, whilst research has shown that those agencies which profess not to use theory offer a non problem solving, wooly and directionless service.'

Since the 1970s, social work has increasingly relied on 'systems theory' as a means of viewing people in the context of their environment (Zastrow & Kirst-Ashman, 1994). While systems theory does not preclude concepts from the medical model or psychodynamic theories being simultaneously applied, it provides a theoretical framework that is generally congruent with social work's values and ethics regarding the role played by people's context. Systems theory is an example of a theory that explains behaviours and interactions, without entailing an explicit set of guidelines for practice. *Explanatory* theories are focused more on development and behaviour (e.g. Erikson's life cycle, Maslow's hierarchy of needs, systems theory, attachment theory), while others are more focused on practice (e.g. Carl Rogers' client-centred theory, and crisis intervention theory). Some theories apply both to interpreting behaviours and to shaping practice (psychodynamic and cognitive-behavioural theories are but two examples). Social workers must understand the appropriate role of theories, and how and when they apply to practice.

The ongoing effort to match theory and practice is actually a reciprocal arrangement, as theory must apply to good practice, just as good practice must reflect sound theory. That equation is not necessarily easily established.

> Theory cannot provide simple answers which tell us 'how to do' practice. Theory can only guide and inform. Theory, practice and the relationship between them are all far too complex for there to be a clear, simple and unambiguous path for practitioners to follow. Theory provides us with the cloth from which to tailor our garment, it does not provide 'off the peg' solutions to practice problems.
>
> (Thompson, 2005: 69)

Necessary components of a theory

A theory comprises a structured set of hypotheses, principles and concepts that serve to explain a given set of phenomena or events. The theory's concepts are based on ideas or observations that are not necessarily provable. The terms and principles used to explain the theory are called *constructs*. The person who developed or created the theory is a *theorist*.

A theory's constructs must be interrelated; they need to be logically consistent and congruent with one another. In that way, the theory provides a coherent framework to organize observations of the relevant factors, by generalizing across them in ways that contribute to the capacity to use the theory to predict future events or phenomena. By doing so, a theory provides a world-view through which the observer can interpret their observations. A theory provides a means of generalizing observations; theories and observations are typically mutually complementary. In order to explain and predict why various phenomena occur, a theory needs to be based on empirically tested or testable principles.

Theories and observations are linked through the basic processes of *induction* and *deduction*. The inductive process entails reasoning based on developing general principles by moving from specific observations to the more general. The deductive process entails drawing specific conclusions by moving from a set of general principles to the more specific. In the scientific tradition, deductions serve to derive a *hypothesis*. A hypothesis (sometimes called an educated guess) is a statement describing a proposed relationship between variables. If that hypothesis is based on theory, then it can be evaluated through the process of conducting further observations and tests.

Some theories are used solely for purposes of classification. For social workers, theories necessarily involve more concepts than classification. Theories ideally are *dynamic*, comprising sets of predictions. By having a sense of causation, theories contribute to social workers being able to anticipate consequences. A dynamic theory is *predictive*.

A good theory also embodies the principle of *parsimony*, which means that it is able to cover the largest range of observations with the fewest possible principles. Parsimony is the way in which the 'less is more' principle is applied to intellectual concepts. In the interests of parsimony, 'simple' really is 'elegant'.

Simultaneously, a good theory is sufficiently *comprehensive* to address a wide array of circumstances. Given the complexity of human behaviour, social workers necessarily rely on theories that have sufficient breadth to address those complexities in an effective manner.

As noted by Polansky (1991: 5), good theories are *concise*; they are sufficiently complex to explain complex concepts, while being sufficiently simple to be remembered and applied correctly. Theories do not have to be adjusted according to which service user a social worker is assessing, but are equally applicable across varied circumstances. Parsimony refers to the reliance on the simplest explanation available, and is sometimes also referred to as *Occam's razor*, after the English philosopher who initially proposed it as an approach to scientific study. Occam's razor is briefly summarized by the premise that the fewer assumptions a theory makes, the better (Gross, 2001).

The functions of theory

For social workers, the primary function of theory is to inform practice. Theory provides ways of understanding people's behaviour that describe, explain and predict. Assessments are necessarily informed by a social worker's theoretical perspectives. For example, if a social worker were to subscribe to the theory that blames Eve for being a moral failure of the worst degree, then that assessment will necessarily shape their assessment and its results. Similarly, if the social worker subscribes to a theory that incorporate Eve's cognitive limitations, her having had a traumatic childhood, along with her living in an oppressive society with a series of exploitative partners, in which she has found alcohol and tobacco to be useful coping strategies, then the social worker's assessment will result in a very different outcome for Eve and her child.

Explanatory theories provide a means of describing why various factors have occurred or resulted in related consequences. Practice theories relate to how specific interventions are best suited (or not) to specific problems.

Aside from theories, *models* describe what occurs in the course of practice in a general way, and applies to a wide range of situations. Models provide a system of classification that facilitates a systematic, pragmatic and concise description and explanation in the interest of consistency in practice (Clark, 1995).

Perspectives tend to reflect professional disciplines' approaches to such complexities as human behaviour. For example, social work perspectives on human behaviour are necessarily reflective of theoretical factors as well as the profession's values and ethics, along with the evidence provided through research and practice wisdom.

Approaches provide perspectives that are not as specific as a theory and which generally embrace two or more distinguishable theories. The components of an approach share some level of congruence, or compatible assumptions or principles. For example, the approaches considered in this text all pertain to understanding facets of people's behaviour.

Implications for practice

The use of theory informs the ways in which social workers interpret people's behaviours and circumstances. Theory also informs the way in which social workers intervene to help people overcome difficulties. The explanatory theories that social workers use inform the selection of practice theory, because they must be congruent in order to provide coherent services. The way a social worker approaches practice will vary according to their theoretical perspectives. A social worker who employs a psychodynamic theoretical perspective will respond to Eve's situation in a very different way from a colleague whose approach is based more on social learning and systems theories.

Social workers tend to apply *microsystems* theories to explain and anticipate the circumstances related to individuals and their immediate environments. *Macrosystems* theories apply to explaining the larger society, and entail ways of looking at the ways in which organizations and governments contribute to the individual's difficulties. Social workers are often in a unique position to intervene on both the micro- and macro-levels. (See Chapter 14 for further discussion of micro- and macro-systems concepts.)

Sometimes social workers are called upon to make use of a medical model when interacting with medical or mental health settings. Being 'fluent' in the medical model is sometimes crucial for the sake of advocating for service users who are recipients of medical or psychiatric services. Social workers sometimes struggle with the authoritarian aspects of the medical model, and its emphasis on diagnostics and 'cures'. Being able to navigate and negotiate with that model does not necessitate social workers' abandoning the integrity of their own theoretical perspectives. It may, however, necessitate the professional equivalent of being 'bilingual' in being able to understand both perspectives simultaneously.

As critical thinkers, social workers must consider an array of factors when evaluating a theory's suitability for application to their assessments and practice. Those factors include (but are not limited to) the theory's actual applicability, its empirical validity, and its value base. Most social workers utilize an 'eclectic' blend of theories, but doing so is not as easy as just 'cherry picking' what suits for the sake of convenience. Being eclectic necessitates considerable finesse in being able to apply components of a number of theories in ways that are consistent and informed.

When evaluating a theory's applicability, social workers must consider whether the theory's principles are suited to understanding and/or responding to their service user's circumstances. Several examples of applicable theories have been mentioned earlier:

- Beginning with systems theory, a social worker could consider whether Eve's family and social supports are positive, and whether she has anyone to whom she can turn in times of crisis. Does social isolation place Eve at risk of greater exploitation and danger from her partner?
  - If so, then good practice would address her isolation. It would also encourage changed behaviours on her part, to include more positive social interactions, and use of available resources.
- By applying the social learning theory, a social worker could consider whether Eve's lacking a sober role model has contributed to her current difficulties. Especially if Eve has never experienced sober, reliable, appropriate parenting, then the prospects of being such a parent may be profoundly challenging.
  - If that is the case, then good practice would address her need for healthy relationships to model 'good enough parenting'. This approach would also look at helping Eve make manageable changes in her parenting skills.
- By applying the self-medication hypothesis to Eve's drinking, a social worker would consider whether Eve's drinking helps her cope, and whether without it she might find her circumstances even more unbearable than they already are. Particularly when Eve's learning disability may compromise her appraisal of her circumstances, her drinking may seem a source of comfort to her.
  - If so, then good practice would address her drinking in a way that would not use ultimatums, but rather help her understand some of the negative consequences of her drinking, especially in relation to her baby. Helping Eve find ways of moderating her drinking, or 'harm reduction', would be a viable consideration.
- By applying learned helplessness theory, a social worker would explore whether Eve perceives herself as being destined to be in demeaning, dangerous partnerships.

  - If so, then good practice would address Eve's sense of herself, and explore ways in which she deserves to be treated respectfully by all concerned. This approach would utilize Eve's strengths as a way of reinforcing her self-esteem.
- By applying psychoanalytic theory, a social worker could explore ways in which Eve's defence mechanisms may be contributing to her difficulties, including such factors as the role of denial in her appraisal of her situation.
  - If so, then Eve's denial of the seriousness of her situation needs to be addressed in ways that are reality-based without being overwhelming. This can be a very delicate balance.

Alternatively, other aspects of psychoanalytic theory could be questioned as to their suitability to Eve. Depending on the particular emphasis and focus of the social worker, some elements of psychodynamic theory could be considered unsuitable when working with Eve.

- By applying psychoanalytic concepts from Freud's topographic concepts (the conscious, the unconscious and the preconscious), a social worker could emphasize the role of the unconscious in Eve's replication of her mother's alcohol dependence. Alternatively, using a psychodynamic approach, a social worker could emphasize Eve's unconscious conflicts with her mother.
  - From a psychoanalytic perspective, Eve could be then referred to a psychoanalytically trained therapist, or for psychoanalysis, which entails a lengthy and often expensive form of insight-orientated therapy. It also typically presumes a cognitive level of understanding that would not necessarily be realistic to expect from Eve.

The complexities of applying a single theory are apparent even from this brief discussion. Especially when applying such a broad and complex ('grand') theory as the psychoanalytic theory, social workers are urged to use caution. Even when some psychoanalytic concepts are readily applicable to an informed assessment, they may not prove relevant or suitable for working with individual cases.

When evaluating a theory's empirical support, social workers are urged to familiarize themselves with both original sources and with current research. Because theories often entail fairly abstract concepts, research is not necessarily going to establish any 'absolute' truths *per se*. Instead, research can provide examples of whether theories are supported through sound research with sufficient numbers to have some validity, and that studies are conducted with the level of rigour to provide confidence in the findings. Such findings will provide empirical or evidence-based support with which to apply the relevant theory.

Finally, when evaluating a theory's value or ethical basis, social workers must consider whether the theory is congruent with social work values and ethics. Specifically, those values and ethics entail social workers' ultimate responsibilities to their service users' best interests, their autonomy, and issues of social justice reflected in anti-oppressive practice. Various socio-economic theories that incorporate advantageous arrangements for the privileged few at the expense of the poor are incongruent with social work values. Theories that discriminate against various groups of people (immigrants, teenagers, gays and lesbians, travellers, etc.) on the basis of their differences or other superficial characteristics are incongruent with social work values and ethics.

Criticisms of a theoretical framework to inform practice

According to some arguments, basic skills are sufficient for social work practice, and thus a theoretical framework is superfluous. From such a perspective, technical competence and familiarity with the law would suffice, making a theoretical orientation unnecessarily complicated. The argument against theory is sometimes couched in ideas such as the sufficiency of 'common sense' (which is a legendarily variable commodity) for effective social work. Sometimes it is absorbed into the will to be helpful being sufficient for social work practice. Such a perspective is more congruent with the approach of a 'streetwise practitioner' than of a professionally trained practitioner. As anyone who has read the preceding pages will have noticed, that perspective is incongruent with the content of this book.

Questions

1 What are the differences between inductive and deductive reasoning?

2 What would be some theoretical perspectives that are incongruent with social work?

3 What do you consider the main differences between a theory and a model? Most of us are constructing or employing theories of our own, or borrowing from others, on a regular basis. What are some theories that you have used to explain or predict the following?
   (a) Do you do your best work ahead of time, or under pressure?
   (b) Is it better to read the assigned readings before lectures or after?
   (c) Is it better to ask the lecturer questions when you don't understand what they've said, or check with a classmate later to see if they understood it (hoping that they did)?
   (d) If you do well on an assignment, is it because you worked hard, or because it was easy?

4 What theoretical perspectives do you consider most relevant to social work practice? Why? (Hint: It's OK to be undecided for now!)

PART I

Biological Dimensions of Human Behaviour

2 Biological and medical influences on behaviour

In this chapter, biological and physical conditions that influence people's behaviour will be considered. From a social work perspective, medical conditions form an important contextual consideration for understanding people's behaviour and circumstances. The strengths model will be considered, as it applies to ways in which social workers are likely to interpret and respond to people's conditions related to medical and other difficulties. Unlike the medical model, social work also emphasizes personal and environmental aspects that influence and are influenced by physical conditions as well as the actual conditions in order to understand the individual more fully.

Relevance for social work

The ways in which social workers approach the assessment of people's needs necessarily entail both the individual and their circumstances. When their circumstances include various medical conditions, social workers must consider ways in which support can be provided to maximize the person's well-being, and to support ways in which suffering can be minimized for all concerned. In order to do so, social workers often need to familiarize themselves with medical conditions that far exceed the parameters of this book.

Using an approach that emphasizes the ways in which a person's humanity and strengths outweigh their illness or condition is an important facet of social work practice. For example, in referring to people with various conditions, social workers typically refer to the person first, and the illness second. Thus, social workers are more likely to refer to 'people with diabetes', rather than 'diabetics', and 'people living with HIV/AIDS', rather than 'AIDS patients'. Thus social work characteristically emphasizes the person, rather than the condition or pathology as a primary focus. Likewise, terms such as 'handicapped' have become antiquated, in part because of the association with going 'cap in hand', or begging for charity.

Effective social work practice entails understanding the importance of the relationships a person with a life-altering condition has with those people around them.

How those people understand and respond to the condition, and their capacity to provide constructive support are also part of social work's perspective on the person's well-being. Similarly, social workers' understanding and responses to life-altering conditions comprise the core of establishing a helping or therapeutic relationship with those with complex circumstances.

Social work's history of approaching people from a contextual framework dates back to the pioneering work of Mary Richmond (1917). In her seminal book, *Social Diagnosis*, Richmond provided evidence of ways in which early social work practice replicated some aspects of the medical model, but with a clear emphasis on the social sciences as they applied to understanding people's circumstances in their community. Thus, in considering the context in which people's health status is often influenced by factors such as poverty and deprivation, social workers are likely to consider points such as whether people have access to medical care, whether they can read the prescriptions they receive, and whether they have adequate nutrition and rest. Examples of non-medical influences on people's health include factors such as those listed in Box 2.1. In many cases, more than one of the factors listed occur simultaneously.

Box 2.1 Non-medical influences on health

Behavioural risks (alcohol, drugs, unprotected sexual activities)
Dietary inadequacies (malnutrition, or reliance on junk food)
Educational deficits (particularly health education)
Employment-related stressors (bullying, exploitation, harassment, long hours)
Exposure to toxins (poor air quality, asbestos, lead)
Family violence
Housing problems (cold, damp, dangerous, overcrowded)
Institutional racism
Lack or loss of exercise
Lack or loss of transportation to medical care
Language and communication difficulties
Literacy problems, inability to read and comprehend instructions
Poverty
Social isolation, loneliness
Stress
Violence

The bio-psychosocial model

While the relevance of any medical condition is fully recognized in the bio-psychosocial model, the essential premise addresses the simultaneous importance of the psychological and social dimensions of an individual's overall health and well-being. Understanding the overlapping areas of people's biological, psychological and social circumstances is a key aspect of social work assessments. Because good health and good medical care are not evenly distributed throughout society, social workers are often called upon to advocate for people whose health problems are influenced by various environmental factors, including exposure to factors such as those noted in Box 2.1.

Approaching questions of health necessitates consideration of factors well beyond the medical circumstances alone. The World Health Organization defines 'health' as 'a complete state of physical, mental, spiritual and social well-being, and not merely the absence of disease or infirmity' (WHO, 1946). By conceptualizing health in a way that transcends factors of medically defined illness, social workers are better placed to appreciate the contextual influences upon people's health or illness. Especially when people are struggling with various conditions associated with stigma (enuresis, hepatitis, HIV/AIDS), or outward disfigurement (amputations, burns, morbid obesity, paralysis, scoliosis), social workers must be both knowledgeable and capable of anti-oppressive practice with individuals and their support systems.

For most people, medical, psychological, and social dimensions frequently overlap. Focusing on one dimension at the expense of the others is likely to produce an incomplete level of understanding. Focusing on the simultaneous roles played by all three dimensions, however, is likely to focus on the interactive roles played by all three in influencing people's health and responses to illness and disability. Much of social work's effectiveness comes from understanding all three dimensions as well as their overlapping points. The overlap being considered is represented in Figure 2.1.

A bio-psycho-social perspective provides a way in which social workers appreciate the inter-relationships between medical, psychological and social factors in a person's life. For example, for a social worker to understand a person's circumstances from a bio-psychosocial perspective, a patient would not simply be considered 'a 60-year-old heart patient', but also as a 'bereaved 60-year-old woman who was unexpectedly widowed last month, whose 30-year-old daughter with autism lives at home with her'.

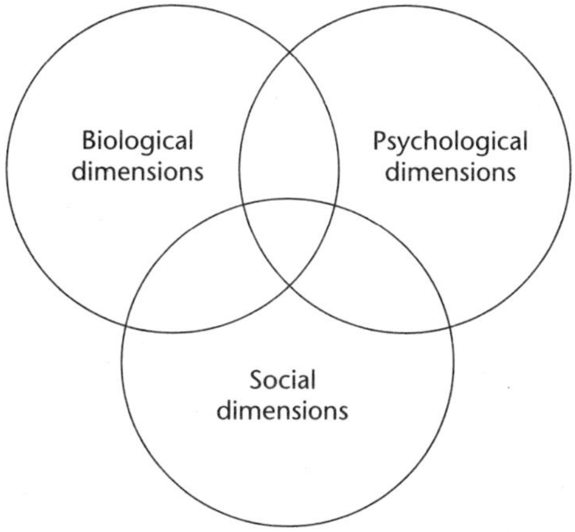

Figure 2.1 The biological, psychological, social model.

The medical model of understanding illness, disease and disability

The key focus of the medical model of understanding illness and disability is based on the premise of some biological abnormality or malfunction, which serves to compromise the individual's health. According to the traditional medical model, that abnormality is generally perceived as impairment, or deficit for the person involved, entailing a comparative inferiority to the general population.

The medical model represents an evolution of mankind's historic efforts to understand and classify individuals and behaviours perceived as differing from the norm. Various examples of such efforts to explain differences have included evil spirits, witchcraft and demonic possession, and an excess of bodily fluids. Typically, such classifications have served to stigmatize and possibly eliminate those who were deemed different. The capacity to make differences fit into medical terms and categories potentially adds considerable authority to such classifications.

While the traditional medical model has operated on the premise of disability entailing inherent deficits, the World Health Organization (2001) has formally redefined its criteria for disability by adopting a new International Classification of Functioning, Disability and Health (ICF). That classification comprises two domains: *Body Functions and Structures*, and *Activities and Participation*. In revising its criteria, the WHO has provided a framework for the various helping professionals to consider multiple domains of functioning, including areas of capability. Such efforts to emphasize wellness and strengths, and the conceptualization of health along a continuum, are generally more congruent with social work values than some traditional aspects of the medical model's emphasis on deficits.

Some basic genetic concepts

Using the term 'genetic' implies an inheritable factor. Sometimes 'genetic' factors refer to conditions or features that are transmitted from parent to child, such as blue eyes or Huntington's disease; sometimes 'genetic' is used to refer to conditions that are present before birth, such as spina bifada, or a club foot. Down's syndrome is an example of a chromosomal abnormality, which occurs during gestation, and would be regarded as a genetic condition.

Current understanding of genetic inheritance dates back to the work of a nineteenth-century Austrian monk, **Gregor Mendel**, who studied genetics by cross-breeding different strains of peas and studying the results of cross-fertilization. The son of a farmer, Mendel was eager to understand the process of crossing different strains of plants to produce new varieties. From his experimentation, Mendel found that the results of crossing green and yellow pea pods were determined by the presence of dominant (green) or recessive (yellow) pea pod alleles. Despite some errors with details, he identified that certain dominant characteristics or traits were passed from parent to offspring (see Table 2.1), which came to be known as the 'Mendelian Law' of heredity

Table 2.1 Dominant recessive genetic traits

Dominant traits	*Recessive traits*
Brown eyes	Blue eyes
Dark hair	Blond hair
	Red hair
Curly hair	Straight hair
Normal vision	Near-sightedness
Pigmented skin	Albinism
Single births	Twin births
Tongues that can be curled	Tongues that cannot be curled
Type A and Type B blood	Type O blood

(Glassman & Hadad, 2004). The ensuing study of genetic transmission has developed considerably, including what is now considered an entire field of behavioural genetics, devoted to the study of the inheritance of traits and characteristics, including behaviour and intelligence (Sigelman & Rider, 2003).

Charles Darwin's subsequent argument that humans and other primates share a common genetic ancestry prompted debate about evolution vs. creationism. Over a century of research has supported the premise of evolution, with considerable evidence in favour of behavioural factors being among those traits that may be genetically influenced. Dating back to William James' (1890) *Principles of Psychology*, research has supported the existence of human instincts, and the inheritance of various instincts and traits (Ginsberg, Nackerud, & Larrison, 2004).

An understanding of some basic genetic principles is helpful before understanding evolution, and that necessitates beginning with conception, or the point at which an egg is fertilized by a sperm. Within hours of fertilization, the combined genetic material of the egg and sperm is transmitted to create a new cell. The tiny new single cell, or *zygote*, contains 46 threadlike bodies called *chromosomes*, which function in 23 pairs, one from each parent. Each chromosome contains thousands of *genes*, which serve as the basic units of heredity. Each gene comprises a stretch of DNA, the 'double helix' molecule that determines development. The mechanisms of genes splitting and then recombining in differing ways depends on the chromosomes, and provides for the variations found between siblings, parents and offspring, and across generations of biological relations (Glassman & Hadad, 2004).

The single-celled zygote formed by the fertilization of the egg becomes a multiple-celled organism through the process of cell division, or *mitosis*, in which the cell (with all its chromosomes) divides into two identical cells. These two cells contain a complete copy of the parental chromosomes. The process of mitosis that enables the cells to reproduce continues throughout life, as new cells are required for growth and the replacement of old or damaged cells.

Genes have varying forms, or *alleles*, which result in different possible versions of *phenotypes*, which are the visible characteristics of the individual. The genetic code that each individual carries in their cells' DNA is called their *genotype*. Because genes function in pairs comprising one from each parent, the gene pair members for various characteristics (height, eye colour, blood type) may vary considerably (Ginsberg, Nackerud, & Larrison, 2004; Glassman & Hadad, 2004).

With the expanding knowledge base about genetic transmission and evolution, changes in the existing gene pool have come to be better understood than was previously the case. Some conditions are linked with genetic transmission (see Box 2.2). Ways in which new genetic characteristics emerge are now understood to result from the addition of new alleles. The processes by which genes are removed from the gene pool include *genetic drift* and *natural selection*. Of these, natural selection is the more familiar concept. It refers to the ways in which, over time, environmental factors are more conducive to the survival and reproductive prospects of those individuals with more desirable characteristics (Ginsberg, Nackerud, & Larrison, 2004).

Thanks to the Human Genome Project, the capacity to understand the causes and mechanisms behind various genetic conditions is rapidly expanding. Basic theories about human development are also likely to evolve as the relationship between human biology and genetics is more clearly understood. This will contribute to a greater understanding of the actual roles of genetics and the environment in the determination of how various conditions are transmitted, understood, and treated.

While conditions such as haemophilia were essentially untreatable in the case of the Tsarevitch in the early twentieth century, medical technology has progressed considerably. Not only are there ways of treating such conditions, but also the means of detecting them *in utero*. In cases where genetic conditions may be transmitted intergenerationally, parents may now choose to undergo testing to determine an infant's risk of various conditions.

A growing number of people are likely to become aware of potentially disturbing genetic information relevant to family planning. Social workers are increasingly likely

Box 2.2 Examples of conditions linked with genetic transmission

Alzheimer's disease
Cystic fibrosis
Deafness
Diabetes
Dwarfism
Glaucoma
Haemophilia
Heart disease
Intellect
Mood disorders
Muscular dystrophy
Osteogenesis imperfecta
Schizophrenia
Spina bifada

Box 2.3 An historic example of inter-generational genetic transmissions

The tragic history of the Romanov dynasty in Russia is among the most historically familiar cases of genetic transmission of an unwanted condition. Haemophilia was introduced into the Russian royal family with the marriage of Tsar Nicholas II to his distant cousin, Alexandra, in 1894. Alexandra, a granddaughter of Queen Victoria, was also a carrier of haemophilia, as were two of her aunts and a cousin. All had sons who inherited haemophilia.

> Hemophilia is a rare inherited blood condition, in which blood does not clot in the normal way. Hemophilia is inherited by way of an X-linked recessive pattern of gene mutation, which causes spontaneous uncontrollable bleeding to occur either internally or externally. Joints are particularly susceptible to bleeding episodes.
>
> (U.S. National Library of Medicine, 2007)

In Alexandra's and Nicholas' case, the X-linked nature of haemophilia meant that their four daughters were spared the condition, which is a recessive gene, and transmitted from mother to son. Their much-wanted only son, however, was diagnosed with haemophilia during the first weeks of life. The entire short life of Tsarevitch Alexei (1904–1918) was shaped by his inheritance of haemophilia. At that time, treatment was essentially non-existent, making his survival to adulthood improbable. For the sole male heir to the Tsar to have inherited haemophilia posed a dynastic dilemma.

Alexandra's despair over his survival contributed to her vulnerability to the influence of the monk, Rasputin, who claimed to have mystical powers to keep Alexei alive. The dissolute Rasputin was perceived as a sinister influence upon Alexandra, who then influenced the Tsar. Rasputin's reputation further eroded their popularity and credibility with the Russian people. The Romanovs became detached from the realities of the people they governed. Following a violent revolution and the Tsar's abdication, the Bolsheviks executed the Tsar and his entire family in 1918. When the family's remains were exhumed in 1991 and 2007, Prince Philip's DNA samples were used to confirm their identities. Philip's genetic links to the Romanovs came through his mother and father being descendants of Queen Victoria and the Romanovs respectively.

to be expected to provide support for people facing some challenging choices in relation to genetic counselling and reproductive decision-making. Social work values such as self-determination, advocacy, anti-discriminatory practice, and confidentiality are crucial aspects of providing support relevant to genetic counselling and family planning.

Twin studies

In cases of twins, the process of genetic transmission varies somewhat from that of individual transmission. Either a single fertilized egg divides to form two genetically matching organisms, which then become *identical twins*, or two eggs are released approximately simultaneously, and a different sperm fertilizes each, resulting in *fraternal twins*. The latter happens nearly twice as frequently as identical twins (Sigelman & Rider, 2003).

Except for cases of identical twins, each individual's genetic composition is unique. This can be seen in variations in eye colours, fingerprints and DNA samples. Shared genetic material, however, explains family resemblances and shared features and traits noted among biological relatives.

While basic structural features, such as the location of teeth and fingers, are relatively strictly determined by our genetic code, traits related to behaviour and intelligence are more likely influenced by environment as well. Thus, the *nature vs. nurture* debate continues. Are people's traits and behaviours decided by biology or environment? How much is determined by genetics and how much by socialization?

Studies that have compared and contrasted the histories and behaviours of twins raised apart have contributed to the understanding of the roles played by genetic and environmental influences, or 'nature vs. nurture'. The strongest studies have been conducted comparing cases of identical twins raised in different environments and reunited during adulthood. Several hundred pairs of twins who were raised apart then reunited have been studied with remarkable findings that support nature or genetic factors as being the dominant influences on human behaviour. Such characteristics as nail biting, headache patterns, food and drink preferences, employment, and even names of pets and spouses have been found to be identical (Sadock & Sadock, 2007). The consistency of such findings argues in favour of biological or genetic influences related to understanding human behaviour.

Many examples can nonetheless be found of twins and siblings being raised together in the same environment, sharing both genetic and environmental factors, and yet still being very unlike one another. Complete reliance on genetic influences can result in a 'reductionist' approach, which reduces arguments of inheritance to biology alone, without consideration of the interaction of genetic influences combined with environmental or social factors. Strict reliance on biological influences having determined characteristics and behaviour also risks overlooking the difference between *predisposition* and destiny. A predisposition to various conditions is just that: an increased vulnerability or chance of having that condition. It is not absolute, and does not entail any certainty that the predisposed individual will actually inherit or develop the condition.

Such variables contribute to the *interactionist* view, which emphasizes the combined interaction of genetic and environmental factors in deciding behaviour (Glassman & Hadad, 2004). An interactionist view is more congruent with social work perspectives than reliance solely on the medical model is likely to be. It is also congruent with the diathesis–stress model of understanding the role of inheritance combined with environmental stressors as a way of understanding the interplay between nature and nurture in influencing traits and characteristics people inherit from their families. For a further discussion of the diathesis–stress model, see Chapter 11.

A bio-psychosocial approach to illness, disease and disability

For most people, the prospect of having a medical condition or physical disability poses some disturbing prospects. Variables such as pain, disfigurement and stigma influence how people face the prospect of illness or disability. The prospect of a painful condition or painful treatment can be both frightening and exhausting. For most people, the additional factor of compromised autonomy, and the prospect of relying on others for various aspects of daily living ('ADLs') can also be demeaning and intimidating.

For children who have no other frame of reference than illness or disability, their conditions may also entail various implications for their families and their social development. Especially when a child's long-term developmental prospects are compromised, families make both internal and external adaptations. A wide range of tasks and responsibilities require consideration and negotiation, making support systems a crucial aspect of their adaptation (Quinn, 1998).

When a child experiences a life-altering condition, their parents are typically faced with an array of reactions, including anger, guilt, distress, and frequently fatigue. Parents faced with their child's having a disabling condition frequently wonder whether they could have done/not done anything differently that would have prevented such a condition. Parents may also seek to allocate responsibility for various genetic factors, when such conditions are known to run in one parent's family, but not the other's. For some parents, a child's medical circumstances amount to a type of bereavement, as they adapt their expectations from their previous anticipations of a child without medical or developmental difficulties to their infant's or child's actual circumstances. Additional challenges arise when one child's medical circumstances dominate the parents' time and energy, and require extensive absences from the family home and other children. Family outings, holidays, and housing options are often influenced by the needs of a family member with disabilities. Parental exhaustion may interfere with marital relations as well as parenting responsibilities with their other children.

If children's medical circumstances require extensive medical attention or prolonged hospital admissions, then their families may also experience disruption and there may be difficult decisions regarding how to allocate time and resources if there are other children in the home. Prolonged absences from the home may interfere with the closeness of relationships between parents and children, and jeopardize attachment between family members. Such absences may also mean that the child does not develop the same social skills that their siblings and peers develop at home and school. In some cases, siblings may feel unable to bring peers into the home because of the affected child's appearance, needs, or behaviour, thus contributing to social isolation and possible feelings of resentment. Some siblings may experience a sense of guilt for their own good health, or for resenting a sibling with a life-altering illness, and ways in which such conditions may dominate family life.

Parents are now capable of advocating for their children in ways that help keep children with special physical or educational needs in mainstream schools. In previous generations, many children with special needs were relegated to segregated schooling or institutional settings, where they were excluded from general society. Awareness of and support for family efforts and complex decision-making on behalf of members with special needs are crucial components of effective social work practice.

An increasing number of people with disabling conditions now survive well into middle age and later life. For example, nearly half of the people with Down's syndrome now live into their sixties or older (Quinn, 1998). Such changed survival prospects have various implications for expectations for the individual as well as their families and carers. If adequate schooling was not available when those individuals were children, their capacity for autonomy may be compromised. Meanwhile, their parents are often of an age when they are likely to be either deceased or physically incapable of providing sufficient physical care for their adult child with Down's syndrome. Adapting to institutional or group homes poses an array of difficulties for an older adult with a disabling condition, especially if they have previously lived only within their family home. Such factors mean that, from a bio-psychosocial perspective, a person with Down's syndrome would be understood in the simultaneous contexts of their developmental stage and medical needs, their cognitive and emotional realities, and their support network.

When life-altering conditions occur later in life, a different array of psychosocial variables influence people's adaptation. For example, when a middle-aged person with teenage children develops debilitating arthritis, and is no longer able to manage basic housekeeping responsibilities, then partners, family members, and various support networks are typically called upon to help with adaptation. When an older parent develops debilitating arthritis, they are more likely to be living with a spouse or partner of a similar age and condition, or be widowed and living alone. Their children may be grown, and either living away or absorbed in the needs of their own children or career, making it difficult to provide the support needed. Such factors mean that, from a bio-psychosocial perspective, a person with arthritis would necessarily be considered in terms of their medical needs as well as their developmental stage, their role and responsibilities, and their support networks.

The network of support available to people experiencing life-altering conditions, whether from illness or disabling conditions, remains crucial to maintain the optimum quality of life available. Attention to developmental needs (education, employment, companionship, leisure activities) remains crucial, regardless of people's physical conditions.

The strengths perspective

Social workers bring a contextual framework of understanding illness that is not limited to it being a deficit, but part of a much larger mosaic of an individual's life and circumstances. Stemming from a humanist or constructionist perspective, Saleebey's (1992) strengths perspective emphasizes the individual's innate capacity to articulate, define and control their choices and environment. While originally applied in mental health settings in the US, the strengths perspective has come to be applied across various practice situations, including medical settings. According to Saleebey (1996: 296), the strengths perspective developed as a reaction to the 'culture and helping professions

[that] are saturated with psychosocial approaches based on individual, family, and community pathology, deficits, problems, abnormality, victimization, and disorder'.

For social workers, the strengths perspective entails an approach to understanding and responding to people's medical circumstances in ways that are empowering, and respectful of the assets people bring to the process of solving problems. Using a strengths perspective, social workers' assessments are likely to differ substantially from an assessment of the same individual along a medical model. The strengths perspective provides an important shift away from assessments that focus solely on the presence of deficits or pathology. In this way, it is an important contrast to the historical precedent of religious charities' emphasis on people's presumed moral failures, the psychoanalytic emphasis on the unresolved conflicts of the unconscious, as well as the medical model's emphasis on disease.

As an example, consider the following case. Table 2.2 provides some contrasts that may be found between the viewpoints of the medical model and a strengths perspective.

'Jimmy', aged 16, was born eleven weeks premature, which resulted in his having cerebral palsy. It affects his left side, causing a pronounced limp, and his poor hand coordination causes difficulties writing. He uses a computer keyboard very well, and is extremely outgoing. Jimmy has begun his own small business, being a disc jockey for children's parties. He is extremely popular, and typically has at least one or two jobs most weekends. He plans to start college in the autumn, to study the business aspect of music production.

Using a strengths perspective, social workers are more likely than their medical counterparts to appreciate the role played by Jimmy's family and their support. The fact that Jimmy completed school in a mainstream school environment points to his academic competence. Likewise, whereas he might be assessed as 'hyperverbal' in a medical interview, Jimmy would more likely be described as 'extraverted' by a social worker, especially as that logically contributes to his success as a disc jockey, and having begun

Table 2.2 Continuum between medical model and strengths perspective

Medical model	*Strengths perspective*
16-year-old male with hemiplegia	16-year-old male with CP due to prematurity
Poor gait	Older of two siblings from intact family
Dysgraphia	Strong parental support
Hyperverbal	Walks unaided despite limp
	Writes fluently with computer assistance
	Above average intelligence
	Finished regular school with As and Bs
	Extraverted, confident
	Has begun DJ business
	Excited about starting college next month

his own business. By considering Jimmy's circumstances from a strengths perspective, his strengths clearly outnumber his medical difficulties. The strengths perspective is also congruent with concepts related to an individual having an internal locus of control, rather than passively relying on others to determine the right course of action for them.

Variables related to stress

Long-term physical and mental health consequences of undischarged levels of stress include high blood pressure, ulcers, colitis, migraines, anxiety, and depression (Sadock & Sadock, 2007). Stress is also associated with exacerbating episodes of various chronic conditions, including arthritis, asthma, Crohn's disease, hyperthyroidism, gastro-oesophageal reflux disease, lupus, and psoriasis (Janson-Bjerklie, Ferkeitch, & Benner, 1993; Sadock & Sadock, 2007). Various highly stressful work environments are also associated with such conditions as coronary heart disease (Bosma et al., 1998). Stress is consistently linked with compromised immune system functions. Vulnerability to various infectious conditions (colds, flu, conjunctivitis, herpes simplex, etc.) appears consistently linked with heightened levels of stress.

Further complicating the role of stress and people's health, stress is also frequently associated with efforts to self-medicate with alcohol and other drugs. While this topic is discussed in some detail in Chapter 10, it is a noteworthy component of the complex interplay between individuals and society, as well as stress and well-being (Wilkinson & Pickett, 2009). Issues of anger management and impulse control, as well as aggression levels associated both with stress and alcohol and other drug usage are often very relevant to social work practice.

The diathesis–stress model

When considering the inter-relatedness of stress and people's vulnerability to various conditions, the *diathesis–stress model* is often useful to understand complex influences on people's circumstances. The diathesis–stress model refers to the vulnerability (diathesis) people have to experience various conditions, combined with exposure to a stressor that serves as a trigger for the condition (Sigelman & Rider, 2003). For example, people with family histories of diabetes are at a greater risk of developing diabetes than people without that family history, or vulnerability (diathesis). In and of itself, however, a family history of diabetes is insufficient to predict that someone will develop diabetes. Usually, some level of stress is also necessary to precipitate the actual development of diabetes. That stress may be lifestyle, diet, weight gain, or health conditions that serve to precipitate the existing vulnerability. For people without the pre-existing vulnerability, that same level of stress could prove inadequate to trigger the onset of diabetes.

The diathesis–stress model provides a means of understanding why some pre-disposing vulnerabilities seem to result in some individuals having a given condition, while the same vulnerabilities do not apply to others. Likewise, some stressors appear to precipitate various conditions among some individuals, but not others. For a person who is vulnerable to a given condition, less stress is generally necessary to precipitate various problems than would be the case for someone without the same level of predisposing vulnerability. For example, someone with a history of fragile, brittle bones is more susceptible to a fracture from a fall that would not necessarily cause a breakage in someone with strong, healthy bones. Thus, low bone density could be seen as the vulnerability (diathesis), and a fall could be seen as a stressor. Consider Table 2.3 as an example of various factors associated with predisposing vulnerability as well as protective factors from a bio-psychosocial perspective.

Table 2.3 Examples of predisposing and protective factors associated with mental health problems

	Factors associated with predisposing vulnerability	*Protective factors associated with lessened vulnerability*
Personal/Individual	Genetic vulnerability Low birth weight Language deficits Chronic physical illness Below-average intelligence Child abuse or neglect	Strong, positive temperament Above-average intelligence Social skills/competence Spirituality or religion
Family/Cultural	Severe marital conflict Overcrowded living conditions Paternal criminality Maternal mental health problems History of having been placed in foster care	Smaller family structure Supportive relationship with parents Positive relationships with siblings Sufficient rule setting and supervision from parents
Social/Environmental	Violence Poverty Community chaos Inadequate academic resources Social exclusion Racism, discrimination	Sufficient commitment to schooling in community Access to health and social resources Social cohesion

Source: Adapted from DHHS (2001).

Criticisms and shortcomings of the medical model

Social workers are agents of change. An inherent belief in people's capacity to learn and change in positive ways is a cornerstone of social work practice. A rigid adherence to strict biological determination of traits and behaviours creates a risk of people's belief that their behaviour or circumstances are so biologically determined that they have no means or responsibilities to attempt change, or challenge biological destiny. Such a belief is incongruent with social work values and ethics, as many people experience both risk and protective factors simultaneously. Such combined variables demonstrate the complexity of understanding the causes of medical and mental health conditions.

Social work's inherent value of *self-determination* necessarily influences the approach social workers are obliged to take in advocating for people at risk of being oppressed on the grounds of life-altering conditions. By advocating for people's self-determination, regardless of illness or disability, social workers continue to challenge the sorts of socially oppressive practices described by Talcott Parsons (1951). Parsons explored the institutional expectations of people perceived to occupy the sick role, which include the following:

- The premise that the sick person cannot be expected to become well/cured by an act of will, but requires care in order to do so.
- That being ill is undesirable, and that the sick person is obliged to wish to be well.
- That the sick/disabled person is obliged to seek technically competent help and to cooperate with the medical establishment.

Institutional biases against people with illnesses and disabilities can be subtle yet powerful means of excluding people because of their being different from the majority. The *social model of disability* is more congruent with social work values. The term itself was introduced by Oliver (1983), and entails an emphasis on removing barriers from the lives of people with disabilities. It also attempts to distinguish disability from sheer biology. The social model addresses the social disparities in power and authority between the medical establishment and those who live with disabling conditions. It emphasizes the importance of all parties' awareness of power discrepancies when dealing with people with disabilities. The social model of disability also advocates for action research, in the quest for establishing empirical evidence that can be applied to enhancing the lives of people with disabilities. In this framework, social workers are empowered to appreciate their own expertise, and encouraged to publish findings of their work with people with disabilities in order to contribute to the existing literature.

Overview of some specific conditions with which social workers are likely to need familiarity

Social workers are increasingly likely to need to understand the roles played by various medical conditions in people's lives in order to support them in the process of getting needs met. The most commonly encountered conditions are: Alzheimer's disease; cancer; diabetes; Down's syndrome; heart disease; HIV/AIDS; and mood swings. The conditions mentioned entail complex psychosocial dimensions, both for patients and their loved ones. You will find it useful to read more about these conditions (Box 2.4).

Box 2.4 Sources of information about health-related conditions

General and specific medical information:

Cochrane Collaboration	www.cochrane.org/reviews
National Health Service	www.nhs.uk/Conditions
BUPA	www.hcd2.bupa.co/uk/fact sheets

Specific conditions:

Alcohol-related conditions	www.intute.ac.uk
Alzheimer's disease	www.alzheimers.org.uk
Children's cancers	www.cancerhelp.org.uk
Down's syndrome	www.downs-syndrome.org.uk
Diabetes	www.diabetes.org.uk
Heart disease	www.bhf.org.uk
HIV/AIDS	www.aidsmap.com

Questions

1 What are some ways in which the strengths perspective is useful in social work assessments? What are some ways in which it could prove counterproductive?

2 What are some reasons that social workers need to know basic genetic principles?

3 Consider the factors noted in Box 2.1. How might those factors vary across age groups? For example, consider the nutritional problems faced by an overweight teenager living in a hostel, compared with nutritional problems faced by a bereaved 80-year-old widower who has never cooked for himself.

3 Developmental models and considerations

Starting with some discussion of infancy, this chapter addresses various developmental influences on behaviour across the lifespan. Because of the importance of what transpires during infancy, attention will first be paid to ante-natal and early development, with particular attention to factors relevant to the first years of life. Some gender differences will be discussed in relation to developmental concerns, using Carol Gilligan's more feminist approach to noteworthy differences. Factors that may influence adolescence, including sexual orientation, will also be considered. Finally, issues related to adult and late adult stages will be considered.

Relevance for social work

Social work places an inherent emphasis on people's context, making their developmental stage an important facet of understanding their behaviour. Having an accurate sense of developmental norms can prove a crucial factor for social workers needing to assess families with problems. When a child's developmental levels are compromised, or when developmental needs are misunderstood by parents, social workers need to be able to understand the implications and conduct their assessments and interventions accordingly.

Because social workers need to understand children in the context of their family, various factors that may influence development and well-being in relation to parental or family factors are crucial components of social work skills. The capacity to recognize developmentally appropriate behaviours throughout the lifespan is a key aspect of good assessment and practice. Expectations that are realistic for a 12-year-old's behaviour are unlikely to apply equally well to a 2-year-old, and vice versa.

Understanding the developmental challenges facing adolescents is another key aspect of good social work practice, especially in cases in which families may perceive developmentally normal behaviours as abhorrent or inappropriate. An awareness of sexual elements associated with adolescence can be a crucial component of a sound social work assessment.

Social workers often work with female-headed families, which necessitates awareness of women's developmental differences. Particularly when working with older people, social workers must have a clear understanding of some of the changing realities faced by people later in life.

Ante-natal factors

Prior to conception, many couples wishing to start a family are faced with reproductive difficulties. *Infertility* involves the inability or diminished capacity to produce offspring, and may occur in the male or female partner, or both. It has a variety of causes, including infections, injuries, organic or age-related factors. Medical technology now offers methods by which previously infertile couples can be helped to conceive and bear children. In some cases, medication is used to stimulate the woman's ovaries to produce more eggs. Other options include artificial insemination, which involves injecting sperm (either from her partner or a donor) into the woman's uterus. These options also make parenthood a more viable prospect for lesbians who wish to be mothers.

When *in vitro fertilization* (IVF) is used, several of the woman's own eggs are removed from her ovary, and then fertilized by sperm in a Petri dish in a laboratory setting, and then returned to the woman's uterus in hopes that one will attach to the wall of the uterus. Because not all IVF attempts are successful, prospective parents are subject to considerable physical and emotional stress when attempts prove unsuccessful. Sometimes reproductive technology results in multiple births, entailing high risks of prematurity and dangerously small birth weights. Prospective parents undergoing such treatments may be faced with some very complex decisions in the process of achieving a successful pregnancy and childbirth (Ginsberg, Nackerud, & Larrison, 2004).

Pregnancy

The safest time for childbearing appears to be between about ages 16 to 35 (Gilbert, Nesbitt, & Danielsen, 1999). Immature physical maturation may account for higher rates of low-birthweight babies born to very young mothers (15 and younger). Even more importantly, pregnant teenagers do not always acknowledge unwanted pregnancies in time to seek ante-natal care, and are also more vulnerable to a variety of socio-economic difficulties than older mothers are likely to experience. Although the vast majority of older women have normal pregnancies, mothers over the age of 35 remain twice as likely to miscarry a pregnancy as younger mothers (Sigelman & Rider, 2003).

Stress, anxiety, violence, and depression are all variables that can have negative impacts on pregnancy, regardless of age. Maternal depression during pregnancy is associated with delayed motor skills in newborns (Lundy, Jones, Field et al., 1999). Mothers with high levels of anxiety appear more likely to have babies of low birth weight, with feeding and sleeping difficulties, and who prove to be hyperactive and irritable than do mothers who have low levels of anxiety (Sadock & Sadock, 2007). The mother's reaction to various stressors appears more relevant than the presence of stress itself, but social workers need to be mindful of the impact of stress and anxiety on a mother's and her infant's overall well-being.

Maternal nutrition is a key variable during and following pregnancy. The effects of malnutrition on the infant depend on when the malnutrition occurred. Children born to malnourished mothers sometimes appear to have cognitive problems during infancy and childhood. During the first trimester, malnutrition can hinder the development of brain cells through the disruption of the formation of the spinal cord. During the later stages of pregnancy, malnutrition is more likely to result in a smaller infant with a smaller brain (Sigelman & Rider, 2003).

Exposure to various teratogens (any disease or substance, including alcohol and tobacco, which can harm foetal development) can influence the outcome of pregnancy. Despite years of warning, pregnant women are still known to smoke during pregnancies. Babies born to mothers who smoke during pregnancy tend to develop more slowly *in utero*, and are prone to prematurity and low birth weight (Haug, Irgens, Skjaerven et al., 2000). Some of the small babies of mothers who smoke experience some catch-up growth by later infancy, but the more heavily the mother smokes during pregnancy, the more likely their child will not catch up completely to their ideal weight (Streissguth, Sampson, Barr et al., 1994). Babies born to mothers who smoke are more susceptible than other babies to respiratory difficulties and breathing problems. Heavy smoking by the mother during pregnancy is associated with higher chances of her baby being at risk of 'crib death', or sudden infant death syndrome (SIDS), in which a sleeping infant suddenly stops breathing and dies (Winborg, Kesmodel, Henriksen et al., 2000).

Maternal drinking during pregnancy means that alcohol consumed by the mother crosses the placenta, where it can directly impact the development of the foetus and impede hormone functions of the placenta. In the worst cases, babies born to mothers who drink during pregnancy will exhibit a range of features that include *foetal alcohol effects (FAE)* and fully-fledged *foetal alcohol syndrome (FAS)*. FAS affects about one-third of infants born to women with alcohol dependence (Sadock & Sadock, 2007). Children born with FAS are typically small from birth, and remain small for their age throughout childhood. Children with FAS often have distinctive facial features including microcephaly (small head circumference), a smooth philtrum, small chins, small and widely spaced eyes, and thin upper lips. Children with FAS often show signs of central nervous system damage, including irritability, seizures, or tremors. The majority of children with FAS score significantly below average on intelligence tests (Day, Zuo, Richardson et al., 1999; Streissguth, Randals, & Smith, 1991).

Developmental delays and learning disabilities are commonly associated with FAS. Such children often present with special needs that may or may not be recognized as stemming from prenatal conditions. Social workers must be particularly sensitive to the complex needs of children and their families in cases involving prenatal exposure to alcohol and other drugs. Maternal use of alcohol and other drugs will be discussed further in Chapter 12.

Ideally, pregnancies are both planned and wanted, although such is not always the case. Spacing of pregnancies between three and five years apart appears to diminish risks such as low birth weight, maternal anaemia and third-trimester bleeding, compared with pregnancies less than two years apart (Sadock & Sadock, 2007).

An array of personal, family, and cultural factors play a strong role in the birth of an infant. Single parenthood, planned or unplanned pregnancies, pregnancies resulting from traumatic relationships, and economic stressors are but a few of the factors that influence the arrival of a newborn. For some families, having the financial wherewithal to support a large family is a status symbol; for others the prospect of another mouth to feed may be a crisis. For new parents who have long awaited a child of their own, the arrival of a newborn often represents pure joy. Sadly, for women in dependent relationships with abusive partners, the birth of a child may be a source of increased dependence and diminished options to leave an unhealthy environment.

The foetal period

For humans, the gestational period is calculated from the first day of the mother's last normal menstrual period, and lasts on average between 259 and 287 days, with a normal range of 37–41 weeks. Infants born prior to the 37th week of gestation are considered premature (Venes, 2005; Sigelman & Rider, 2003).

By the eighth week of development, the human embryo undergoes a tremendous development. Every major organ of the body begins to take shape during the embryonic period. During the first month of pregnancy, the neural plate folds up to become the neural tube, the bottom of which becomes the spinal cord. The areas at the top of the spinal cord go on to form those parts of the brain that control such functions as digestion, breathing, elimination, and the sleep–wake states. In rare cases (approximately 1 in 1,000 pregnancies), the neural tube does not fully close, resulting in spina bifada (Sigelman & Rider, 2003). In cases of spina bifada, the protective covering around the spinal cord does not fully develop during the early weeks of gestation, resulting in a condition involving various functions of the brain, nervous system and spinal cord, including the ability to walk.

The foetal period begins at the ninth week of pregnancy, and continues until birth. Organ systems continue to develop and begin to function. Because major organs have already formed during the first trimester of pregnancy, harmful agents (such as infection, alcohol or drugs) consumed from that point onward are unlikely to result in malformations, but may slow foetal growth, or hinder the development of the nervous system. Although only about three inches long, the foetus has begun to develop a human appearance, and can swallow, digest food, and urinate.

During the second trimester (months four, five and six), the foetus grows rapidly, the respiratory system develops in ways that will sustain life outside the womb, and the brain develops in ways that will serve the baby's ability to communicate and respond to stimuli. The foetus typically becomes very active during this period, moving inside the mother's womb. The point traditionally known as the *age of viability* refers to that point at which the brain and respiratory system are sufficiently developed that a premature infant's life can be sustained outside the uterus.

During the third trimester, the foetus grows in size, and the brain continues to develop in ways that contribute to survival and development. The foetal heart rate becomes more variable, and responds to stimuli outside the mother's womb (Sigelman & Rider, 2003).

Pre-eclampsia and eclampsia are among the pregnancy-related conditions that may be of particular concern for social workers. They are related conditions that occur in a small percentage of pregnant women in the later stages of pregnancy. Detection and treatment are essential to prevent pre-eclampsia from becoming eclampsia, which typically results in maternal and/or infant death. Symptoms include alarming rates of blood pressure, headaches, seizures, oedema of the lower limbs, and ultimately coma. Treatment includes bed rest and careful monitoring throughout the remaining pregnancy. Both conditions are associated with pre-existing hypertension, but sometimes happen in cases with no known predisposing risk. The birth of the mother's child is the only known means of fully resolving the condition, which may entail a premature or induced delivery (Ginsberg, Nakerud, & Larrison, 2004; Venes, 2005).

Prematurity

A small percentage of infants are born prior to 37 weeks of gestation. When that is the case, the infant is considered *preterm* or *premature*. Some of the conditions associated with premature births include maternal diabetes, pre-eclampsia, trauma, and multiple births (Beers et al., 2006). Infants who are born prior to 23 weeks of gestation remain less likely to survive, and more likely to have chronic lung disease and/or severe neurological complications (including cerebral palsy, blindness or severe myopia, and deafness) than infants born at 24 weeks or more of gestation (Hack & Fanaroff, 1999).

Advances in medical technology have enhanced the survival rates and health of babies born prematurely. Despite medical advances, however, premature infants are often born with medical complications that necessitate lengthy stays in special neonatal units, apart from their parents. Those early weeks and months are often the very times at which full-term infants are beginning to establish attachment to their parents, and their parents are bonding (and falling in love) with their newborn. In cases of prematurely born infants, hospitalization may complicate physical access to newborns who may be connected to various pieces of equipment, making cuddling and bonding more complex. Furthermore, some parents find the atmosphere of hospitals very intimidating, and feel frightened by their medically fragile infant's appearance at the same time they feel intimidated by the hospital environment.

Birth weight

Low and very low (<1500 grams) birth weights are worrying for babies regardless of prematurity (NHS, 2006). Even though low-birthweight babies are a minority of births (approximately 8 per cent), they remain the majority (65 per cent) of all infant deaths (Murphy, 2000; Sigelman & Rider, 2003).

Low birth weight (< 2500 grams) is associated with various conditions, including prematurity, multiple births, mothers with eating disorders, and maternal smoking (Harrigan & Baldwin, 2003; NHS, 2006). Problems resulting from low birth weight include respiratory problems, blindness, deafness, autism, and cognitive difficulties (Parrish, 2004). These problems are consistently complicated by poverty and by maternal alcohol misuse during pregnancy. Fortunately, most infants are born healthily, without genetic or prenatal injuries or complications.

Newborns

A newborn's adjustment to life outside the womb is generally measured by means of the *Apgar Scale*, which is assessed at intervals immediately after birth. The Apgar Scale provides a standardized means of determining whether a newborn is breathing satisfactorily, maintaining a regular heart rhythm, and maintaining a stable temperature, or whether resuscitation is necessary (Harrigan & Baldwin, 2003).

The arrival of an infant marks significant changes in most new parents' relationship. Patterns of eating and sleeping, availability of leisure time, and sexual energy are all subject to enormous changes. Many first-time parents experience doubts about their competence to provide for the many needs of the demanding creature they have brought into the world. When newborns and infants have special medical needs, such doubts may be even more acute. Such special needs may occur in cases of premature infants with respiratory or sleeping irregularities, or children born with special medical conditions, such as spina bifada, Down's syndrome, or cleft palate.

Many new fathers acknowledge considerable strain experienced during the pregnancy and delivery, especially if they were uninformed about what to expect, or if any medical difficulties occurred. For most new fathers, though, the overall experience of new parenthood is a positive and life-affirming experience (Sigelman & Rider, 2003).

For most new parents, the mother is still the parent who spends the most time with the infant. Whereas in 1965 fathers reported spending about half as much time with their children as the mothers did, in 1998 they were spending about two-thirds as much time with their children (Bianchi, 2000). Newborn humans demonstrate an array of proximity-seeking behaviours and preferences for nearness to their mothers. Experiments with infants of breast-feeding mothers indicate early preferences for their mothers that appear based on the combined features of feeding, scent, taste, and proximity (Polan & Hofer, 1999).

Post-natal depression

The majority of new mothers (60 per cent) report experiencing episodes of tearfulness, irritability, anxiety, fatigue, and mood swings that include depression in the immediate days and weeks following childbirth (Najman, Williams, Nikles et al., 2000). Such episodes are still sometimes referred to as 'baby blues', and while they are to be taken seriously, they are within the normal hormonal process most women experience following childbirth; episodes typically last for a matter of days, and resolve with time.

In stark contrast to the relatively normal, time-limited episodes of maternal depression following childbirth, the experience of *post-natal depression* is a considerably more serious condition. Approximately 10–20 per cent of new mothers experience levels of depression severe and prolonged enough to meet the criteria for post-natal depression (Sigelman & Rider, 2003). Post-natal depression is not psychotic, but often comprises feelings of despondence and inadequacy, suicidal thoughts, and sleep disturbances (Sadock & Sadock, 2007). Post-natal depression typically occurs within the first 12 weeks, and persists for months. It may hinder the mother's ability to perform the physical and emotional functions necessary to attend to a newborn's needs. Preoccupations with fears of harming the infant may become a focus of thoughts and obsessions. Risks of experiencing post-natal depression are increased for women with histories of depression prior to pregnancy, and are exacerbated by simultaneous stressors, such as social isolation and problematic relationships with their baby's father. Experiencing severe post-natal depression increases the risks of future episodes (Sadock & Sadock, 2007; Sigelman & Rider, 2003).

Importantly, episodes of post-natal depression have been found to impair the capacity for establishing secure mother–infant relationships. Children of mothers with post-natal depression have been found to have subsequent problems with attachment and lowered levels of responsiveness to interactions with their mothers in early childhood. Children of mothers with post-natal depression have also been found to have social disadvantages throughout childhood, entailing such factors as engaging in less creative play, and demonstrating lower levels of social confidence when approached in friendly manners by other children (Sigelman & Rider, 2003; Rutter & O'Connor, 1999). Such factors may play a crucial role in the lives of children with whom social workers interact. An awareness of the roles played by post-natal depression is a crucial component of good social work assessment skills.

Infancy

Vast and rapid changes occur during the first year of life. More information is processed during those months than during any other time of life. Infants' emotional and social development begins with their capacity to respond to those around them, and the ability to imitate expressions and movements. Babies' smiling responses begin spontaneously within the first two months of life. Initially, infants' *endogenous* smiling occurs regardless of stimulation. Beginning around four months, infants' *exogenous* smiling occurs in response to stimulation from their surroundings or caregivers.

Unlike other animals, human infants remain totally dependent on those around them for their survival for a long time. Infants' ability to comprehend and respond to their environment and their ability to begin expressing themselves comprise crucial aspects of their ability to survive. Advances in motor skills, or the ability to move and manipulate themselves and objects around them tend to progress in a fairly orderly way, entailing *developmental milestones*. While milestones tend to be predictable (such as speaking, sitting up, walking), they also vary considerably. Examples are provided in Table 3.1. Certain reflexes, including sucking, and *rooting* (the turning of the head toward stroking of their cheek or mouth) also contribute to survival.

Infants' stages of emotional development often parallel their cognitive development. During the first year of life, infants' emotional states are closely linked with basic needs, such as hunger, tiredness, or fullness. During the later part of the first year, the infant's moods grow increasingly responsive to their external environment, and social cues provided by parents and caregivers. The infant's primary caregiver, who is most often their mother, heavily influences both emotional and cognitive development. Prolonged separation from the mother or other primary caregivers during the second six months of life is associated with heightened risks of depression that may persist into adulthood (Shaffer, 1996).

Table 3.1 Developmental aspects of responsiveness and expression

Age and stage	*Response*	*Expression*
Birth–6 months	Startle response to loud or sudden noise Effort to locate sources of sounds by turning head, eyes Appearing to attend to those speaking, may smile at sound of voices Recognition of warning, angry, or soothing voices Responds to sound of own name	Makes sounds other than crying Makes different cries for hunger, pain Makes distinct sound to express pleasure Experiments with making different sounds Babbles
7–11 months	Show selective listening Shows interest in music or singing Recognizes 'no', 'hot', and own name Looks at pictures being named for up to 1 minute	Responds to sound of own name with sounds Imitates sounds Invents sounds (own language) Begins using gestures (shaking head for no) Uses exclamations ('oh-oh') Plays games requiring language (peek-a-boo, pat-a-cake)
12–18 months	Shows ability to distinguish between sounds (bells vs. voices, dog vs. mother) Understands basic body parts, names of common objects Adds new words to vocabulary each week Can identify basic objects from a group or from pictures Has acquired an understanding of up to 150-word vocabulary by 18 months	Uses single words (beginning around 11 months; by 18 months, is using up to 20 words) 'Talks' to self, toys, others, using own language About 25% of expressions are intelligible Vowel sounds are pronounced correctly Beginning and ending consonants are often dropped

Source: Adapted from Sadock & Sadock (2007) and Rutter & Hersov (1985).

Consequences of maternal rejection or prolonged absences have long been understood as being problematic for infants' emotional development. From his work with infants who were foundlings, or abandoned by their parents, **Rene Spitz** (1945, 1946) originally outlined the developmental hazards associated with emotional deprivation stemming from maternal rejection, and the subsequent syndromes he referred to as 'hospitalism' and 'anaclytic depression' in infants. Spitz studied infants placed in regimented institutions, where strictly antiseptic conditions were maintained, and physical contact was limited to scheduled feedings. Babies deprived of mental or visual stimulation became very passive and unexpressive. They also proved more susceptible to infections, and were developmentally delayed by age 2, demonstrating limited verbal skills, and lacking the ability to feed themselves. Spitz's term 'hospitalism' referred to the combined features of infants whose development had become thwarted while institutionalized (Polansky, 1991). More recently, infants who have been placed in institutional settings with inadequate staff-to-infant ratios to provide consistent emotional care, and where frequent staff turnovers compromise relationships with infants have also demonstrated delayed developmental progress. The same infants, when placed in settings where consistent care and nurturing were provided, demonstrated remarkable developmental resilience (Sadock & Sadock, 2007). Further dimensions of attachment and mothering are addressed in greater detail in Chapter 5.

Failure to thrive

In rare instances, infants either do not gain necessary weight to maintain steady growth, or they may actually lose weight. *Non-organic failure to thrive (FTT)* refers to the state when an infant's or child's weight is consistently below the 3rd to 5th percentile for age, and no medical or organic cause can explain their growth failure. Failure to Thrive generally reflects inadequate caregiving, and is most evident between 3 and 12 months (Beers et al., 2006; Woody, 2003b). It results from environmental neglect (inadequate food) or understimulation, similar to the 'hospitalism' already discussed. Risk factors for children with FTT include maternal depression, maternal malnutrition during pregnancy, relationship problems between parents, and mental illness and/or substance misuse in the primary caregiver (Woody, 2003b).

Temperament

Temperamental differences can be noted during the early weeks of life. Basic constructs of temperament refer to the individual's characteristic level of expressiveness and affect (both positive and negative) in response to their environment. Because temperament also determines arousal/activity and the response to soothing, theorists consider temperament a key factor in determining both the quality and quantity of exchanges between the infant and their caregiver(s). In a reciprocal pattern, the quality and quantity of those exchanges can also influence the infant's temperament and its expression. Infants and children who are considered more temperamentally difficult (i.e. prone to distress, difficult to soothe, and emotionally reactive) appear less likely to utilize their caregivers for comfort and safety than less temperamentally difficult children (Vaughn & Bost, 1999).

Temperamental differences between infants, including siblings raised in the same environment, are important factors in understanding parent–child interactions and subsequent behaviour. Given the crucial role played by temperament throughout infancy and childhood, overlapping issues of attachment and disposition serve to influence subsequent personality development. Other factors (environment, safety, intellect, genetics, etc.) also play crucial roles, with a variety of reciprocal influences playing a part in personality development and behaviour, thus furthering the ongoing debate of nature vs. nurture (Sadock & Sadock, 2007). The concept of *goodness of fit* refers to the expectations and responses that evolve between infants and parents/caregivers that facilitate or confound the process of emotional or temperamental expressions (Thomas & Chess, 1986).

Fears

Basic fears of certain stimuli appear to serve adaptive purposes. The experience of alarm may then serve to precipitate the child's awareness of and reliance on the protection of their caregivers, and thus facilitate attachment. Normal sources of alarm for babies and small children include an awareness of aloneness, darkness, loud noises, and sudden looming movements (Cassidy, 1999). Toddlers frequently experience fears of the dark at night-time, which may create bedtime difficulties. Such fears are generally remedied by the use of night lights or parental reassurances.

A developmentally normal fear of strangers is often noted from about 26 weeks, but becomes noticeable at around 8 months. The typical response usually entails crying and clinging to their mother or primary caregiver. Babies who are accustomed only to one parent or caregiver appear more susceptible to fearfulness of strangers than those exposed to a variety of people. Stranger anxiety is believed to indicate babies' increasing capacity to distinguish between their caregivers and other people. *Separation anxiety*, which typically occurs between 10 and 18 months, differs from stranger anxiety, although they are connected.

Toddlers

During the second year of life, children acquire both intellectual and motor skills that accelerate their social and emotional development. By being able to walk independently, toddlers gain considerable independence for purposes of play and exploration.

During their second year of life, toddlers' verbal repertoires are typically expanding dramatically, with 'no' preceding 'yes', and 'mine' preceding 'yours'. While toddlers' newfound ability to protest and challenge may test parents' and caregivers' patience, it also provides the means by which children experiment with independent thought and action. Either extreme – the absence of expressed opposition, or persistent oppositional behaviour – can prove problematic for children's emotional and social development.

Developing language skills is a primary task for toddlers, and their ability to articulate clearly usually increases during this period. Nearing age 2, children often use short but complete sentences to express themselves.

In addition to spoken words, toddlers often engage in symbolic play, where toys or dolls represent something or someone else. They are also increasingly capable of listening to explanations, including reasons for not achieving immediate gratification. By doing so, toddlers are likely to demonstrate the beginnings of self-regulation and frustration tolerance that will serve them throughout life.

Among the other areas of toddlers' exploration, their own anatomy typically becomes increasingly interesting to them. Age-appropriate curiosity about anatomical differences often leads to questions about genitalia. *Gender identity*, which is the ability to label oneself and others correctly according to being male or female, usually begins to be evident around 18 months, and is generally established around age 2. *Gender stability*, by which a child understands that gender remains a lifelong constant, generally occurs around ages 3–4 (Shaffer, 1996).

During their second year, toddlers are capable of expressing increasingly distinct emotional responses, differentiating between pleasure and displeasure. Exploratory excitement, pleasure in discovery and new behavioural achievements become part of their expressive repertoire. The capacity to tease and surprise others becomes an important social skill. Toddlers also develop the capacity to demonstrate affection (by such behaviours as running up to and simultaneously smiling, kissing and hugging others) as well as protest (by turning away, crying, yelling, biting and kicking). Meanwhile, fine motor skills are also advancing, enhancing the ability to run, navigate stairs alone, and pull on simple garments independently.

Most toddlers generally need about 12 hours sleep a day, which may include a daytime nap. During this same period, toddlers are also usually gaining increasing control of their urination, with control of night-time urination usually complete around age 4. Daytime control of urination is usually earlier, at around 2½–3, depending on individual variations (Sadock & Sadock, 2007).

Early childhood

For children moving past the tasks of toddlerhood, the period between about ages 2 and 6 entails considerable physical, mental and social development as well as consolidation of those aspects of development already achieved. Baby teeth have come in, and some begin to fall out in order for permanent teeth to grow. Primary social skills, such as bladder and bowel control, and the ability to dress and feed oneself are typically established. Most children have begun to gain control of tearful outbursts and temper tantrums during this stage, along with learning to be helpful to others, and putting toys away to some degree (Woody, 2003a).

Between ages 3 and 6, children are increasingly aware of their bodies, and of differences between the sexes. Discovery and rediscovery of their own anatomy are a primary interest during this phase. Natural curiosity associated with this developmental stage may lead to exploratory play with others, such as games of 'doctors and nurses'. Fascination with illness and injuries may lead to a wish to have any scrape or cut fully examined and elaborately bandaged. Curiosity about bathrooms may lead to repeated visits to public toilets while parents may wish to be engaged in other activities (Sigelman & Rider, 2003).

The first three years appear to be particularly important for the brain's development. By age 5, the brain's functioning has become increasingly specialized. By age 6, children's vocabularies have expanded greatly, and they have begun to think more analytically, thanks to the development of the brain's left hemisphere. Simultaneously, the brain's right hemisphere is more engaged in tasks involving emotional expression, visual imagery, and spatial skills. Children's perspectives remain primarily egocentric, however, and they lack the ability to imagine themselves in another's circumstances in an empathic manner (Woody, 2003a).

During this phase of development, some children have 'imaginary friends', usually children with above-average intelligence. These imaginary friends are generally human, but may be animals or anthropomorphized toys. Imaginary friends typically emerge among children between ages 3–10. They are typically a positive, friendly presence, and their significance remains unclear. They usually seem to diminish loneliness, and often serve to reduce anxiety. Their need typically ends by age 12 (Sadock & Sadock, 2007).

Peer relations during this phase are often gender-based, with boys gravitating to friendships with other boys, and girls with other girls. Much of the essence of children's friendships during this phase relates to playing together. Thus, the capacity to play well with others provides children with a certain 'social capital'. Children with aggressive tendencies have greater difficulty making friends than children capable of cooperative play (Woody, 2003a).

Middle childhood

During the phase called 'middle childhood' (ages 6–puberty), aspects of academic accomplishments and skill building are often the focus of children's attention and efforts. By age 9–10, the capacity to concentrate has expanded considerably, and often determines academic success. The ability to understand abstract concepts also influences children's behaviour during middle childhood because of the increased ability to apply reason.

School occupies the majority of most children's weekdays, and provides a crucial backdrop to academic and social achievements. Because of various social and economic factors, such as parents' employment, many children do not leave school and return home to individual parental supervision. The quality of intellectual stimulation afforded to children after school can have a considerable influence on children's social and academic progress. High-quality childcare is associated with cognitive gains that contribute to children's better performance on standardized cognitive tests (Charlesworth, Viggiani, & Wood, 2003). Simultaneously, children's growth and increased coordination during this phase contribute greatly to engaging in increasingly complex tasks. Improving motor coordination and strength contribute to improvements in tasks such as writing and playing musical instruments, as well as playing increasingly complex games and activities (cycling, swimming, dancing, and gymnastics).

While school provides the primary context for children's social and intellectual development, during this phase children are exposed to an increasingly diverse array of social contacts, including peers, team members, and adults other than family members, including teachers and other children's parents. During this phase, peers become an increasingly important influence on children's behaviours and activities. Social acceptance by peers becomes increasingly important to children during this phase, making the development of the social skills needed for successful interaction with peers and others crucial. The capacity for empathy and concern for others typically emerges during middle childhood, which can facilitate social interactions.

Because of Freud's influence, middle childhood is still sometimes referred to as the *latency period*, implying a moratorium on sexual exploration and interest. During this phase, however, considerable sexual play and interest are common among both boys and girls. Boys often find ways to compare their genital areas, and jokes regarding body functions, toilets, and body sounds are often popular among children during this phase.

Adolescence

Some of the stereotypes of adolescence as a period of emotional crises and drama stem from the work of the psychologist and educator G. Stanley Hall (1904), who defined adolescence as a turbulent period of 'Storm and Stress'. Hall considered the instability of adolescence a natural precursor to a more stable period of adulthood. While the accuracy of Hall's premise remains contested, considerable research indicates that adolescence entails distinct bio-psychosocial shifts. Particularly for girls, adolescence appears to be a time of stress and lowered self-esteem (Durkin, 1995; Gilligan, 1993). For most, the drop in self-esteem appears to be temporary, but some of the consequences are not.

The onset of puberty is typically associated with the onset of menarche (menstruation) for girls, and the appearance of secondary sex characteristics, including body hair. The onset of puberty marks the physical capacity for reproduction. A delayed onset of puberty may be a source of teasing or sense of inadequacy for both sexes, and should be medically evaluated in order to determine any physiological problems. For girls, the onset of puberty varies widely, and may occur comparatively young (ages 9–10) or later (15–16). For most, menarche starts between ages 9 and 16. Typically, girls enter puberty about two years earlier than boys. For girls, the onset of puberty may be the source of some confusion and awkwardness, particularly if their emotional functioning remains young for their age, or if their growth spurts entail suddenly towering over their peers. Girls may also be mistaken for being older than they are when they mature early, thus placing them at some risk of being sexually pressured before they are emotionally prepared to respond.

Cognitive development during adolescence typically entails a gradual transition toward increasingly abstract thinking, along with an increasing capacity to apply logic in relation to problem-solving and anticipation of consequences. Along with cognitive development during adolescence, a growing sense of self and identity typically emerges. During adolescence, concepts of the future become increasingly prominent, along with increasing awareness of talents, aptitudes, and interests that will become future occupations, means of earning income, and lifelong interests.

Elkind (1967) applied Piaget's concepts of formal operational thought to his observations of how *adolescent egocentrism* influences their interpretations and behaviours. Elkind proposed that adolescents engage in a form of reflection related to themselves and others that differs from the egocentrism of younger children. Two outcomes of those differences can be found in what Elkind called the *imaginary audience phenomenon* and the *personal fable* (Durkin, 1995).

The imaginary audience phenomenon refers to a sense to which many teenagers allude, in which they are keenly aware of the scrutiny of others. Such a sense of being scrutinized sometimes creates high levels of self-consciousness, and sometimes actually blurs perceptions of the self as distinct from others. The imaginary audience phenomenon creates a sense of continually being on show, and contributes to some adolescents' preoccupation with their appearance, dress, and social approval based on their sense that others are critically appraising their every outfit, hairstyle, and blunder. This is that phenomenon that contributes to a teenager's sense that everyone in school is aware that he or she has a spot (which is almost imperceptible) on the first day of class. Because their peers are also similarly preoccupied with their own appearance, feelings and behaviour, the ironic reality is that such scrutiny rarely occurs.

The personal fable is another form of adolescent egocentrism noted by Elkind (1967). According to Elkind, adolescents tend to consider their thoughts and feelings as being absolutely unique. In some ways, the personal fable reflects the reverse of the 'imaginary audience', in that it represents an excessive distinction between the self and others. It may entail a sense that rules and norms that apply to others are not relevant to oneself because of one's unique feelings and perceptions. For example, such adolescents may perceive their first love as being so totally unique and wonderful that such a romance has never occurred before. As a function of that uniqueness, practising 'safe sex' or contraception may appear unnecessary for them, because their love is too special to be sullied by such mundane matters as a sexually transmitted infection or an unplanned pregnancy. The personal fable may contribute to some adolescents' sense of personal invincibility, which may contribute to various forms of risk-taking including speeding and not wearing seat belts (because 'it can't happen to me'). For most teens, the personal fable phenomenon appears to resolve in later adolescence, but may be more problematic for people with insecure relationships with their parents that may contribute to a lack of self-confidence (Elkin & Bowen, 1979).

Some of the issues related to identity and self-esteem during adolescence appear gender-related (Gilligan, 1993). Girls' developmental processes appear more linked with intimacy and relationship, while boys are more focused on role and autonomy. Developing and maintaining relationships represents an inherent strength for girls and women (Gilligan, 1993; Brown & Gilligan, 1993). It also determines more than attachments, and links with decision-making and personal priorities, in ways that are quite distinct from boys and men. For that reason, Gilligan (1993) questions the applicability of traditional male-focused developmental theories for considering girls and women.

Social development during adolescence takes on increasing importance, with peer groups' influences often outweighing those of parents and families. Teenagers frequently prefer the company of their peers to that of their parents. Social affiliations, inclusion and interactions are key components of adolescents' sense of identity. For some, compatibility with a positive peer group proves a personal and social asset. For others, negative influences from peers may jeopardize academic and social aspirations, and place the adolescent at risk of danger, exclusion, or exposure to sexual or drug-related behaviours for which they are not prepared.

Meanwhile, as adolescents gain experience and competence, they also become increasingly independent, and capable of choosing their own friends and relationships outside their family of origin. This growing social autonomy may become a source of conflict with parents, especially when teens choose peers or romantic partners who do not conform to parents' norms or expectations. Adolescents' choices of peers and boyfriends/girlfriends are frequent sources of conflict with parents. For adolescents from families in which cultural norms dictate that parents select their children's peers and spouses, western norms of increasing social autonomy may prove particularly problematic. Peer conformity is consistently a strong component of most western adolescents' behaviour patterns (Beckett, 2002).

Alcohol and drug usage are often crucial components of adolescent experiences. During adolescence, drinking tends to occur outside the home, and is linked with social activities. While some are able to experiment without negative consequences, alcohol and drug-related problems often link with peers' usage patterns. Binge drinking is particularly associated with peer-driven behaviours (Gill, 2002; Weber, 2001). Particularly for girls, combined issues of social pressures, poor refusal skills, and coercive partners often contribute to personal and sexual vulnerability related to drinking.

Adolescents often receive an array of mixed messages related to sexual behaviours. They are often simultaneously urged to be popular with their peers and members of the opposite sex, while watching media presentations that glamorize sexual behaviours, along with being told to value their virginity, avoid pregnancy, sexually transmitted infections, and bad reputations. And despite common awareness of the likelihood of sexualized behaviour during adolescence, many well-intended adults avoid discussing sexual information with teenagers from fear of saying the wrong thing, or appearing either ignorant or encouraging undesirable behaviour.

Sexual orientation

The term *sexual orientation* refers to the objects of a person's sexual urges (Sadock & Sadock, 2007). (The term 'sexual preference' is not being used, as it implies a matter of choice.) While sexual orientation exists along a continuum, most people develop some awareness of their sexual orientation before or during adolescence (McCarter, 2003).

The majority of people identify themselves as heterosexual, or sexually attracted to the opposite sex. A minority of people identify themselves as homosexual, or sexually attracted to the same sex; another minority identify themselves as being bisexual, or attracted to both sexes.

Some level of sexual behaviour and attraction is typical during adolescence. Acknowledging homosexual attachments may be difficult, depending on environmental factors, including peers and family attitudes. While gay and lesbian adolescents appear to be acknowledging their homosexuality ('coming out') at younger ages than before, being different from the majority of their peers remains a complex aspect of their identities for most adolescents (Durkin, 1995). Homosexuality was once considered a mental illness, and was listed in the APA's *Diagnostic and Statistical Manual* until 1980 (Sadock & Sadock, 2007). Homosexuality is still sometimes associated with stigma in a predominantly heterosexual society. The 'coming out' process can be traumatic for adolescents, particularly if it is associated with internal conflicts or rejection by family or friends (Ryan & Futterman, 1998). The process is further complicated by the probability that repeated disclosures across the lifespan are often necessary.

Sexual orientation crises during adolescence are associated with heightened risks of suicide, with estimates of suicide attempts among homosexual youths as much as four times higher than among their heterosexual counterparts (Bagley & Tremblay, 2000; Parrish & Tunkle, 2005). Such risks emphasize the need for social workers to be keenly aware of personal, family, and cultural implications of adolescents' sexual orientations. Familiarity with resources such as Parents, Families and Friends of Lesbians and Gays (PFLAG) and their publications may be useful. Such tools as 'Questions to Ponder Prior to Coming Out' (PFLAG, 2001) may prove useful (Box 3.1).

Box 3.1 Questions to Ponder Prior to Coming Out

1. Are your sure about your sexual orientation?
2. Are you comfortable with your gay sexuality?
3. Do you have support?
4. Are you knowledgeable about homosexuality?
5. What is the emotional climate at home?
6. Can you be patient?
7. What is your motive for coming out now?
8. Do you have available resources?
9. Are you financially dependent on your parents?
10. What is your general relationship with your parents?
11. What is their moral society view?
12. Is this your decision?

Source: Parents, Families and Friends of Lesbians and Gays (2001).

Young adulthood

Suggestions of when adolescence ends and adulthood begins vary considerably. According to some, adolescence ends with the capacity to be financially self-sufficient; others argue that adolescence ends when an individual becomes a parent. Given current trends in lengthy education, the prospects of financial self-sufficiency and starting a family are often delayed for those pursuing higher education. This means that young adulthood is generally a time of physical, emotional and social changes.

Across Western cultures, young adulthood is associated with leaving the parental home to set up one's own. It is also a time during which most people establish enduring sexual relationships or marriage, and begin having children. It is also a time in which many people focus on developing marketable skills and establishing careers (Beckett, 2002).

According to the developmental psychologist Levinson (1986), the selection of a credible mentor is an important feature of young adulthood, particularly for men, who are focused on achieving 'the dream' to which they aspire. For young women, choices between identity, relationships, motherhood, and careers may be more complex. While women's social networks have traditionally been strong components across the lifespan, those networks are rarely validated by society at large. Often, women are expected to substitute their own social networks with those friends or associates chosen by their male partners (Brown & Gilligan, 1993; McGoldrick, 2005b).

Alcohol consumption generally peaks during young adulthood, particularly for men. Young adulthood is the time of peak physical health and performance for most people, but during their thirties, many are likely to begin noticing subtle physical changes, such as diminished eyesight, less physical stamina, and slower metabolism (Matto, 2003).

Middle and late adulthood

Clear chronological definitions of middle and late adulthood remain varied. Many of the developmental aspects of middle adulthood relate to family relationships; some are defined by occupational status (i.e. employed or retired). Roles and relationships of middle adulthood are often linked with contributions to the family or the greater society. Eriksonian views on the crises of 'generativity vs. stagnation' are discussed further in Chapter 4. Social workers are urged to resist stereotypes of older people as grannies/granddads, or frail helpless creatures, when they are not.

While many women find gratification from volunteering (at hospitals, charity shops, historic sites) in later life, for most women the prospects of old age are considerably poorer than those of men in the UK. Some of the differences are discussed further in Chapter 13. On a developmental level, however, women's health is an important variable. Older women are more likely than men to have chronic conditions that are not necessarily responsive to treatment. These include arthritis and fractures that often compromise mobility and autonomy. Increasing immobility may further complicate older women's circumstances when they depend on public transport. Women are also subject to more medication-related problems, such as dizziness and sedation. With age, however, women appear to feel that medical professionals pay them less attention, and ascribe complaints to stereotypical assumptions about ageing, rather than taking them seriously (Maynard, Afshar, Franks, & Wray, 2008).

Alcohol misuse is an often overlooked factor related to problems in later life. While many older people abstain from alcohol, a significant number drink problematically. Alcohol-related problems among older people may be complicated by interactions with prescribed medications, poor nutrition, and social isolation. Metabolic changes associated with ageing also compound people's assessments of their drinking patterns and problems (Goddard, Plant, Plant, Davidson, & Garretsen, 2000).

We live in an 'ageist' society, meaning that age often determines social divisions. Old age is often socially constructed simply by being over age 65. Older people (over 65) are frequently subjected to arbitrary decisions regarding retirement, unfair dismissal, bank loans, car hires, and medical options based solely on age. This ironic reality persists despite changing social structures, including remarriages, later parenting, social mobility and mid-life career changes that sometimes mean that people in later life are more vitally engaged with new activities and ideas than their younger counterparts.

Implications for practice

Social work practice involves working with people of all ages, and families of varying configurations. Social workers need considerable awareness of developmental norms and patterns in order to be effective with diverse service users. Social work often entails working with complex multi-generational situations, which makes having a clear understanding of developmental implications a crucial element of providing accurate assessments of problems.

Social workers must be mindful of gender, ethnic, and socio-economic differences across the lifespan, in order to practise in ways that are affirming and empowering for service users. Inequities regarding support and services for women and older people contribute to social workers' need to advocate for vulnerable populations. Social workers must be mindful of the implications of high rates of poverty among pensioners in the UK (Tanner & Harris, 2008).

The ability to listen carefully and the capacity to understand people in the context of their history and their current circumstances are among the valuable skills social workers bring to their practice. Understanding and responding to the meanings older people place on their experiences and expertise are vital to good practice.

Questions

1 What would some of the survival-related advantages be for an infant who is able to attend and respond to caregivers' voices and faces? What would some survival-related disadvantages be for a child who does not respond to caregivers' efforts?

2 What are some of the ways in which an infant whose mother experiences post-natal depression may be disadvantaged during childhood?

3 What are some protective factors that may serve to balance the risks posed by negative peer influences during adolescence?

4 In small groups, returning to the case mentioned in Chapter 1 (p. 5), reconsider the following:
   (a) What are some of the developmental concerns you have for Eve's baby?
   (b) How/why might her baby's needs be complex?
   (c) What are some of your developmental concerns for Eve?
   (d) What factors could complicate Eve's ability to meet her baby's needs?

5 In small groups, discuss:
   (a) When do you think childhood ends and adolescence begins?
   (b) When do you think adolescence ends and adulthood begins?

6 What are some of your ideas about being 'old'?
   (a) How do you define 'being old?
   (b) What do you like/dislike about being around older people?
   (c) What are some positive and negative aspects of being old?

PART II

Psychological Dimensions of Human Behaviour

4 Freud's psychoanalytic and Erikson's developmental theories of behaviour

While classical psychoanalytic theory originally evolved from Sigmund Freud's work with patients in Victorian-era Vienna, some of his basic concepts continue to influence current approaches to understanding people's behaviours and difficulties. In her own right, Anna Freud expanded upon her father's work, and contributed to the evolution of 'ego psychology', which is discussed in Chapter 5. The subsequent work of Anna Freud's protégé, Erik Erikson, built upon Freudian theories, to provide a framework for understanding the developmental process across the lifespan. While clearly distinct from one another, Freud's and Erikson's theories are considered in juxtaposition because of their combined relevance to understanding behaviour as a dynamic and developmental concept.

Relevance for social work

Regardless of their specific area of expertise, most social workers rely on some level of familiarity with psychoanalytic concepts, because they have influenced so many aspects of twentieth-century psychological thinking. While a minority of social workers would likely consider themselves 'purely' psychoanalytic in their approaches, the majority would likely acknowledge being influenced by concepts stemming from Freud's works, including such concepts as the ego (ego strengths), the unconscious, and the defence mechanisms. Dating from Mary Richmond's (1917) premise that 'uncovering the cause will reveal the cure', social work has historically relied on psychoanalytic theory to provide a more scientific and intellectually credible basis for its approach to assessing problems and helping people in need.

Many of Freud's ideas and terminology have permeated western cultural beliefs, literature, and vocabularies, which should not be mistaken for the direct application of his actual theories. Social workers need to be familiar with his concepts as well as ways in which those concepts have evolved and been interpreted (and possibly misinterpreted) over the past century, regardless of the theoretical perspective they employ to shape their practice.

While Erikson was initially considered among the mainstream of psychoanalytic orthodoxy, his conceptual approaches differed significantly through his emphasis on a developmental approach to ego mastery. Unlike Freud's psychosexual developmental concepts, Erikson expanded the concept of life stages to include stage-related tasks as well as old age. Especially as social work practice increasingly entails attention to the needs of older people, Erikson's more optimistic theory has particular relevance to the appraisal of behaviour relevant to characteristic stages of later life. Erikson also emphasized the significance of relationships across the lifespan, referring to a 'radius of significant relationships' (Erikson, 1982) to describe the expanding array of emotional connections established across the lifespan. His attention to interpersonal relationships is congruent with social work's emphasis on the importance of social networks in people's well-being.

Freud's historical background

Sigmund Freud (1856–1939), the son of a Jewish wool merchant, spent most of his life in Vienna. He was the oldest of his parents' eight children born during a ten-year period. Freud's family of origin provides ripe material for speculation, as his mother was nearly 20 years younger than his father, with whom Freud had a distant and possibly uneasy ('Oedipal'?) relationship (Ewen, 1998). At age 30, Freud married the woman whose brother subsequently married Freud's sister Anna. The Freud family's genogram can be found in Chapter 12.

Freud trained as a neurologist, and studied hypnosis. As a newly married young neurologist in Vienna, Freud's practice relied heavily on referrals from other physicians. Many of those patients sent to Freud were considered 'hysterics', whose presenting symptoms lacked physical explanations. The context of his practice with those patients necessarily shaped his approach to understanding human behaviour, and thus formed the backdrop for the development of his *psychoanalytic theory*.

With the exception of his daughter Anna, Freud's relationships with his various protégés generally ended acrimoniously (see Chapter 5). Freud's final years were spent in considerable pain, resulting from cancer of the mouth and jaw. Some question the linkage of his cancer to his smoking habits. His final years were made even more traumatic by the Nazi invasion of Vienna in 1938; the Freud family escaped to London, where Sigmund Freud died the following year.

Key psychoanalytic concepts

Freud's psychoanalytic theory evolved into a broad framework comprising clinical observations and basic theoretical propositions about people's thinking and behaviour as well as a therapeutic technique used in clinical practice. Among the key tenets of Freud's theories is the premise that all behaviour is driven by innate instincts that express themselves through actions. Based on that premise, Freud proposed that all behaviour is purposeful, as a means of fulfilling instinctual needs, drives and urges;

furthermore, behaviour is also subject to interpretation and explanation by applying the concepts contained in his theories.

In working with patients in late nineteenth-century Vienna, Freud came to rely on the use of hypnosis to delve into patients' buried memories that were unavailable to them in a regular waking state. Hypnosis was not universally successful for all Freud's patients, however; in fact, not everyone is even susceptible to entering the hypnotic state necessary for its practice. Freud also used the cathartic method of *free association*, in which patients explored their thoughts in a quiet room in which even the physician was out of sight. Patients responded to simple suggestions or questions using whatever words, thoughts or images entered their minds. The analyst refrained from influencing the patient's accounts of their thoughts, but listened intently in order to interpret the dynamic patterns of associations that occurred in the patient's explorations. By engaging in free association, the patient sought to experience a *catharsis*, or a release of the emotional tension with which they had been struggling.

From his work with 'hysteric' patients, Freud introduced the term *neurosis* to refer to various disorders in which anxiety was the most prominent symptom. Although dropped from the diagnostic lexicon in the early 1980s because it lacked an empirical measure, the term 'neurotic' remains closely associated with psychoanalytic concepts. It also tends to be applied in dismissive and potentially derogatory and patronizing ways, inferring that the person's distress is less than real or legitimate. As employed by Freud, the concept of neurosis often pertained to the premise that the root of much of adult pathology could be found in early childhood experiences. The uncovering and interpretation of those experiences became a key component of psychoanalysis.

The psychoanalytic process entailed an intense working relationship between the patient and the psychoanalyst, who was expected to interpret and explain the presenting problems and uncover their origins in a corrective way. To practise psychoanalysis necessitated considerable self-awareness; at a minimum, psychoanalysts were expected to have undergone psychoanalysis themselves (Greene & Ephross, 1991).

Some of the material patients explored in the course of free association included content that had previously been 'forgotten'. Freud proposed that some of the highly emotional content of patients' previously forgotten recollections contained memories that had been *repressed*, rather than actually forgotten. Repression was considered an unconscious means of blocking events or thoughts from conscious memory or awareness. Freud believed that patients' presenting problems typically reflected some symbolic representation of conflictual repressed material, which was previously excluded from their conscious awareness. *Psychic determinism* refers to the psychoanalytic premise that actions or behaviours stem from the individual's earlier experiences and thought processes, rather than just happening at random or as a coincidence (Payne, 1997).

The content of dreams often arose in patients' sessions of free association, leading Freud to regard them as a significant means of uncovering relevant material that would otherwise remain repressed or unconscious. He referred to dreams as the 'royal road' to understanding the unconscious. Freud's theory of dreams preceded his development of a comprehensive theory of the functions of the ego. His views on dreams emphasize the importance of discharging unconscious drives and wishes through their symbolic content. Freud's (1900) monumental work *The Interpretation of Dreams* is a reflection of his work interpreting the unconscious content of dreams and issues of repressed impulses and wish fulfilment. The subsequent role of Freud's seminal book also represents an intellectual and social history of the psychoanalytic movement and Freud's considerable efforts to shape the intellectual content of that movement (Franklin, 2005; Marinelli & Mayer, 2003).

Freud's regard for dreams' content remained a key component of his understanding of the mind's efforts to express unconscious material. According to Freud, the content of dreams frequently represents *wish fulfilment*, or fantasies that were otherwise considered unacceptable or socially inappropriate in a conscious context. Freud saw the various figures within an individual's environment (such as parents, teachers, religious authorities) as influences and monitors of how the individual's needs and wishes were approached, and how their acceptability/unacceptability was defined and understood.

The content of the material revealed through dreams, hypnosis and free association initially convinced Freud of the incidence of childhood sexual seduction and its relevance to subsequent dynamic difficulties and psychopathology. In the later 1890s, however, Freud's thinking shifted from being convinced of the occurrence of childhood sexual experiences toward minimizing some of the accounts he had heard, and regarding them as being too fantastic for belief. While Freud did not actually deny the occurrence of childhood sexual molestation, he placed greater emphasis on the role played by childhood sexual fantasies as the foundation of subsequent neuroses.

Freud's capacity to revise his ideas provides a dynamic example of how theories develop and grow. An example of this can be found in his approach to bereavement. In his essay *Melancholia and Mourning*, Freud (1917) proposed that both mourning and melancholia shared common features, including profound sorrow, loss of interest, and the loss of the ability to love. He viewed mourning as more within the 'normal' range of emotions, and melancholia more toward the pathological, and proposed that mourning reached its conclusion when the bereaved reached a point of emotional detachment that allowed for the reinvestment of the freed libidinal energy in a new love object. In his essay *The Ego and the Id* (1923), however, Freud revised his concept of mourning, and acknowledged the possibility of mourning persisting without necessarily entailing melancholia (Clewell, 2004). Historically, Freud's shift in perspective coincided with the events of World War I that dramatically influenced people's first-hand experience of bereavement on an unprecedented scale, providing an example of the interactions between political history, personal experience, and the development of a theory.

Freud's aspiration to explain the content of people's thoughts as rigorously as he would people's behaviour represented a dramatic development, even among his contemporaries in the study and practice of psychology. As a significant portion of his efforts to explain people's thoughts, Freud proposed a model of understanding the mind that divided its functions into three components: the conscious, the preconscious, and the unconscious. Two of the primary components of Freud's theories are his Topographical Conception and his Structural Conception. While both contain explanatory concepts of the mind's workings, they refer to different dimensions. To quote Polansky (1991: 28): 'Put another way, it is always the same cake you are cutting. But the stroke of the knife yields different kinds of information about it. A vertical cut makes the layers stand out; a horizontal one makes its roundness apparent.'

Freud's topographical concept of the mind

First introduced in his *The Interpretation of Dreams* (1900), Freud's topographical concept involves a division of the mind into three areas: the conscious, the preconscious, and the unconscious, each of which has its own unique functions and characteristics. From the geological term 'topography', 'topographical' possibly refers to the imagery of a mountainous landscape, in which the highest ground (the conscious) is the most visible, and most readily available to sunlight. Parts of the hillsides (the preconscious) receive partial or reflected sunlight in the course of the day, and the lower valleys (the unconscious) are hidden in darkness (Polansky, 1991).

The conscious

In Freud's topographical model, the conscious is that part of the mind in which ideas and perceptions resulting either from the outside world or from within the individual are brought into awareness. Freud proposed that the conscious entails those thoughts and feelings about which the individual can focus direct attention. The conscious is readily accessible to the individual. Examples of conscious material include names, whereabouts, and intentional activities.

The preconscious

Unlike the conscious, the preconscious represents those aspects or ideas that can be focused upon at will, but require some deliberate effort to summon forward. Examples include the name of one's first pet, or a childhood neighbour, which can be remembered, but are not likely to be foremost in conscious material. Conceptually, the preconscious interfaces with the conscious and unconscious or seemingly forgotten areas of the mind, and can serve to link material that has previously remained unconscious. It can also function as a barrier to material maintained in the unconscious that may be unacceptable to the conscious, through *repression* of that content.

The unconscious

In Freud's topographical model, the unconscious represents a dynamic array of content and processes that are kept from conscious awareness through a form of mental censorship or repression. In some older references, the unconscious was also referred to as the 'subconscious', which is more aptly used to refer to the preconscious and the unconscious combined.

The unconscious processes extend from such mundane tendencies as forgetting names and misspeaking and misreading words, to the content of dreams, jokes, and choices of life partners who resemble a parent, the motivations for which remain outside an individual's actual awareness. Importantly, various urges or wishes may represent some degree of conflict (with society or the self); that conflict may likely remain unconscious, and thus influence behaviours in ways that are covert rather than overt. The mental material that remains hidden or unconscious is considered *latent content.*

Freud proposed that the unconscious content of the mind was manifested through dreams, free association, or possibly through erroneous slips of the tongue. Such comments are also sometimes referred to as 'Freudian slips', whereby someone says something less than socially or politically correct, but which contains a more suggestive or symbolic content that would normally have been left unspoken (or *repressed,* in Freudian terms). An example would be a wife calling her husband by her previous husband's name during a heated argument. As expressed by a common pun: 'A Freudian slip is saying one thing, and meaning your mother.'

In proportion to the conscious and preconscious, the unconscious is considered the far larger portion of the mind. The conscious is more the 'tip of the iceberg', with the preconscious and unconscious being far more substantial. The unconscious is considered the source of much of the personal conflicts experienced involving relationships, instincts and behaviour. Being unconscious, however, conflictual material is generally only expressed symbolically, or through physical symptoms. Those conflicts often involve the id, the ego, and the superego addressed in Freud's *structural concept.*

Freud's structural concept

With his structural concept of the mind, Freud sought to explain what was going on beyond the individual's presenting problems or symptoms. Unsurprisingly for someone who lived during the Industrial Revolution, Freud relied on somewhat mechanical imagery to describe his ideas of the id, the ego, and the superego. Each aspect serves a distinct function, and together they comprise a key component of psychoanalytic *personality theory.*

The *id* denotes the more primitive instinctive urges, sometimes known as the 'party animal' of the psyche. Regarded by Freud as entailing unorganized instinctive drives, the id is regarded as being dominated by the *primary processes* of thinking. The primary processes are the more primitive, illogical, irrational, less mature levels of thinking. Examples include childish logic (I can't see you, so you don't exist), severe regression, and some psychotic thinking. In such instances, the id is detached from the external world and its rules, reasons, realities or consequences. Along with controlling a large portion of the mind's energy, the id is associated with the *pleasure principle,* which focuses on immediate gratification of urges, pleasure seeking, passions and aggression. Thus the id is associated with impulsive acts and irrational behaviours. It is also the psychic home of those drives that result in a state of tension, and which compel the individual to act in ways that reduce tension, regardless of reason or consequences. The *libido* refers to the sexual energy and drives among the id's biological instincts, and is a key component of the id.

In contrast to the id, the *ego* serves an adaptive function, balancing the urges of the id with the demands of the superego. Psychic energy is shifted from the id to the ego in order that the ego can function in an executive role for the personality. The ego plays the role of 'preceptor' or 'traffic warden' to the conflicting tensions of the id and the superego. Unlike the id's reliance on the pleasure principle, the ego is governed by the *reality principle*, which entails the ability to delay gratification, and constrain impulses until appropriate release is possible. In order to do so, the ego operates according to *secondary process thinking*, which entails the capacity to anticipate consequences of behaviours, or *reality testing*. Thus the ego serves to coordinate the psyche's mastery of impulses, along with the capacity to distinguish between fantasy and reality.

The ego serves a complex function, by balancing the challenges of the internal drives and urges of the id, and external realities, including social norms, legalities, and such mundane realities as personal and public safety. In doing so, the *ego functions*, such as frustration tolerance, boundaries, and coping skills are applied to coordinate the person's behaviour. Those personality functions also have great relevance to a person's capacity to live in harmony with others, which relates to Freud's purported definition of wellness, which was the capacity *to love and work* (Erikson, 1950). Ego functions are essential components of the capacity to love and work effectively.

Developing after the id and the ego, Freud proposed that the *superego* fulfils the equivalent of a judicial branch of the psyche, representing those external values and ideals embraced by the individual's parents and greater society. The formation and development of the superego are key aspects of a child's socialization process, helping to restrain impulses and aggression. As a child develops, an increasing array of influences serves to shape the evolving superego (teachers, religious leaders, coaches, role models). Ideally, the superego functions in much the same way as a 'conscience'; it alerts the individual to behaviours that are 'bad' or immoral, and distinguishes between good and evil. The development of the superego during childhood entails both physical and mental rewards (associated with reduced tension) and punishments (associated with increased tension). Throughout life, however, examples of under-developed or overly harsh superego functions may be found in the content of people's appraisals of their experiences. Examples of overly harsh superegos would entail adults whose sense of right and wrong is excessively judgmental or punitive, with an unforgiving element over-riding issues of justice or compassion. Examples of underdeveloped superegos may be found among people who have no regard for the rights or safety of the vulnerable, or who operate solely on the basis of their own gratification at the expense of others.

As an illustration of the id, the ego and the superego, visualize a child at a checkout counter in a shop, where sweets are displayed in various attractive packages at her eye level. If her id were to say 'The sweet is delicious; grab a handful!', her ego would look to see if her mother or the clerk might be looking. Her superego, however, would be that voice that says, 'good children don't steal.'

Defence mechanisms

Defence mechanisms play a crucial part of the psychoanalytic personality theory's proposal of how the ego manages conflict on a day-to-day basis. Freud's daughter Anna Freud (1895–1982), a prominent psychoanalyst, teacher and author, is credited with having introduced the term (Glassman & Hadad, 2004). According to psychoanalytic thought, conflict results from the efforts of the ego and superego to control the id in relation to various aspects of social acceptability, responsibility and propriety. Those conflicts subsequently result in *anxiety*, which is associated with a sense of being somehow threatened. Sigmund Freud proposed that anxiety is biologically based, and that it serves a protective or adaptive function, to warn the ego of potential danger. The perception of threat associated with anxiety may be internally or externally generated, but is usually experienced as an undesirable emotional state, and potentially overwhelming. In order to make the anxiety more manageable, the ego calls upon an array of defence mechanisms, including denial and repression.

While defence mechanisms are an adaptive and necessary feature of healthy egos, not all defence mechanisms are created equal. The defence mechanisms vary in their level of sophistication and function. Denial is considered the most primitive, and possibly the most over-utilized of the defence mechanisms. (Witness the most typical response to bad news: 'I don't believe it, but . . .') Important defence mechanisms include those shown in Table 4.1.

Table 4.1 Psychoanalytic defence mechanisms

Defence mechanism	*Defence mechanism behaviour*
Denial	Involves refusal to acknowledge the reality of thoughts or urges that raise anxiety
Displacement	Involves redirecting or refocusing energy from one subject to a less anxiety-invoking substitute
Projection	Involves attributing one's own undesirable or unacceptable thoughts or urges to another as their own
Rationalization	Involves offering an explanation or reason that is more acceptable to the ego than the actual cause of the anxiety
Reaction formation	Involves reacting to anxiety-inducing situations or people in ways that are the opposite to one's characteristic impulses
Regression	Involves reverting to behaviours associated with an earlier developmental phase
Repression	Involves excluding or blocking out threatening thoughts, memories, or impulses that would exacerbate anxiety from conscious thought
Sublimation	Involves redirecting energy (especially sexual energy) toward a more consciously acceptable activity or creativity that is less anxiety-inducing for the ego

The developmental constructs of Sigmund Freud

When Freud developed his theories of the developmental aspects of the human psyche, his formulations linked human drives with those of other animals, with an emphasis on their serving basic survival needs. He also proposed that the personality's basic structure was essentially established by about age 6. In what proved to be one of his more controversial concepts, Freud's (1905) *Three Essays on the Theory of Sexuality* outlined his ideas that came to be considered the *psychosexual stages*. His concepts of sexual energy are more to do with drives and gratification derived from bodily functions (sucking, feeding, and elimination) than erotic or adult sexuality, but the application of the term 'sexual' during infancy is sometimes confusing to those unfamiliar with Freud's works. Freud considered sexuality the most powerful of the biological forces that shaped behaviour.

Freud introduced the constructs of a psychological model based on stages of development. He based his premise on sources of gratification that dominated different stages of development. Freud's concepts of gratification were defined around the area of the body that was the focus of pleasure or stimulation. Thus, his phrase the *erogenous zones* referred to many parts of the body, rather than solely genital pleasures. He proposed that psychosexual development occurs over the course of five distinct stages. These stages are outlined in Table 4.2 on p. 65, along with those of Erikson.

Freud's psychosexual stages

Aside from Freud's focus on the conflicts resulting from unresolved issues related to each stage, he also suggested that those stages were essentially completed by adolescence. Within Freud's psychosexual stages, his concept of the *Oedipal complex* remains highly controversial. Reflecting various factors relevant to his era and culture, Freud's expectations of fathers included considerable authority, with males typically representing the disciplinarian functions in many Victorian families. Freud's theory possibly reflected early childhood struggles with authority and power, rather than an overtly sexual component of the child's relationship with his mother (Segall et al., 1999).

One of Freud's key concepts linked with his Oedipal complex is the idea of boys experiencing *castration anxiety*, entailing fears that their sexual organs will be removed as punishment for their Oedipal wishes. The Oedipal complex refers to the Greek myth of Oedipus, who unwittingly killed his father and married his mother. Some analysts referred to the female equivalent of this dynamic 'the Electra complex', but Freud applied the term Oedipal to both sexes.

Freud's oral stage of psychosexual development

During the *oral stage* (birth–18 months), the infant's primary source of gratification is the mouth, through which nourishment is sought, and through which he or she is able to express hunger, distress or pleasure. During early infancy, crying may or may not appear purposeful. As the infant comes to associate crying with obtaining attention and being fed, however, crying appears to become more intentional. During this phase, the infant is also increasingly capable of distinguishing between her/himself as a physical being apart from their environment. Such distinctions serve as the beginnings of an individual's *self-image*.

During Freud's lifetime, breastfeeding was the norm, and thus feeding also necessarily entailed intimate body contact between mother and child. With weaning, children experienced the loss of the pleasure, intimacy and gratifications associated with nursing, and were expected to be increasingly able to tolerate frustration of meals and other pleasures being delayed. Likewise, children who are currently fed from bottles are similarly exposed to aspects of more regimented, delayed meal times during this proposed stage.

The dominance of pleasure associated with infantile oral gratification relates to Freud's concept of the *id*, which he described as that part of the personality that is driven by instinct and pleasure-seeking. The *id* is considered a more primitive drive than its counterparts the *ego* and the *superego*, which are presumed to develop later. Infants are not expected to apply these more sophisticated aspects of judgment or boundaries in their quest for food or pleasure during the oral stage of their development.

From Freud's perspective, premature or overly delayed weaning could result in a subsequent *oral fixation*, which reflects unresolved conflicts associated with the oral stage. Fixations are typically associated with either overly rigid or overly permissive expectations on the part of adults, and thus may reflect either insufficient or overwhelming levels of gratifications associated with a particular stage of development, and are associated with some evidence of *regression* back to the unresolved stage. Regression is particularly associated with people's response to stress. A 5-year-old resuming sleeping with a pacifier following the birth of a new sibling would be an example of regression to an oral stage-related behaviour. Examples of oral fixations include people who continue to engage in behaviour focused on that mode of gratification, including compulsive over-eating, smoking, or possibly nail-biting.

Freud's anal stage of psychosexual development

According to Freud's concepts, a shift in the focus of energy occurs at around 18 months, signalling the transition to the *anal stage* (18–36 months). During the anal stage, the infant is increasingly focused on factors associated with elimination (both producing and withholding urine and faeces). At this stage, many children experience some distress at the prospect that the bowel movement that they have so proudly enjoyed producing is simply going to be discarded, rather than admired and appreciated.

Along with their increasing capacity to control body functions (i.e. with meal times and with toilet training), Freud proposed that children's *egos* were also developing in maturity. The ego functions proposed by Freud entailed a capacity to balance the demands of the external environment with the instincts and pleasure-seeking drives produced by the id. In balancing the competing demands of the physical pleasures associated with producing bowel movements and the personal pleasures associated with gaining approval from adults, Freud asserted that children's ego functions were becoming increasingly sophisticated.

Learning to accommodate adults' expectations, timing, and instructions may bring about some conflict for children who are particularly intent on sharing the products of their bowel movements. Adults' preoccupation with hygiene and smells may not seem reasonable to a 2-year-old. A child who experiences punishments that exceed praise and rewards may develop a sense of shame or confusion associated with bodily functions, and possible resentment of those in a position to exert their authority. From

Freud's perspective, such conflicts could lead to an *anal fixation*, which would typically entail behaviour related to control of the environment, and possibly involve preoccupation with cleanliness or routine.

Freud's phallic stage of psychosexual development

According to Freudian concepts, by about ages 3–5, children's focus of gratification has shifted from the mouth (oral stage) to the elimination process (anal stage) to the genital area (phallic stage). The gratification associated with genitalia that children experience during the *phallic phase* is quite distinct from adult sexual pleasure. For one thing, children's physical immaturity precludes the sexual gratification experienced by adults. During this phase, however, children consistently experience delight in exploring, touching, and even comparing their bodies in general, including their genitalia.

The primary area of conflict Freud associated with this phase related to what he called the *Oedipal complex*. According to Freud, children between about ages 3 to 5/6 are likely to develop strong attachments to the parent of the opposite sex, and fantasize about growing up and marrying them, thus rendering their same-sex parent either irrelevant or a rival.

According to Freudian concepts, the resolution of the ambiguous feelings of either resentment or jealousy of their same-sex parent thus represents a primary task during this stage. *Ego* functions are necessary in order to contribute to sufficient reality testing to recognize that the same-sex parent has sufficient power to maintain their relationship, and thus the child can proceed to cope with anxiety through *identification*. Through identification, the child effectively incorporates or adopts the values of the same-sex parent as their own, thus precluding any hostilities from arising. As part of the process of identification, the opposite-sex parent becomes a prototype for future attractions.

Simultaneously, according to Freud, the child's *superego* begins to be manifest, by incorporating some of the parental values and norms relating to acceptable behaviour. The child begins to apply the ideas of 'shoulds/should nots' and 'oughts/ought nots' associated with the functions of the superego. As it applies to the child's development, the superego is likely to function as an internalized sense of what thoughts or behaviours would or would not be considered acceptable, and thus serves to support the process of identification and the suppression of the child's desire for their parent of the opposite sex.

Freud also believed that children experienced *castration anxieties* and *penis envy* during this developmental phase. For boys, castration fears related to their developmentally normal fascination with their own genitalia as well as their awareness that females' genitalia differs from their own. Freud proposed that the awareness of boys' penises prompted a sense of envy on the part of girls. As part of the identification process, boys were presumed to identify with their fathers' continued evidence of possessing an intact penis. Likewise, Freud proposed that girls were faced with evidence of their mothers having also suffered the loss of their penis, and thus formed a closer sense of identification based on their mutual loss.

When challenged by those who insisted on having no such recollections, feelings or fears during childhood, Freud proposed that they existed, but had been relegated to the *unconscious*, and were therefore not accessible to the conscious memory of childhood. Freud's concepts of penis envy and the Oedipal complex remain among his more controversial concepts, and have been strongly criticized by the more feminist theorists of development.

Freud's latency stage (5–12 years)

During this phase of development, Freud proposed that children's sexual energy is repressed, while the ego and superego become more developed. Conscious energy is primarily focused on academic and practical skills. Children become increasingly autonomous during this period. Freud saw the *latency stage* as a time during which previous psychosexual development can be consolidated, in preparation for a successful transition into adulthood.

Freud's genital stage (12–20 years and onward)

From Freud's perspective, the *genital stage* represented the physical maturation of the child, entailing puberty, and the physical capacity to reproduce. The primary objectives of this phase have to do with diminished dependence on the child's parents, the achievement of an adult identity and role, as well as the establishment of sexually gratifying (non-incestuous) relations with adults. Freud did not expand upon further stages of development following the genital stage. However, his concept of normal adulthood was defined by the capacity 'to love and work'.

Erikson's historical background

Erik H. Erikson (1902–1994) was the son of a Jewish mother from Denmark and an unnamed Danish father who abandoned them before Erikson's birth. In 1904, Erikson's mother, a trained nurse, married her son's paediatrician, Dr Theodor Homberger, who adopted her son. Erikson went by the name Homberger, and was apparently not informed of the details of his birth until later in life. Erikson's mother never revealed his birth father's identity to him (Sadock & Sadock, 2007). The man who went on to devote the majority of his career to the understanding of identity and development was teased as a boy for looking Nordic by his classmates at his Jewish Temple School, and for being Jewish by his Gentile grammar school classmates.

After completing his education, in the years following World War I, Erikson travelled through Europe as something of a social rebel, long before 'gap years' became the norm. While teaching art in Vienna, Erikson obtained a certificate in Montessori education as well as another from the Vienna Psychoanalytic Society, where Anna Freud both psychoanalysed and taught him. He trained to become a child psychoanalyst in Vienna, becoming the first non-university-trained psychoanalyst. While studying in Vienna, he also met his future wife, the Canadian Joan Serson (1902–1997), with whom he had three children.

In 1933, the Eriksons fled the Nazis and moved to America, where he was the first child psychoanalyst in Boston. Upon taking American citizenship, he changed his name from Homberger to Erikson during the 1930s, and eventually converted to Christianity (Ewen, 1998). Erikson taught at Yale and then at the University of California at Berkeley. He also studied the Oglala Lakota and Sioux tribes in the American West. During the politically divisive McCarthy era, Erikson returned to the Boston area and taught at Harvard. His seminal book, *Childhood and Society*, written in 1950, reflected his exposure to an array of childhood experiences, from wartime Europe to Native American traditions. In 1951, Erikson began working with severely disturbed children and adults at the Austen Riggs treatment centre in Stockbridge, Massachusetts. He retired from Harvard in 1970, and continued to write and work collaboratively with his wife Joan until his death in 1994.

Key concepts of Erikson's psychosocial theory: the life cycle

Erik Erikson's psychosocial theory represents a distinct generational shift from the initial Freudian tradition. While Erikson is generally considered among the vanguard of ego psychologists, he is also sometimes referred to as a 'neo-Freudian' or a 'Freudian ego psychologist' because of his adherence to some of the more controversial Freudian concepts, including the Oedipal complex. He is also noted for including more sociological, developmental and anthropological concepts related to environmental influences.

Erikson's basic premise entailed a bio-psychosocial view of lifelong development. He emphasized the dynamic relationship between the individual and his or her social environment, including a core concept of the 'nourishing exchange of community life' (Erikson, 1964: 89), especially as it pertains to mental health. From his exposure to socially diverse aspects of development and behaviour, Erikson introduced a more multi-cultural perspective to the formulation of his theory of the life cycle than his predecessors' or contemporaries' theories had contained. Importantly, Erikson envisioned eight stages occurring across the lifespan, rather than Freud's five stages.

Erikson's theory reflects an inherently optimistic view of people's capacity to grow and be well. This alone distinguishes his approach from the psychoanalytic orthodoxy that emphasizes conflict, neuroses, and psychic determinism. Erikson's premise that 'there is little in inner developments which cannot be harnessed to constructive and peaceful initiatives if only we learn to understand the conflicts and anxieties of childhood' (Erikson, 1959: 83) represents a significant theoretical shift away from his psychoanalytic origins. Erikson is credited with focusing more attention on social factors in contemporary psychoanalytic thought. Thus his work serves as something of a theoretical bridge between traditional psychoanalytic theory and ego psychology.

Some of the more important distinctions between Freud's and Erikson's approaches include the following:

- Erikson placed more emphasis on social influences such as peers, siblings, teachers, role models and the broader culture than Freud did, and thus placed less emphasis on sexual urges to explain behaviour.

- Erikson's emphasis on the ego's adaptive power was greater than the attention he paid to the role played by the id.
- Erikson's overall view of human nature was considerably more positive than Freud's, with a particular emphasis placed on the capacity for rational, adaptive development.
- Erikson proposed that development continued during adulthood, over the course of eight stages, rather than Freud's proposed five.

Erikson's terminology reflects a logical and contextual progression, rather than a strict psychological emphasis. The eight stages are also sequential, which relates to his theory's *epigenetic effect*, which entails the ways in which earlier decisions or outcomes influence subsequent stages. Erikson's stages entail aspects of developmental 'crises' that are normal, rather than signs of neuroses or pathology (Polanksy, 1991).

Erikson proposed that development follows a bio-psychosocial trajectory across the life cycle, and that development is essentially propelled by various biological factors. His theory proposed that the role played by the ego entailed a quest for competence and mastery of the environment. Erikson viewed individual development as being positively supported by society, as well as contributing reciprocally to society. Erikson's theory proposes that the individual's personality is the result of the resolution of the proposed stages through which they progress. Each stage builds upon the previous stage, on a continuum from positive to negative. Psychosocial health is seen as a function of the reciprocal interaction of ego strengths and social supports, and entails inter-generational supports and interactions. Distortions in self-identity are seen as arising from inadequate resolutions of developmental crises, and/or estrangement from constructive social interactions and support (Greene & Ephross, 1991).

Erikson's life stages of development

In contrast to Freud's emphasis on gratification and possible conflictual content (Table 4.2), Erikson focused on tasks and *phase-specific* life crises associated with development. Erikson focused on a more psychosocial approach to understanding people's development, entailing environmental influences on the experiences of each phase. Instead of conflicts or neuroses, Erikson described the possibility of *crises* associated with the different stages' resolutions. He also believed it was always possible to renegotiate unresolved issues from previous stages at a later date.

Erikson's trust vs. mistrust stage (birth–1 year)

According to Erikson, the initial stage of an infant's development revolves around the establishment of trust or mistrust, both internal and external. By this, he referred to the attitude adopted by the infant in relation to the self and others. Does the infant come to expect those around him or her to be reliable in their attentions, feedings, etc., or does he or she express a characteristic reluctance to trust or rely on them? Elements of consistency, reliability, and parents' capacity to anticipate an infant's needs are all

Table 4.2 Comparison of Freudian and Eriksonian stages of development

Age	*Freud*	*Erikson*
Birth–18 months	Oral Stage Focus of gratification: mouth Early ego formation, weaning, beginning to tolerate delayed gratification	Trust vs. Mistrust Initially called 'inner confidence' Development of trust of self and others; attachment to reliable caregivers (Hope)
18 months–3 years (toddler)	Anal Stage Source of gratification: elimination Focus: continued ego formation, toilet training	Autonomy vs. Shame Exploration of environment, learning self-control (Willpower)
3–5 years (early childhood)	Phallic Stage Source of gratification: genitalia Focus: formation of superego Emergency of Oedipal complex likely	Initiative vs. Guilt Learning to plan, initiate and follow through with activities; learning to share with others, and to tolerate frustration (Purpose)
5–12 years (puberty)	Latency Stage Source of gratification: repressed sexual urges in interest of skill building Genital Stage Focus of gratification: genitalia Capacity for symbolic gratification of drives; secondary process thinking	Industry vs. Inferiority Preoccupation with activities such as education, sports, play; expanding sense of competence in multiple spheres (Competence)
12–20 (adolescence)		Identity vs. Role Confusion Formation of clear sense of self, values, aspirations (Fidelity)
20–25 (young adult)		Intimacy vs. Isolation Learning commitment and sharing relationships with others (Love)
25–65 (middle adult)		Generativity vs. Stagnation Making contributions to family and society (Care)
Over 65 (late adult)		Integrity vs. Despair Development of a sense of completeness, contentment towards life; reconciliation with past (Wisdom)

relevant to the emergence of *external trust* or mistrust during this stage. Erikson considered this stage crucial in the infant's sense of self-reliance, hopefulness, and frustration tolerance. Being able to influence the environment by crying in order to get needs met was one of the ways that Erikson understood infants' sense of *internal trust*. The capacity for hope is an essential result of this stage's successful resolution. Problematic outcomes associated with this stage being unsuccessfully resolved include psychoses, autism, substance misuse, and depression.

Erikson's autonomy vs. shame, doubt stage (18 months–3 years)

During this stage, Erikson proposed that the main focus of energy was on the acquisition of self-control. While the initial emphasis of self-control is likely to do with toilet training, and the mastery of bladder and bowel functions, toddlers are also expanding aspects of self-control that impact on their social relations. Their ability to play with others and to learn from their explorations also necessitate an emerging capacity to control basic urges. Erikson emphasized the importance of learning about *holding on and letting go* during this stage of development. Successful resolution of this stage is associated with the capacity to exert willpower. Difficulties associated with problematic outcomes from this stage include paranoia, obsessions, compulsions, and impulsivity.

Erikson's initiative vs. guilt stage (3–5 years)

While Erikson initially included Freud's concepts of an Oedipal complex during this stage, he emphasized the focus of energy on learning, exploring and experimentation. By this stage, most children are less aggressive than they were in the previous stage, and have mastered increasing degrees of self-control, language and physical dexterity. Children at this stage are likely to be taking increasing initiatives in their increasingly complex and ambitious efforts. Simultaneously, children at this stage are also likely to be developing the capacity for self-observation, self-regulation, and self-punishment that are frequently referred to as a conscience (or in Freudian terms, a 'superego'). The natural curiosity and eagerness to explore new tasks during this phase also necessitate considerable patience and encouragement from the adults interacting with the child. A balance between encouraging appropriate expectations and discouraging potentially dangerous activities is sometime a challenge for parents of children during this stage. Overly harsh criticism or setting unrealistic expectations can prove problematic.

According to Erikson, the desired outcome of this stage would be the acquisition of a sense of purpose. Problematic outcomes from unresolved aspects of this stage would include phobias, inhibitions, and psychosomatic conditions.

Erikson's industry vs. inferiority stage (5–12 years)

During this phase, Erikson proposed that children's energy was focused primarily on aspects of productivity and skill-building. Increasing attention spans and the capacity to concentrate on task completion bring increasing gratification to children during this stage. The capacity to contribute to teams, and to work alongside others also provide important social dimensions to this stage of development. Teachers and other role models play important roles for children in this stage, who often engage in hero-worship of same-sex role models (sports figures, political leaders, and fashion influences).

Conversely, children who struggle with academic achievement and other areas of achievement may experience a sense of inferiority in relation to their peers. Successful navigation of this stage results in a sense of competence. Problematic outcomes from difficulties during this stage may include a lifelong sense of inadequacy or stifled creativity.

Erikson's later psychosocial stages

Erikson's theory proposed a significant progression beyond Freud's genital stage, adding four additional stages representing the continued lifelong developmental process. This alone represents a noteworthy expansion on the theoretical frameworks that preceded him. The later stages incorporated in Erikson's theory are shown in Table 4.3.

Erikson's identity vs. role confusion stage (approximately 13–20 years)

From an Eriksonian perspective, adolescence entails challenges that include a quest to establish a secure sense of self in relationship to the society in general. This often entails philosophical, religious, and social exploration, experimentation and debates. Simultaneously, adolescents are typically experiencing rapid physical changes and developments that entail outward signs of their approach to adulthood. Integrating the physical, mental and social dimensions of their experiences entails the challenge of establishing 'Who am I?'

Erikson believed that teenagers were primarily occupied in the complex tasks of establishing their own sense of identity in relation to the world around them. Erikson was among the early observers of adolescents' preoccupation with their peers' esteem and approval. Affiliations with various groups, cliques, or causes are typical ways in which adolescents express their sense of identity.

According to Erikson, the primary danger of this stage is identity confusion, which may be manifested in a number of ways. Some of the ways in which that confusion

Table 4.3 Erikson's later psychosocial stages

Stage	*Crisis*	*Task*	*Desired outcome*	*Negative outcome*
Adolescence	Identity vs. role confusion	Peer relationships	Fidelity	Fanaticism, estrangement
Young adulthood	Intimacy vs. isolation	Enduring relationships	Commitment (Love)	Promiscuity
Middle adulthood	Generativity vs. stagnation	Parenting and productivity	Contribution (Care)	Over-extension, exhaustion, rejection
Old age	Integrity vs. despair	Reflection on and acceptance of life	Wisdom	Bitterness, hopelessness

could be evidenced include resisting increased responsibilities and insistence on immature, childish behaviours; other ways include impulsive selections of peers or behaviours without considering consequences, or neglect of acquiring skills or abilities that would contribute to employability and self-sufficiency. While identity development entails a lifelong process, Erikson saw adolescence as the stage most defined by the quest for identity.

Successful resolution of this stage is associated with the capacity for what Erikson referred to as 'fidelity', or the ability to sustain loyalties despite challenges posed by society or circumstances. He saw fidelity as also applying to the sense of self. Erikson regarded the identity crises experienced during adolescence as being developmentally normal. He saw problematic negotiations of such identity crises as placing adolescents at risk of suffering from a confusion regarding their inherent identity, including such problems as running away, criminality, gender identity disorders, or psychoses.

Falling in (and out) of love is generally an important part of the process of establishing a sense of self-identity. Questions of sexual orientation often come into play during this stage. Choices of interests and occupations are also typical during this stage. Such choices often entail experimentation, and sometimes surprises and even disappointments. Risk-taking necessarily features as a factor in developing confidence in personal and social situations. Experimentation during adolescence may entail use of alcohol and other drugs. Body piercing and tattoos may be acquired during adolescence as outward indicators of self-expression (regardless of subsequent regret). Religious, political, and philosophical identities are also subject to question during this stage, with adolescents challenging and sometime rebuking the beliefs or affiliations of their parents as a means of establishing what they wish to claim as their own. Ultimately, a sense of *fidelity*, or trueness to a chosen set of values, relationships, or identity is considered the indication of a successful resolution of this Eriksonian stage.

In order to establish a sense of identity with some integrity, most adolescents engage in behaviour and questions that challenge the *status quo*. Idealism and cynicism are often found in nearly equal portions. A yearning for a better social outcome than their parents achieved is normal during this stage. Without considerable trial and error along these lines, adolescents are faced with two ends of Erikson's continuum: either unquestioning acceptance of someone else's sense of who one should be (cult membership would be an example), or a chaotic absence of a sense of self that lacks any coherence (withdrawing into alcohol- and drug-related destructive behaviours, or psychotic fantasies would be examples). Various rites of passage are associated with this stage: first dates, passing exams, learning to drive, first jobs, etc.

Ideally, identity is established in the process of navigating an array of questions, doubts, and relationships in an environment that is sufficiently safe and tolerant, so that the adolescent is allowed optimum opportunities for self-exploration. The capacity to tolerate imperfections in oneself and society are often hallmarks of accomplishing these developmental tasks. Ultimately, the adolescent will achieve a sense of who they are, how they fit into the society around them, and find that their contribution to their society is valued.

Young adulthood: intimacy vs. isolation (approximately 20–25)

The primary developmental tasks associated with young adulthood (around 18–around 30–35) entail the capacity to achieve some degree of intimacy as opposed to existing in isolation. By 'intimacy' Erikson referred to the capacity for emotional closeness or 'mutual devotion', rather than simply being sexually active. In this context, intimacy also entails a genuine and unselfish interest in another's well-being, and a sense of joy in their company that transcends romantic attraction.

A 'fear of commitment' is often seen as a sign of emotional immaturity during this stage, in which a person is consistently reluctant to become emotionally connected in a lasting way. Ideally, during this stage, the young adult brings some of the lessons learned through trial-and-error during previous stages, and has a sense of self that transcends simply being one half of a couple. Erikson regarded the inadequate development of the capacity for intimacy as *promiscuity*. By this, he referred to the tendency to establish superficial relationships without the capacity for depth. An example of this might be seen in the emotionally immature young man in his late twenties or early thirties who continues to date a series of 16-year-old girls who are likely to be in awe of his comparative sophistication. In short, this stage is defined around the difference between a 'one night stand' and the capacity to enjoy breakfast together for years on end.

Ideally, Erikson's (1982) 'radius of significant relations' expands to include intimate partners as well as friends, colleagues, and neighbours, in addition to the family and friends with more historic associations. When this stage is not resolved, some of the risks include what Erikson considered 'exclusion', or the tendency to be isolated from loving relationships and a sense of belonging; this exclusion is often associated with a characteristic selfishness, hostility or even hatefulness toward society.

Middle adulthood: generativity vs. stagnation (approximately 25–65)

The primary developmental tasks Erikson associated with middle adulthood (approximately mid-thirties–sixties) entail finding a balance between the crises he defined as 'generativity vs. stagnation'. In western society, this phase is often associated with raising a family and establishing a legacy that will contribute to those who follow. Erikson concurred with Freud's view of the criteria for maturity as the ability to 'love and work' (Erikson, 1968).

During this stage, the healthy individual has found ways of looking after their own needs as well as those of others with a degree of balance. Engaging in a rewarding activity, raising a family, having a job, or mentoring a younger person are a few examples of ways in which Erikson saw individuals successfully navigating this phase. Generativity necessarily entails a sense of foresight and hope for the future. In that sense, this phase entails a degree of selflessness in the service of leaving a legacy that was not relevant in previous stages.

'Mid-life crises' are perhaps the most stereotypical example of people experiencing an unsatisfactory navigation of this phase. Men often provide the more dramatic examples of this behaviour pattern. During a man's late forties or in his fifties, a previously respectable, hard-working married father will suddenly abandon his wife and children, buy a sports car, and move in with a much younger woman, often jeopardizing his career and his children's inheritance. These often-told scenarios rarely end with the phrase, 'happily ever after'.

Ideally, healthy individuals have developed sufficient coping skills and sources of gratification, that they find satisfaction through middle age. That does not mean they necessarily welcome the various signs of ageing, but that they are satisfied with the person they have become and are still becoming, and find gratification in what they are contributing to future generations. For some, seeing their children growing into happy, healthy lives will reflect such fulfilment. For others, career, community, and artistic involvements bring deep satisfaction. Adults who are generative tend to be caring parents, devoted partners and friends, and productive workers. They tend to be enthusiastic, and remain open to new experiences, and generally rank low on measures of what Freud would have considered 'neuroticism' (see Erikson, 1950).

Erikson's stages were confirmed by the research conducted by the psychoanalytic theorist and researcher George Vaillant (1977). According to Vaillant's longitudinal studies of mentally healthy men who attending Harvard, those men's twenties were devoted to issues of relationships and intimacy; their thirties were spent focused on careers, and their forties were spent with more focus on long-term legacies they would leave behind. As one of Vaillant's subjects commented, 'At 20 to 30, I think I learned how to get along with my wife. From 30 to 40, I learned how to be a success in my job. And at 40 to 50, I worried less about myself and more about the children' (Vaillant, 1977: 195).

Late adulthood: integrity vs. despair (over 65)

The primary tasks Erikson associated with old age entailed confrontation of issues entailing 'integrity vs. despair'. By that, Erikson proposed that people of this age group were engaged in some reflection over the life they had led, and found some grounds for contentment. Coming to terms with their experiences and with themselves was not meant to imply that people of this age group are preoccupied solely by the distant past. Rather, people at this stage are likely to have engaged in what has come to be considered a 'life review' in which they have evaluated and integrated the factors of their lives as a means of preparing for life to end satisfactorily (see Erikson, 1950).

Successful navigation of this phase is associated with older people who are philosophical and generally at peace with themselves and their circumstances. They also tend to stay active and engaged with the world around them. Close friendships that have endured over many years are important among this group. Remaining helpful to others is another consistent element of satisfactory navigation of this stage, along with the capacity to 'grow old gracefully'. Wisdom is the hallmark of integrity during this stage, and that wisdom usually entails a sense of fearlessness regarding death. Unsuccessful navigation of this phase is generally associated with people who are disinclined to reflection, and who are easily preoccupied with various examples of life having treated them poorly. They rarely achieve a sense of meaning or spiritual wholeness (Greene & Ephross, 1991). Such people are often lonely, embittered, and regarded as 'difficult' and 'complainers' by those around them, especially if they are preoccupied with poor health. If you were to consider people living in a nursing home, which group would you expect to receive the most visitors?

By considering the final stage of Erikson's proposed eight stages, the epigenetic nature of his theory becomes clear. Without having successfully navigated previous stages, an individual is unlikely to find a way to negotiate later stages in a rewarding manner. The intertwining of generations' reciprocal influences throughout the stages is perhaps best summarized by Erikson's own statement, 'Healthy children will not fear life if their elders have integrity enough not to fear death' (Erikson, 1950: 269).

Criticisms and debates regarding psychoanalytic and Eriksonian perspectives

Some subsequent theorists consider the influences of psychoanalytic, Eriksonian, and medically dominated perspectives as overly dominant, especially in relation to the majority of the world's cultures, which are not Euro-American (Roland, 1988; Robinson, 2007). The impossibility of proving any of Freud's concepts remains a primary criticism levelled at psychoanalytic theories. His approach relied on interpretation and inference, and his constructs lack empirical measurability. Psychoanalytic hypotheses defy testing, and lack predictive value for purposes of application (Kenny & Kenny, 2000).

Freud's response to reports of childhood sexual trauma now appears both patronizing and potentially detrimental to women's experiences. By attributing memories of childhood sexual abuse and assaults by adult male family members to the realm of 'fantasy' and 'wish fulfilment', Freud certainly delayed a great deal of effort to address the implications of childhood sexual abuse. By attributing women's reports of sexual abuse to falsified memories associated with their 'hysteria', Freud essentially 'blamed the victim' (Good, 1995). Feminist thinkers and authors have critically scorned the psychodynamic implications for the status of women (particularly in relation to the authority given to the traditionally male-dominated medical profession).

In Freud's controversial concept of the Oedipus complex, his premise that young boys have both lustful fantasies about their mothers and wish to replace their fathers has raised long-standing debate, doubt, and criticism. Conceptually, the mechanism by which Freud asserted that a boy's resolution of his Oedipal feelings resulted in the formation of the superego was never clarified. Culturally, for the many children currently being raised by a single parent (most often their mother), and for whom contact with fathers is an inconsistent factor in their lives, Freud's theory has questionable reliability. A primary flaw associated with Freud's approach is that he focused on the individual, rather than considering the interactions of individuals within families, relationships or society. In this, he also disregarded the importance of power discrepancies among individuals, particularly between men and women (Milner & O'Byrne, 2002).

Similarly, Erikson's lifespan approach to development has been criticized for its emphasis on male development, and its Euro-American bias. Because of subsequent explorations of gender differences, some of Erikson's suppositions about the progression from identity to intimacy have been challenged. His racial biases have also been questioned (Milner & O'Byrne, 2002). Another risk associated with an overly simplistic interpretation of Erikson's theory would be that of presuming that the stages are chronologically fixed. Various life events with which social workers are often engaged result in people renegotiating such issues as roles and identity.

As important as Freud's and Erikson's concepts have proven to the evolution of psychology, many of their ideas now seem slanted toward a male, Eurocentric perspective, with an implicit adherence to western individualism. In an increasingly multi-cultural society, their more conventional late nineteenth- and early twentieth-century perspectives on gender and culture reflect a more patriarchal view than is currently the norm. An example of cultural differences would be Freud's emphasis on the unconscious, which is an altogether unfamiliar concept in traditional Asian societies. A social worker applying Freudian concepts must necessarily be conscious of relevant cultural implications, including such examples as traditional Asian regard for elders and family cohesion.

The inherent psychoanalytic premise that the patient necessarily depends upon the psychoanalyst to interpret their innermost thoughts and wishes is perhaps the most noteworthy of the discrepancies between psychoanalytic principles and social work values and ethics. This premise disregards issues of self-determination and a strengths-based model that are fundamental to social work values and practice. Ultimately, psychoanalytic theory's implicit sanctioning of white and male privileges is incongruent with an awareness of oppressive practices or social justice that are inherent to social work values.

Implications for practice

With such shortcomings in mind, social work students are encouraged to avoid the academic equivalent of 'throwing the baby out with the bath water' when it comes to their regard for psychoanalytic and Eriksonian concepts. Applying a critical appraisal does not necessitate discarding a theory altogether because a broader perspective has emerged since its introduction. Freud's and Erikson's theories entail a very complex and sophisticated array of concepts, and provide a fascinating area of study for social workers and other helping professions, regardless of whether they are applied directly in practice.

Regardless of social workers' areas of practice, an understanding of defence mechanisms is crucial, especially when working with people who are vulnerable and oppressed. Social workers must also be mindful of their own use of defence mechanisms, including denial and rationalization of our own foibles. An appreciation of conscious and unconscious mental material applies to understanding behaviour in general. Social workers are not immune to unconscious preferences and avoidances of some service users vs. others. Self-awareness of one's own behaviour and coping strategies is congruent with good practice.

Erikson's developmental concepts, while imperfect, have contributed greatly to social workers' understanding of age-related tasks and emphasis. Erikson's inherently optimistic view of people's capacities is essentially congruent with social work values and efforts to avoid pathologizing people because of their behaviour.

Questions

1 Following a severe trauma (such as a serious car crash, or assault) some people describe being unable to remember events surrounding the traumatic event. To what part of the mind would Freud attribute such an inability to recall important details?

2 Match the following defence mechanisms with their examples:

____	'Sadie' is very angry with her boss, but instead shouts at her husband when she gets home	(a) Repression
____	'Zoe', aged 6, begins bedwetting when her parents separate	(b) Sublimation
____	'Joe', a heavy drinker, insists that he actually drives better after having a few pints to drink	(c) Projection
____	'Tom' resents his father's violent treatment of his mother, but begins to punch and slap his little sister	(d) Reaction formation
____	'Chris' is very sexually frustrated and feels inadequate, but lectures and authors books on keeping the romance in marriage	(e) Denial
____	'Keith' cannot remember being sexually abused by his uncle during childhood, although his siblings have shared recollections of this being the case	(f) Regression
____	'Jill', who is married, is attracted to her colleague 'Jack', but accuses their mutual colleague 'Mary' of flirting with him	(g) Rationalization
____	'Cleo', whose partner accuses her of compulsive shopping, refers to her shopping trips as 'retail therapy'	(h) Displacement

3 What are some examples of behaviour you can think of in yourself, family, or friends that might be interpreted as indicating fixations from Freud's oral or anal stages of development? What other explanations might apply?

4 Read the following case study and, from an Eriksonian perspective, address the questions that follow.

> At 14, Beverly was much more interested in singing in a local band and in her boyfriend Ken (age 16) than she was in school. Following considerable conflict with her parents, both of whom were teachers, Beverly left school and moved in with Ken and his family.

She became pregnant at 15. Their baby, Darren, was born prematurely, and has mild cerebral palsy. Now age 2, he has some developmental delays. For example, he has difficulty walking and feeding himself without help.

Both Beverly and Ken are trying to build their musical careers in two local bands, around which alcohol and tobacco are prevalent. They have relied heavily on both sets of grandparents to baby sit Darren, and for keeping many of his medical appointments. The situation has become more difficult in recent months, since Ken's mother died suddenly of heart failure. Last month, Beverly's father was injured in a serious car crash, and is expected to need extensive physiotherapy during the coming months. He may not be able to resume teaching until next year.

Now 17, Beverly has recently learned that Ken has fathered another child by a local girl, and is not sure where she will move, or how she will care for Darren when she does so. Her parents have made it clear that they consider her behaviour very immature, and that they would expect her to assume more responsibility for Darren if she is living with them.

(a) What are some of the developmental tasks Beverly and Ken are facing?
(b) What are some of the developmental tasks Beverly's and Ken's parents are facing?
(c) How would you envision conflicts arising from Beverly's parents' circumstances if she continues to keep late hours and expects them to care for Darren's needs?
(d) What might Darren's developmental priorities entail, and how might that create some tension with Beverly and her parents?

5 Read the following case study and, using Erikson's framework, answer the questions that follow.

Kate and Lois are widowed sisters. Both are in reasonably good health. Kate (84) is the older of the two, and has been widowed over ten years, after a long, happy marriage. She moved from her house into a flat near her daughter's home five years ago. Her son lives in London, but he has installed email on Kate's computer, and they communicate each day by phone or email. Her grandchildren routinely drop by on their way home from school. She keeps up with their friends and school activities. Their school routinely asks her to come talk with their classes at school about her experiences as a young woman during World War II.

Kate regularly visits Lois in a nearby nursing home. Lois (81) broke her hip two years ago, and could no longer manage the stairs in her home. She had long since lost contact with the people in her neighbourhood, often criticizing them for being 'terribly common', and voicing racist remarks about neighbourhood children. Lois and her husband divorced when their son Basil was 14. She remains bitter about her ex-husband, and blames his infidelity for Basil's lifelong reluctance to marry or be in a committed relationship. Basil (now 60) rarely visits, and when he does, arguments often arise resulting in Lois threatening to 'cut him out of the will'. He usually goes home by way of his Aunt Kate's, where he unburdens himself over a sympathetic cup of tea. His and Kate's are the only visits Lois receives. Few people in the nursing home seek out her company, and the staff regards her as being 'difficult'. Even Kate's daughter's family avoids coming to see their aunt, because she is 'so grumpy'.

(a) At what stages would you say the two sisters' experiences started to differ?
(b) How would you describe the two sisters' current life stages?
(c) What do you think explains the two sisters' contact with those around them?
(d) What developmental stages may have proven difficult for Basil?

5 Neo-Freudian or ego psychology perspectives

An array of psychological theories evolved from the Freudian tradition, including assorted revisions of the original psychoanalytic perspective. This broad array of ideas is called by various titles, including neo-Freudian and ego psychology; some refer to it more broadly as a psychodynamic perspective. Some of Freud's original protégés developed distinctive approaches to defining and responding to problems that are included in this discussion, which embraces a wide range of concepts, including attachment theory and object relations, as well as the works of Adler and Jung. The various contributors to this broad array of thought expanded upon Freud's emphasis on the unconscious and conflict, to address external factors such as relationships, as well as resilience to adversity based on ego strengths.

Relevance for social work

Social work has been strongly influenced by a wide range of concepts that stemmed from neo-Freudian thinking and ego psychology. From such views as Hartmann's (1978) emphasis on people's capacity to adapt to the outside world serving as a marker of health, social work has historically emphasized the importance of ego strengths, rather than focusing solely on pathology.

Social work has also placed tremendous emphasis on the role played by attachment, particularly involving children born into disadvantaged families. Because of social work's traditional association with the protection of children, a clear grasp of attachment and attachment theory is fundamental to good practice. The ability to observe and interpret key indicators of attachment (or lack thereof) throughout the lifespan is an essential assessment skill for social workers.

Historical background

Several of the early contributors to neo-Freudian perspectives and ego psychology (including Adler and Jung) were originally protégés of Freud who subsequently had bitter departures from his intellectual circle. Some (such as Hartmann and Klein) maintained some of Freud's more orthodox concepts, and expanded upon them. Others (such as Ainsworth and Bowlby) effectively pioneered aspects of childhood attachments that had not been explored. The following discussion provides a brief overview of a wide array of thinkers and their concepts.

As you may notice, quite a few of them escaped the Nazis and pursued careers in the UK and the US. Had it not been for Hitler, perhaps ego psychology and developmental psychiatry would have remained an overwhelmingly German school of thought. Instead, it has shaped subsequent understandings of children and families around the world, along with some of the core concepts of social work practice.

The British School (also known as the 'Independents') evolved from Melanie Klein's emphasis on infants' earliest ('pre-Oedipal') relationships with their mothers. While the British School is not considered a unified approach, it represents a definitive move away from the Freudian structural approach, toward an emphasis on the interaction of the self with others (Fonagy, 1999). Concepts associated with *object relations theory* evolved from the work of Fairbairn, Bowlby, Winnicott and others associated with the British School.

Key concepts

Originally promoted by Anna Freud, *ego psychology* emphasized the mechanisms used by the ego as a means of adapting to and coping with external demands, with particular emphasis on the role of defence mechanisms. While ego psychology does not deny the existence of intrapsychic conflict, its focus is much more on the ego's striving for mastery and competency over the environment than the traditional Freudian approach. By addressing the complexity and variety of mechanisms employed by the ego to avoid unacceptable wishes or feelings, Anna Freud drew attention away from the role played by the unconscious, and expanded upon the appreciation of the complexities of the ego's functions (Polansky, 1991). By addressing the ego functions as a healthy, adaptive dimension of functioning, Anna Freud's interpretations contributed to a more positive application of psychoanalytic thinking, and thus led the way toward what came to be referred to as ego psychology (Masten, Burt, & Coatsworth, 2006).

Ego psychology developed in relation to various thinkers' concepts regarding the adaptive functions of the ego. Those functions specifically related to the potential for wellness, as well as difficulties. Examples of ego functions are provided in Table 5.1.

Attachment refers to the ability to form and maintain emotional bonds with others. Developmentally, attachment refers to the bond between children and their primary caregivers/parents (Bowlby, 1988). Attachment is also associated with Erikson's first developmental stage of 'Trust vs. Mistrust'. John Bowlby introduced attachment theory,

Table 5.1 Ego functions

Function	*Examples*
Control and regulation of instinctual drives	The capacity to delay gratification The capacity to test reality Closely linked with infants' socialization process and development of logical thinking
Judgement	Capacity to anticipate consequences Typically develops in conjunction with *secondary process thinking* Closely linked with development of logical thinking and capacity for delayed gratification
Relation to reality	Sense of boundaries between internal and external, self and others Perceptions of reality (Crucial) capacity to mediate between the internal world and external reality Closely linked with infants' emerging bodily awareness Reality testing capacity (including capacity to distinguish between fantasy and reality) Adaptation to reality (entails capacity to respond to changing reality based on interpreting experience)
Object relations	Capacity to form mutually satisfying relationships with others Capacity to integrate both positive and negative aspects of self and others Capacity to maintain an internal sense of others even when apart from them Capacity to employ transitional objects for comfort during times of distress
Synthetic functions of the ego	Capacity to integrate diverse factors into a unified sense of self and others Capacity to organize, coordinate and generalize information about self and others
Primary autonomous ego functions	'Conflict-free' functions described by Hartmann Perception Learning Intuition Language Motor control
Secondary autonomous ego functions	Follow development of primary autonomous ego functions Capacity to engage defensive responses to impulses and drives
Defence mechanisms Narcissistic defences Denial Distortion Projection	Serve to manage anxiety in ways that are acceptable to the ego May be grouped hierarchically according to the degree of maturity associated with them Narcissistic defences are associated with primitive levels of functioning found in infancy and severely disturbed adults
Immature defences Blocking Hypochondriasis Passive-aggressive behaviours	Immature defences are associated with childhood, adolescence and some non-psychotic conditions

Regression	
Somatization	
'Neurotic' defences	'Neurotic' defences are associated with obsessive-compulsive conditions, severe stress responses, and maladaptive interpretations
Controlling	
Dissociation	
Intellectualization	
Rationalization	
Reaction formation	
Repression	
Mature defences	Mature defences are associated with normal functioning
Altruism	
Anticipation	
Asceticism	
Humour	
Sublimation	
Suppression	

Source: Adapted from Sadock & Sadock (2007).

and his colleague Mary Ainsworth expanded upon it. Much of what Bowlby referred to as 'attachment', Balint (1965) referred to as 'primary love', Fairbairn (1952) referred to as 'object seeking', and Winnicott (1965) referred to as 'ego relatedness'.

The capacity for attachment is considered developmentally and dynamically crucial, especially because it is such a fundamental component of subsequent social development and a predictor of functioning. Both the quality and character of children's attachments and relationships influence subsequent development (Howe et al., 1999).

While sometimes used interchangeably with attachment, *bonding* is a very different phenomenon. Bonding refers to the parent's/caregiver's affection and feelings for the infant. Because that affection does not reflect the same physical dependence as the infant's experience of attachment, the distinctions between attachment and bonding are noteworthy.

Attachment behaviours stem from biological instincts, to which both infants and parents are predisposed (or 'biologically biased') (Bowlby, 1969). By engaging in attachment behaviours, infants increase the probability and frequency of contacts with the attachment figure (usually the mother), who is also a source of food and comfort. This survival function dates back to the historic eras when humans and their young were in danger from predators. Thus attachment functioned to enhance the chances of survival. Attachment behaviours entail a behavioural repertoire that elicits positive responses from parents/caregivers. Many are evident before babies become verbal. Examples include smiling and cooing. Some attachment behaviours are also signalling behaviours, such as crying and whimpering. Some attachment behaviours, such as approaching, clinging and following serve to gain physical closeness to the attachment figure (Cassidy, 1999).

Distress tends to activate characteristic attachment behaviours. When individuals experience anxiety, their response is likely to be indicative of those strategies they have found effective in response to anxiety and distress. Their response to stress is also likely to indicate whether they see themselves as worthy and effective, and whether they regard others as potentially caring and accessible. Their experience of attachment is likely to influence their comfort-seeking behaviours and shape their expectations (Howe et al., 1999). According to Bowlby (1988), the central feature of parenting entails providing a *secure base* from which to explore their world, along with confidence in being able to return to a welcoming, nurturing environment.

Ainsworth (1973) and Bowlby (1979) proposed that children's patterns of attachment develop and change dramatically during the first two or three years of life. They proposed that four distinct stages of attachment patterns emerge. Those stages are outlined in Table 5.2.

According to attachment theory, young children with close relationships develop mental representations of themselves based on their own sense of worthiness as reflected by others' responses to them. Those representations are called *internal working*

Table 5.2 Stages in the formation of attachment

Age range	*Stage*	*Key features*
Birth–2 months	Pre-attachment	Indiscriminate social responses Capacity for prosocial responses Preference for human faces and voices (tracking)
3–6 months	Attachment-in-the-making	Recognition of familiar people Increased vocal responses More smiling and crying directed toward familiar faces than strangers Growing interest in and preference for primary caregiver Increase ability to 'read' moods of primary caregiver
7 months–3 years	Clear-cut attachment	Protest at separation Wariness of strangers Intentional communication Widening repertoire of attachment behaviours Increasingly selective attachment (including seeking-out behaviours) Increasing ability to match behaviour to needs and intended outcomes Increasing ability to select behaviours intended to engage with others
3+ years	Goal-directed partnership	Increasingly reciprocal relationships Increasing understanding of parents' needs Emerging ability to envision others' perspectives Increasing capacity to distinguish between their plans and others' wishes Increasingly sophisticated relationships resulting from capacity to discuss, negotiate and share

Source: Adapted from Howe et al. (1999).

models. They often reflect the child's sense of the availability of protection and approval based on their closest attachments. In the course of developing attached relationships with others, children are likely to develop mental representations of themselves and others, as well as of the relationship they have with others (Ainsworth et al., 1978; Howe et al., 1999).

By being in attached relationships with others, children learn to understand others as well as themselves more accurately. Increased understanding of others generally serves to enhance understanding of the self, and vice versa; hence the quality of relationships experienced in early childhood for the child's sense of self as well as subsequent social competence is crucial. The resulting internal working models serve to inform the child's expectations and beliefs including their own sense of the kinds of relationships they deserve to have (nurturing and constructive or unreliable and punitive). Essential beliefs about their own inherent lovability and acceptance, as well as the emotional availability and reliability of others stem from the child's internal working model during the first months and years of life. Some contrasting examples of responses to an infant's distress can be found in Table 5.3

When infants and children have experienced positive responses to their signalled needs or distress, they are likely to form secure attachment patterns. Those patterns help them organize their behaviours in order to maintain a partnership with trusted caregivers. Children who have not experienced positive responses to their signalled needs or distress are more likely to show avoidant or *defensive strategies* as means of coping with distress or anxiety. One of the best defensive strategies appears to be that of minimizing attachment behaviour and expressiveness. Such strategies can be seen when children learn to deny or refrain from expressing their emotions including distress. Such children become quite stoic, or impassive, even when experiencing strong emotions (Howe et al., 1999).

Table 5.3 Examples of basic responses to infants' distress

Responses associated with strong attachment	*Responses associated with problematic attachment*
Availability	Absence
Accessibility	Conditional acceptance
Comforting	Critical
Consistent	Demeaning
Emotional availability	Disinterest
Expressed pleasure	Emotional unavailability
Proximity	Inconsistent
Recognition of feelings	Indifference
Reliable	Insensitivity
Responsiveness	Rejecting
Sensitivity	Resentment
Sympathy	Unreliable
Unconditional acceptance	

Children's internal working models are subject to modification and adaptation, depending on their circumstances, both positive and negative. While they are formed during infancy and childhood, models serve to inform lifelong relationship patterns. According to George (1996), the internal working model predicts people's interactions with their own children when they become parents themselves. Intergenerational transmission of relationship patterns is not necessarily automatic, but with age, internal working models appear to become increasingly resistant to change, underscoring the lifelong importance of early relationship patterns (Gerhardt, 2004; Howe et al., 1999).

Questions arise about the transferability of attachment from one parent or caregiver to another. Variables such as temperament and parental discord make such questions difficult to answer conclusively. Babies' attachments to their parents also appear to differ according to roles. Generally, mothers appear more likely to hold infants for purposes of caregiving, while fathers are more likely to hold babies for purposes of play. Following a separation from both, most babies usually gravitate to the mother when given the choice (Sadock & Sadock, 2007). In an interesting review of multiple studies, however, Fox, Kimmerly, and Shafer (1991) found that infants classified as having secure attachments to one parent rarely demonstrate insecure attachments to the other parent. They also found that specific types of insecure attachment tend to apply from one attachment object to others; infants who are insecurely attached to one parent tend to be insecurely attached to both.

Object relations theory

Object relations theory encompasses a variety of ideas proposed by several theorists. Its key emphasis is on the importance of internal images ('representations') of one's self and *objects* (significant others with whom emotions and actions can be exchanged). Developmental progress as well as the capacity for subsequent relationships is seen as being related to the earliest experiences (or lack thereof) of relationships (Gross, 2001).

Both Winicott (1958) and Mahler (Mahler et al., 1975) emphasized the role played by an infant's total dependence on the reliability of those around them as a crucial basis of the primary and lifelong process of achieving adult autonomy. The infant's internalized images of others ('objects) begin as primitive and possibly even intimidating images. According to Mahler, they may not be distinguishable from the infant's sense of self (Mahler et al., 1975). When successful separation and individuation between the infant and mother have occurred, however, the individual is more likely to be capable of empathy and realistic appraisal of others. Mahler subsequently introduced the concept of *separation–individuation* to explain the process of mother–child interactions.

Rather than focusing on the traditional Freudian concepts of psychosexual instincts, object relations theory focuses more on the earliest experiences of relationships with specific *love objects*. At the time of the original writings on those relationships, the love objects (or objects of affection) were primarily the infants' mothers.

Transactional analysis

In the late 1950s, Dr Eric Berne, an American psychoanalyst, introduced the concept of transactional analysis, proposing that people operate from three basic ego states, which develop throughout childhood. The three states are parent, child, and adult. Berne ([1961] 1978) suggested that the three states form a key part of the personality. The three ego states share some similarities with concepts of the ego, the id and the superego.

The *child* ego state serves as a repository of all childhood experiences, both positive and negative; interpretations of the self and others are those formed during childhood. The *parent* ego state serves to retain both positive and negative messages spoken and modelled by parental figures during childhood. The *adult* ego state assesses current inner and outer realities, and uses knowledge and experience to interpret and respond appropriately to current situations.

Berne (1973) proposed that people's beliefs that become fixated at the child or parent state preclude functioning fully as adults. An example would be someone who prefers relying on functioning as a child, in order that others take responsibility; another would be someone who overcompensates for ('parents') a partner whose drinking precludes adequate functioning. According to Berne, people's *ulterior transactions* are psychological games, and represent unconscious ways of gaining recognition ('strokes') by using repetitive patterns of interaction. Ideally, when people interact with one another as adults, they are able to communicate in ways that are authentic, appropriate and genuine (see Berne, 1973).

Historical contributors

The array of contributors are discussed in alphabetical order, rather than attempting to group them by particular interests. Their lives spanned a remarkable historical period, dating from Alfred Adler's birth in 1870 to Mary Ainsworth's death in 1999.

Alfred Adler (1870–1937) was among a number of Viennese doctors who initially studied under Sigmund Freud. After completing his medical degree (1895), and originally practising ophthalmology, Adler's interests transferred to neurology and psychiatry. Upon entering the realm of psychiatry, however, Adler quickly gained prominence within the Freudian circle, and was initially regarded as the likely 'heir apparent' to Freud's status. As with Freud's subsequent protégés, however, Adler expressed theoretical views that differed from those of Freud, with acrimonious results. Despite his earlier acceptance of Freudian concepts, he rejected Freud's emphasis on the libido theory, or the importance of infantile urges and wishes.

Strongly influenced by Darwin's ideas of organic superiority and inferiority, Adler proposed that children initially experience a sense of *inferiority* because of their relative smallness and dependence on those around them. From that sense of inadequacy or inferiority, Adler proposed that children engage in *compensation* as a means of overcoming their inherent disadvantages (an example would be a child with a limp who lacks athletic skills developing musical talents). According to Adler, childhood attempts at compensation entail a *striving for superiority*, which he considered a universal drive to achieve and adapt. Unlike Freud's emphasis on psychosexual development, Adler focused on individuals' motivation being based on the desire for autonomy or mastery of oneself, and a healthy striving for competence.

Adler considered the childhood experience of inferiority or inadequacy as a crucial determinant of the personality. According to Adler, an unresolved sense of insecurity resulting from feeling inadequate or inferior can develop into an exaggerated sense of deficiency, which he called an *inferiority complex*. In some cases, when an individual relies on masking their sense of inadequacy by pretending to feel superior or powerful, despite inwardly feeling inferior, then this would reflect a *superiority complex* (Ewen, 1998).

Adler's contributions to psychological theories included his concept of *sibling rivalry*. The first theorist to address the relevance of birth order, Adler argued that the first-born child responds to the arrival of the subsequent siblings with anger and resentment about having to surrender the powerful position of being the only child. Adler proposed that second children struggle with competition with older siblings in what amounts to a lifelong quest for identity, lifestyle and character formation. (As a second-born child, Adler presumably had an informed perspective on this topic.) Adler referred to his theory of the personality as 'Individual Psychology', which was derided by Freud (Polansky, 1991; Adler, 1924).

Mary Ainsworth (1913–1999) was an American-born developmental psychologist educated at the University of Toronto. During the 1950s, she conducted research with Bowlby at the Tavistock Clinic. They studied infants and their mothers in hopes of gaining a greater understanding of 'normal' mother–child relationships from which to expand their understanding of problematic relationships. Ainsworth contributed significantly to the development of attachment theory by developing a means of measuring attachment security in infants. Her empirical measure provided clinicians and researchers with a means of examining the strength of relationships in ways that had scientific validity and rigour. She returned to the US during the 1960s, where she had an illustrious academic career (see Ainsworth, 1991).

Ainsworth expanded upon Bowlby's ideas, and observed that the infant's and mother's interactions during the attachment period have profound, long-term implications for the infant's behaviour and emotional prospects. According to Ainsworth, unresponsiveness from the mothers was associated with emotional immaturity and lower intelligence, and was also associated with more anxious infants (Ainsworth, 1973).

Ainsworth's 'strange situation' experiments entailed a series of situations in which the mother and child were observed (Ainsworth et al., 1978). The experiments involved the following situations:

- Mother and child are placed in a room with toys with which to play.
- An unfamiliar adult enters the room and engages in conversation with the mother, then plays with infant.

- The mother leaves the room, while the stranger interacts with the child.
- The mother returns and the stranger leaves the room.
- The mother leaves the infant alone in the room.
- The stranger returns to the room.
- The mother returns and the stranger leaves the room.

From the 'strange situation' experiments, children's responses were measured in relation to the following variables:

- How close does the child stay to the mother in the initial arrangement?
- How does the child react to the initial approach of the stranger in the mother's presence?
- How distressed is the child when the mother leaves the room?
- How does the child react when alone with the stranger?
- Is the child happy upon the mother's return?

From the child's responses to the cumulative stress of the experiment, their behaviour patterns were categorized according to three different types of attachment. Those types were:

1. *Anxious/Avoidant* (Indicating a child who did not pay much attention to the mother's presence. If distressed, the child may have sought comfort from the stranger. The child did not actively endeavour to reunite with the mother upon her return.)
2. *Anxious/Resistant* (Indicating a child who tended to stay close to the mother and became clearly distressed upon her departure. The child was difficult to console, took a long time to settle down, and remained anxious about the mother's whereabouts.)
3. *Securely Attached* (Indicating a child who remained calm and unthreatened by the stranger's presence. When the mother departed, the child was unlikely to be comforted by the stranger. When the mother returned, the child was eager for their reunion, and settled down and relaxed quickly thereafter.)

Ainsworth proposed that the securely attached infant uses the parent as a *secure base*, which provides an internalized sense of security in the strange situation. The hallmark of the securely attached infant appears to be the capacity to use their attachment object as a means of regaining a sense of equilibrium when distressed. The Anxious/Resistant child, however, is more likely to appear anxious or distressed even when the parent returns, which is likely to inhibit the child's capacity for exploration and self-confidence. This child's resistance and possible anger with the parent may inhibit the parent's sense of attachment and competence. The Anxious/Avoidant infant also reflects difficulties between the parent and child. They do not appear to use the parent as a secure base from which to explore. Their seeming disregard for the parent may also serve to inhibit further closeness on the parent's part. Their willingness to seek comfort from the stranger poses further potential for risk of vulnerability to strangers.

According to Ainsworth, parents who routinely responded caringly and sensitively to their child's signalled needs during the early years were more likely to have a child with a secure sense of attachment. Examples include behaviours such as feeding, face-to-face play times, physical contact and comforting. Such parents typically responded spontaneously to their infants' signals; they were readily accessible to the children, and exhibited warmth and acceptance. For the secure infant, the quality of the mother's responses contributed to their internal working model of the self and others as being caring, capable, responsive and reliable (Shaffer, 1996).

John Bowlby (1907–1990) is generally regarded as the 'father' of attachment theory. The son of an affluent family, Bowlby spent his first four years being cared for by a devoted nanny who then left the family. He subsequently described that loss as particularly difficult, along with being sent to boarding school at age 7 (Coates, 2004). Bowlby was a paediatrician, and although trained as a psychoanalyst, he became disenchanted with the psychoanalytic emphasis on hypothetical fantasies and conflicts during infancy and childhood. Although influenced by Klein's work, Bowlby went on to propose that observations of actual parent–child interactions would be much more applicable to understanding a child's development, and scientifically methodical (Fonagy, 1999). He emphasized the importance of inter-generational transmission of attachment difficulties.

According to Bowlby's theory, attachment is linked to the infant's basic survival instincts associated with the need for nurturance and protection. His particular interests included the effects that separation from their parents had on children. Many of his original ideas stemmed from his work with the World Health Organization (WHO) during the 1950s on behalf of children who had been traumatically separated from their families or orphaned during World War II (Hinde & Stevenson-Hinde, 1991).

Bowlby's interest in *maternal deprivation* included children having experienced either physical loss or separation from the mother, as well as neglectful or abusive parenting. One of his more frequently quoted observations was that 'mother love in infancy and childhood is as important for mental health as are vitamins and proteins for physical health' (Bowlby, 1951).

Among his early observations related to attachment, Bowlby noted that young children separated from their parents appeared to go through a similar progression of responses to the distress of those separations (Robertson & Bowlby, 1952). Bowlby observed that children went through the following predictable responses to separation from their mothers:

- *protest:* crying, screaming, striving to find or reunite with mother;
- *despair:* becoming listless, resigned to the loss, and possibly apathetic;
- *detachment:* becoming indifferent to the parents, preferring to focus on some other activity that may be of little actual interest.

Bowlby was keenly aware of and responsive to many child care practices that were considered normal at the time, which he considered detrimental to children's best interests. For example, he challenged the practice common during the 1950s and 1960s of dissuading parents from visiting children in hospital. He argued against the claim that parental visits were disruptive to the children, and observed that children who became distressed upon their parents' departure were simply sufficiently confident to express their actual feelings (as opposed to those whose passive resignation may have been more convenient for the staff to manage). He was influential in bringing about changes such as the following:

- distinguishing between poverty and neglect of children;
- increased awareness of the negative impact of institutional care on children;
- including children's views and feelings in the assessment process;
- avoiding placing children in temporary care without long-term plans being in place (Beckett, 2002).

Anna Freud (1895–1992) was the sixth of the Freuds' six children. Originally trained as a teacher, she was their only child who pursued a career in psychoanalysis.

Anna Freud was admitted as a member of the Vienna Psychoanalytical Society in 1922. She greatly expanded upon her father's original consideration of the defence mechanisms. While her father emphasized the importance of repression, Anna Freud stressed other concepts, including reaction formation, projection, and sublimation. She published *The Ego and Mechanisms of Defense* in 1936, which contributed greatly to the emerging field of ego psychology (Zangwill, 2004).

Anna Freud also contributed to the field of child psychoanalysis and the understanding of ego development during childhood. She also established a psychoanalytic training institute, at which Erik Erikson subsequently became her protégé.

Heinz Hartmann (1894–1970) was born in Vienna and trained by Freud as a psychoanalyst. He fled the Nazis in 1938, and spent the remainder of his illustrious career in the US. Hartmann came to have a concept of normality that varied considerably from the psychoanalytic tradition (Blank & Blank, 1994). Hartmann (1978) referred to various autonomous functions of the ego as being fundamental for mental well-being. According to Hartmann (1958), various psychological functions are present from birth, and represent a conflict-free dimension of the mind. Those functions include perception, intuition, comprehension, and certain features of motor development and intelligence. The conflict-free ego functions Hartmann explored apply to the individual's capacity for mental well-being by serving an array of adaptive functions. By helping the person adapt to external demands and reality, those ego functions serve to enhance the prospects of autonomy and mental well-being. Hartmann's concepts of ego functions help understand and interpret aspects of childhood resilience and trauma, through an appreciation of relevant ego strengths.

Karen Horney (1885–1952), along with Anna Freud, was among the first women trained as psychoanalysts. Horney (pronounced 'Horn-eye') entered medical school against her parents' wishes and against the social norms of her era. After training as a psychoanalyst, Horney lectured at the Berlin Institute for Psychoanalysis. In 1926, Horney was the first to challenge the male dominance of Freud's theories.

Distinguishing between *penis envy* and *privilege envy*, Horney (1967) argued that women are actually physiologically superior to men partly on the basis of being able to give birth to their young. She also proposed the existence of *womb envy* as the male alternative of penis envy (see Horney, 1967). In 1930, Horney immigrated to the US, and settled in Brooklyn, New York.

According to Horney (1950), individuals develop characteristic ways of dealing with others and managing anxiety, depending on their early interactions and relationships with their caregivers. She proposed that individuals tend to rely on one of three primary, characteristic patterns of interacting with people: (1) sociability, or the tendency to *move towards* others; (2) isolation, or the tendency to *move away from* them; and (3) mistrust/aggression, or the tendency to *move against* others. Her views of people's inherently constructive nature were congruent with some of Adler's views, although she rejected his more holistic views of neurosis in favour of a more Freudian position (Ewen, 1998).

Horney's concepts of *neuroses* expanded considerably upon the psychoanalytic tradition. She proposed that neuroses are basically purposeful ways of coping, based on needs that are taken to counterproductive extremes. She specified a variety of needs that relate to neuroses, including needs for admiration, approval, control, prestige, partners, and perfection. By addressing the irrational extreme to which such needs were taken in cases of neuroses, Horney believed that psychoanalytic treatment was beneficial. Her *self-theory* entailed a contrast between the *real self* and its healthy quest for self-realization, and the (neurotic) *idealized self* and its vacillation caused by inordinate neediness.

Horney's work strongly influenced both humanists and feminist writers. Her concepts of the real self and the ideal self (an image of what we should be) were particularly influential in Carl Rogers' subsequent work.

Carl Jung (1875–1961) was the fourth of his parents' children, but the only one to survive. His father was a Swiss Lutheran pastor, and his mother's mental health was evidently delicate, and she spent prolonged periods hospitalized and absent from the home. Jung's father's approach to parenting appears to have been somewhat distant and unapproachable. Jung subsequently described feelings of isolation and introversion during his childhood, and regarded those experiences as influential in his psychological concepts. Jung received his medical training at the University of Basel, and did a psychiatric internship under Eugen Bleuler (who introduced the term 'schizophrenia'). Jung initiated contact with Sigmund Freud in 1907, and their first meeting reportedly turned into a 13-hour discussion. Despite their initial affinity for each other, and Jung's early status as Freud's protégé, they had a bitter clash in 1912, not unlike Adler's earlier experience.

Jung developed and expanded upon his own theories and techniques of conducting therapy, which came to be known as *analytic psychology*. Much of Jung's emphasis was more spiritual than scientific, and included elements from psychology, philosophy, religion and mythology. In a radical departure from traditional psychoanalytic concepts, Jung proposed that the personality is essentially present from birth as a complete entity.

Unlike Freud's emphasis on the unconscious and conscious, Jung proposed that the psyche comprises three major, interactive levels: (1) *consciousness*; (2) *the personal unconscious*; (3) and the *collective unconscious*. Jung regarded childhood experiences and their unconscious implications as relatively unimportant. Instead, Jung emphasized the importance of the *collective unconscious*, which he viewed as stemming from the evolutionary history of humanity as a collective whole.

Jung had a long-standing fascination with the content of dreams, and had a very vivid dream life, which he carefully recorded. Various aspects of death featured heavily in Jung's dream life, and he came to believe this represented the collective unconscious, representing not just his own personal unconscious, but that of humanity in general (Jung & DeLaszlo, 1993). As Europe was being torn apart by World War I, Jung reported having had had a premonition of the carnage of that war in a dream in 1913. His philosophical approach was influenced by his observations of the tragedies of World War I. Jung's theory included concepts of the *collective unconscious* and *archetypes* and the *persona* (see Jung & DeLaszlo, 1993).

Along with Adler, Jung dismissed Freud's emphasis on sexuality as a source of conflict. Instead, he proposed that the collective unconscious comprises various archetypes, which refer to various innate, untaught tendencies to experience things in a particular way. Jungian theory relies heavily on the use of symbolism to represent ideas. Some of the more prominent of Jung's archetypes include the following:

- *Anima* (the female archetype)
    - experienced as a feminine voice within the psyche;
    - serves to compensate for male persona in ways that support understanding female perspectives.
- *Animus* (the male archetype)
    - experienced as a male voice within the psyche;
    - serves to compensate for female persona in ways that support understanding male perspectives.
- *The Shadow* (derived from a pre-human past)
    - 'dark side', primitive dimension of the personality;
    - amoral content, which may be frightening or unacceptable to the conscious or the persona, and thus often repressed;
    - symbolic examples: dragons, demons, serpent (in Eden).
- *The Persona* (from the Latin for 'mask')
    - entails a public image;
    - ideally: 'good impression';
    - risk: 'false impression' (exaggeration, inflation, etc.).
- *The Hero* (defeater of evil)
    - represents the Ego;
    - often in conflict with the Shadow.

Jung is probably best known for his popular personality typology. Jung distinguished between people's personal dispositions, specifying differences between *introversion* and *extroversion*. Jung proposed that introversion and extroversion shape an individual's characteristic way of interpreting and understanding the world. Introverted people tend to prefer a more inward focus on thoughts, feelings, dreams, philosophies, etc., while extroverted people tend to prefer engaging with the external world of people, places, things, and activities, often using logic and practicalities. Jungian usage of 'introversion' and 'extroversion' entailed much more complex characteristics of the ego than just shyness or being outgoing. He proposed that introverts and extroverts have characteristic ways of gathering information and interpreting the world around them (Ewen, 1998).

Jung specified four basic ways, which he called *functions*. The four Jungian functions are *sensing, thinking, intuiting,* and *feeling*. According to Jung (who was very intuitive), each person has a *superior* function, which provides the primary and preferred way of perceiving; likewise, people also have *secondary, tertiary, and inferior* functions, in diminishing order of prominence (Jung & DeLaszlow, 1993).

Melanie Klein (1882–1960) represents something of a transitional figure between Freudian instinct theory and the object relations school of thought. Born and educated in Vienna, Klein underwent psychoanalysis in Budapest during the early years of World War I.

Klein adapted several Freudian techniques in order to explore children's unconscious, and introduced the idea of play therapy in working with young children. Her assertion that the superego and the Oedipus complex were present during the first two years of life proved controversial (Segal, 2004).

Much of Klein's work stemmed from her work with young children, in which she focused on the symbolic meaning of their unconscious fantasies. She proposed that children's fantasy world was already well developed between ages two and three years. According to Klein, infants engage in a form of projection, and fear attack from the '*bad mother*' in what she termed '*persecutory anxiety*'. Klein proposed that this anxiety was a component of infants' mental functions during efforts to organize all aspects of themselves and others into good and bad dichotomies. She considered the resulting anxiety to be part of the *paranoid-schizoid position,* which related to subsequent emotional vulnerabilities. As infants begin to integrate good and bad as coexisting realities, they are then capable of viewing the mother as possessing a mixture of good and bad qualities, as well as being able to experience both love and resentment toward her. Many of Klein's concepts of children's early fantasies reflected their quests for relationship (Guntrip, 1973).

Another of Klein's controversial ideas involved her counterargument to Freud's concept of *penis envy* among females. According to Klein in *Envy and Gratitude* (originally published 1957), envy is an innate or inborn factor of the psyche, and therefore resistant to change. It reflects inborn destructive impulses, and is counterbalanced by the presence of gratitude. Klein proposed that, contrary to the traditional concept of penis envy, men were subject to womb and breast envy (Guntrip, 1973; Segal, 2004).

Konrad Lorenz (1903–1989) was an Austrian zoologist and ethologist who studied the instinctive behaviours of animals. His work with young goslings has informed some of the thinking about childhood attachment. Lorenz observed that young fowl do not have to be taught to follow their mother, but they have an automatic response based on *imprinting*. According to Lorenz (1935), imprinting occurs only during a *critical period* shortly after hatching. The goslings Lorenz studied automatically followed a particular object, and remained attached to it, regardless of whether it was their mother, and regardless of food being provided. Lorenz found the imprinting was irreversible, and that once goslings had imprinted upon an object (in some cases, Lorenz himself), they remained attached to it. Lorenz proposed that imprinting is biologically determined, having evolved from survival strategies. The critical period identified by Lorenz has been likened to the first three years of human life, which Bowlby viewed as a *sensitive period* for attachment (Sigelman & Rider, 2003).

Margaret Mahler (1897–1985) was born in Hungary. She taught widely and wrote prolifically, and her concepts influenced developmental theory in Europe and the US (Stepansky, 1988).

Mahler's *separation–individuation* theory expanded upon the object-relations concepts, and represented a radical shift from traditional psychoanalytic thinking about the psychosexual stages of development. Mahler et al. (1975) proposed that infants' 'psychological birth' was independent from their physical birth. Thus, Mahler's stages of 'normal autism' (not to be mistaken for the pervasive developmental disorder with the same name) and 'normal symbiosis' are not considered pathological, but rather they are universal stages that precede the infant's achievement of an independent identity (Polansky, 1991). Symbiosis refers to a state of fusion, in which there is no clarity as to where one and another start and stop.

Mahler (1965) proposed that separation-individuation is the desired result of children gaining a sense of identity distinct from their mothers. Her concept of *Object Constancy* represented a crucial variable in the understanding of children's perceptions of themselves in relation to others. Mahler proposed that Separation–Individuation began somewhere around age 5–6 months. By its successful completion, separation-individuation represents the internalised sense of object constancy, with which emotional stability is possible. Through the achievement of object constancy, a child is capable of calling upon internal representations of the loved object (typically mother) in ways that are soothing or comforting in times of distress.

Mahler regarded significant mismatching between infants and their mothers during the stage of normal symbiosis as a potential risk factor for regression (back to the shell-like state), including possible autism or psychosis. She associated inadequate matching during the symbiotic stage with borderline states, self-mutilation and self-starvation. The emotional availability of the caregiver throughout the process was an essential component of Mahler's concepts (Fonagy, 1999).

Harry Stack Sullivan (1892–1949) was the only surviving child of Irish parents who immigrated to the US following the potato famine. His childhood has been described as poor, lonely, and socially isolated. Sullivan received his medical training in Chicago, and originally trained in the psychoanalytic tradition.

Sullivan's theoretical approach, referred to as *interpersonal psychiatry* emphasized social factors related to the development of the personality. Unlike Freud, Sullivan considered the developmental implications of parent–child as well as peer relationships

Table 5.4 Margaret Mahler's stages of separation–individuation

Age	*Stage*	*Characteristics*
Birth–2 months	Normal autism	Longer periods of sleep than wakefulness Similarities to life in the womb Internal stimuli (e.g. hunger) more dominant that interest in external stimuli Goal: Homeostasis
2–5 months	Normal symbiosis	Emergence of perceptions Gradual perception of external world (e.g. mother's presence) Perception of mother–infant relationship remains undifferentiated Importance of 'matching' of infant's and mother's needs and dispositions
5–10 months	Differentiation	Expanding neurological development Increased alertness Attention increasingly drawn to others Physical and psychological distinctions from mother increasingly obvious Beginnings of object permanence Increasing usage of 'transitional objects'
10–18 months	Practising	Increasing physical mobility and autonomy results in greater exploration of surroundings Crawling, walking episodes typically interspersed with returns to mother for 'emotional refuelling' Increasing levels of busy-ness and autonomy Infant's 'love affair with the world'
18–24 months	Rapprochement	Surge in physical and verbal capacities Increasing curiosity Increasing cognitive abilities to understand environment and consequences of behaviour 'Terrible twos' Alternating sense of helplessness and dependence with growing sense of autonomy and independence Possible stranger anxiety Repeated explorations followed by returning to mother
2–5 years	Object constancy: Identity	Gradual comprehension of and reassurance by the mother and others, even when apart Achievement of *identity* entails achievement of separation–individuation Enduring concepts of self and others linked with a strong foundation for the personality

Source: Adapted from Sadock & Sadock (2007).

critical influences on the personality. Sullivan introduced the term 'significant other' to refer to important relationships (Sullivan, 1953).

Sullivan proposed what he called *the chum period* in order to describe the psychologically important aspect of same-sex friendships that occur by about age 10. Beginning with the significance of having companionable playmates in order to learn crucial social skills, Sullivan considered the experience of 'chums' essential for subsequent emotional and social well-being. Because such relationships can provide opportunities to develop trust, caring, and loyalty, Sullivan argued that close chumships could actually counteract some of the detrimental effects of poor parent–child relationships, and prepare children for subsequent partnerships with loved ones. Similarly, Sullivan argued that a child who is deprived of chumships would be at risk of subsequent social difficulties as an adult.

Sullivan was well known for his clinical work with people with severe psychoses. He approached therapy with the premise that even those people with the most severe forms of schizophrenia could benefit from the human relationship provided in psychotherapy (Evans, 1996). Sullivan's emphasis on the role of interpersonal relationships in the healing process is congruent with social work values. His attention to cultural influences on mental illness, which was quite radical at the time, is also congruent with social work approaches because of its focus on social factors rather than pathology alone.

Donald Winnicott (1897–1971) was among the prominent contributors to the British School of object relations. His second marriage was to a psychiatric social worker who was also a psychoanalyst.

Winnicott proposed a theory of 'multiple self-organizations', which included a *true self*. According to Winnicott (1965), the true self represents the successful development of various ego functions, and entails a sense of integrity. The true self can develop in a setting in which a responsive *holding environment* is provided. The holding environment provides a setting in which both aggression and love can coexist, thus providing a means of the infant safely experiencing and tolerating ambivalence and frustration. The alternative *false self* is primarily a defensive function, which is potentially disruptive, and generally associated with paranoia and pathology.

Winnicott (1958) also introduced the concept of the *good enough mother* as one who is capable of being adequately emotionally present for the infant, and thus capable of providing a holding environment sufficient for the development of the infant's true self. Based on his ideas about sufficiently sensitive caregiving, Winnicott emphasized that attachment did not necessitate maternal infallibility. In fact, maternal errors are both inevitable and potentially instructive. The comparison between good enough and not good enough mothering has been likened to the difference between a gentle loosening of an embrace and the dropping of an infant.

Winnicott also introduced the concept of the *transitional object*, which infants and children may use as a substitute for the mother in times of duress or experimental separations. Transitional objects often include familiar items, such as blankets, a teddy bear, or a 'dummy' to provide a sense of security and comfort during the mother's absence (Winnicott, 1958).

Implications for practice

Many of the concepts inherent to ego psychology and attachment theory are related to social work with individuals in need. Basic concepts of the therapeutic alliance between the worker and the service user are inherent to ego psychology. Providing ego support for people in crisis is typically congruent with good practice. Being able to appreciate ego strengths in service users is also necessary for good practice. By having the ability to recognize defence mechanisms (both used and abused), social workers are likely to be able to provide suitably matched interventions without invoking excessive anxiety on the part of service users. By attending to such factors as relationships and ego strengths, social workers can make time-limited services and closures considerably more effective than they would be if those factors were unappreciated.

Many of the basic concepts of attachment theory and object relations are fundamental to sound assessment for purposes of identifying and describing circumstances with which social workers routinely intervene. Beyond assessment skills, however, social workers are called upon to be keenly aware of the relevance of past relationships for present and future relationships and behaviour. Even when past experiences of relationships with parents have been painful and destructive, children typically continue to prefer being in the company of the parents with whom they are most familiar, and the most attached. That reality may prove profoundly bewildering to anyone unfamiliar with the basic concepts of attachment theory.

Social workers typically appreciate attachment as a lifespan concept (Howe et al., 1999). Understanding the levels of reorganization necessary to enter into and succeed with new and multiple relationships (remarriages, new step parents, new siblings and step-siblings) forms an essential component of social workers' interventions with children and families. Balancing an awareness of risks and resilience is a fundamental factor of sound social work practice.

Winnicott's concepts of a 'holding environment' are particularly applicable to much of social work practice. In his approach to therapy, Winnicott (1968) likened the helping or therapeutic relationship to the relationship in which the good enough mother provides a holding environment for a child. In a therapeutic relationship, the holding environment is intended to provide a sufficiently safe setting for the client to develop and meet those ego needs that have been previously unmet. Importantly, Winnicott emphasized that the clinician's patience was a crucial factor in the helping relationship, much as is the case with mothers.

Much of Mahler's theory of separation–individuation has been applied in clinical work with survivors of childhood trauma. It is also associated with working with people with personality disorders, particularly the assessment and treatment of borderline personality disorders (see Blank & Blank, 1994; Polansky, 1991).

As it applies to the helping relationship, Mahler's theory provides a way of facilitating growth by attending to the unmet needs to achieve a secure identity. Especially when working with survivors of childhood trauma, such work can prove pivotal, by focusing on the client's capacity to adapt and grow, along with providing a safe and trustworthy environment in which they may do so.

Berne's transactional analysis theory lends itself to social work practice with people who repeatedly find themselves in unhealthy relationships. It also provides a framework for understanding some of the work social workers do when working with people with severely damaged ego functions. By using a strong adult ego state, social workers can support service users who are struggling to resolve past traumas and deficits.

The Myers–Briggs Type Indicator is many people's primary frame of reference for Jung's work. Based upon Jung's ideas of psychological types, it comprises a 125-question paper-and-pencil test, and is among the most popular tests of its kind. The Myers–Briggs Indicator is designed to identify a person's primary inclination (either introversion or extroversion), as well as the primary and secondary functions (Myers, McCalley, Quenk, & Hammer, 1998). Because the test tends to frame people's inclinations in terms of strengths, rather than deficits, it is often well regarded among social workers.

Criticisms and debates regarding ego psychology and neo-Freudian perspectives

Not surprisingly, Freud was among the foremost critics of his various former protégés' ideas. He reportedly dismissed Adler's theories about over-compensatory behaviour by commenting that there would 'always have to be a psychology for the Hausfrau, and Adler has created it' (Polansky, 1991: 10).

Although Klein's concepts provide inspiration to many, her emphasis on infants' and children's fantasies has been criticized for its conceptual vagueness. Its abstractness distinguishes that component of her theory from the applicability of much of Bowlby's and Ainsworth's research on attachment. Also, because she mainly observed older children, some argue that her findings are more descriptive of the outcomes of insecure attachment than the cause *per se* (Fonagy, 1999).

While Bowlby's theory of attachment is widely held dear to social workers and developmental specialists alike, it is also criticized for some of its sexist implications. Bowlby's work was primarily produced and introduced during the 1950s, at a time when men were returning to the workforce following World War II. By arguing that separation from the mother posed lifelong risks to children's physical and mental well-being, Bowlby has been criticized for effectively excluding women from competing with men for employment. Bowlby's ideas about the consequences of maternal deprivation precluded many conscientious mothers' consideration of meaningful employment outside the home, and reinforced many women's financial dependence on men. The near-exclusive emphasis on the mother–child relationship also excluded the consideration of infants' relationships with fathers, thus overlooking the critical factors of paternal roles and contributions (or lack thereof) (Burman, 1994).

Another criticism of Bowlby's theory of attachment is its inference that any break in the early relationship between the mother and child poses risks for the child's subsequent emotional well-being. Little if any empirical evidence supports that premise; even Bowlby's own work with children following early and prolonged separations indicated tremendous variations among children, with a small minority developing serious personality problems as a result of early separations (Hughes, 2003).

Questions of predisposing genetic and environmental factors that could preclude attachment behaviours are largely unaddressed in Bowlby's and Ainsworth's research. Issues such as newborns' medical states or genetic predispositions to extreme responses are not explored in relation to complex attachment patterns (Reiss et al., 1995).

The language usage of the time when the British School was most prolific was generally sexist, especially in the premise that mothers were necessarily the primary caregivers. While developmental psychologists have addressed that bias in the intervening decades, the original 'mother-centric' wordings remain very patriarchal in their implications, and can be interpreted as very mother-blaming.

The majority of research into attachment has been conducted with Euro-American samples. Very little attachment research has included cross-cultural information. Of the available cross-cultural information, the variations are noteworthy. For example, in Japanese studies, children rarely exhibit behaviours considered consistent with 'secure attachment', but more often are categorized as 'resistant'. Because most infants in Japan are almost continually in their mother's presence, questions arise about whether the experience of separation is even more stressful for them, thus skewing the findings (Shaffer, 1996). Further questions arise about whether the premise of 'secure' attachment is necessarily ideal or adaptive across cultures. Especially in cultures in which single-family dwellings are not the norm, measures of 'adaptive' attachment might be more informative than the Euro-American norm of 'secure' (Robinson, 2007).

The research methodology employed in the exploration of infants' attachment also raises ethical questions. In order to examine different styles of attachment, Ainsworth placed children in settings in which some distress was virtually necessary on the infant's part. By current ethics committee standards, that practice could be considered dubious. The research procedure of comparing children of employed vs. non-employed mothers would probably be considered a confounding variable by today's research standards, whereas it was not regarded as problematic at the time Ainsworth was conducting her studies (Burman, 1994).

Jung's theory has been criticized for its mysticism and lack of empirical measurability. Some have suggested that his emphasis on communication with ghosts and death in general is indicative of his being quite ill at the time he was writing.

Any effort to review the entire array of neo-Freudian or ego psychologists' work entails a vast and varied body of work. Students are encouraged to consider areas of their particular interest, in order to review the original sources and construct their own critical appraisal.

Questions

1 Match the following concepts and psychoanalysts:

	Concept	Psychoanalyst
____	Ego psychology	(a) Mary Ainsworth
____	Internal working model	(b) Harry Stack Sullivan
____	Attachment theory	(c) Donald Winnicott
____	Archetypes	(d) Karen Horney
____	'Good enough mothering'	(e) Margaret Mahler
____	Separation–individuation	(f) Anna Freud
____	Imprinting behaviours	(g) Alfred Adler
____	Inferiority complex	(h) Konrad Lorenz
		(i) Melanie Klein
		(j) John Bowlby

2 What are some of the ways in which the following settings might complicate the application of Bowlby's and Ainsworth's concepts of secure attachment?
   (a) Infancy spent living in a commune or kibbutz.
   (b) Infancy spent in a small day care setting, with the same people each day.
   (c) Infancy spent living with both parents, two grandparents, an aunt and cousin in the home.
   (d) Infancy spent living next door to extended family and close friends.
   (e) A six-month-old infant's mother dying in a car crash, following which a devoted but bereaved family member assumes the caregiving role.
   (f) Infancy spent with teenage mother completing her education, while very caring attentive grandparents share primary caregiving roles.
   (g) Infancy spent with parents running a busy shop or pub, in which many familiar faces are a routine occurrence.
   (h) Infancy spent with a mother experiencing post-natal depression, for whom social interactions are overwhelming and avoided.

3 Consider some examples of children and parents with whom you are familiar. Can you identify some aspects of attachment behaviours that you consider relevant? These may be positive or negative.

4 What could be some of the ways in which social workers might risk imposing Eurocentric standards of attachment behaviours in ways that could be culturally inappropriate when working with families from different cultures?

5 How do you see Berne's transactional analysis concepts of the child, parent and adult ego states in relation to Freud's id, ego and superego? Compare and contrast how the two theories would be applicable to working with service users.

6 Behaviourism

As an approach to psychology, behaviourism revolutionized the understanding of people's behaviours by concentrating explicitly on measurable components. With its focus on the interactions of environmental variables ('stimuli'), observable behaviour ('responses') and consequences ('reinforcements'), behaviourism provided an early alternative to traditional psychoanalytic emphasis on the internal workings of the mind. By focusing on observable behaviour, psychology thus moved into the realm of scientific methods for studying and verifying human behaviour.

While some would argue that behaviourism has come to be intrinsically linked with cognitive models of understanding behaviour, there are some inherent distinctions that require consideration. This chapter's focus is primarily on classical and operant behaviourism and their origins, which may seem rather limited in its scope, but which correlates with the material on cognitive-behavioural models discussed in Chapter 7.

Relevance for social work

The behaviourist approach gained considerable popularity during the 1950s and 1960s, in part as a reaction against the psychoanalytic tradition (Coulshed & Orme, 2006). By focusing on specific observable behaviours, the behaviourist approach introduced a more empirical means of predicting behaviour and assessing change than the psychoanalytic tradition could offer. That led the way to conducting experiments to measure behavioural changes, leading toward the use of outcome measures as a means of support in the realm of evidence-based practice.

The behaviourist tradition has contributed to several methods of therapeutic interventions that represent noteworthy departures from the psychoanalytic tradition that preceded behaviourism. For social workers who are working with people with various anxiety-related conditions, including phobias, behavioural approaches have considerable appeal based on evidence of their effectiveness (Barlow et al., 2002).

Historical background

Compared with their neo-Freudian or ego psychology counterparts, the key contributors to behaviourism were less likely to be contemporaries. For purposes of this discussion, they will be discussed in approximate chronological order.

Shortly after Sigmund Freud proposed the concepts that evolved into psychoanalytic theory, an array of work was being conducted in the realm of what subsequently evolved into behaviourism. While most of that work occurred in America, the Russian physiologist **Ivan Pavlov** (1849–1936) is among the most well-known names associated with psychology. As part of his study of the digestive processes of dogs, Pavlov noted that the dogs salivated not only at the sight and taste of food, but also at the sound of footsteps associated with their feeders' arrival, prior to seeing or smelling the actual food. Pavlov carried out experiments to understand the dogs' responses, and came to establish what eventually formed the core concepts of *classical conditioning*.

According to Pavlov, a *conditioned response* (e.g. salivation) is one that is elicited under conditions in which a particular *stimulus* is present (e.g. the sound of feeders' footsteps). Finding this area more intriguing than the chemistry of saliva, Pavlov continued his study of conditioned responses; he introduced assorted variables, including the sound of a bell ringing just prior to the dogs being fed. Under experimental conditions, though, Pavlov demonstrated that when dogs came to associate the sound of the bells ringing with the imminent arrival of food, they came to salivate upon hearing the bells ring, even when food did not arrive. Importantly, the bell ringing is neither normally associated with dogs' feeding, nor does it normally induce salivation. Over time, the dogs came to salivate at the sound of the bell alone, which Pavlov referred to as 'psychic salivation'. The dogs' salivation represented a conditioned response. Pavlov's observations led to the emergence of what is now considered classical (or Pavlovian) conditioning (Gross, 2001).

The term 'Pavlov's dog' is often used when someone's behavioural response to a given situation is virtually automatic, rather than being based on intent, consideration or analysis. Examples include responses to phones ringing, alarm clocks, or the sound of seat belt buzzers in automobiles. Most people find that their reactions to such 'stimuli' are instinctual, rather than considered responses. On a more pleasant level, the sight of an outdoor barbecue or a bakery's window may elicit similarly unconsidered responses, including salivation for some of us.

In 1904 (the year of B.F. Skinner's birth), Pavlov received the Nobel Prize in Medicine, based on his doctoral thesis, 'The Centrifugal Nerves of the Heart', although his earlier work had been far over-shadowed by his subsequent work on behavioural conditioning. He continued to conduct physiological studies well into his later years, and was held in high regard during the Stalinist era in Russia. His laboratory in St Petersburg remains a museum to his work.

Edwin Thorndike (1874–1949) was educated at Harvard and Columbia Universities. Thorndike conducted animal studies in the newly established psychology department at Columbia University. Using an approach that was less directly focused on physiological responses than Pavlov's, Thorndike studied animals' problem-solving capacities through the use of 'puzzle boxes'. His experiments included placing cats in boxes from which they could learn to escape by pressing a lever, resulting in his (1898) doctoral thesis entitled 'Animal Intelligence'. Thorndike studied the situation in which the cats used a *trial and error* approach to solving problems, which involved interacting with their environment. For example, as most cat owners can attest, the cats proved remarkably skilled at finding ways to escape from the boxes. Thorndike used that skill, along with incentives of food placed outside the puzzle boxes, to test their intelligence and reinforce their behaviours (Thorndike, 1911).

Thorndike framed his questions and findings in an experimental context, and emphasized the measurable or empirical aspects of the behaviours being studied. His basic premise foreshadowed Skinner's subsequent concepts of reinforcement associated with operant conditioning. Thorndike introduced the term *law of effect* to refer to any response that leads to an outcome that the organism (animal or person) finds gratifying, and thus likely to be repeated. Likewise, any response that the organism finds aversive or unpleasant is unlikely to be repeated. His basic premise was that behaviour is determined by its consequences (Garvin, 1991). Thorndike's emphasis on reinforcement became a dominant approach in the US in the early twentieth century.

John Broadus Watson (1878–1958) is generally regarded as the founder of behaviourism. Originally from a poor, rural, deeply religious South Carolina family, Watson was a precocious student. He entered the University of Chicago for his doctoral studies at a time when that meant being in an intellectually exciting environment, and a centre of the functionalist perspective on psychology. Watson was offered a full professorship in psychology at Johns Hopkins University in 1909, just a few years after completing his PhD, and he subsequently became the chair of the psychology department. While there, he strengthened the department's ties with the biology department, rather than its historical ties with philosophy. Such a shift in affiliations was in keeping with his vision of psychology as a science linked more with behaviour than the mind alone (Passer et al., 2009).

Watson rejected the idea of introspection as a necessary component of psychology. Similar to John Locke's (1693) premise, Watson believed children lacked any inborn tendencies, and that their development and functions resulted entirely from their environments and their treatment by those around them. In fact, his work included specific experiments to explain several of Freud's psychoanalytic concepts through basic learning principles (Ewen, 1998).

A very dynamic and assertive personality, Watson began publishing in the area of behaviourism in 1913, and quickly received considerable attention in the field of psychology through his insistence on observable, measurable behaviour being more relevant than any mysterious mental processes. Watson's (1913) 'Behaviorist Manifesto' established a move toward psychology being based on a rigorously empiricist approach, whereby objective measures were considered a necessary aspect for scientific validity. The key components of Watson's Behaviorist Manifesto included an emphasis on pure objectivity, with the goal of psychology being the ability to predict and control behaviour, and the inherent similarity between human and non-human (i.e. laboratory animal) behaviour for purposes of study (Gross, 2001).

Watson published widely in the area of early child behaviour and parenting. He applied many of his behavioural concepts to his own children's early lives, insisting on very regular habits for sleeping, eating, and elimination. An example of his bold assertions can be found in the following frequently quoted passage:

> Give me a dozen healthy infants, well-formed and my own special world to bring them up in and I'll guarantee to take any one at random and train him to become any type of specialist I might select – doctor, lawyer, artist, merchant-chief and, yes, even beggar-man and thief – regardless of his talents, penchants, tendencies, abilities and vocation and race of his ancestors.
>
> (Watson, 1925: 82)

Watson collaborated with Johns Hopkins postgraduate student Rosalie Rayner, who subsequently became his second wife. Their experimentation to demonstrate the modification of behaviour through the process of associative learning included the well-known example of 'Little Albert'. By means of experimental methods that would no longer receive the approval of institutional ethics committees, the Little Albert experiment entailed demonstrating that fears could be learned, rather than being inborn. To demonstrate this classical conditioning premise, Watson and Rayner showed a white rabbit to 9-month-old infant Albert, who initially showed no fear of the rabbit. They proceeded to show Little Albert the rabbit while simultaneously clanging a steel rod with a hammer out of his sight. Little Albert responded with predictable fear and distress with which infants with normal hearing typically respond to loud noises. In the course of the experiment, however, he came to respond fearfully to the sight of the rabbit, regardless of any loud clanging noise accompanying its appearance. The fearful response to the rabbit was experimentally expanded to include other white, furry objects, including a Santa Claus mask. Thus, Watson asserted the basic principles of learned or conditioned (emotional) responses to a given stimulus (Schaffer, 1996). In doing so, he provided a stark challenge to the role of the psyche, introspection, and most of the prevailing psychological concepts of his time.

Watson's subsequent research endeavours reportedly included experimentations in the field of human sexual behaviours, some of which entailed participant observation. His methods attained some notoriety, and were not socially or ethically approved by his university's administration (Glassman & Hadad, 2004). Meanwhile, Watson's divorce from his socially prominent first wife in order to marry his graduate student Rayner (who was only five years older than his oldest daughter) was the source of considerable notoriety in conservative 1920s Baltimore. Despite his distinctions in the field of psychology, Johns Hopkins dismissed Watson. He subsequently joined a New York advertising firm, where his skills in influencing behavioural responses were quite useful. Following Rayner's death in her mid-thirties, Watson eventually retired to a farm in Connecticut, where he became increasingly reclusive. Their oldest son died of suicide just four years after his father's death. By most accounts, Watson's later years were in stark contrast to the promise of his early career.

Of the behaviourists, the work of the American **B.F. Skinner** (1904–90) remains the best known. As a child in Pennsylvania, he displayed an interest in animals and in inventing gadgets and toys. After graduating from university with honours, Skinner aspired to become a novelist, but concluded that he had nothing literary to say after a year's effort. He subsequently pursued postgraduate studies at Harvard, where he became interested in the ideas of Pavlov, Watson and Thorndike. Along with inventing laboratory equipment that bears his name, Skinner published widely and spent a distinguished career on the Harvard faculty (Ewen, 1998).

Skinner began conducting experiments that eventually evolved into *operant conditioning* during his postgraduate studies at Harvard. His emphasis on strict empirical measures of behaviour was strongly influenced by Thorndike's and Watson's work. Skinner's concepts of operant conditioning stemmed from his work with laboratory animals. He conducted experiments with animals and later with humans under carefully controlled experimental conditions. Skinner's experiments ultimately led to the creation of a technology designed to modify behaviour through what he termed 'operant conditioning', including the use of the 'Skinner Box' (which he preferred to call an operant conditioning apparatus).

Based on his experiments, Skinner proposed that behaviour results from basic principles of reinforcement. The term *radical behaviourism* refers to Skinner's proposition that variables pertaining to emotions, sensations, and various personal events are essentially irrelevant to the explanation of behaviour because such factors are neither observable nor measurable (Gross, 2001). According to Skinner, while 'radical behaviourism' may recognize the role played by personal events, it nonetheless asserts that 'so-called mental activities are metaphors or explanatory fictions and that behaviour attributed to them can be more effectively explained in other ways' (Skinner, 1987: 91).

Key concepts

While 'behaviourism' actually refers to several different theories to explain various aspects of people's behaviours, some core concepts apply across the approach. One of those core concepts is that behaviour is defined in ways that are observable and measurable. By emphasizing specific, measurable and quantifiable aspects of behaviour, behaviourism is closely associated with a more empirical approach to defining problems and measuring change.

Behaviourism is often associated with the scientific principle of *parsimony* (discussed in Chapter 1) because it approaches the study and understanding of people's behaviour in ways that utilize the simplest possible explanation for the most comprehensive approach. An example of this might be a behaviourist explanation for eating a bag of crisps being a response to a given stimulus (i.e. hunger, or seeing an advertisement). That is a considerably more parsimonious explanation than the consideration of unconscious motivations stemming from a repressed childhood experience, or possible oral fixations dating from infancy that could be applied to the understanding of the same behaviour from a psychoanalytic perspective.

Classical conditioning

Both *classical* and *operant conditioning* address observed behaviour (responses) in relation to external causation (stimuli). The two approaches define the stimulus–response (S–R) relationship quite differently. Both types of conditioning entail a level of learning from experience (*associative learning*). In classical conditioning, however, the stimulus is seen as activating the response in a predictable, automatic manner, whereas in operant conditioning, the response is seen as learned and subject to change.

Some understanding of *unconditioned* and *conditioned responses* helps to understand classical conditioning. Unconditioned responses include those reflex responses that often entail basic neurological reactions to a given phenomenon. Responses such as salivating when tasting a slice of lemon, or a startle response to the sound of thunder are examples of unlearned, involuntary unconditioned responses to a given experience (or trigger), which serves as an *unconditioned stimulus*.

Conditioned responses entail some level of learning in their acquisition. Before that learning occurs, the given experience (such as Pavlov's bell ringing) remains a *neutral stimulus*. To function as a stimulus, there must be some demonstrable awareness of that entity (the bell, or the thunder) on the part of the individual. That awareness is demonstrable through what is called an *orienting response*, which entails the turning toward the sound, or other ways of evidencing attention toward the stimulus.

When a stimulus was repeatedly paired with a given experience (such as bell ringing being associated with food), the sound of the bell came to elicit salivation from the dogs, thus representing a *conditioned response*, as distinguished from salivation that would occur in response to food alone. The basic ideas involved in these processes are represented in Figure 6.1.

Without conditioning

Neutral stimulus (NS) (rabbit) → Orienting response (Little Albert observes the rabbit)

Unconditioned stimulus (UCS) (loud noise) → Unconditioned response (UCR) (fear, distress at loud noises)

During conditioning

NS/CS (Conditioned stimulus) (rabbit appearing PLUS loud noise) → UCS → CR/UCR (Conditioned response) (fear, distress)

After conditioning

Conditioned stimulus (CS) (rabbit appearing without loud noise) → Conditioned response (CR) (fear, distress)

Figure 6.1 Basic classical conditioning concepts.

Operant conditioning

Operant conditioning has come to be the more dominant approach since the 1950s. Unlike classical conditioning's emphasis on involuntary response, operant conditioning is more focused on self-generated or voluntary behaviours, and how they are subject to change. Operant conditioning is generally regarded as a more easily applicable approach to behaviourism than classical conditioning, and is associated with most behavioural treatment approaches.

Strongly associated with Skinner's work, operant conditioning relies on the premise that behaviour is determined by prior conditioning, which is operant or learned. According to Skinner (1972), behaviour is shaped and maintained by its consequences. Skinner's (1965: 111) famous summary of his views was: '[I] simply say that he behaves because of the consequences which have followed similar behavior in the past . . . [Thus] no behavior is free.' Key concepts of operant conditioning relate to ways in which new behaviours can be learned, altered, and regulated according to the consequences they elicit. Operant conditioning relates to ways in which weak behaviours can be *reinforced*, strong behaviours can be sustained, and undesirable behaviours can be discouraged and eliminated. According to operant conditioning, the *consequences* of behaviour provide the key means by which behaviours are influenced (Skinner, 1972).

Reinforcement refers to a result or consequence of behaviour that influences the likelihood of that behaviour being repeated. Reinforcement can be positive or negative. If the behaviour is already occurring, then *positive reinforcement* serves to maintain that occurrence. If behaviours are desired, then positive reinforcement serves to strengthen them by increasing the likelihood of their being repeated. Skinner made no assumptions about inner workings of the psyche in terms of insight, satisfaction or drives.

Negative reinforcement refers to the removal of a negative event or consequence that serves to increase the frequency of a particular behaviour. Negative reinforcement entails two components. First, some variable must be eliminated from the situation. Second, the frequency of a particular behaviour must be increased in response to the removal of the variable mentioned. Examples of negative reinforcements can be found in automobiles equipped with buzzers that sound until seat belts are fastened, and bells that ring when keys are left in ignitions when doors are opened. Most people respond to those sounds in order to avoid or stop the sounds, by increasing the frequency with which they fasten their seat belts or remove their keys from the ignition. Thus the sounds provide negative reinforcement by increasing the frequency of the desired behaviour.

Punishment and negative reinforcement are easily confused with one another. *Punishment* is designed to reduce the probability of an operant occurring, and functions as the opposite of reinforcement. It refers to the introduction of either an aversive event or the removal of a positive reinforcement in response to a given behaviour, which serves to decrease the undesired behaviour. Examples include verbal scolding, spanking, or changing the will that determines a dependant's inheritance. While punishment generally results in a direct reduction in the undesired behaviour, it is generally more reinforcing to the punisher than the punished. Punishments necessitate careful monitoring, as they may sometimes elicit adverse reactions, and because they serve only to deter behaviours, rather than contributing to the learning of new behaviour (Skinner, 1972).

An important distinction between punishment and negative reinforcement relates to the decreased frequency of behaviours associated with punishment, rather than the increased frequency associated with negative reinforcement. While somewhat counter-intuitive, the distinction is noteworthy. Also, punishments may be administered either through the introduction of aversive responses to behaviours (such as through slaps, electric shocks, extreme heat, or public humiliations), or through the removal of a positive reinforcement (such as desserts, play time, prestige, or social privileges) (Table 6.1). The result of punishment is the decreased frequency of behaviours, while the result of negative reinforcement is an increase (Skinner, 1987).

Shaping refers to the process of reinforcing subsequent approximations of behaviour to a desired response. Shaping presumes that the person influencing the behaviour (i.e. researcher, parent, or tutor) has an ideal goal in mind, and can influence the delivery of reinforcements according to the behaviour's approximation of the goal. Generations of animal trainers can attest to the applicability of shaping to reinforce desired behaviour on the part of their animals. Examples include the practice of distributing treats to a puppy when she comes when called, but gradually withholding treats until she comes when called *and* sits at her owner's feet, then progressing to treats being given only when she comes when called, sits *and* lifts her paw to be shaken. With babies, the glee with which most parents greet their taking a first step typically generates babies taking more and more, and thus learning to walk.

Schedules of reinforcement refer to intervals at which reinforcements are given. *Continuous reinforcement* provides reinforcement after every correct response, but is not the most common form of learning. With *intermittent reinforcement*, the reinforcements are given for some correct responses, but not all. With *fixed-ratio reinforcement*, a specific number of correct responses are needed before the reinforcement occurs. *Variable-ratio schedules* reinforce the behaviour at the first correct response after a varying interval of time, which provides a schedule of intermittent reinforcement. Skinner considered the scheduling of reinforcements more important in changing behaviours than the amount or type of reinforcement used.

Conditioned positive reinforcements are sometimes employed in *token economies*.

Table 6.1 Examples of consequences of reinforcements and punishments

	Pleasant stimulus	*Unpleasant stimulus*
Administered	*Positive reinforcement:* Adding a pleasant stimulus (Strengthens behaviour)	*Positive punishment*: Adding an unpleasant stimulus (Weakens or deters behaviour)
Withheld or withdrawn	*Negative punishment:* Withdrawal of a pleasant stimulus (Weakens behaviour)	*Negative reinforcement:* Withdrawal of an unpleasant stimulus (Strengthens behaviour)

Particularly when working with young people, or people in institutional settings (schools, psychiatric units, residential settings, and jails), token economies are used by providing specific reinforcements for desired behaviours. For example, for getting a certain number of spelling words right, a student may receive extra time doing their favourite activity. For staying out of fights for an entire day, a troubled young person may receive telephone or television privileges as reinforcement. In order to work, token economies presume that there are (a) desired behaviours, and (b) desired items or privileges that can be used as incentives for behavioural change.

Extinction refers to the termination of reinforcement of a response, which contributes to the eventual decrease in frequency and possible elimination of the behaviour. Extinction entails the simple stopping of reinforcement, rather than the removal of positive reinforcement associated with punishment. With extinction, the behaviour elicits no consequence. Examples include ignoring behaviour that had previously elicited attention, or not rewarding the aforementioned dog when she comes and sits at her owner's feet. Research indicates that the behavioural changes previously achieved will likely remain for a short while, but then decrease in probability. The drop in the rate of behavioural response when reinforcement is discontinued is referred to as extinction.

Implications for practice

Based on operant conditioning, *behaviour modification* remains a prominent approach to the treatment of behaviour problems, and is considered a mainstay of many clinicians' repertoires. Behaviour modification has been applied across an array of conditions, including phobias, obsessive-compulsive disorders, substance-related conditions, and sexual disorders such as paraphilias (Sadock & Sadock, 2007).

Systematic desensitization is based on the concepts of classical (or respondent) conditioning, and is often used in work conducted with people experiencing anxiety and severe avoidance. Desensitization refers to techniques employed to reduce anxiety associated with specific stimuli. By teaching someone in real life (*in vivo*) that gradually increased exposure to specific stimuli can be tolerated without adverse effects, desensitization techniques have proven effective in the treatment of anxieties and phobias (Coulshed & Orme, 2006). An example would be the case of 'Bill':

> 'Bill' has an irrational fear of cats that is causing him problems in his relationship with his girlfriend, who has cats. Using systematic desensitization, working with Bill might begin by showing Bill photographs or other representations of cats. He might then watch a video of cats in a garden. Bill might then be asked to sit through a meeting with a life-like stuffed toy cat in sight. Gradually, he would be introduced into a setting when a cat would be present, but from which Bill could easily leave. Ultimately, through a gradual but progressive exposure to cats, Bill would be helped to overcome his fear, and be able to gain comfort in the presence of a real cat.

Biofeedback is a non-medical treatment derived from studies of ways in which to apply operant techniques in order to modify rats' autonomic physiological functions. It involves the use of instruments to record and display information about normally involuntary body functions, such as muscle tension, heart rate, and skin temperature. It has evolved into a sophisticated technique sometimes used in the treatment of a variety of conditions, including stress-related symptoms, migraines, bruxism (teeth-grinding), and urinary incontinence (Gross, 2001; Maxmen & Ward, 1995).

Criticisms and debates about behaviourism

Behaviourism has been criticized for its emphasis on external factors that influence behaviour, at the expense of other variables, including genetic factors, increased insight, internal motivations, and emotions. One of Watson's and Skinner's premises that has been criticized is their assertion that human behaviour can be predicted and modified in the same way that non-humans' behaviour can. Their emphasis on a single type of learning and their seeming disregard for the roles played by thought, memory, and communication remains a point of considerable debate (Gross, 2001; Sigelman & Rider, 2003).

The 'Skinner Box' remains one of the more controversial aspects of behaviourism. Its controversial aspects are in part because of its association with the premise that behavioural frequency is a sufficient measure, without consideration of the implications of intensity, quality, or length. Such debates necessarily entail questions of 'quantity vs. quality'.

Ultimately, the question of actual implementation of behavioural techniques raises questions of skills, methods, and ethical soundness. Despite the seemingly elegant simplicity of stimulus–response, altering environmental or personal stimuli in the real world requires considerable finesse and sensitivity. Questions of coercion and potential oppression must be considered. Very high levels of communication skills are needed in order to monitor effectiveness and service user consent and readiness to change. In an environment of increasing case loads and bureaucratic demands, the seeming simplicity of behavioural social work may appear quite tempting to inexperienced workers who may not fully appreciate the ethical and logistical demands it entails (Watson & West, 2006).

Questions

1 Match the following with the theorist or concept with which they are associated:

____	Law of effect	(a) Reinforcement
____	Behaviorist Manifesto	(b) Ivan Pavlov
____	Classical conditioning	(c) B.F. Skinner
____	'Trial & error' process	(d) John B. Watson
____	Intermittent reinforcement	(e) Edwin Thorndike
		(f) Schedules of reinforcement

2 Consider the following scenario:

> Sam (age 3) and his mother find a long queue at the supermarket checkout counter. Sam had his nap before coming shopping, and has been quite content during their time in the store. Upon reaching the checkout counter, he asks for his favourite sweet. His mother tells him that he cannot have sweets until after tea. He tries to convince her, but without success. He then begins to cry loudly, and cannot be consoled. His mother tries to reason with him, and even threatens that he will not have a sweet after tea if he continues his outburst. Several people have turned to stare. The elderly lady ahead of them in the checkout line looks particularly distressed by Sam's crying. Exasperated, Sam's mother finally reaches over to the sweet display, and hands Sam the sweet he wanted. His crying stopped.
>
> The next time Sam's mother took him to the supermarket, and they were approaching the checkout line, Sam began to cry.

(a) What do you consider the unconditioned stimulus?
(b) What do you consider the conditioned stimulus?
(c) What do you consider the conditioned response?
(d) What do you consider positive or negative reinforcements?

3 The noted psychologist John B. Watson ended his career working in the advertising industry, applying concepts of behavioural modification to the ways in which consumers were persuaded to make various purchases. Can you think of ways in which your purchasing behaviours have been influenced by advertising campaigns?

4 Match the following scenarios with the four concepts of operant conditioning.
(a) Positive reinforcement
(b) Negative reinforcement
(c) Positive punishment
(d) Negative punishment
(i) ____ When Billy the bully uses intimidation and threats with the younger children at school, they give him money to leave them alone.
(ii) ____ One teacher at school is aware of Billy's bullying tactics, and intervenes to stop the bullying, but Billy has found a way of activating that teacher's automobile's alarm system, which distracts him from attending to the younger children during play time, and allows Billy to continue his intimidation tactics.
(iii) ____ The teacher confiscates Billy's cash during recess, in front of other children who then shun Billy.
(iv) ____ Knowing that Billy does most of his bullying during recess, the teacher arranges for Billy to stay inside while all the other children are at recess.

5 Consider a behaviour in which you routinely engage for pleasure (sports, computer games, 'Free Cell', shopping, clubbing, etc.).
   (a) What are some stimuli that promote your behaviour?
   (b) What are the reinforcements that promote your behaviour?
   (c) What would serve to extinguish that behaviour?

7 Cognition and theories of learning

Cognition and cognitive development are those areas of psychology most associated with how and what people think, and the ways in which thinking skills change and develop over time. By its nature, cognition entails both the mental activities involved in acquiring, interpreting and retaining information, as well as the thoughts and beliefs that result from those processes. Cognitive development is often associated with concepts of 'intelligence', which may be defined in ways that are culturally influenced or defined. While much of cognition is conscious or intentional, much occurs without people's conscious awareness. In this chapter, topics having to do with the process of acquiring, retaining, and interpreting information will be discussed, along with the implications those processes have for people's behaviour. Distinct from the traditional psychoanalytic emphasis on drives and the unconscious, as well as from behaviourism's emphasis on consequences and reinforcements, cognitive theory addresses how people's behaviour is influenced by the complex role played by their thoughts and interpretations of their experiences.

Relevance for social work

As a very broad area of human functioning, cognition necessarily plays a crucial role in social work approaches to human behaviour. Cognitive theory reflects the breadth of the relevance of cognition, and entails a variety of concepts and perspectives that sometimes overlap and sometimes differ widely. Those theoretical concepts address both the acquisition and functions of thought, and the influence those thoughts have on what people do and feel. Core components of various aspects of cognitive theories, such as perceptions of the environment, memories, emotions, and interpretations support many social work approaches to understanding people's personalities and behaviour, as well as approaches to helping people solve problems and achieve change.

Social workers often apply *social learning theory* in order to understand people's behaviour, and how it evolves in the context of having observed others' behaviours and their consequences. Social workers often engage with service users through understanding the ways in which they attach meaning and value to various factors. By doing so, social workers are employing cognitive elements in their practice. Cognitive and cognitive-behavioural approaches are prominent in effective practice with an array of mental health and substance-related problems with which social workers are frequently involved. Through approaching behaviour as something learned and reinforced, the simultaneous premise is that learned behaviour can be adapted, relearned, or changed for the better through changed consequences.

Social work's inherent values of self-determination and self-actualization also relate to understanding the role played by learned helplessness, which is a cognitive concept related to how people perceive themselves as being destined to experience suffering. As agents of change and advocates for vulnerable populations, social workers are often in powerful positions to challenge the underlying premises of learned helplessness among service users.

Historical background

An American contemporary of Pavlov, **William James** (1842–1910), served as a pioneer in the teaching of psychology as a subject in its own right. The son of a wealthy and intellectual family, James was educated at Harvard during the American Civil War. James's struggle with recurrent depression began in his youth. Although American born, James was keenly associated with European thought, and he spent long periods of his adulthood in Europe.

In 1875, James established the first laboratory devoted to experimental psychology in the US. James wrote and spoke eloquently, and his considerable contributions to the field of psychology include his discussions of instinct, brain function, habit, the stream of consciousness, attention, memory, perception, and self-esteem. In 1894, James became the first American to draw favourable public attention to the recent work of the fledgling Viennese neurologist, Sigmund Freud (Gross, 2001).

Both William and his brother, the novelist Henry James, were intrigued by the challenges of articulating the complexities of the individual consciousness. James emphasized the role of introspection as a fundamental aspect of knowing and achieving individual potential. James contributed to psychology being increasingly considered as a science through his (1890) publication of *Principles of Psychology*, which he wrote over a period of 12 years, and in which he included the definition of psychology as the *science of mental life* (Hunter, 2004).

Jean Piaget (1896–1980) is widely regarded as a pioneer in the field of childhood cognitive development. Born and educated in Switzerland, Piaget's first publication (at age 11) was a letter to the editor about an albino sparrow. With about 20 articles published by age 20, Piaget earned a doctorate in biology at age 22. Although his interest in psychology initially remained secondary to his interest in biology, his continued studies and research included work at the Sorbonne in Paris and with Eugene Bleuler, who subsequently introduced the term 'schizophrenia' (Sadock & Sadock, 2007). He also worked with a colleague of Binet (of the well-known Stanford–Binet IQ test), where working on standardizing test questions led to his interest in the intellect, and how and why errors on those tests occurred (Vourlekis, 1991).

With his background in biology, Piaget viewed intelligence as a process that evolves in order to enhance an individual's adaptation to the environment. Much of his early work was based on his *naturalistic observations* of his own three children as infants, and how they explored and navigated the world around them. He subsequently developed what he called his *clinical method*, which entailed a flexible question-and-answer technique that he employed to explore how children approach and solve problems through asking questions specifically relevant to the individual child's line of reasoning.

Piaget devoted his career to developing a broad theory of intellectual development and the implications of intellectual development for children's emotional, social, and moral development. While more recent theories have evolved to explain the processing of information, Piaget's theory of the development of cognition provided a fundamental basis of subsequent cognitive and child development theories. Despite his historical prominence in the area of child development, developmental psychology and education, Piaget regarded himself as a *genetic epistemologist*, which he defined as the study of the development of abstract thought on the basis of a biological or innate environment.

The eminent Russian psychologist **Lev Vygotsky** (1896–1934) was a contemporary of Piaget. Because of a combination of his work having been censored for political reasons in Soviet Russia, and because of a lack of sufficient translations for his work to be appreciated in the West until the 1970s, his name is far less familiar to most than his work deserves (Durkin, 1995). Combining Marxist ideas with psychology, Vygotsky focused on the developmental tensions between the individual and the larger society, or nature and culture. Vygotsky argued that cognition is a social function, because of the interweaving of learning and social activities, which are shaped by culture and the social instrument of language usage (Durkin, 1995). His ideas were later appreciated for their importance both to clinical and educational psychology. Vygotsky's promising career was tragically brief; he died of tuberculosis at age 37.

Lawrence Kohlberg's (1927–1987) work is strongly associated with studies of moral development, which was an area of study traditionally avoided by most psychologists, out of fear of placing value judgements that are laden with biases and cultural presumptions. Kohlberg chose the area of moral development for his doctoral studies at the University of Chicago after helping to smuggle Jewish refugees through the British blockade into Palestine. During that time, Kohlberg and his crew mates along with the refugees were once captured and held captive in Cyprus, before escaping to Palestine and eventually returning to the US (Kroger, 1996).

Having studied with Piaget, Kohlberg expanded upon the Piagetian cognitive stages to describe cognitive and moral development. He proposed that children had to reach an appropriate stage of logical thought before being able to proceed to a comparable stage of moral reasoning, thus linking moral development and cognitive development (Schaffer, 1996). In an era in which Freudian concepts of the superego remained predominant, Kohlberg's ideas of moral development and social justice were considered quite revolutionary. He spent the majority of his career on the psychology faculty at Harvard University.

Perhaps the most prominent of the learning theorists, **Albert Bandura** (1925–present) is a Canadian-born psychologist. His work, which he originally referred to as 'social cognitive theory', challenges the Skinnerian premise of controlling external environments in order to shape behaviour. A pioneer in the area of *social learning* and *self-efficacy*, Bandura has been on the psychology faculty of Stanford University in California since 1953.

Two of the names most commonly associated with cognitive-behavioural approaches to mental health difficulties, particularly depression, are **Albert Ellis** and **Aaron Beck**. Both are American psychologists, and their work shares many common premises.

Albert Ellis (1913–2007) was born in Pittsburgh, Pennsylvania, and trained in psychology at Columbia University. Originally trained in the psychoanalytic tradition, Ellis departed from that practice during the 1950s, and came to refer to himself as a 'rational psychologist'. Ellis's development of rational-emotive therapy represents a crucial application of cognitive theory, with his emphasis on irrational thinking as the source of much unnecessary suffering. His rational-emotive therapy is based on the premise that negative emotions and problematic relationship patterns arise from inaccurate interpretations of experiences, rather than from the experiences *per se*.

Regarded by some as the 'father of cognitive therapy', Aaron Beck (1921–present) trained as a psychiatrist and psychoanalyst. Similar to Ellis, he also became disenchanted with the psychoanalytic approach and began focusing more intently on people's conscious belief systems, rather than their unconscious conflicts. From his work with cognitive behavioural processes, Beck came to consider that dysfunctional thinking resulted in problematic behaviours, and that underlying beliefs were the source of dysfunctional thinking. According to Beck, changes in symptoms result from changes in thinking (Fenichel, 2000).

Aaron Beck is renowned for addressing the cognitive aspects and measurement of depression, an important aspect of cognitive theory. Beck explains depression as a condition resulting from faulty evaluations or interpretations. His cognitive triad of depression addresses the negative and illogical thoughts that seem to come involuntarily and automatically. In his cognitive triad, Beck proposes that depression is shaped by the negative interpretation of the self, the world and the future. The cognitive triad that he proposed entails a catastrophic evaluation of the self, based on a faulty interpretation of the past, which influences the negative expectation of world in general (Gross, 2001).

Key concepts of cognition and learning

Piaget's theory of cognitive development

Prior to Piaget's revolutionizing contributions, children's thoughts and understanding were presumed to follow in the same vein as those of adults. Paradoxically, adults often presume(d) that children were not necessarily attending to adult discussions that they did not (or were not meant to) understand. Far from considering children to be miniature adults, Piaget considered children naturally curious explorers and experimenters, who are constantly trying to make sense of their observations and experiences. Stemming from Piaget's work, we are more likely to appreciate that children are consistently trying to interpret the world around them in an increasingly systematic way. Their interpretations rely on their own evolving logic as a means of explaining their observations.

According to Piaget, children's learning is essentially experiential; it takes place when they actively construct their own cognitive realities and understandings of their environment. Hence, Piaget's concepts are sometimes referred to as *constructivism*. He considered development an ongoing, dynamic process resulting from the ability to adapt thinking and form new ideas in ways that are responsive to the demands of a changing environment. Each of Piaget's *cognitive stages* represents an essential reorganization of how a child 'knows' the world. He considered these stages universal, or applicable to all children, regardless of culture or environment, although that point has since been argued by some (Robinson, 2007).

Piaget's stages are *epigenetic*, meaning that progression from one stage to the next necessitates both physical and mental maturation through the previous stage. Achieving the previous stage is a prerequisite for progression to the next, although the rate at which children move may vary according to innate abilities and environment. Piaget believed that children would reach the same cognitive conclusions and develop their thinking along essentially similar routes, regardless of their circumstances.

Piaget identified four factors that influenced the developmental process:

1. Physical maturation of the brain, resulting in new capacities.
2. Experiences that resulted in developing knowledge.
3. Social transmission of knowledge (education).
4. Equilibration or equilibrium.

According to Piaget, these four factors are mutually interactive. For example, the physical maturation of the brain that would allow for cognitive development is not sufficient without opportunities to undergo experiences that contribute to that development. Likewise, experiences typically reinforce the social transmission of knowledge, and vice versa. Finally, the interactions between maturation, experiences and social transmission of knowledge are kept in balance through 'equilibration', or the capacity for establishing equilibrium.

Accommodation, assimilation and equilibrium

Piaget referred to the basic building blocks of children's learning as *schemata*, which provide the basic organizational patterns used to interpret observations and experiences. He saw each *scheme* as the result of two inborn and complementary intellectual functions, which he called organization and adaptation. Within Piaget's theory, schemata continue to be subject to change or adaptation when newly acquired knowledge no longer fits within the previously sufficient scheme. Through organization, an existing scheme can be combined with a pre-existing or subsequently acquired scheme to make more complex frameworks for understanding. Piaget regarded adaptation as the intellect's process of adjusting to the changing demands of the environment.

Piaget regarded knowledge as the product of the simultaneous and corresponding mental processes he called *assimilation and accommodation*. Assimilation involves the way new information is absorbed into the existing intellectual organization. Accommodation refers to the modifications required to deal with the new material. According to Piaget (1970: 8), *there is no accommodation without assimilation.*

Intrigued by his observations of children of the same age making similar errors in reasoning, Piaget questioned whether these errors actually reflected age/developmental patterns of intellectual development. He proposed a universal sequence of four stages of cognitive development: (1) sensorimotor; (2) preoperational thought; (3) concrete operations; and (4) formal operations. According to Piaget, the four stages provide an invariant sequence of intellectual development, meaning that they necessarily occur in the same order for all children, and that progression to the next stage necessitates having successfully completed the previous stage.

The sensorimotor stage (birth to 2 years)

Piaget described the first stage as entailing an infant's learning through sensory observation and experience. During this stage, cognitive development evolves primarily through such sensorimotor structures as sight, hearing, ingestion (sucking and swallowing), mobility, and vocalization (crying, cooing) being in place. The infant's attention is primary focused on bodily sensations. According to Piaget, intelligence develops through action, when the child learns by doing and experiencing.

The ultimate aim of this stage is *object permanence*, when a baby comes to know that objects and people continue to exist even when they are out of sight. During the later part of the first year, infants begin to demonstrate some signs of distress upon their mother leaving the room; they no longer appear to operate on the 'out of sight, out of mind' principle (Shaffer, 1996). Ultimately, a baby comes to understand that balls roll under chairs, but can still be found there when sought; likewise, parents may leave the room, but can then be found in the next room when sought. The capacity to learn where to look is an important feature associated with object permanence.

Infants begin to demonstrate a grasp of *causality* through their growing awareness of the relationship between causes and effects. Similarly, infants demonstrate an increasing level of *intentionality*, entailing the emergence of goal-directed behaviour. Behaviours such as proto-declarative pointing, in which babies direct others' attention to objects or events of significance to them, are examples of intentional behaviours, reflecting an expanding cognitive capacity. During this stage, infants' thinking appears to entail a growing capacity for mental representations of objects, as well as the ability to solve sensorimotor problems (hungry, hot, etc.). These elements represent *representatational intelligence* (Vourlekis, 1991).

The preoperational stage (approximately 2–6 or 7 years)

Piaget proposed that the preoperational stage was the point during which conceptual thinking actually begins. The emergence of language provides the means by which children express otherwise symbolic ideas through fantasy and play. The preoperational stage marks a time during which a child becomes increasingly interested in the people and things around them. A typical marker of increasing curiosity during this stage is the perpetual 'why' questions asked by young children. Thinking tends to be 'prelogical' during this phase, and typically fairly concrete (Vourlekis, 1991).

Some key aspects of cognitive development during this stage include Piaget's concept of *conservation*, referring to the capacity to understand that physical quantities remain the same regardless of whether they change shape or appearance by being placed in different positions or containers. The experiment most commonly associated with this Piagetian concept is the way in which children can observe water being poured from a container into a taller, thinner container, and believe that the taller, thinner container is holding a larger amount of water. Piaget also noted children's tendency to focus on a single aspect of a problem during this stage of development, which he called *centration*. Because of the ease with which they may be distracted from a task, children during this stage are unlikely to be able to focus on more than one task at a time (Shaffer, 1996).

Piaget also noted that this stage was defined by evidence of innate *egocentrism* by children. Their world-view is defined by children's own experience, and they lack the capacity to imagine it from another's perspective. They also presume that if they know something from a particular perspective, then others know it in the same way (Durkin, 1995). According to Piaget, intelligence during this stage is defined primarily by perception, which is dominated by what children see. Egocentric interpretation of what they see tends to be fairly concrete, and divided into 'right' and 'wrong'.

During the later part of this stage, children are typically engaged with an increasingly broad social array of people, and are thus likely to become more socially adept and less egocentric in their perspectives. Their vocabularies expand rapidly, along with their ability to use numbers to add and subtract. Symbolic play becomes a prominent feature during the sub-stage referred to by some as the 'stage of intuitive thought' (approximately ages 4–7) (Robinson, 2007). The child's expanding verbal and numerical repertoires contribute to the capacity to think in increasingly symbolic ways, and to the ability to reason intuitively rather than logically during this stage. Examples of these capacities may be found in children's elaborate fantasies and their solutions to dilemmas, as well as imaginary playmates that sometimes arise during this stage.

The concrete operations stage (approximately 7–11 years)

According to Piaget, the concrete operations stage represents a time during which children begin to master an array of logical operations such as classifications of objects, speed, and mathematical multiplications and divisions (in addition to adding and subtracting). Children also gain the capacity for *seriation*, or the ability to arrange objects according to increasing or decreasing size. They are also capable of *decentration*, which facilitates being able to focus simultaneously on more than one dimension or task.

Because of the capacity for *transformational thought*, children in this stage are able to understand the process of change from one state to another, and through the capacity for *conservation*, they are likely to grasp the concept of water remaining the same, regardless of the shape of its container (Robinson, 2007).

During this stage, children are likely to acquire an array of skills to work with assorted objects, people, and events. They are likely to rely heavily on trial-and-error learning to solve problems. They are also likely to demonstrate increasingly logical reasoning in their approach to problem-solving. During this stage, children typically demonstrate an increasing capacity for *deductive reasoning*, through which they draw conclusions based on the logic of cause and effect.

During this stage, children are likely to be increasingly exposed to social settings (school, play groups, siblings, etc.) in which they are required to become increasingly aware of and responsive to the needs and feelings of others. During the concrete operations stage, Piaget argued that children become less egocentric in their capacity to recognize other people's perspectives.

The formal operations stage (approximately age 11 onward)

Piaget proposed that during the formal operations stage, children develop the ability to apply logical thought across an array of situations, including the future. The capacity for hypothetical and abstract thought leads to the ability to engage in more systematic *scientific thinking* from this stage onward (Vourlekis, 1991). Piaget proposed that intuitive thinking is replaced by scientific reasoning as children age. Especially during adolescence, the capacity to engage in reality- and hypothesis-testing contributes considerably to academic as well as social success. This stage is associated with *hypothetical-deductive reasoning*, which contributes to the capacity to plan ahead, and to anticipate consequences.

During adolescence, concepts of past, present and future are likely to become much more sophisticated, allowing for much more hypothetical thinking. Values, morality, and concepts of social justice gain significance during the formal operations stage, and relate to the evolving capacity for reflective thought often noted among adolescents and young people. Whereas concepts of 'fairness' often dominate younger children's sense of right and wrong, an awareness of justice is likely to evolve during this stage that entails a growing awareness that justice and fairness are not always the same thing. Sometimes a quest for absolute truth emerges during the formal operations stage, during which some young people approach very complex concepts with a sense of mission: if only they apply their minds with sufficient determination, or ask the tutors the right questions, they will find answers to existential dilemmas and a sense of absolute truth. (Such quests are typically a source of considerable frustration for all concerned.) This stage is also associated with an increased appreciation of possibilities, rather than straightforward realities. This may also contribute to an increased appreciation for absurd and sometimes silly humour.

Piaget's formal operations stage is associated with the capacity during adolescence to gain a sense of identity and to understand complex issues and circumstances. It is also associated with increasingly autonomous and independent thinking, which is sometimes associated with teenage rebellion and risk-taking (discussed in Chapters 3 and 4 in relation to developmental variables and Eriksonian stages).

Piaget also proposed three further stages for children's moral development. His basic premise was that children develop a system of reasoning about moral issues. Piaget's three stages were the *amoral stage* (early childhood), the *heteronomous stage* (middle childhood), and the *autonomous stage* (late childhood). According to Piaget (1932), young children remained essentially amoral in their reasoning, and responded primarily to externally imposed values and morals. By the heteronomous stage, Piaget argued that children are increasingly aware of rules and the capacity to distinguish 'right from wrong' (Table 7.1). By the autonomous stage, Piaget proposed that children had assimilated various rules and their implications sufficiently to be able to apply them in an autonomous fashion. Kohlberg further developed Piaget's stages of moral development.

Vygotsky's social cognition learning model

In his *social cognition learning model*, Vygotsky asserted that children acquire knowledge according to their cultural environments, as well as what he considered the tools of intellectual adaptation. According to Vygotsky, culture shapes both what and how children think (Doolittle, 1997). He proposed that cognitive development is a result of children's shared experiences of problem solving, in which they are provided guidance by a parent, teacher, or peer. According to Vygotsky, language is the primary form of interaction in which knowledge is exchanged, and children's learning occurs in the

Table 7.1 Piaget's stages of cognitive development and moral development

Age	*Cognitive stage of development*	*Moral stage of development*
Birth–2 years	Sensorimotor World is explored and understood through physical experiences	Amoral
2–7 years	Preoperational Capacity for symbolic thought Capacity for imaginative play Egocentricity Centration	Middle childhood: Heteronomous morality
7–12 years	Concrete operational Capacity for logical thought Expanding vocabulary and numbers Deductive reasoning Less egocentricity More empathy	Late childhood: Autonomous morality
12 onwards	Formal operational Capacity for logical and abstract thought Can form hypotheses and test them	

process of gradually assuming autonomy in the course of the problem-solving exercise. Simultaneously, according to Vygotsky, the child's language comes to serve as a primary tool of intellectual adaptation during the learning process, leading to an expanded internal vocabulary serving their learning processes (Durkin, 1995).

Vygotsky distinguished between what a child can do independently and what they can do with help, and referred to this difference as the zone of proximal development. Interactions with the child's surrounding culture and social environment, such as family and more capable siblings and peers, play crucial roles in the child's intellectual development (Luria, 2004).

Lawrence Kohlberg's stages of moral reasoning

Kohlberg's (somewhat controversial) technique for studying moral development entailed asking children and adults to try to solve various moral dilemmas from vignettes he provided. He would ask them to do so aloud, so that he could follow their reasoning. Less concerned with their specific answers, Kohlberg was eager to learn the process by which they reached their conclusion (Kroger, 1996).

Perhaps the best known of his vignettes, Kohlberg told the story of a man named Heinz, whose wife was dying of a disease that could be cured if only he could obtain a certain medicine. When Heinz asked the chemist, he was told that the medicine could only be obtained at a prohibitive price. So the next evening, Heinz broke into the chemist's and stole the drug in order to save his wife's life. Kohlberg's question was whether Heinz was right or wrong to steal the drug.

From his collection of hundreds of interviews, Kohlberg proposed three broad levels with sub-stages in each related to the process of moral development. Each successive stage of moral reasoning was increasingly cognitively complex. During childhood, Kohlberg believed that moral development entailed *preconventional* and *conventional* stages, in which moral reasoning was primarily influenced by rewards and approval or punishment and disapproval by others; during adolescence, moral development reached a *postconventional* stage. At that point, individuals become capable of moral reasoning based on social contracts and cooperation, and could base their principles on broader, universal ethics rather than externally generated norms. Ultimately, according to Kohlberg's premise, people progress from acceptance of social rules for the greater good to a level of universal benevolence that is equitable for all (Thomas, 1999). The progression of Kohlberg's stages is provided in Table 7.2.

Kohlberg also proposed a theory of *gender-role development* that has subsequently been contradicted by various proponents of social learning theory. Kohlberg (1963) applied a cognitive theory to explain what he considered 'gender typing' to explain why some children of both sexes adopt traditional or even stereotypical gender roles, even when they are not encouraged to do so by their parents. Kohlberg also proposed that children engage in *self-socialization,* in which they actively undertake socializing behaviours, rather than being passive targets of social and gender-related influences. Kohlberg further proposed that gender-role development progressed in stages, and that children attain certain perceptions about gender *before* being influenced by their social experiences related to gender roles *per se*.

Table 7.2 Kohlberg's stages of moral development

Level	*Stage*
Level One: Preconventional (Pre-school age)	Stage 1: Reward or punishment stage Moral reasoning based on consequences of behaviour to determine right or wrong (right is permitted; wrong is punished)
	Stage 2: Exchange stage Moral reasoning based on potential benefits for self or loved ones Reciprocity of benefits is a strong component of this stage
Level Two: Conventional (School age onward)	Stage 1: Moral reasoning based on approval from those in authority; 'The Golden Rule' is often applied Being 'good' means fulfilling others' expectations
	Stage 2: Moral reasoning based on conforming to accepted social norms; law-and-order are key determinants of right and wrong Fulfilling agreed-upon duties and responsibilities is 'right'; contributing to society is 'good'
Level Three: Post-conventional (Some adolescents and adults)	Stage 1: Moral reasoning is based on social contracts and reciprocal cooperation 'The greatest good for the greatest number' becomes a key concept Injustices can be corrected
	Stage 2: Moral reasoning is based on abstract universal ethical codes Universal principles take precedence over social law or customs Self-chosen ethical or moral principles determine what is 'right' or 'wrong'

Source: Based on Kohlberg (1976).

According to Kohlberg's theory of gender-role development, a child's basic *gender identity* is established around age 2–3, at which time the child recognizes her/himself as being female or male. The child's sense of gender subsequently evolves into what Kohlberg considered *gender stability*, which entails a child's awareness that girls become women and boys become men. Kohlberg proposed that around ages 5–7, children attain *gender consistency*, with the realization that their sex remains constant, and is not subject to superficial alterations through such activities as dressing up as members of the other sex, cutting or growing their hair, or pretending to be the other sex in play (Sigelman & Rider, 2003).

Most social learning theory proponents subscribe to the premise that children are first influenced by those around them to adopt 'male' or 'female' roles prior to perceiving themselves as girls or boys, and identifying with same-sex role models.

Social learning theory

Social learning theory places a strong emphasis on defining problems according to behaviours that can be identified and measured in some way that will also contribute to defining the desired changes that are needed. Social learning theory is sometimes associated with role theory as both incorporate ways of defining problems in relation to expectations and reinforcements.

Albert Bandura's social learning theory

Bandura proposes that behaviour, interpersonal factors (such as beliefs, thoughts, and self-perceptions), and the environment are all linked in what he refers to as *reciprocal determinism*. If Skinnerian conditioning could be represented as a straight line between cause and effect, Bandura's social learning model would be more triangular, incorporating behaviour, environmental factors, and personal factors interacting reciprocally. Bandura specifically proposes that humans learn in distinctly different ways from rats, whose learning styles previously influenced much of the behaviourists' experiments and findings. He points out that this is because humans consider and anticipate consequences of their behaviour, and because they develop *beliefs* about what happens, rather than just responding to stimuli. Bandura argues that human cognitive capacities are necessarily more sophisticated than those of the rats on whom so many experiments had been performed. He simultaneously considers behaviours much less mysterious and unobservable than psychoanalytic theory would infer (Shaffer, 1996).

Unlike the behaviourist perspective, social learning theory addresses the contextual influences on people's behaviour, with particular attention paid to environmental influences. An important aspect of social learning theory for social workers is its capacity to explain both why behaviour occurs as well as ways in which behaviour can be changed by altering environmental influences. In this way, social learning theory has contributed to social workers' abilities to observe, measure, and document the effectiveness of some of their efforts with service users in ways that other theoretical perspectives do not offer (Garvin, 1993).

Bandura expanded upon the behaviourist tradition by his emphasis on *observational learning*. He proposes that people's behaviour changes through the results of observing others' behaviour ('models'). By imitating the model's behaviour, speech, dress, etc., people expand upon their existing cognitive and behavioural repertoires. By observing and replicating behaviours, they may learn to smoke, to use correct (or incorrect!) grammar, dance, or where to get a tattoo. Unlike orthodox behaviourist ideas, social learning necessitates the individual having paid attention, constructing, and remembering mental representations of what they observed, and being able to retrieve them for future reference in order to replicate what they observed (Bandura, 1969).

Bandura and the learning of aggression

One of Bandura's well-known experiments entailed children watching an adult play with a large, plastic clown (the 'Bobo doll'), treating the doll very aggressively (hitting, kicking, etc.) without any explanation. One woman even shouted 'Sockeroo!' as she attacked the Bobo doll. When the children were subsequently allowed to play with the Bobo doll, those who had observed the aggressive adult proceeded to play much more aggressively than children who had not observed the adult's aggression. Those who had observed the aggression also engaged in repeating some of the specific acts they had observed earlier, even shouting 'Sockeroo!' as they did so. This 'modelling' of behaviour applied in other examples, including altruistic and gender-related behaviours observed by children (Shaffer, 1996).

Bandura's studies of aggression and how children learn to replicate acts of aggression have proven valuable for social workers, especially when working with families in which violence occurs. His experiments demonstrated variations such as ways in which some parents actively encourage and condone violence and aggression when their highly aggressive teenage sons were aggressive toward other boys, but punished the same behaviours when they were directed at the parents (Bandura & Walters, 1959).

Bandura and self-efficacy

Another of Bandura's major contributions to cognitive studies stemmed from his attention to how people's self-appraisal amounted to a belief system about themselves. Bandura (1977, 1986) introduced the term *self-efficacy* to refer to individuals' perceptions of their own capacity to succeed at a given task or effort. According to Bandura, self-efficacy entails beliefs about the self that can shape behaviour by influencing willingness to try new behaviours. Self-efficacy entails a sense and expectation of some competence, and a capacity to envision succeeding at a given task (Vourlekis, 1991). It can also determine the level of persistence, or willingness to tolerate frustration a person is willing or able to devote to practising unfamiliar or difficult changes. People with higher levels of self-efficacy are more likely to take on challenges that others might avoid, because they are more likely to see challenges as surmountable, rather than overwhelming.

Bandura's concept of self-efficacy is of prime importance for social workers trying to facilitate change on the part of service users. By utilizing existing strengths, social workers are in pivotal positions to enhance a person's self-efficacy by encouraging them to see themselves as being competent and capable of new behaviours. This has direct relevance to anti-oppressive practice, as does the concept of 'learned helplessness'.

Learned helplessness theory

In a somewhat ironic contrast to Bandura's movement away from animal experiments, Martin Seligman's (1979) experimentations with dogs resulted in the important introduction of *learned helplessness theory*. In Seligman's study, dogs were exposed to an electrical shock in the course of trying to cross a room. They came to perceive the pain inflicted by the electrical shock as being unavoidable, and resigned themselves to its inevitability, even after it was discontinued. Even in other settings, the dogs appeared apathetic and helpless, seeming always to expect punishment regardless of their behaviour (Seligman, 1979).

Seligman's theory of learned helplessness has important implications for social workers. For children who have come to perceive themselves as being incapable of succeeding at school, the expectation of failure, regardless of effort or practice, can prove a powerful disincentive, sometimes amounting to a self-fulfilling prophecy. For people in violent relationships, a childhood history of family violence and/or previous partnerships involving violence can also relate to the theory of learned helplessness. When people have come to perceive themselves as being effectively destined to be in punitive, unhealthy relationships, their expectations of partners may also amount to self-fulfilling prophecies.

Role theory

Role theory helps explain people's behaviour by addressing how the social environment influences behaviour by creating various roles to be fulfilled. Roles refer to ways in which people behave in relation to a socially defined position or set of expectations. Those positions and expectations may be defined by relationships, such as parents, students, lecturers, service users, clients, or managers. Roles may also be defined by the dynamics between people, such as 'dominant', 'victim', 'bully', or 'clown'. Role theory provides a social context in which psychological aspects of people's behaviour can be considered. Role theory is closely linked with social learning theory (Garvin, 1991). Through its emphasis on the positions people occupy within social structures, role theory is also related to structural-functional theory in sociology (Payne, 1997).

Shakespeare's line, 'All the world's a stage, And all the men and women merely players' (*As You Like It*, Act II, Scene 7), is often quoted to refer to the patterns of people's behaviour. Roles create a sense of identity, reflecting both how we see ourselves and how others perceive us. By addressing some of the structures provided by society, role theory also serves as a means of understanding the person-in-environment concept, by conceptualizing the ways in which relationships may establish patterns of behaviour and expectations. Those behaviours and expectations may contribute to 'places' or allocated status that people occupy in their social setting. Examples may include such positions as troublemaker, drug user, thief, 'Asbo', do-gooder, rescuer, or teenage mother. Different roles have varying sanctions or levels of approval within different settings. For example, having a juvenile criminal record may be a rite of passage in some settings, but a stigma in others.

Roles may be *ascribed* according to innate circumstances (such as being female, or British, or having a disability); likewise, they may be *attained* through something a person has done (such as being a parent, a graduate, or a pensioner). *Role sets* refer to clusters of roles that are inter-related, such as simultaneously being a mother, wife, the person who does the household grocery shopping, cooks most meals, maintains most of the family's personal correspondence, attends school performances, along with being a daughter, daughter-in-law, sister, and sister-in law. *Role complementarity* refers to the balance that occurs when roles, expectations, and behaviour form a congruent whole with the surrounding environment and people. *Role ambiguity* occurs when there is uncertainty about what a role entails. When one role is incompatible with another, then *role conflict* occurs. When the various roles held by one person are incompatible, then *inter-role conflict* can be found (Payne, 1997). An example of this could be found when a middle-aged woman enrols in a university degree programme. If her teenage children and her husband continue to expect to arrive home to find tea prepared for them, and her elderly mother continues to expect to rely on her to drive her to the shops each Tuesday morning, then some inter-role conflict may occur when she is attending classes at those times. Importantly, role theory provides a means of addressing the numerous roles most people occupy simultaneously.

Attribution theory

Attribution theory helps to explain how people perceive and assess the causes of behaviour and its consequences. The term attribution theory refers to a collection of theorists' work, including Kelley (1971, 1992) and Weiner (1986) among others. Attribution theory's primary purpose is to explain how people gather and refine their beliefs about what causes human conditions and behaviour. According to attribution theory, people are likely to attribute changes in their own behaviour to external influences, but are likely to attribute changes in others' behaviour to internal characteristics or traits (Passer et al., 2009).

By attributing the cause of various behaviours and events to specific influences, people are able to avoid the premise that bad things happen totally randomly and therefore uncontrollably. According to Weiner's (1986) concepts of attributional structure, causation can be located along several dimensions, among which the internal/external dichotomy is often used to explain attributions. Internal, personal attributions infer that people's individual characteristics determine their behaviour or experiences. An example would be: 'My A on the test resulted from my hard work', or 'I got a C because I didn't study hard enough.' External or situational attributions infer that external influences determine people's behaviour or experiences. An example would be: 'My A on the test came from the test being so easy', or 'I got a C because the subject is so boring.'

The idea that causation can be attributed either to the person's inherent characteristics or outside forces (or to a combination of both) is a key component of the theoretical construct known as *locus of control*. The person's attribution of causation to their own inherent factors would relate to *internal* locus of control, whereas the attribution of causation to outside influences beyond the individual's control would relate to *external* locus of control (Thomas, 1999). The locus of control typically serves to shape whether an individual perceives a situation or difficulty as something within or beyond their control (Vourlekis, 1991). Examples of internal and external attributions are listed in Table 7.3.

People's *attributions* entail beliefs about causes of behaviour or events. Those beliefs are generally based on experience or observations. They serve as hypotheses or frameworks for explaining why things happened or will happen in a certain way. They may or may not be accurate explanations. Misattribution entails the inaccurate perception of a sequence of events in which causation is attributed incorrectly (Vourlekis, 1991).

Table 7.3 Some internal and external attributes associated with causation

Internal causation	*External causation*
Genetic or inherited characteristics	Environmental influences
Inherent traits or features	Peers
Personal diligence, perseverance	Social setting
Honesty	Supernatural powers (God, angels, spirits of deceased loved ones)
Preparation	Chance (luck, fate, magic, 'on the cards')
Adherence to prescribed treatment	Medication alone
Intelligence, learning, aptitude	

For example, misattribution may play a part in a service user's perception of a social worker's efforts to provide services. Consider the following scenario:

> Ms X insists that if the social worker had not visited her home, she would not have proceeded to get drunk. If she hadn't been drunk, then she wouldn't have hit her child. She insists that her having hit her child is the fault of the social worker for having come to her home.

Thus, Ms X is employing an *external* locus of control, and is misattributing causation for hitting her child to someone else's actions, rather than her own behaviour.

Another example may be found in the following scenario:

> Ms W recently learned that her partner sexually abused her 9-year-old daughter. In the course of your discussion, Ms W discloses that her own stepfather sexually abused her between the ages of 9 and 14. She has blamed herself for the sexual abuse ever since. She now believes there must be something inherently wrong with her that she did not detect the abuse of her own child when it first started. Her self-blame persists, even when you point out that she responded assertively and constructively upon first learning of the abuse.

In this scenario, Ms W is employing an *internal* locus of control, and is misattributing causation for her stepfather's and her partner's behaviours to herself.

Attributions and misattributions can play vital roles in shaping people's behaviours and their expectations or hypotheses about experiences. Using an 'If ____, then ____' formula to understand the attribution process, most of us are very familiar with ways in which we seek explanations for events, feelings and circumstances that we otherwise find threatening, overwhelming, or unjust. In some cases, a pattern of self-attribution consistently contributes to an excessive level of self-blame or internalized pejorative self-regard or labelling (Vourlekis, 1991). Examples of this can be seen in cases where people regard themselves as 'losers', 'useless', or consistently along the hopeless–helpless continuum.

Some basic ideas about intelligence

There are many theories to explain intelligence, ranging from informal 'folk psychology' approaches to formal models proposed by educators, psychologists, anthropologists and sociologists. Some theories rely on genetic inheritance, others address experiential or learning factors.

Because measures of cognitive development and skills are sometimes used to classify children and students, social workers also need to be familiar with various aspects of those measures, especially when they are used as means of justifying oppression. From a Euro-American perspective, intelligence generally refers to a variety of functions, including knowledge, abilities and aptitudes. In other cultures, however, the whole concept of intelligence is defined quite differently. Many of the most prevalent standardized measures of intelligence (IQ tests) are culture-specific, in that they were explicitly designed and validated for use with white middle-class subjects (Robinson, 2007). Because standardized measures (such as the Wechsler Intelligence Scale for Children-Revised, WISC-R) rely heavily on verbal performance and cultural knowledge, when they are applied in cross-cultural settings, the findings are not necessarily going to provide a reliable measure of other cultural or ethnic groups' performance. Social workers need to be aware of such factors when asked to accept the relevance of such findings.

Howard Gardner's theory of multiple intelligences

Howard Gardner (1943–present) was born in the US, following his parents' escape from Nazi Germany. Educated at Harvard, Gardner studied under Erik Erikson (Smith, 2002). In an era in which psychometric measures were considered the gold standard of understanding intelligence, Gardner questioned the idea of intelligence comprising a single (inherited) entity, or being measurable by a standardized test. He proposes that the question of 'How smart are you?' is less relevant than asking 'How are you smart?' (Chen & Gardner, 2005).

According to Gardner, intelligence is actually an array of factors better referred to in the plural 'intelligences'. He challenges Piaget's sequential model of development, arguing that intelligences are more about people's different capacities than stages of progression. Gardner proposes that there are at least eight distinct intellectual abilities or intelligences, as noted in Table 7.4. He also notes that of these, only the first two or three are generally valued in traditional Euro-American schooling.

While Gardner emphasizes the complex nature of intelligences, he does not claim that his model is definitive. He also argues that there are clear exceptions to his categories, such as those seen with cases of *savant syndrome*. In such cases, an individual may be profoundly limited in all but one of the different dimensions, but have

Table 7.4 Howard Gardner's types of intelligence

Intellectual abilities	*Typical markers*	*Examples*
1 Linguistic intelligence	Language skills, written and spoken	Ability to learn new languages, expressive use of words Teachers, speakers, authors, poets
2 Logical-mathematical intelligence	Abstract thinking, fluency with numbers	Analytical skills Scientific investigation of problems Deductive reasoning Mathematicians, computer scientists
3 Musical intelligence	Acute sensitivity to sound patterns	Ability to perform, compose, and appreciate musical patterns; recognition of pitches and rhythms Musicians, conductors, disc jockeys
4 Spatial intelligence	Recognition and use of patterns of space and proportions	Ability to draw, design, decorate, sculpt Architects, artists, interior decorators, clothes designers, tailors, engineers
5 Bodily-kinaesthetic intelligence	Skilful use of the body to solve problems or create new objects	Ability to coordinate mental and physical activities Craftsmen, repair workers, dancers, surgeons, athletes
6 Interpersonal intelligence	Understanding of others' emotions and intentions	Ability to work well with others through a well-developed sense of self and others Educators, salespeople, religious and political leaders
7 Intrapersonal intelligence	Capacity to understand one's own emotions and intentions	Ability to use one's own self-knowledge for self-regulation and effective relations with others Carers, parents, and mentors often exhibit such traits
8 Naturalistic intelligence	Expertise in the natural world of plants and animals	Capacity to recognize, grow and tend animals, plants, gardens Animal trainers, gardeners

Source: Based on Gardner (1983).

extraordinary talents or skills in a relatively narrow cognitive realm (such as counting, music, or calculating dates or schedules).

In contrast to Piaget's developmental premise, Gardner suggests that different intelligences have distinct developmental trajectories. For example, musicians and artists often demonstrate their talents during childhood, whereas logical-mathematical talents are generally evident much later in life. Gardner proposes that the various intelligences are neurologically linked (Passer et al. 2009).

Cultural variations in assessing intelligence also have important implications for social workers. Non-western cultures do not necessarily rely on test-taking to the same extent as Euro-Americans do for estimating intelligence. Culturally biased interpretations of intelligence often reflect this dichotomy. Dating back to Margaret Mead's landmark anthropological studies of people in Samoa, Eurocentric approaches have led to some crucial misinterpretations of people's intelligence. The ways in which Mead asked the questions were not congruent with Samoans' conceptual approaches, and led her to believe that they were intellectually simple, when in fact their answers reflected a culturally different approach to interpreting others' behaviours (Thomas, 1999).

A widening cognitive-behavioural perspective

While behavioural theorists are discussed separately in Chapter 6, the overlap between cognitive and behavioural theories necessitates some consideration. The two theories are often joined together as an approach to practice and therapeutic interventions, especially in mental health settings.

From a strictly behaviourist perspective, abnormal behaviour and mental health difficulties are not attributed to any particular underlying cause. From a cognitive perspective, however, various thoughts and beliefs are seen as influencing problematic behaviours and relationships (Coulshed & Orme, 2006).

Albert Ellis proposed what he called the *A-B-C principle* to explain how problematic interpretations result in problematic emotional and behavioural outcomes. In his A-B-C principle, an Activating Event ('A') triggers a Faulty Belief ('B'). The Faulty Belief ('B') subsequently triggers the problematic Emotional Consequence ('C'). The common irrational premise is that the Activating Event (A) is responsible for causing the distressing Emotional Consequence (C). According to Ellis's theory, however, the intervening variable of irrational beliefs is the actual source of distorted expectations and consequences (Ellis, 1962). Ellis's rational-emotive therapy is based on the premise that negative emotions and problematic relationship patterns arise from inaccurate interpretations of experiences, rather than from the experiences *per se*.

When asked to summarize his concepts of irrational beliefs, Ellis identified the following as the core irrational beliefs:

> I must do well.
> You must treat me well.
> The world must be easy. (Fenichel, 2000)

According to Ellis's approach, unrealistic expectations from such irrational beliefs are the most common source of distress, including depression. When taken into a person's viewpoint on the world, Ellis described a resulting preoccupation with negative events as 'awfulizing', as a semi-humorous description of how irrational thinking can distort a person's general outlook. In response to such distortions, Ellis argued that flawed beliefs could be modified in ways that he called *cognitive restructuring*. Through the use of cognitive restructuring, Ellis proposed that people could be helped to develop more realistic expectations as well as an enhanced sense of self-worth (Ellis, 1962).

For social workers, Ellis's approach has proved useful in understanding how people come to interpret events and experiences. For example, when working with service users with limited problem-solving skills, helping them to understand the role played by their own interpretations, as distinct from actual outcomes, may prove very beneficial in helping them to change behavioural patterns. Such distinctions can prove very empowering for people who tend to ascribe considerable power to others at their own expense. Consider the following example:

> Joe (age 6) recently learned that he was adopted following his having been abandoned by his birth parents. He has become preoccupied with the prospect of his adoptive parents abandoning him, either through desertion or death. He states that his recent outbursts and uncharacteristic temper tantrums are actually intentionally designed to provoke them into deserting him, to 'get it over with'.

Joe's Activating Event (A) would be learning of his having been abandoned. His Faulty Beliefs (B) would likely include such thoughts as his having done something that caused him to be abandoned, or that being abandoned is an arbitrary event that could happen to him again, and his adoptive parents being prepared to abandon him now. Joe's Emotional Consequences (C) include his apparent distress, as evidenced by his behavioural outbursts and temper tantrums, and his belief that abandonment is apparently inevitable.

Aaron Beck's *cognitive triad* of depression addresses the negative and illogical thoughts that seem to come involuntarily and automatically, and which result in unnecessary suffering. In his cognitive triad, Beck proposes that depression is shaped by the negative interpretation of the self, the world and the future. The cognitive triad that he proposed entails a catastrophic evaluation of the self, based on a faulty interpretation of the past, which influences the negative expectation of world in general (Beck, 1963).

An example could be seen in a social work student's response to getting a poor grade in a recent test. By applying Beck's negative triad to the situation, the following pattern of beliefs can be seen:

Past: 'Having got a C on the test is a disaster for my academic prospects of becoming a social worker.' (Even though the test included some questions that were asked in a way that the student hadn't understood at the time, and that they now comprehend.)

Self: 'I am incompetent because I failed the test.' (Despite the fact that a C is not failing, and having previously outstanding marks in all other areas of the programme.)

World: 'I am unfit to practise social work because of my catastrophic performance.' (This is despite being highly motivated and capable thus far!)

Beck's cognitive model has been particularly influential in the area of cognitive behavioural therapy, with particular emphasis in the treatment of depression. His *Depression Inventory* is frequently used as a means of measuring the existence of depression. Beck's model has also been successfully applied in the treatment of alcohol and drug-related conditions, post-traumatic stress disorder, obsessive-compulsive disorder, and schizophrenia (Barlow et al. 2002).

Implications for practice

When working with people in distress, the cognitive theories provide social workers with a perspective that is both optimistic and non-deterministic. The cognitive theories operate on the premise that change can be achieved through the individual's innate capacity to construct knowledge and meaning that relate to solving problems (Vourlekis, 1991). Especially when working with people who have depressive conditions, social workers are advised to consider the role played by learned helplessness to interpret people's expectations of themselves and others, as it provides a means of addressing some important aspects of how people view themselves, their potential, and what they consider reasonable to expect from others. Some research indicates brain differences determine the release of endogenous opiates, meaning that some people with depression may have decreased immune functions and increased pain thresholds, which may compound their expectations that suffering is unavoidable (Sadock & Sadock, 2007). Such biological factors would need to be balanced by attention to psychosocial dimensions such as cognitive and environmental factors.

For social workers, role theory may apply to working with people who have come to occupy an unhealthy role in repeated settings, as a way of helping them explore alternative ways of relating with others. Examples include working with women in sequential violent or demeaning relationships, in which they have consistently acquiesced to enacting the role of 'victim'. Role theory may also apply to working with people who resist the idea of occupying the role of needing help, and for whom social workers may represent a challenge to the way in which they see themselves as being self-sufficient. Examples include people in later life, who have taken pride in their self-sufficiency throughout lifetimes of adversity and challenges, who may now be facing the unwanted prospect of depending on others, and find the role of being in need of help or 'helpless' quite disturbing.

Role theory also applies to working with people whose identities entail various aspects that are considered undesirable or disadvantaged. Roles may be ascribed on the basis of skin colour, gender, disability, illness, or physical appearance in ways that entail *labelling*. Goffman (1963) worked extensively in the area of stigma, and its influences on identity as well as expectations. He studied the implications of visible markers (burns, amputations, physical malformations) and invisible markers of difference (such as homosexuality, former mental hospitalizations, imprisonment, etc.), and proposed that stigma is necessarily associated with *stereotypes*, and that both are directly linked with conscious and unconscious expectations that influence all social interactions. In relation to role theory, social workers are in a position to function as powerful advocates on behalf of those who would otherwise be vulnerable to stereotyping and labelling by society and potentially oppressive and demeaning individuals and systems.

For social workers, an awareness of different types of intelligence can be a crucial aspect of appreciating different people's inherent strengths and diversity. It can be a critical component of understanding how and why some children do or do not flourish in conventional classroom settings, as a function of context rather than intelligence *per se*. It may also influence how social workers choose to approach explaining important concepts and ideas to service users, in ways that are most likely to be congruent with the ways in which people are best equipped to understand new or difficult information. For example, when working with groups from ethnic minorities, social workers are called upon to be particularly sensitive to the implications of language (including accents) when communicating with people in need. Particularly when communications are about personally sensitive topics, language barriers can pose significant difficulties. Use of interpreters is a very delicate prospect, and social workers are encouraged to avoid using children to serve as their parents' interpreters, as this can be a source of role confusion for all concerned.

The cognitive-behavioural approach to viewing problems and their origins according to maladaptive learning processes is supported by a growing array of empirical research (Bandura, 1969; Sheldon, 2000). In keeping with core concepts of evidence-based practice, professionals who provide cognitive-behavioural therapy (CBT) are trained to use quite explicit definitions of their objectives and desired outcomes, employing a contractual approach to defining problems and expectations in order to establish quantifiable changes in thinking and behavioural patterns (Coulshed & Orme, 2006).

Cognitive-behavioural therapy represents a prominent approach to the assessment and treatment of emotional and behaviour problems, and is considered a mainstay of many clinicians' repertoires. Far from simple, CBT necessitates considerable and intense involvement with service users and their social support networks that often exceeds the parameters of social service agencies' capacities and budgets (Sheldon, 2000). As with any other practitioner who employs CBT methods, social workers are expected to adhere to the *Code of Ethics* of the British Association of Behavioural and Cognitive Psychotherapies (BABCP).

Criticisms and shortcomings of cognitive models

While most social workers find the cognitive framework relevant to understanding people's behaviours and problems, the cognitive models are not without their shortcomings. Perhaps the caveat 'necessary but not sufficient' applies to the application of cognitive theory for social work practice.

Piaget's cognitive development theory has been criticized for its cultural bias, as his theory paid so little attention to children's culture, language, or social environments, and his measurements were based on children's transactions with inanimate objects (Burman, 1994; Durkin, 1995). For children who are unaccustomed to

European-style testing, the distress associated with taking standardized tests may actually compromise their performance (Robinson, 2007). Some argue that children need not necessarily reach Piaget's concrete operations stage of cognitive development in order to understand gender stability. Bem (1989) argues that if children possess even rudimentary knowledge of female and male anatomy, they inherently recognize that anatomy explains gender. Piaget's neglect of various social factors remains a key argument against the applicability of his theories.

Kohlberg's premise that children only begin actively seeking out same-sex role models upon having fully grasped the concepts of gender constancy is perhaps the most controversial aspect of his theory. Many developmental researchers find that children learn various gender-role stereotypes and develop distinct preferences for same-sex playmates and activities long before mastering the idea of gender stability or constancy (Sigelman & Rider, 2003).

Role theory has been criticized for its application in ways that placed people in static roles defined by gender, age, or various traditional frameworks. It has also been criticized for not providing a technique with which to approach practice (Payne, 1997). The implications of non-traditional family roles and norms have challenged the application of role theory in ways that are potentially stereotypical and obsolete. Role theory, however, has historically emphasized the ways in which people typically occupied multiple roles, both in families and in social settings. In this sense, role theory has remained potentially fluid in its application in contemporary practice (Hockey & James, 2003).

Although outcome studies have supported the effectiveness of cognitive models' usefulness in the assessment and treatment of depression, they have been criticized for their lack of attention to social factors (Gross, 2001). Nonetheless, considerable evidence supports a cognitive approach across a wide array of conditions relevant to individuals and families who are often seen by social workers, including medical as well as mental health patients.

Questions

1 Match the following:

____	A-B-C principle	(a) Albert Bandura
____	Schemata	(b) Martin Seligman
____	Zone of proximal development	(c) Aaron Beck
____	The 'science of mental life'	(d) Bobo doll
____	Social learning theory	(e) William James
____	Learned helplessness	(f) Lev Vygotsky
____	Multiple intelligences	(g) Howard Gardner
____	Modelled aggressive behaviours	(h) Albert Ellis
____	Cognitive triad	(i) Basic organizational patterns used to interpret observations and experiences

2 What are some of the ways in which Bandura's concept of self-efficacy could be said to apply to the following experiences?
   (a) Learning to ride a bicycle.
   (b) Learning to drive.
   (c) Accepting an invitation to dinner at a new friend's home.
   (d) Choosing to apply for a university degree programme.
   (e) Studying for an exam.

3 What are some of the ways in which Seligman's theory of learned helplessness could be said to apply to the following experiences?
   (a) Children who are told by teachers that they are not good at maths.
   (b) Children who are bullied at home and then at school.
   (c) Teenagers to whom the 'popular' students never speak or include in their socializing.
   (d) Women who have been abused during childhood, exposed to parental violence growing up, and then have partners who abuse them and their children.

4 Can you think of ways in which faulty beliefs may have influenced your own expectations in various circumstances? How would you describe your own experiences in relation to Albert Ellis's A-B-C principle?

5 Please consider the following scenario:

> 'Trisha' (age 14) is the oldest of her widowed father's three children. She is her father's primary carer, as he has chronic mental health and alcohol-related problems. Trisha is a strong student, along with providing most of her younger brothers' care and support. She wants to be a doctor when she grows up, and to care for children in Africa.
>
> You have found Trisha sobbing in the doorway of her father's apartment building. She came home with news of having won a distinction for an essay she wrote for a competition at school. She came home expecting to enjoy sharing her good news with her father, and to have a celebration. Instead, she found him passed out from drinking all day, and her two younger brothers had gone into her room to play with her music system, leaving her room a shambles. She is weeping and insisting that nothing she does is ever good enough to make a difference, and that she might as well give up school, as she will never be able to finish or go to university, or become a doctor.

   Using Ellis's rational-emotive perspective, identify the following:
   (a) What could be identified as an A-B-C pattern for Trisha?
   (b) What are some of the irrational beliefs that could be influencing how she is feeling?
   (c) What are some ways of approaching cognitive restructuring that could serve to empower Trisha to focus on her own self-worth and development?

6 What are some ways in which high levels of self-efficacy would be an asset to social workers?

8 Humanist and existentialist perspectives on behaviour

Stemming from early twentieth-century philosophy, both humanism and existentialism approach behaviour in ways that incorporate people's ability to make conscious, rational decisions in keeping with a quest for the greater good of all concerned. Both humanism and existentialism approach the human condition with an inherent appreciation of the importance and complexity of context and the quest for meaning. Individuals' unique subjective experiences are seen as shaping their equally unique psychological perspective. The role played by motivation in people's behaviour also features prominently in both approaches. This chapter offers a rudimentary introduction to two quite complex theoretical approaches to understanding people's behaviour and to practice based on the respective concepts.

Relevance for social work

For most social workers, the *humanist* perspective is most closely associated with the work of Carl Rogers. His emphasis on non-judgemental acceptance and unconditional positive regard as core therapeutic ingredients remain fundamental aspects of good practice. Listening and communication skills associated with sound social work practice often entail application of Rogerian concepts of attentive listening in order to gain understanding of the individual's perspective and achieve informed decisions (Coulshed & Orme, 2006). Rogers' inherently optimistic regard for people is congruent with the strengths perspective associated with social work practice.

Part of the *existentialist* perspective's congruence with social work comes from its complexity and its inherent acceptance of ambiguity and uncertainty. Because social work often operates in circumstances involving loss, abandonment, and seemingly random suffering, the existentialist perspective can prove quite relevant, particularly when no explanations suffice, and no absolute solutions apply. Many of the complex human dilemmas addressed by social workers defy tidy, formulaic resolutions. In such circumstances, 'tick box' approaches are woefully inadequate, while an existentialist perspective may provide a more applicable response for people in crisis.

Existentialism addresses reflections on the simultaneous challenges posed by unavoidable suffering and eventual death. They are seen as realities of life, rather than any unconscious conflicts or fixations. When working with people in the midst of adapting to overwhelming tragedies and loss, this may prove an essential component of social work practice.

Historical background of humanism

Humanistic psychology evolved following World War II, stemming from and differing from the psychoanalytic tradition. Its emphasis on subjective meaning distinguishes it from the traditional psychoanalytic and behavioural approaches to psychology. Humanistic psychology challenges the *deterministic* tradition, which refers to the premise that behaviour has specific causes. For example, from a psychoanalytic perspective, those causes include unconscious conflicts, drives, defences, etc., which operate as psychic determinism. From a behavioural perspective, the determining factors are more likely to be influences such as stimuli, reinforcement, and the environment that shapes behaviour in a more chess game-like manner. From a humanistic perspective, free will makes such determining factors irrelevant.

The humanistic perspective encompasses several theorists' influences, and traces its philosophical roots to the Enlightenment concepts of individualism, reason and progress. Humanism's key emphasis on potential and choice, rather than pathology or determinism, is inherently congruent with social work values of strengths and self-determination. While humanism is not associated with any single theorist, Gordon Allport, Abraham Maslow and Carl Rogers are among the most familiar proponents of humanistic practice. All gained prominence in America following World War II.

Gordon Allport (1896–1970), an American psychologist, is considered the founder of the humanistic school of psychology, and its emphasis on each individual's inherent capacity for autonomous growth and function. According to most biographers, Allport arranged a meeting with Sigmund Freud while in Vienna at age 22. That single meeting apparently served to dissuade Allport from subscribing to psychoanalytic theory and practice.

Allport is widely associated with the *trait theory*, which evolved from his having painstakingly studied the English dictionary in search of any and all words that could be used to describe personal traits. From that search, Allport produced an extraordinary list of 17,953 words (Allport & Odbert, 1936). According to Allport, people's only assurance of personal existence is based on their possessing a sense of self.

Carl Rogers (1902–1987) is perhaps the name most associated with humanistic psychology. He grew up in a rather strict, religious family in the American Midwest. After completing his PhD in psychology from Columbia University, Rogers attended a seminary and studied for the ministry before returning to study psychology. He spent 12 years providing counselling in a child guidance centre, from which many of Rogers' ideas of personality and providing therapy evolved. Throughout his long and productive career, Rogers remained a popular lecturer and published widely. He founded the Center for the Studies of the Person in La Jolla, California, which remains strongly associated with Rogers' approach to counselling. Rogers devoted considerable efforts throughout his career to promoting world peace, and conducted international peace workshops. His death followed hip surgery resulting from a fall (Ewen, 1998).

Abraham Maslow (1908–1970) has long been considered among the foremost contributors to humanistic psychology. Originally from New York, Maslow was the son of uneducated Russian immigrant parents. His childhood has been described as isolated and unhappy. Having completed his PhD in psychology at the University of Wisconsin in 1934, Maslow was originally an ardent behaviourist. He came to consider behaviourism inadequate to explain the personality, and following a profound reaction to the suffering he witnessed during World War II, Maslow resolved to establish the human capacity for something far grander than hate and destruction. To do so, he studied the most psychologically healthy people he could find, from whom his concept of the *hierarchy of needs* evolved (Ewen, 1998).

Key concepts of humanism

Humanism emphasizes free will in the quest for personal growth and meaning, and relies on a *phenomenological* perspective to understand how the individual perceives and experiences the world in the here-and-now. This perspective renders consideration of unconscious or behavioural determinism unnecessary. While humanistic psychology does not exclude the effect of past influences, it does not consider those influences sufficient to explain the individual's unique experience and perceptions. The phenomenological perspective reflects the role of conscious awareness in the process of making choices and decisions. According to Rogers (1951: 485), 'we live by a perceptual "map" which is never reality itself'. That experiential map, however, serves as a reflection of our perceptions of reality, and is expressed through our phenomenological field in order to influence our behaviour.

A further component of humanistic psychology is its emphasis on the individual's subjective experience as a scientifically legitimate means of understanding behaviour. Unlike the behaviourist emphasis on objective, measurable changes, humanistic psychology emphasizes the individual's own unique interpretation of their perceptions. Nor does humanistic psychology attribute the capacity to interpret others' behaviours to a third person, as with psychoanalytic practice. From a humanistic perspective, the therapist serves more as a facilitator and encourager than as an analyst (Glassman & Hadad, 2004).

Allport referred to *traits* as the main units of the personality structure. Personality traits reflect those relatively stable features of a person's thinking (cognition), feelings (emotions), and actions (behaviour). Those features help to establish the individual's identity in ways that distinguish them from others. According to Allport (1937), each individual has an array of general, relatively consistent traits that serve to shape their responses to most situations.

Allport referred to *personal dispositions* as reflecting individual traits that represent the real meaning of their personality. Allport proposed that emotional maturity represents the capacity to relate to others with warmth and intimacy as well as an authentic sense of self. According to Allport, that sense of self entailed a sense of security, humour, insight, enthusiasm and 'zest' (Allport, 1937, 1963).

Allport proposed that the individual's personality traits exist in a hierarchy comprising *cardinal*, *central*, and *secondary traits*. Cardinal traits are those that are so inherent as to be dominant. For example, from the Harry Potter stories, Dumbledore's cardinal trait could be considered wisdom, while Voldemort's central trait might be evil. Secondary traits are those that are not necessarily evident on a regular basis. For example, an otherwise quiet, studious student who confronts a group of bullies on behalf of a classmate with a disability could be responding according to traits of bravery and conviction that are not often evident to others. Central traits are those major traits that generally characterize an individual's personality.

An integral part of the humanistic approach is its emphasis on *meaning*, or the inherent purpose or value that individuals attribute to their experiences or perceptions. Traditional psychological approaches typically avoided the discussion of 'meaning' *per se*, possibly because it is necessarily such an idiosyncratic and subjective concept. Meaning defies empirical measurement, and thus falls well outside the traditional scientific approaches. The quest for meaning necessarily entails a subjective endeavour, and the humanist approach first acknowledged its importance as a dimension of human behaviour.

Finding 'meaning' in tragedy

Lieutenant C., age 30, was dedicated to his work as a Royal Marine. He met his wife while both were at college, and they have two sons, ages 6 and 8. Because of Lt. C.'s dedication, he worked late into most evenings, and often spent part of his weekends at the base. He was ambitious, and was highly regarded by his unit. His wife complained that he was missing out on most of his sons' childhoods, and that she often felt like a lone parent. She often commented that she would rather have less money and more time together with her husband.

Two years ago a freak gas explosion destroyed the tank in which he was doing manoeuvres. The fire spread before alarms could be raised, and two of Lt. C.'s men died in the fire, including his closest friend. Others, including Lt. C., were severely injured. He suffered full thickness burns over 50 per cent of his body, and very nearly lost one hand. His vision was damaged, and the explosion caused him to have a hearing loss. He now receives a disability allowance.

When interviewed over a year after the fire, Lt. C. calmly explained his injuries, and described the various treatments he required, some of which will be ongoing for life. He then described his involvement with his sons' sports groups and school. Following the fire, Lt. C. began including his friend's son on family outings, and started attending church for the first time.

Lt. C. acknowledged that his marriage was probably at risk when the explosion occurred, and that the problems were caused by his 'workaholism'. He stated that he would give anything he has to be able to have prevented the fire from happening in the first place. Since it happened, though, he says that his world-view of what really matters has changed completely. His wife and family are invaluable to him, and he now realizes that he took them for granted before the fire. He reports often reflecting upon his own good fortune to have survived to see his sons grow up, and the sadness of his friend being deprived of that joy. Lt. C. states that he believes he is a better person because of having been through the fire, and that he intends to spend the remainder of his life trying to justify his good fortune to have survived.

From a humanistic perspective, Lt. C. provides an example of a phenomenological approach, including a sense of how some people find meaning from adversity. While that meaning is typically very individual or idiosyncratic, it nonetheless provides a sense of purpose. Otherwise, suffering could seem arbitrary and pointless, leading to bitterness and despair. For some people meaning has religious overtones, for others it has to do with relationships or philosophical insights. From a humanistic or phenomenological approach, the uniqueness and the validity of Lt. C.'s experiences and perspectives would shape how his behaviour is interpreted.

The *person-centred theory* of personality and psychotherapy introduced by Rogers (1951) is based on core concepts of self-actualization and self-direction. Rogers proposed that people have an innate capacity to direct themselves in the healthiest way available toward their greatest potential, which he called *self-actualization*. In stark contrast to the psychoanalytic premise of unconscious conflicts and neuroses, Rogers proposed that people had an innate capacity for wellness, and that the therapeutic process was ideally intended to facilitate that capacity, rather than to focus on pathology. Sometimes referred to in conjunction with *client-centred therapy*, Rogers' emphasis was on the autonomy of the person seeking help, rather than the authority of the therapist.

Because so many of Rogers' ideas about behaviour relate to the individual self, his views are sometimes referred to as *self theory*. According to Rogers (1985), any event that can be agreed upon by two or more observers has scientific validity, even though each observer is reacting from their own subjective perspective. Rogers referred to this process of agreement as *intersubjective verification*. From the humanistic perspective, intersubjective verification is the essential basis of all observations, including the more traditional scientific techniques.

Unlike more traditional theorists, Rogers did not view the self as a fixed state, but rather as a fluid, changing entity, comprising various elements at any given time. According to Rogers (1951), the self serves to reflect our view of who we are at a given moment, depending on a range of influencing circumstances, past, present and future. To Rogers, the past is only as relevant as the individual chooses to perceive it to be. Thus, if we choose to focus on the influences of the past, then they are highly relevant to our perceptions. If, however, we choose to relinquish the past, and concentrate on present or future opportunities, then the past will play a less significant role. Thus

Rogers emphasized the individual's personal authority and autonomy to focus on defining the self according to their own perceptions.

Rogers (1985) proposed that each individual's inherent humanity entailed a capacity for growth, which he considered the *actualizing tendency*. He saw this manifested in people's creative efforts as well as relationships and achievements, starting from infancy. Rogers regarded the actualizing tendency as the mobilizing force behind the curiosity that leads people to explore new efforts and places, including human relationships. He considered the capacity to be 'in touch' with that tendency essential to maximizing human potential. Borrowing from geometrical concepts, Rogers proposed that the extent to which the sense of self and the ideal self match provides a sense of *congruence*. A mismatch between the sense of self and the ideal would likewise produce a sense of *incongruence*. Congruence and incongruence relate to levels of emotional balance or imbalance.

Abraham Maslow introduced a hierarchical organization of needs that he considered universal to the human experience. Maslow proposed that as the more fundamental physical needs are reasonably satisfied, the more abstract personal and psychological needs can be addressed, culminating in what he called *self-actualization*. While Maslow's premise that the human quest for self-actualization may entail an ideal, he also considered it universal, stating,

> We have, all of us, an impulse to improve ourselves, an impulse toward actualizing more of our potentialities, toward self-actualization, or full humanness or human fulfilment, or whatever term you like. Granted this, then what holds us up? What blocks us?
>
> (Maslow, 1971: 35)

According to Maslow, the reluctance to seek the level of fulfilment represented in self-actualization is a sign of unhealthiness.

Both Maslow and Rogers shared a basically optimistic view of human nature. While the traditional psychoanalytic view proposed that a child must be led against its will into maturity, Maslow's premise is that healthy children naturally seek out new skills congruent with their personal potential.

The hierarchy that Maslow proposed in order to explain personal growth and motivation is typically represented by a triangle (see Figure 8.1).

Maslow (1971) considered the four lower levels of need '*Deficiency Needs*', suggesting that until those needs were met, progression to the increasingly abstract *Growth Needs* would be unlikely. At the more basic end of Maslow's hierarchy, the emphasis of people's needs is focused on physical and social survival. In the level of *Physiological Needs*, food, drink, air, and shelter are among the essential needs that Maslow proposed must be met before people are likely to engage in more abstract levels of personal growth and development. Examples would be cases involving homelessness or malnutrition that could threaten actual survival. The next level addresses *Safety Needs*, in which both physical and psychological safety issues are essential areas of people's priorities. Examples would include people living in fear of crime, assault or abuse. At the next level, *Needs for Love and Belonging* represent the

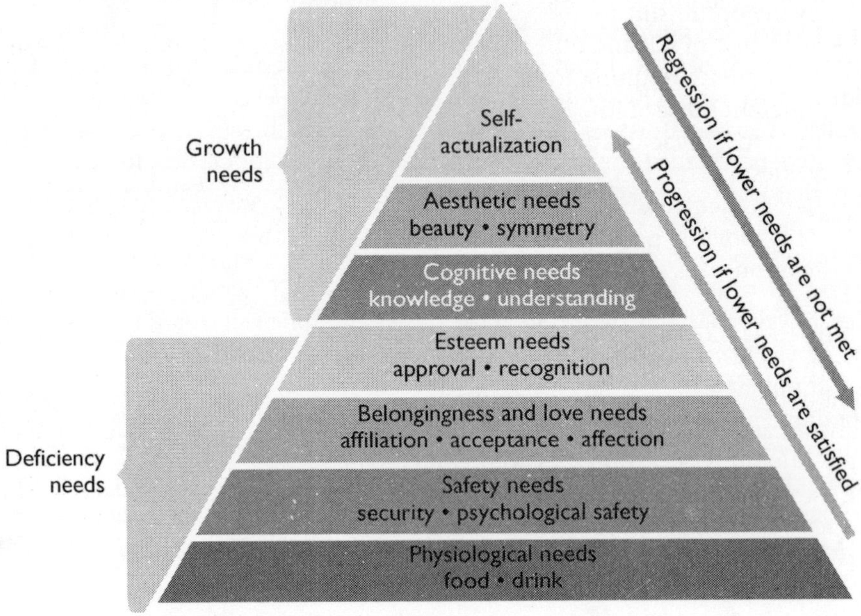

Figure 8.1 Maslow's hierarchy of needs.

dominant source of motivation. Examples would include barriers to relationships, isolation, and abandonment. The next level comprises *Esteem Needs, in* which needs for recognition and approval are essential. Examples of such needs include children who live without praise or reward, or people working in punitive or harshly critical environments.

Maslow referred to the remaining levels of needs as *Growth Needs*, representing essential elements in the process of attaining personal fulfilment. *Cognitive Needs* address quests for knowledge and understanding. Access to education and skills needed to attain personal potential would be relevant to this level of need. The next level, *Aesthetic Needs* addresses the need for beauty and order. Needs on this level may include the lack of artistic, natural, or musical pleasure. According to Maslow, the level of *Self-Actualization* represents the ultimate human motivation. It motivates people to achieve their best efforts, to explore their potential, and to live deeply meaningful lives. According to Maslow, most people remain so preoccupied with needs that are lower in the hierarchy that they never actually consider the possibility of self-actualization. Maslow proposed that rare individuals actually achieve self-actualization. Examples would include Abraham Lincoln, Jane Addams, Albert Einstein, Mahatma Gandhi, Mother Teresa, Martin Luther King, and Nelson Mandela.

Maslow cautioned 'There are no perfect human beings' (1971: 50), and that even self-actualization is not an all-or-nothing state. According to Maslow, self-actualizing ('fully human') individuals share some key characteristics. Some of those characteristics include the following:

- accurate perceptions of reality, free of defensive distortions, that are neither overly optimistic nor overly pessimistic;
- accepting of self and others in ways that are tolerant and non-judgemental;
- spontaneity resulting from self-awareness and self-knowing, which entails an inherent sense of integrity, regardless of popular conventions;
- need for privacy stemming from a tendency to rely on their own feelings and values;
- heightened autonomy and resistance to external rewards of social approval;
- deep, loving personal relationships rather than superficial contacts; their relationships are non-possessive and genuinely affectionate.

According to Maslow's model, when people reach the level of self-actualization, they are also more likely to have 'peak experiences', which serve to provide powerful, potentially transcendental states of awareness. Euphoria and a sense of oneness with the universe are characteristics of such experiences. Having such experiences does not preclude situations occurring that could entail regression to lower levels of needs, but having experienced such a powerful state also provides considerable motivation to resume a level of functioning that reflects self-actualization.

Maslow remains one of the few theorists who considered the area of work in relation to people's levels of self-fulfilment or self-actualization. According to Maslow (1971: 208), 'If you are unhappy with your work, you have lost one of the most important means of self-fulfilment.' According to Maslow, work places should provide settings in which not only basic safety needs are met, but also such factors as belonging, dignity, and respect in order to support people optimizing their potential.

Historical contributors to existentialism

Historically, existential psychology emerged in between the World Wars in Europe, but became prominent in the US following World War II. Well-known existentialist writers include Søren Kierkegaard, Friedrich Nietzsche, and Jean-Paul Sartre (Thompson, 2000). Less well known perhaps, the writings of Binswanger, Buber, Heidegger and Tillich also influenced the theoretical perspective that came to be regarded as existential psychology (May, 1983).

In the wake of the horrors of World War II, French philosopher **Jean-Paul Sartre** (1905–1980) proposed that life lacked any inherent meaning or purpose other than whatever an individual was able to construct through his or her own actions. Sartre denied the presence of a god or the relevance of an unconscious, and made no distinction between psychology and philosophy (Sadock & Sadock, 2007). According to Sartre, the capacity to reflect and make individual choices provides meaning in people's lives.

The existentialist psychologist most associated with individuals' quest for meaning is **Viktor Frankl** (1905–1997). A Viennese doctor trained in neurology and psychiatry, Frankl's lifework stemmed from the suffering he endured and observed in Nazi concentration camps (Frankl, 1992). Unlike Freud's emphasis on anxiety and unconscious conflicts, however, Frankl traced the source of people's suffering to a lack of meaning or sense of responsibility in their existence.

The remarkable life of Viktor Frankl

By the time Frankl had finished what was the equivalent of secondary school in Vienna he had already published an article in the *Journal of Psychoanalysis*, and had begun corresponding with Sigmund Freud. As a prodigious young Jewish doctor, Frankl's career in psychiatry appeared destined for great things. He earned doctorates in both philosophy and medicine.

By the time he completed his medical degree at age 25, Frankl had already established counselling centres for teenagers in Vienna and elsewhere. He was placed in charge of the treatment of suicidal women at Vienna's Psychiatric Hospital during the 1930s. Despite having a visa to travel to the US in 1939, Frankl remained in Vienna because of his concern for his elderly parents, despite the threat of the Nazi invasion.

In 1940, Frankl was appointed head of the neurology department in the only hospital for Jews in Vienna under the Nazis. While there, he endeavoured to protect patients from Nazi regulations requiring that people with mental illness be euthanized. During this period, Frankl began writing *The Doctor and the Soul*, which was a reflection on some of the professional, moral and ethical dilemmas with which he was struggling.

In 1942, the same year in which he married, Frankl, his bride, his brother and his parents were arrested and transported to a concentration camp. He was the only family member to survive the camps; his sister survived by having immigrated to Australia. Frankl's manuscript for *The Doctor and the Soul* was found and then destroyed during his transfer to Auschwitz.

Frankl managed to reconstruct his manuscript, writing on stolen fragments of paper. His theory and therapeutic practices stemmed from his harrowing experiences facing death and observing survival in the Nazi death camps.

His hopes to complete his work and to be reunited with his loved ones provided Frankl with motivation to endure his ordeal. Quoting Nietzsche, Frankl (1963) proposed that 'he who has a why to live for can bear with almost any how.' Only upon returning to Vienna in 1945 did Frankl learn of his family's fates.

Having survived the ordeal of the Nazi death camps, Frankl returned to Vienna, where he continued to teach at the University of Vienna until age 90. He was a prolific author, and dictated his famous *Man's Search for Meaning* in only nine days. Although Frankl originally intended to publish it as an anonymous memoir of his experiences in the death camps, he eventually determined that his personal context was necessary to give the work its full meaning.

Following his return to Vienna, Frankl remarried and had a daughter. He earned a pilot's licence at age 67. His second wife and their daughter, grandchildren and great-grandchildren survived him when he died at age 92.

Rollo May (1909–1994) was a prominent American existential psychologist, whose extensive writing contributed greatly to the fields of psychology and theology. May was originally from the Mid-Western state of Ohio, but travelled in Europe after his undergraduate studies, including a brief time spent studying under Alfred Adler in Vienna. May attended the Union Theological Seminary in New York, where he was strongly influenced by the existential theologian Paul Tillich. May served as a Congregationalist minister before beginning his doctorate in psychology. While studying for his PhD, May contracted tuberculosis, which resulted in his spending three years in a sanatorium. During that time, he read widely, and particularly focused on the existentialist writings of Kierkegaard. He was awarded the first PhD in clinical psychology from Columbia University in 1949 (Robbins, 1999).

Originally trained in psychoanalysis, May went on to practise and teach existential psychology at a number of American universities, including Princeton, Harvard and Yale. In much of his writing, May sought to reconcile Freudian and existentialist thinking. According to May, both psychoanalysis and existentialism share a common focus on the analysis of 'anxiety, despair, alienation of man from himself and his society', and both seek 'a synthesis of integration and meaning in the person's life' (May, 1983: 60).

Of the post-war generation's contributors to existentialism, perhaps the best known would be **Sheldon Kopp** (1929–1999). Writing as a widely experienced psychotherapist, Kopp verged on the realm of 'pop psychology', as his books were intended much more for the popular self-help market than for academic study. He proposed that people seeking wisdom are often inclined to seek a mentor to whom they can effectively become disciples. According to Kopp (1976), this poses an existential dilemma, as the quest for insight entails autonomy, and precludes reliance on others for second-hand wisdom. Kopp emphasized the importance of engaging in an existential struggle for authenticity. He proposed that part of that process is to take personal responsibility for finding and defining meaning and living as a 'grown up' in a world in which fairness and meaning are not guaranteed. A prolific writer, some of Kopp's books include *An End to Innocence: Facing Life Without Illusions; Mirror, Mask,* and *Shadow: The Risks and Rewards of Self-Acceptance*; and *If You Meet the Buddha on the Road, Kill Him!*

Key concepts of existentialism

Existentialism refers to a broad philosophical school of thought, involving the exploration of human existence with particular emphasis on immediate experiences. Profound universal themes such as aloneness, death, despair, and moral accountability figure prominently in existential considerations. Especially for social workers, who often work with people who are profoundly isolated from loved ones or even from society in general, such themes can prove highly relevant. From an existentialist perspective, the human condition is defined by a continual struggle to sustain some level of rational or coherent meaning amidst a confusing and confounding world. That struggle is a dynamic, continuous factor of the existentialist perspective, which emphasizes the ongoing nature of people's quest for truth and self-understanding. Humanism and existentialism clearly have a number of overlapping concepts.

The existentialist perspective presumes that people have the capacity to reflect on their circumstances in a profound and critical fashion. From that capacity for reflection on our own lives and those around us, a realization of mortality is essentially inevitable. On an existential level, then, the certainty that we and all those we love are inevitably going to die represents a fundamental concept, as is the awareness that suffering is an inevitable fact of life. The combined realities of those two realizations combine to create the existential question of meaning or purposefulness. What makes life worth living? Furthermore, the answers to those existential questions are often elusive and inevitably subject to individual interpretations. The quest for meaning in our lives is a very individual undertaking, lacking simple or uniform answers. People's quest for meaning that serves to redeem experiences of suffering or despair provides an essential element of existential psychology.

Frankl introduced the term *logotherapy* to refer to the form of therapy he conducted. From the Greek word *logos*, denoting 'meaning', Frankl's approach was sometimes referred to as 'The Third Viennese School of Psychotherapy', after Freud's and Adler's. His rejection of the levels of determinism found in both psychoanalysis and behaviourism is a key component of Frankl's approach. While he acknowledged that various conditions may serve to limit personal freedom, Frankl argued that the essential point, 'is not freedom from conditions, but it is freedom to take a stand toward these conditions' (Frankl, 1992: 132). Pointing to the suffering experienced in the death camps, Frankl argued that individuals exercised choices in the attitudes they took towards given sets of circumstances. In his emphasis on personal choice, Frankl's approach is congruent with the humanist theorists.

Frankl also emphasized the importance of having a *phenomenological framework* in order to interpret behaviour. By that, he referred to the role of personal experience as a means of determining subjective meaning. Frankl distinguished between the objective 'facts' that had traditionally been considered scientifically necessary, and subjective 'experiences', which are secured in an individual's perspective on events and their meanings. Frankl acknowledged that psychology as a science had traditionally relied on detached observations and measurements of objective facts, but suggested that some experiences defy objectivity. Survival of trauma (including the death camps) was a case in point, to which Frankl pointed out that the individual alone is capable of determining the meaning of such experiences.

Ultimately, Frankl viewed meaning as a personal outcome related both to the context of individual experiences as well as to the attitudes chosen with which to respond to those experiences. His emphasis was very much on the here-and-now, as it contributes to finding future fulfilment. In this respect, Frankl's is an innately optimistic perspective. It is also distinct from psychoanalytic perspectives' focus on past experiences, or behaviourism's emphasis on modifying future responses.

According to Frankl, the endeavour to 'find a meaning in one's life is the primary motivational force in man' (Frankl, 1992: 104). He also considered a degree of tension between one's current state and one's potential a necessary component of mental health. This view distinguishes some of Frankl's perspective from that of Carl Rogers, who suggested that optimal mental health entailed congruence without the presence of tension. It is also distinct from Maslow's perspectives on self-actualization, which

Frankl saw as a possible outcome of seeking meaning, rather than an attainable end in itself.

Frankl's existentialist perspective does not propose to impose or assert any particular meaning to life or even a set of values necessary to attain meaning. He suggests, however, that some experiences are congruent with discovering meaning in life. Those experiences include:

- achievement;
- having a transcendent ('mountain top') experience (e.g. love, an aesthetic or natural experience of delight);
- the attitude one takes to unavoidable suffering (e.g. death camp experiences, of someone facing a terminal condition or profound bereavement).

Rollo May emphasized the concepts of *will* and *myth*. By will, he is referring to a basic feature of human existence, and relies on some of Nietzsche's concepts of core human features that serve to define humans as being distinct from other animals. For social workers, May's concepts resonate with the basic premises of self-determination and 'starting where the client is'. According to May (1983: 77), 'The acorn becomes an oak regardless of any choice, but man cannot realize his being except as he wills it in his encounters.' May (1969) proposes that will plays a key role in individual motivations, and entails the ability to organize oneself in such ways as to be capable of achieving one's goals, or even to 'make wishes come true'. Such executive functions are comparable to the Freudian concepts of ego functions and reality testing, but with a greater level of individual self-determination and positive energy. As used by May, the role played by will has to do with self-determination and hopefulness.

May's (1991) concepts of myths are similar to Jungian terminology. May regarded myths as stories that give meaning or sense to our lives, and that serve as 'guiding narratives'. This usage differs considerably from the traditional usage of myth as a made-up story or fairy tale lacking reality. In May's usage, myths serve to provide stories that illustrate themes and values. For some people, Aesop's fables provide examples through myths that serve to demonstrate timeless truths. Some people find relevant myths in *The Simpsons*, or in biographies of historic figures who overcame adversity. According to May, the purpose of myth is to provide meaning that relates to truth and core values.

Implications for practice

Perhaps best summarized by May's (1991) chapter, 'I Never Promised You a Rose Garden', both humanism and existentialist practice focus on change coming to the individual through internal rather than external solutions. Both approaches emphasize the individual's autonomy in the change and healing process.

By de-mystifying and de-medicalizing psychotherapy, Rogers empowered an array of other professions including social work to engage in mental health practice. Rogers' contributions to social work practice remain enormously important. His *client-*

centred approach to working with people is based on the premise of providing people with environments in which they can endeavour to attain self-actualization. His emphasis on providing *unconditional positive regard* and a non-judgemental acceptance of people are fundamental aspects of social work values. Rogers' approach to interactions with clients (as opposed to the traditional medical model's references to 'patients') remains a fundamental aspect of effective therapeutic practice (Watson, 2007). Simple but elegant, Rogers urged therapists to be genuinely and empathically *present* with their clients, and to regard them as valued fellow human beings, rather than as mere objects of diagnostic assessment (Brown, 2007). He also introduced an awareness of the therapeutic value of working alongside people, rather than maintaining the patriarchal or authoritarian role that was the norm established by the psychoanalytic tradition.

According to Rogerian methods, the therapeutic environment is shaped by the therapist's unconditional positive regard for the client. Rarely experienced outside infancy, unconditional positive regard entails totally non-judgemental acceptance of the individual as they are. Such practice entails a primary focus on the present, and an inherent confidence in the individual's potential for wellness. The process of treatment is a key feature of the client-centred approach, with considerable attention paid to the client's feelings throughout. Philosophically, the Rogerian approach is essentially based on a positive attitude toward the client's potential, without the traditional psychoanalytic emphasis on past conflicts or neuroses. Using a client-centred approach, the power differential between therapist and client is more egalitarian than traditional therapeutic relationships, and thus congruent with social work values (Coulshed & Orme, 2006).

For social workers, Maslow's hierarchy of needs is readily applicable to an array of practice priorities. In the course of assessing needs, a failure to attend to basic survival needs could prove disastrous. Similarly, presuming to focus on basic needs without attending to service users' more advanced priorities could also prove counterproductive. Essentially, Maslow's model provides an optimistic approach to understanding people's motivation and growth. He also provided a model in which the role of the environment is an essential component of understanding people's motivation.

From asking patients about what precluded their opting for suicide, Frankl approached psychotherapy with them on the premise that certain factors (love for their children, religion, etc.) provided a crucial dimension to their lives. Having faced the extreme brutalities of Auschwitz and Dachau, Frankl brought a profound sense of authenticity to his work with others, which he called logotherapy (Frankl, 1992). The quest to find meaning that redeemed personal suffering, and counteracted despair represents a fundamental aspect of Frankl's approach to existential psychology.

Addressing key concepts surrounding questions of meaning and explaining suffering are key components of existentialist practice. According to Yalom (1985), anxiety is the outcome of tensions stemming from struggling with the simultaneous realities of suffering and death.

When working with the 'messy' complexities of people's lives, social workers are called upon to practise in ways that are reflective, acknowledging that easy answers do not apply (Schön, 1983). In such circumstances, existentialism provides an approach that acknowledges the inadequacies of the options available in response to the complexities of people's dilemmas. The quest for meaning is the primary distinction between the humanistic and the existentialist approaches to practice.

Criticisms and debates regarding humanism and existentialism

Humanistic psychology has been criticized for being best designed for people who are actually coping reasonably satisfactorily, sometimes called 'the worried well'.

The focus of humanistic psychology is rarely applicable when working with people experiencing conditions such as autism or psychosis (Polansky, 1991). When working with people with severe impulse control problems, including paedophilia, the humanistic premise of self-direction, self-determination and choice may prove unrealistic as it presumes a level of ego functioning that may not be readily available.

According to some critics, the trait theory associated with humanism is overly simplistic, and lacks the intellectual rigour sufficient for a genuine theory. Some critics argue that the trait theory lacks sufficient depth for consistent application because of the inherent complexity of personalities and the numerous circumstances that influence people's personalities and behaviours (Zastrow & Kirst-Ashman, 1994).

Humanistic and existentialist approaches both emphasize the unique role of the individual as a key concept. For some cultures, the very western focus on self-determination and self-disclosure may remain very difficult to apply (Coulshed & Orme, 2006). In some aspects, that same emphasis on the individual and the therapeutic process make measurement of motivation and therapeutic effectiveness virtually impossible for purposes of research into reliability (Watson, 2007).

From a feminist perspective, much of Rogers' work, despite its potential value, is inherently weakened by its apolitical content, and its failure to address inherent dimensions of social 'incongruence' caused by sexism and male dominance. Rogers' failure to comment on the implications of the oppression of women, and the human suffering resulting from gender-based inequities has compromised the integrity of the humanist tradition for many feminists (Brown, 2007).

Some find the semi-religious elements in both Maslow's and Frankl's work contradictory to scientific rigour as well as basic existential concepts. Both writers' works have been subjected to an array of 'pop psychology' interpretations that could be considered detrimental to the intellectual strength of their works. Arguably, religion's fundamental premise of a God who imbues life with meaning or redemption is inherently at odds with existentialism's core concepts.

Questions

1 Match the following:

____	Trait theory	(a) Abraham Maslow
____	Unconditional positive regard	(b) Viktor Frankl
____	Peak experiences	(c) Rollo May
____	Logotherapy	(d) Gordon Allport
____	Hierarchy of needs	(e) Carl Rogers
____	Will and myth	(f) Self-actualization

2 In small groups, please discuss your ideas of Allport's trait theory.
  (a) What are those traits that you consider your 'primary traits'?
  (b) What are those traits that you associate with effective social workers?
  (c) What are those traits to which you aspire?

3 Given the life story of Viktor Frankl, to what do you attribute his proposal that meaning can contribute to the capacity to survive?

4 Have you ever had a particularly difficult experience, which at the time seemed insurmountable, but from which in retrospect you consider yourself stronger or wiser? How do you see this relating to Frankl's view of the role of attitudes toward unavoidable suffering?

5 Based on the following scenario, consider the existential implications for the elderly neighbour.

> On a brief visit to her former hometown, Alice paid a visit to her old neighbourhood. Upon stepping out of the car, she encountered a former neighbour, an older woman with whom she had been friendly. Alice was aware that her elderly neighbour is the primary carer for her husband, a former judge, who is in the mid-stages of Alzheimer's disease. Upon greeting her former neighbour, Alice asked how her family was, to which the woman blurted out, 'You probably haven't heard, but our son's house burned down last month, and his two youngest children died. He is still in intensive care, but we think he'll survive. It was touch and go at first.' Trying to imagine the enormity of her neighbour's loss, Alice tearfully hugged her friend and said, 'Words fail.'

  (a) What meaning would you consider possible to assign to the elderly neighbour's experience?
  (b) Do you think anyone who has not experienced such a profound loss is in a position to offer any suggestions or comments?
  (c) What are some ways in which trying to respond with some positive platitude would risk ignoring the woman's existential sense of despair?

6 Sometimes groups of people develop an array of myths or legends that provide illustrations of ways in which they (or their members, ancestors, role models, etc.) overcame adversity, or established meaning. What are some of the myths that you find meaningful?

9 Influences of trauma on behaviour

Social workers often work with people who have experienced various types and degrees of trauma. That trauma may take the form of abuse, assault, rape, or violence, to name but a few. This chapter addresses just a few of the areas with which social workers are most likely to interact: child maltreatment, domestic violence, sexual assault (rape), and traumatic bereavement. Various types of trauma are considered by using a bio-psychosocial framework, such as developmental variables, psychological concerns, and social factors relevant to adaptation and coping following trauma. From the topics addressed in this chapter, readers are encouraged to explore the applicability of some key concepts across other contexts, such as schools, mental health settings and the criminal justice systems in which people's behaviour may reflect earlier traumatic experiences.

Relevance for social work

Social workers are often in a position to work with people following trauma, yet the core features of trauma often go unspoken. There are countless ways in which people are overtly and covertly exposed to trauma. This chapter sets out to address a few of the traumatic experiences frequently found in social workers' case loads. Traumatic experiences may include a house fire, forced immigration, disfiguring injuries, war, and terrorism, to name but a few of the more overt examples; job loss, racism, sexism, and homophobia are among a long list of the more covert ways in which people may experience trauma on a regular basis.

Regardless of where social workers work, they are often in a position of responding to and advocating for people who have experienced trauma. A growing body of literature attests to the linkages between trauma and mental, medical, and behavioural problems (Everett & Gallop, 2001; Teicher et al., 2006). Social workers are often in crucial positions to understand the developmental and emotional roles played by trauma, particularly among children who may otherwise be regarded very unsympathetically by society and the media because of their behaviour. An awareness and application of some of those trauma-related assessment concepts can contribute to social workers practising in ways that are empowering and healing, rather than contributing to a system whereby 'blaming the victim' is perpetuated.

For purposes of this discussion, people who have experienced trauma are referred to as 'survivors', rather than 'victims'. This is an intentional word choice, meant to emphasize strength, and to reflect empowerment rather than victimization.

Key concepts related to child maltreatment

Definitions of child maltreatment sometimes vary according to culture, generation, and developmental stages. It is generally considered according to specific aspects of neglect and abuse, which are not mutually exclusive; many children experience multiple forms of maltreatment, sometimes simultaneously. Neglect may entail physical, educational, or medical dimensions related to parental or carer acts of omission. Extreme examples of neglect include malnutrition, failure to thrive, and abandonment. Abuse may entail physical, emotional, or sexual dimensions. *Physical abuse* entails non-accidental injury or harm to a child; *emotional* or *psychological abuse* entails a child's health and development being jeopardized, and is usually present with all other types of abuse (Scannapieco & Connell-Carrick, 2005). *Sexual abuse* entails children under age 17 (England and Wales) being in sexual or sexualized relationships to which they are not fully capable of giving informed consent (Waterhouse, 2008). As with *sexual assault* (rape), sexual abuse entails a violation of power between those involved.

Because families living in poverty or receiving social support are more likely to come to the attention of authorities, they appear over-represented among reports of child maltreatment. Child maltreatment is not restricted to families living in poverty or lone-parent households; those families are, however, more likely to be reported than those living in more affluent circumstances. Most families living in poverty neither abuse nor neglect their children. Being in a large family living in relative poverty increases children's risks of being abused (Howe, 2005). As with alcohol- and drug-related conditions, child maltreatment is no respecter of culture, race, or socio-economic status, although financial privilege often prevents its detection.

Physical abuse

Some of the biological, visible indications of *physical abuse* include injuries such as bruising (especially in infancy), cuts, fractures (especially those indicative of twisting, and those nearer the torso), and burns. Head injuries, loss of hair from violent pulling, subdural haematomas (blood collected inside the outer covering of the brain following shaking or hitting), and detached retinas are also indications for concern. Children at the greatest risk of abuse include children born prematurely, children who are born unwanted, children with disabilities, and children who are born sick or under-sized (or all of the above) (Roberts, 1988; Howe, 2005). Parents who were abused during childhood are more likely to be abusive than parents who were not abused (Howe, 2005; Scannapieco & Connell-Carrick, 2005).

Experiencing the level of aggression associated with being injured is frightening at any age. During childhood it is both frightening and bewildering. The younger the child is, the more fear and agitation are associated with being abused (Howe, 2005). The child's reaction to fear may involve aspects of the fight-or-flight response.

The *fight-or-flight* response to a critical event or perceived threat includes an intense stimulation of the sympathetic nervous system and the adrenal gland. The physical components of the fight-or-flight response entail a rapid, yet elaborate process involving the brain, the emotions, the autonomic (ANS) and central nervous systems (CNS), among other organs. The brain communicates the message of alarm through the CNS, travelling through the pituitary gland, which then produces adrenaline. The subsequent secretion of the neurotransmitters serotonin and norepinephrine then results in a mobilization of fats and an increase in oxygen and blood to the necessary cells, which fortifies the body's capacity to withstand the challenges it is facing (Lawrence & Zittel-Palamara, 2002). Those physical reactions also raise heart, blood pressure and respiratory rates, along with blood flow to muscles, in order to facilitate the body for either fighting or fleeing from the situation. It may also be associated with higher levels of aggression (i.e. 'fight') among children who have been exposed to trauma (Teicher, 2000). Extreme watchfulness and wariness sometimes associated with 'hypervigilance' among those who are on guard for further danger are often noted among abused children. In some cases, this can prove adaptive, as it facilitates self-defence. Some children run away, freeze, or even dissociate (i.e. flight) in response to abuse (Howe, 2005). Many of these same responses are characteristic of post-traumatic stress disorder (see Chapter 10).

Childhood maltreatment, especially among very young children, is associated with irreversible damage to the neurological functions of the brain related to verbal and emotional memories (Teicher, 2000; van der Kolk, 1994). Such neurological consequences appear linked with the higher incidences of problems including antisocial behaviour as well as dissociative identity disorder ('multiple personality disorder'), and borderline personality disorders that are associated with childhood histories of severe physical and sexual abuse.

Children who have been abused manifest high rates of depression and suicidal behaviours, especially during adolescence. Boys who have histories of abuse appear more angry and prone to violence. Children with histories of abuse are more likely to experience academic problems and disruptions than their peers without abusive histories (Scannapieco & Connell-Carrick, 2005).

Some of the behavioural indicators associated with children who have been physically abused include over-compliance, passivity, exceptional quietness and docility (to avoid further dangerous attention). Extremely aggressive, hyperactive, demanding and angry behaviours are also associated with children who have been subjected to physical abuse (Gerhardt, 2004). During adolescence, both boys and girls appear at heightened risks of aggression and delinquency (Herrera & McCloskey, 2001).

Some children who have been abused are so preoccupied with coping and survival skills that basic developmental tasks are delayed. These may include social skills, language skills, problem-solving skills, or motor skills. Reading and writing may be jeopardized during early school years if the child is more focused on survival than on school achievements (Everett & Gallop, 2001; Teicher, 2000).

Child abuse is consistently linked with parents with distorted or inappropriate expectations of children's behaviours. Highly authoritarian and coercive styles of parenting are also associated with limited parenting skills, which can contribute to abuse (Scannapieco & Connell-Carrick, 2005).

Without the opportunity to achieve object constancy, many abused children also lack the important ability to comfort themselves in times of duress (Everett & Gallop, 2001). The emotional and behavioural results can entail severe anxiety, self-harm, overly intrusive demands of others, and self-medication with alcohol and other drugs, among other problematic behavioural patterns. Problems with attachment are consistently linked with histories of abusive childhoods (Scannapieco & Connell-Carrick, 2005). When abused children have not experienced caring, consistent parents who are capable of providing protection and comfort, those children often lack the experience of internalizing comforting, caring representations that comprise object constancy (discussed in Chapters 5 and 7). Children who have experienced a sense of helplessness in the face of abuse may find strong emotions (positive or negative) overwhelming and frightening, which is likely to make attachments to others very complex (Fahlberg, 1991; Howe, 2005). Some abused children do not appear to distinguish between familiar people and strangers, and engage in 'promiscuous bonding', which often entails seeking attention from people with whom they are not sufficiently familiar, and who may be potentially dangerous. Children with ambivalent attachment styles stemming from abuse may also prove to be so emotionally needy and demanding that their behaviours overwhelm people with whom healthy relationships would otherwise have been beneficial.

Sexual abuse

Child sexual abuse (CSA) refers to sexual relationships involving a child (under age 17 in England and Wales) and a more dominant partner, who is usually an adult. Child sexual abuse may involve physical contact (including penetration, fondling, or masturbation), or may be non-penetrative, or non-contactual (including exhibitionism, being forced to witness violent sexual activities, or making or using pornography) (DOH, 2006).

Current estimates of sexual abuse remain underestimates, because of various elements of shame, fear, ignorance, and stigma serving to dissuade its being reported or acknowledged. The majority of perpetrators of CSA are either immediate or extended family members, or someone who is familiar to the child, who occupies a position of trust and authority. Estimates of sexual abuse perpetrated by women remain particularly vague, despite evidence that women can and do abuse children. Nearly a quarter of the CSA perpetrated against boys is attributed to women (McManiman, 2001). Older children and teenagers also perpetrate sexual abuse against younger children; some children who have experienced abuse become sexual offenders during adolescence, but this appears to apply to a minority (Scannapieco & Connell-Carrick, 2005). The majority of known perpetrators of CSA are male; most CSA is perpetrated by fathers, stepfathers, mothers' partners and men known to the child's family (Howe, 2005).

Children appear more vulnerable to sexual abuse between ages 7 and 13, but boys appear to be more vulnerable around age 8, while girls' vulnerability rises at age 11 (Scannapieco & Connell-Carrick, 2005). Children with physical and learning disabilities are at nearly double the risk of CSA as other children (Howe, 2005). Family-related risk factors for CSA include parental separation or divorce, low maternal educational achievement, family isolation, paternal unemployment, frequent house moves, role reversals between the child and parent, and parental substance misuse (Howe, 2005; Scannapieco & Connell-Carrick, 2005).

Some physical manifestations of child sexual abuse include bruising, genital pain and itching, difficulties sitting, bleeding, and sexually transmitted infections. Enuresis (lacking bladder control) and encopresis (lacking bowel control) are also associated with CSA (Zastrow & Kirst-Ashman, 1994). Behavioural indicators of sexual abuse vary enormously. Young children with premature sexual knowledge may engage in sexualized behaviours with their peers. Temper tantrums and difficulties playing are commonly noted problems. Some children become fearful of men following abuse by a male (Sadock & Sadock, 2007).

While the psychological effects of sexual abuse can be lifelong and devastating, they also vary enormously. Depression is frequently noted among survivors of CSA, along with post-traumatic stress disorder and dissociative identity disorder (Everett & Gallop, 2001). High rates of impulsivity, self-destructive behaviours and suicidal tendencies are frequently noted among adolescent survivors. Sgroi (1988) referred to the perpetually 'damaged goods' element of CSA survivors' self-evaluation. Especially around ages 3–4, when emotions such as shame, distrust and embarrassment are likely to be emerging, the effects of sexual abuse may be particularly complex (Scannapieco & Connell-Carrick, 2005). Problematic outcomes are heightened when children engage in dissociation (fractured consciousness involving a splitting away from the here-and-now) as a coping strategy for CSA. Dissociation is associated with subsequent risks of self-mutilation during adolescence as well as subsequent mental health difficulties (Howe, 2005).

The outcomes of severe childhood maltreatment vary enormously, and variables such as severity, duration, and protective responses by others influence the outcomes. The age at the onset of trauma as well as the duration are key considerations in any assessment, with trauma at a very young age (especially preverbal) and prolonged trauma being associated with a poorer outcome. The best outcomes are associated with children who do not sustain cognitive impairment, and when the trauma is recognized and promptly stopped (Howe, 2005). With that in mind, children's resilience in the face of adversity and trauma must never be underestimated. Social workers are urged to emphasize the role of resilience and children's inherent strengths and coping skills in understanding the complex consequences of childhood trauma.

According to Finkelhor and Brown (1986), some of the factors associated with more problematic psychological outcomes for children following CSA include the following:

- prolonged duration of the abuse;
- multiple incidents of abuse;

- perpetrator being a father or stepfather;
- lack of support from the family;
- removal of child (victim) from the home rather than the perpetrator.

Gender differences among survivors of CSA are noteworthy. The historic and persistent under-reporting of male CSA makes accurate estimates of its prevalence unreliable (McManiman, 2001). Sexual abuse may represent more of a violation of sex roles for males than is the case for females. Especially when working with male survivors, issues of anger management and the capacity to experience and acknowledge the emotions of fear and sadness may entail even more attention than when working with female survivors. Regardless of sexual orientation, male survivors of CSA may experience confusion regarding the homosexual implications of childhood sexual abuse, and somehow hold themselves responsible for its occurrence (Briere, 1992). Similarly, female survivors may hold themselves somehow responsible for having enticed the abuser. Reports of CSA are further complicated when children experience being physically aroused by the experience, and regard themselves as having therefore consented on the basis of having experienced pleasure. Children need clear messages about the perpetrator's responsibility for sexualized behaviour with underage partners, and that the children were not equally responsible for what occurred. Perpetrators of CSA often blur the emotional boundaries between love, coercion and sex, which can lead to profound confusion for the children they abuse.

Some perpetrators of sexual abuse engage in behaviours known as *grooming*, whereby they find ways and means of gaining a child's trust and affection. This may entail gradually rewarding the child, by making her/him feel special or singled out for attention. Purchasing special clothes or sports equipment, or spending large amounts of time with the child prior to the actual sexualization of the relationship may also occur. Especially when a child is lonely, vulnerable, or neglected, grooming often serves to meet strong emotional needs.

Problematic relationships are often a consequence of CSA, resulting from a child's trust having been betrayed (as is necessarily the case when an adult uses a child as a sexual partner). Issues of self-blame are particularly relevant when survivors of CSA see themselves as having somehow attracted the sexual abuse, and therefore being unworthy of healthy relationships thereafter. Having experiential knowledge that people are capable of harm may have lifelong implications for survivors' capacity to trust or engage in healthy relationships. When early, primary relationships have been defined by unpredictability, exploitation, and cruelty, sexual relations may be linked with the expectation of pain and trauma, or something to be avoided altogether (Everett & Gallop, 2001). Issues of sexual orientation may be particularly confusing for male survivors.

Adolescent survivors of CSA may appear their actual age, or even older. That does not necessarily mean that their emotional or social development is on course developmentally. Many adolescent CSA survivors struggle with articulating emotions and with communication in general (Wieland, 1997). During adolescence, when most children experience both physical maturation and the onset of romantic and sexual relations with peers, issues of trust and intimacy may be problematic for survivors of sexual abuse. In some cases, the prospect of sex is intensely stressful and overwhelming; in some cases, adolescents use sex as a means of gaining approval or social acceptance. Sexually promiscuous behaviours can result in further social alienation for sexually abused teenagers (Scannapieco & Connell-Carrick, 2005). This can be further complicated when teenagers are also using alcohol and drugs for self-medication ('forgetting') and/or social acceptance by partners or peer groups whose usage is potentially problematic. The following scenario depicts a few of the complexities of working with survivors of CSA.

'Ben' (age 17) is the youngest of his parents' four children; his older brothers, Carl and Alf are now ages 23 and 28. His sister (Dora) is 20. All four are of mixed race. Their parents divorced when Ben was 6, and his father served time in prison on drug-trafficking charges when Ben was 8. Around that time, their mother's mood swings and her drinking worsened dramatically, and Ben and Dora often attended school with facial bruises inflicted by their mother in fits of drunken anger, but no one intervened. During that time, their mother was diagnosed with bipolar disorder, but she has always laughingly insisted that alcohol and cocaine are better than prescribed medication for managing her mood swings.

When Ben was age 9, Alf began sexually abusing him. Ben tried to tell their mother, but she did not believe him. The early episodes of sexual abuse were usually accompanied by marijuana, which Ben started smoking regularly at age 10. The abuse continued until age 14, by which time Alf had introduced Ben to alcohol and then heroin. The main reason Ben continued attending school was to sell marijuana, in order to support his own growing heroin habit.

Although regarded as a bright and likeable child during junior and early primary school, at around age 10, Ben seemed to lose interest in school. He came to be regarded as a discipline problem, and his family's troubled reputation in the community added to his difficulties.

When Ben was 14, Alf and Carl were both sent to prison for a gang-related murder conviction. Left without a regular heroin supplier, Ben resorted to male prostitution in order to support his usage. Although Ben considers himself heterosexual by orientation, and has several female partners, being very attractive and likeable, he is quite successful in his role as a 'sex worker'. He often finds ways to slip extra money to Dora, who is now a lone mother. Ben left school at 15 with no qualifications.

Last year, Ben was charged with solicitation by the local police. Both his parents were shocked by the charges, and both refused to allow Ben to continue living with them. Let off with a warning, Ben moved in with his maternal grandmother (Bess, age 67). Although she worries about Ben and Dora, she doesn't wish to 'interfere' with their behaviour. She is aware of Ben's heroin use, but they have agreed that he will not use in front of her, and that he will not bring any drug-using friends into her home. Bess is aware that Ben works as a male prostitute several nights each week. They spend much of their time together smoking cigarettes and drinking cider, which Bess provides. Bess is the only person in whom Ben has confided that he has been diagnosed with HIV. She is also aware that Ben's mood swings are very like his mother's were at the same age, and she worries that he may also have bipolar disorder, which runs in her family.

As 'Ben's' case demonstrates, many survivors of child sexual abuse have complex family and social lives, and not all perpetrators of abuse are parental figures. Some of the very skills that have served their survival are not necessarily socially rewarded, legal, or marketable. Their support networks are not always as secure as Bess, who is not necessarily equipped to meet Ben's looming health crises. Much of Ben's life story could have been prevented had his early behavioural changes been noted as indicators of abuse, rather than his being dismissed as a 'problem child' from a 'bad' family.

Domestic violence

Domestic violence (DV), or family violence, is of profound relevance to social workers. Domestic violence represents a source of tremendous suffering across the lifespan, and across all ethnic and socio-economic categories. Although DV varies enormously, it generally entails elements of physical, sexual and emotional abuse and intimidation between partners.

> It can be understood as the misuse of power and the exercise of control by one partner over the other in an intimate relationship, usually a man over a woman, occasionally by a woman over a man (though without the same pattern of society collusion) and also occurring amongst same sex couples.
>
> (Mullender & Humphreys, 1998: 6)

Risk factors for DV include substance misuse, pregnancy and recent or proposed separation (Milner & Myers, 2007). At its worst, DV results in death; in England and Wales alone, nearly two women die each week as a result of injuries inflicted by a current or former intimate partner (Humphreys, 2008). That number exceeds the number of policemen killed in the line of their work in England and Wales. Women's issues related to DV are further discussed in Chapter 13. This chapter's discussion of family/domestic violence pertains more to children than women because of the well-established links between child maltreatment and DV. For purposes of this discussion, children's exposure to DV is meant to include overhearing as well as witnessing episodes of violence.

The most common form of family/domestic violence to which children are exposed entails harm to their mother. The tactics of the abuse often compromise both parents' roles and abilities as parents (Rowsell, 2003; Humphreys, 2008). Examples besides physical violence include witnessing the mother being humiliated or sexually violated. The abuse of animals is strongly linked with DV in families (AHA, 2002). In such cases, perpetrators may use cruelty to the animals as a way of controlling other family members' behaviour.

Not all children exposed to DV manifest the same responses (Rowsell, 2003). Some behaviours associated with childhood exposure to DV include social withdrawal, clinginess, bed wetting, asthma attacks, stuttering, and nightmares. Developmental regressions (such as eating, toilet habits, and emotional neediness) may also occur

(Mullender, 1996). Children exposed to DV also show higher levels of phobias, depression, insomnia, and post-traumatic stress syndrome than children not exposed to DV (Osofsky, 1999).

Children who have been exposed to chronic DV have been consistently found to have higher rates of cognitive and behavioural problems when compared with children from non-violent homes. Exposure to DV appears linked with poorer verbal skills during childhood (Huth-Bocks et al., 2001). The highest levels of behavioural and emotional disturbances are linked with the children themselves having been physically abused along with witnessing violence (Mullender, 1996; Rossman, 2001). As with other forms of maltreatment, children's developmental stages and tasks are often disrupted in the course of finding ways to cope with parental violence. Disorganized and controlling attachment patterns, and heightened levels of aggression and antisocial behaviours are associated with children being exposed to parental violence (Herrera & McCloskey, 2001; Howe, 2005). As when experiencing other forms of maltreatment, children's *fight-or-flight* responses are often activated by witnessing DV.

Parental substance misuse (particularly alcohol and cocaine) often contributes to incidents of domestic violence (Baty et al., 2008; Howe, 2005). Children's experiences are likely to be compounded by both factors. Particularly when children are exposed to patterns in which violence is 'justified' by the usage ('he only does that when he's drunk'), or when usage is a consistent strategy for coping with the violence (I wouldn't need to drink/use if it weren't for the pain of having just been assaulted'), problem-solving skills and patterns of social learning can take on some ominous prospects. Confusing issues of role reversals (i.e. where children become their parent's carer) and children's emotional needs going unmet are commonly noted problems among abused children in general; additional factors of DV and parental substance misuse can intensify such risks (Cleaver et al., 2000).

Exposure to parental violence tends to complicate children's social prospects. Domestic violence tends to impede children's ability to establish strong friendships with their peers, which can persist into lifelong difficulties (Howe, 2005). Children who have tried to intervene (phoning the police, trying to alert authorities, etc.) may also have had their trust of helping professionals undermined. Particularly during adolescence, externalized behaviours (aggression and delinquency) appear linked with exposure to DV at home (Baldry, 2007).

Linkages between perpetrators having witnessed DV during childhood are better documented than is the case for their partners (Baty et al., 2008; Cleaver et al., 2000; Howe, 2005). The implications for the continued perpetuation of DV are ominous for both the sons and daughters who witness parental violence. Issues of identifying with the aggressor (i.e. perpetrator), distorted views on what does or does not represent love, issues of learned helplessness ('just learn to live with it; he was just teaching her a lesson') and emotional dependence are all relevant to children's exposure to domestic violence. Social learning theory has been applied to the *inter-generational transmission of violence* by observing how children who witness violence used as a means of getting what they want by the adults around them see that violence is an acceptable, even rewarded behaviour (Jasinski, 2001).

Domestic violence is consistently linked with issues of misused power, distorted aspects of affection, trust, and loyalty. The power and control wheel in Figure 9.1

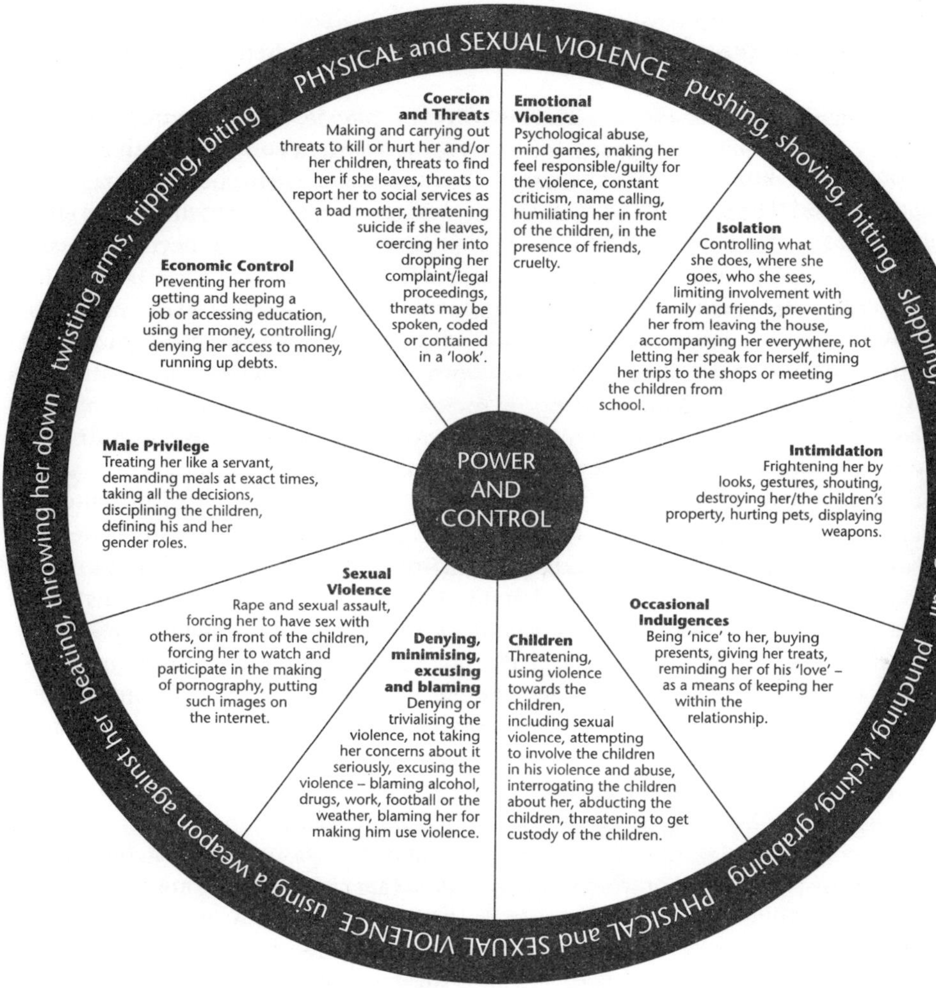

Figure 9.1 The power and control wheel of domestic violence (adapted from Pence, 1987).

Source: Harne & Radford (2008).

provides a visual representation of the ways in which DV can and does distort family functioning. While it primarily addresses the partners, children's experiences are necessarily influenced by the dimensions of intimidation and coercion in relationships.

Social workers must be mindful of the insidious nature of such lessons, as well as children's resilience and strength in coping with and moving beyond violent family norms. Protective factors include high levels of self-efficacy, problem-solving skills, strong attention spans, religious affiliations, and strong personal relationships with non-violent adults and children (Howe, 2005; Osofsky, 1999; Scannapieco & Connell-Carrick, 2005).

Sexual assault (rape)

Rape is often mistaken for a sexual crime involving violence, which misses the point of it being a violent crime of aggression in which sex is used as a weapon. It usually occurs alongside other crimes, including threats and non-sexual assaults and life-threatening injuries (Sadock & Sadock, 2007). One of the timeless features associated with sexual assault (rape) is that assessments of its true incidence and consequences are under-estimates of the reality. Less than 10 per cent of all rapes are ever reported to the police, and less than 1 per cent result in convictions of the rapist (Erooga & Print, 2001). The complex reasons for rape being historically under-reported include issues of fear of retribution, stigma, shame, and the abuse of power (both personal and societal). Rape is no respecter of age, gender, ethnicity, or socio-economic status, although all those factors can influence a survivor's willingness to report what happened. And what we know is only the proverbial 'tip of the iceberg' of the prevalence and consequences of rape across the lifespan.

Rape entails forceful coercion of a person to engage in a sexual act, which is usually penetrative (vaginal or anal), by using a penis, a finger, tongue, or an inanimate object. Most rapes involve the use of force, intimidation, or violence. The survivor's acquiescence in response to threats or incapacity does not equal consent (Venes, 2005).

Most rapes are premeditated (planned); most are perpetrated by a known assailant (over half are partners, ex-partners or acquaintances), and a minority by strangers. Rape can occur between married couples and between members of the same sex. Women who are raped by a partner or spouse are much more likely to experience repeated rapes than those raped by strangers (Kernsmith, 2008). They are also more likely never to disclose having been raped (Myhill & Allen, 2002). While rape can occur at any age, women aged 16–24 are at the highest risk (Myhill & Allen, 2002). Acquaintance (date) rapes are particularly prevalent on university campuses, and are among the most common and least reported rapes (Parrish, Felice & Feroli, 2001).

Rape typically places victims (mostly female) in a life-threatening situation, in which their prime motivation is survival. Rape survivors often sustain internal injuries as well as fractures, dislocated joints, and broken teeth (Kimmel, 2008). Most rapists are larger than their victims, who are subject to intense shock, fear, and possible panic during the rape. Some survivors dissociate during the experience; by doing so, they mentally place themselves somewhere outside their body. Sometimes they have a sense of witnessing the assault as if hovering outside their physical body. A history of having been raped, especially during childhood or adolescence, is consistently linked with subsequent alcohol and drug misuse, raising questions of self-medication for trauma (Preto, 2005).

Women who knew their rapist report higher levels of residual anger and distress when compared with those raped by a stranger (Myhill & Allen, 2002). Issues of self-blame remain an insidious aftermath of rape. Particularly when some social myths assert that women are somehow responsible for rape's occurrence, the tendency to blame oneself lends itself to a potentially self-destructive pattern of misplaced responsibilities.

Social consequences following rape include avoiding places associated with having been raped, going out less than before, and feeling the need to take additional personal security measures (Myhill & Allen, 2002). Stranger rapes appear strongly linked with women's ongoing sense of needing to take additional safety precautions. Fears of being raped again are prevalent among victims (Myhill & Allen, 2002; Zastrow & Kirst-Ashman, 1994).

In addition to any physical and emotional injuries sustained during the rape, survivors are also subject to varying degrees of scepticism, doubt, and even blame for their ordeal. Rape remains the only crime in which the victim is frequently subjected to equal if not more scrutiny than the perpetrator. Especially in cases involving alcohol, some women's reports of rape have met with a 'blame the victim' response. Social workers must be aware of and responsive to the double standards that often apply to rape survivors, and to find ways of resisting the sometimes subtle aspects of oppression that are inflicted on vulnerable people following rape.

Following a rape, survivors often report experiences of shame, confusion, fear, self-blame and rage. Such reactions vary according to circumstances, but often persist for a year or longer. Many women experience symptoms of post-traumatic stress disorder, in which they have flashbacks, nightmares, repeated sightings of the rapist, and maintain a state of hypervigilance (McNally, 2001). Post-traumatic stress syndrome and substance use disorders frequently co-exist, and may make assessment very difficult. Traumatic memories may preclude successful efforts at sobriety, as usage may provide a means of managing intrusive memories and flashbacks (Schumacher, 2008). Ironically, usage also elevates the risk of being re-victimized while under the influence of substances. Social workers must be very mindful of such correlations among vulnerable populations (Stewart & Israeli, 2002).

While the sedative rohypnol is commonly regarded as the 'date rape drug', alcohol is much more statistically prevalent in reported cases of rape by acquaintances. Especially on university campuses, a combination of alcohol and jealousy appears to be the most frequently cited precipitant for 'date rape' (Pittman & Wolfe, 2002; Wood & Sher, 2002). Alcohol is also associated with a reluctance to report rape, especially when women who have been drinking fear that their drinking will result in their being more harshly scrutinized or even blamed for provoking the rape. At a time when young people are beginning to establish autonomy (including drinking habits) as well as relationship patterns, the incidence of relationship violence among students is a cause for concern. Dates that include alcohol and other drugs are more likely also to involve sexual aggression (Pittman & Wolfe, 2002). Risk factors include lacking refusal skills, limited perceived options, and low levels of self-efficacy among young women.

The reported reasons for rape vary. Alcohol remains a predominant culprit. Social learning theory has frequently been used to explain how and why rapists perceive their behaviour as acceptable: they have witnessed it being tolerated or even glamorized elsewhere. Social workers must empower survivors of sexual violence to appreciate that it is neither erotic nor acceptable.

Traumatic bereavement

As most people who have experienced bereavement can attest, it is rarely uncomplicated, but some traumatic circumstances associated with bereavement can make the process even more difficult. Examples include unnatural and violent deaths, such as murder, suicide, or consequences of terrorism. Such circumstances are linked with bereavement being further complicated by fear, horror, anger, and heightened risks of post-traumatic stress disorder (Sadock & Sadock, 2007).

Some clarifications between bereavement and depression are important. Some of the same symptoms associated with depression are often noted during bereavement, including appetite disturbances, sleep disturbances, and irritability (Polansky, 1991). For some people, bereavement is accompanied by impaired immune functioning (Sadock & Sadock, 2007). And while bereavement may trigger depressive episodes for some people, it is nonetheless a very different experience. While depression is a condition (typically cyclical, and often with genetic factors), bereavement is a response to the loss of an important relationship or attachment. While they are not mutually exclusive, the differences are important to remember.

Given the closeness of family relationships and attachments, adjustment to family members' deaths is typically among the most difficult of all life changes (Holmes & Rahe, 1967). Issues that influence the bereavement process include: (a) the timing of the loss; (b) the simultaneous occurrence of multiple losses or other major life cycle changes; (c) a history of traumatic losses and unresolved bereavement; (d) the nature of the death; and (e) the role or function of the person who has died. Untimely losses, such as deaths that occur outside chronological or social expectations (such as the death of a parent's child, or early widowhood) often result in profoundly complicated bereavements for individuals and families. Questions of 'why', survivor guilt, or a sense of inherent injustice often complicate an already difficult process of mourning. The death of a child is probably the most painful type of bereavement (McGoldrick & Walsh, 2005: 187).

A loved one's death by suicide represents one of the more complex forms of bereavement. Some families collude to keep the suicide a secret, although with varying degrees of success. Suicide remains more whispered about than discussed. Unlike cases when death results from illness or accidents, bereaved family members are often the ones who discover the body of their loved one. At that time, the setting becomes a crime scene, and family members implicitly become 'suspects' until proven otherwise. Meanwhile, the family may be facing the prospect of continuing to live in the home where their loved one died violently, along with such reminders as visible blood stains, bullet holes, etc.

The traditional phrasing of someone having 'committed suicide' perpetuates the criminal implications associated with suicide, as no other form of dying does (Parrish & Tunkle, 2003). The Compassionate Friends (2000) guidelines encourage clinicians working with people bereaved following a suicide ('survivors of suicide') to refer to the death in a form similar to that used to refer to any other death. So rather than referring to having 'committed suicide', the preferred phrasing would be 'died of suicide'.

The aftermath of a family member's suicide is often further complicated by the absence of social support that often follows, when neighbours, classmates and colleagues are often at a loss for the right words to say, and opt for saying nothing. In some cases, the very people who would otherwise be supportive at a time of bereavement actually avoid contact, fearing saying the wrong thing. In many cases, the bereaved family members come to feel uncomfortable referring to the deceased by name.

Most parents regard the idea of their child's death as their worst fear. A child's death by suicide represents a prospect that most parents consider unimaginable, despite rising rates of adolescent suicides in recent decades. Among adolescents, exposure to domestic vilence, family histories of suicide, and a history of child sexual abuse are among the factors that increase the risk of suicide (Parrish & Tunkle, 2005). They are also factors that would complicate a family's capacity to cope with such a traumatic bereavement as a child's suicide.

Feelings of guilt and anger are among the factors that may complicate bereavement, especially following a violent or self-inflicted death. Thoughts of things done or undone, or words said or unspoken may preoccupy the bereaved, along with a sense of having missed opportunities to have prevented the death. Existential dilemmas of injustice and a sense of unreality may also complicate bereavement, particularly when families have no body to bury, and no means of finding meaning in what has happened. Social workers must be sensitive to issues of anger and forgiveness that may impede some individuals' and families' bereavement process.

Implications for practice

Social workers are often ideally placed to appreciate that children with histories of trauma are not necessarily functioning at their predictable age or developmental level. This can be particularly relevant when working with adolescents, who are sometimes regarded as 'manipulative' or unsympathetic, when in fact, they are angry at the injustices they have experienced at the hands of both personal and societal perpetrators of trauma.

The high rates of reported abuse that are either unsubstantiated or retracted for various reasons remain among the dilemmas and stressors of working with children and adolescents who have reported sexual abuse. Social workers are urged to remember that sexual abuse typically occurs in the very complex context of a child's home or closest relationships. Neither the report nor the recanting of a report alone is sufficient to 'prove' or 'disprove' the alleged abuse. Social workers must listen very carefully in order to respond to children whose needs and lives are often complex. Particularly when working with adolescents, social workers are urged to consider their developmental age (which may be considerably younger than their chronological age or physical appearance!) when trying to assess what has actually occurred. For some children, the prospect of the shame and stigma associated with disclosure is a higher price than ongoing abuse, particularly when the perpetrator holds financial power over the family.

When working with survivors of abuse and violence, the use and abuse of power is a crucial element of the discussions that must take place. Social workers are often in a crucial position to discuss the distinctions between healthy and unhealthy use of power to survivors of abuse and violence. When adults choose to have sexual relations with children, then it is a breach of power, as they are not equals in the decision-making process. Such clarifications may diminish lingering issues of self-blame among children. Children's innate sense of justice and fairness can often be applied to understanding the imbalance of power in sexually abusive relationships in terms of its inherent injustice based on adults having more authority.

Domestic/family violence has far-reaching implications for most social workers' case loads. Unless sensitive questions are asked, many children's lives will continue to be complicated by its effects. Effective staff training has been known to double the number of reported cases (Hester, 2006). In cases of family violence, what we don't know really can hurt others. Social workers cannot afford to minimize the implications of domestic/family violence, or its impact on children. Particularly in cases involving black women and their families, social workers must address the systemic barriers to help that are even greater than is typically the case for white women and their families.

When working with violent families, social workers are ideally suited to recognize issues of insecure attachment and developmental difficulties, in addition to women's issues of safety. When working with women and children in refuges, social workers are in crucial positions to emphasize the strengths that mothers and children bring, having survived such extraordinary circumstances. Individual, family and group interventions are generally considered relevant for working with women and children in refuges following domestic violence. Such work entails considerably more than routine child-minding or play time for children exposed to violence (Mullender, 1996).

While research does not indicate that any specific racial or ethnic groups are more or less prone to domestic violence, services remain very inequitable. Many Asian and African Caribbean women have found social workers unhelpful when responding to domestic violence in their homes and communities, which has not helped families at risk (Mullender, 1996). Social workers must exercise cultural and racial sensitivity with assessments and services provided to black women and their families at risk of violence.

When working with rape survivors, social workers must remember the importance of immediate support and finding ways in which survivors can relay their fears and rage to responsive loved ones, compassionate medical professionals, and understanding law enforcement personnel. Knowing that justice has occurred, including the arrest and conviction of the rapist is generally beneficial for the survivor. Group therapy with other survivors has proven effective for many (Sadock & Sadock, 2007).

When working with individuals or families following a traumatic bereavement, social workers are urged to approach families in ways that diminish shame and stigma. Special attention to pointing out the ways in which the suicide could not have been realistically anticipated or averted may facilitate families' adaptations and processes of forgiveness.

Understanding the roles played by the mental and physical responses to stress is crucial to effective social work practice. On an individual basis, stress may be experienced as various forms of anxiety. Such anxiety may be *acute* or sudden, or it may be *chronic* or long-term. The ways in which it is manifested will vary according to developmental, personal and social variables. While crisis interventions are generally brief, social workers often encounter people both during and after traumatic events. A biopsychosocial perspective is crucial to social workers grasping the complexity of people's circumstances, particularly when trauma is involved.

Social work is a demanding profession, and involves hard work that often goes unthanked. Especially when working with multiproblem families amidst trauma, social workers may find themselves overwhelmed, to the point of questioning their own effectiveness. The capacity for genuineness and empathy remains essential to good practice, which involves facilitating service users to achieve their maximum potential despite adversity.

Stress management remains one of the concerns that often applies to social workers whose case loads entail high levels of trauma. When professionals reach a saturation point with various responsibilities, risks of 'burnout' become a serious concern. Burnout entails an array of symptoms and attitudes, including apathy, exhaustion, cynicism, feelings of helplessness/hopelessness, and a loss of enthusiasm about work and even life in general (Zastrow, 2007). It can also reflect what is sometimes called 'secondary trauma', which has been noted among emergency workers responding to massive trauma (such as the 7 July 2005 bombings in London, and 11 September 2001 in the US), as well as those whose case loads involve intense levels of personal trauma. Such workers have an experiential knowledge of just how unfair life can be. Professionals may find themselves experiencing symptoms similar to those of their service users, including intrusive traumatic thoughts, a generalized state of anxiety, a sense of impending danger, avoidance of trauma-related events or places, or some degree of emotional numbing. This may be further compounded by difficulties in personal relationships and home life (Everett & Gallop, 2001). Social workers remain human, despite some super-human expectations, and issues of stress management must be taken seriously in relation to how they relate to good practice.

The following vignette represents an example of how difficult case loads and personal difficulties can take their toll, even among capable and well-intended professionals.

Kate is a social work student whose practice learning placement is in a team working with asylum seekers, many of whom are children and young adults. Many of the children have been orphaned by civil wars, and quite a few have undergone amputations from land mine explosions. Her supervisor has been working with this population for over ten years, and is a very capable professional. Kate considers herself very fortunate to be able to observe some of the adroit ways in which her supervisor (Julia) interacts with the children and young people, to establish the level of rapport that is necessary for them to begin the disclosure of their traumatic circumstances. Some of the necessary discussions are emotionally exhausting and Kate sometimes finds herself in tears after listening.

Julia is well known as a compassionate and dedicated supervisor for social work students. Kate finds supervision sessions rewarding and supportive. She is amazed at Julia's fortitude in the face of repeated disclosures of torture, bereavement and loss. Kate is also aware that Julia has a teenage child with severe learning disabilities living at home and that Julia's marriage recently ended bitterly.

About three months into her placement, Kate began noticing that Julia was delegating an increasing number of cases to the students, and that her paperwork was no longer being kept up to her usual high standards. Julia also seemed unable to shake off a chest infection and cold, and had a chronic cough about which her students worried. There were times when Kate wondered if perhaps Julia was finally overwhelmed, and too exhausted to absorb any more traumatic cases. Kate was assigned the assessment of two sisters who had recently arrived, in order to begin arrangements for their being granted asylum. The morning she was to begin their assessment, Kate arrived at her office on time, but when she went to go meet the two sisters, she burst into tears at her desk. When Julia found her there, still weeping after nearly an hour, Kate confessed to her that she was in something of a state, following her aged but beloved cat's death the night before. To Kate's despair, Julia berated her for thinking the death of a pet was anything to compare with what the two sisters she was assigned to assess had experienced.

The following day, Julia apologized sincerely to Kate, and confessed that she was experiencing tremendous strains maintaining her professional responsibilities. She wondered aloud whether she had reached a point of professional burnout, but also commented on how she truly loved her work. Julia observed that her work with asylum-seeking young people gave her a sense of purpose, and that even during the worst days of her recent divorce, her sense of professional gratification had sustained her sense of self-worth, even when her personal life did not.

Kate's and Julia's case is an example of how some highly skilled professionals are also human, and can become overwhelmed by professional and personal demands. Julia, a dedicated professional and gifted supervisor, reached a point of mental and emotional overload, and was consequently unable to appreciate the emotional circumstances of a young student. Prolonged periods of high stress are also associated with impaired immune system functions and susceptibility to infections (Sadock & Sadock, 2007). As most social services agencies can attest, infections and illness are associated with higher rates of absenteeism and the subsequent staffing difficulties those entail.

Finding and maintaining equilibrium between over-involvement with vulnerable, highly demanding case loads and a balanced personal life is not easy. Social workers and students are strongly encouraged to seek out supervision from seasoned professionals who have found healthy strategies to maintain both professional and personal commitments simultaneously. At the very least, social workers must learn to look after their own health and well-being with the same diligence with which they propose to look after those of others.

Questions

1 Identify some of your concerns for 13-year-old 'Letty' whose history includes the following:
- Sexual abuse between ages 5 and 9 by two different 'boyfriends' of her mother.
- Early physical maturation (looks older than her age).
- She now dresses very seductively.
- She is preparing to meet a 30-year-old married man whom she met on-line last week, who believes she is 18.

2 Try to recall an incident that evoked a sudden rush of fear or excitement for you (a near-miss car accident, a suspected burglary, a sudden perceived threat, etc.). What do you recall of your physical responses? How do these reactions relate to the fight-or-flight response?

3 Read Mary, Queen of Scots' history and form small groups to discuss the following questions:

> The early life of Mary, Queen of Scots (1542–1587) is among the more familiar historical examples of complicated bereavement. Her father died during the first week of Mary's life. The child-queen's early life was spent in the care of various nobility and monks, assigned to protect her from such dangers as kidnapping, attack, religious conversion, or murder. At age five, her French mother sent Mary to live in the safety of the Catholic court in France, where her uncles were influential, and where she spent the next twelve years. One of the highlights of Mary's remaining childhood was her mother's only visit when she was seven. She was betrothed to the Dauphin of France at age 12, and married him at age 15. Within an 18-month period (1559–60), Mary's father-in-law, her husband, and her mother all died. During her husband's brief reign, Mary's uncles were responsible for the deaths of 1200 men following a rebellion. Following her husband's death (1560), Mary returned to her Scottish homeland in 1561. She remarried (against advice) in 1565. Her second husband, Lord Darnley, proved to be unstable and violent. While Mary was pregnant with their only child, her husband killed her Italian secretary inside her apartments. She fled from Darnley shortly after giving birth (1566), and he was murdered soon thereafter (Feb. 1567). Twice-widowed, orphaned, and mother to an infant son, Mary was abducted by still another violent, jealous man, the Earl of Bothwell, who was suspected of murdering Darnley. Mary married Bothwell three months after Darnley's death. Two months later, at age 24, Mary abdicated her throne in favour of her year-old son, whom she never saw again.

(a) How might unresolved grief have influenced some of her decisions (such as relationships, remarriage, religion, etc.)?
(b) How might her age have influenced Mary's bereavement processes?
(c) How might complicated bereavement have influenced Mary's capacity to parent her newborn son?

4 Read the following scenario:

> 'Stan' (age 45) was married with three children, ages 3 months, 12 and 14. His 15-year marriage to 'Sue' was turbulent, and they had separated on three different occasions during the final two years. Their 3-month old son had been an unplanned pregnancy that resulted from a brief reconciliation. Their two daughters (April and Abby) spent much of their time living with their paternal aunt and uncle, with whom they were very close.
>
> Stan and Sue recently asked that the girls spend the bank holiday weekend with their aunt and uncle, in order that they could have some private time with the new baby. Several bitter arguments erupted, and Sue left the house on Saturday with the baby, without telling Stan where she was going. He phoned his sister, his parents, and various friends during the weekend, trying to locate Sue. On one of his calls, his oldest daughter (April) answered the phone. She could tell that her father was distressed, and that he had been drinking, and asked if he wanted her to come home to keep him company, but he insisted that she stay where she was. Although a bit of a rebel, April was closer to Stan than to her mother, and generally took his side in any argument. Abby typically tried to distract them from their disagreements, and found ways to placate all concerned.
>
> No further calls came from Stan, so his sister Frances and his daughters presumed he and Sue had resolved their differences. Abby and April had spent the day with friends, and had been pleased to be invited to a care-free swimming outing that both had thoroughly enjoyed. When neither Stan nor Sue arrived to collect the girls on Monday evening, however, Frances became concerned. She could not get through to Stan's or Sue's mobile numbers, and eventually phoned their neighbours to ask if they could tell if Stan was at home. Stan's neighbours phoned back about an hour later, to tell Frances that the police and ambulance had been called, as it appeared that Stan had collapsed on the kitchen floor.
>
> The emergency crews discovered that Stan had died of a deliberate ingestion of poison on Sunday night. Because she had spoken with him on Sunday afternoon, April became convinced that she should or could have said or done something to prevent her father's suicide. Both his sister and their parents had similar convictions about their own conversations with Stan. Both April and Abby blamed their mother for her having left Stan at the time, despite knowing that their arguments could sometimes erupt into extreme verbal savagery.

Form small groups to consider and discuss the following questions:

- What are some of the important family dynamics displayed in Stan's family?
- What are some areas of blame and shame that you think have been or will be relevant to this family?
- What are your concerns for Stan's children?
- Why?

Following Stan's suicide, Sue moved with the three children to a different area, where she said they could start life anew. The girls were instructed that they should only tell people that their father died in an accident; their baby brother was not told how his father died until the subject arose for purposes of a family medical history when he was in his thirties. April and Abby rarely saw their aunt and uncle during the following years, until both were adults. Even then, they never discussed their father's death with anyone but each other for the rest of their lives. Meanwhile, April embarked on three unhappy marriages to much older men. Abby married very young and later looked after their mother through a prolonged final illness. Only when faced with prospects of teaching their own young children to swim did the sisters realize that neither had gone swimming again since the day their father died.

Please consider the following concepts in relation to Stan's family and traumatic bereavement:

Developmental implications

Relationship implications

Issues of anger, guilt, and secrecy

How was the family's bereavement likely to differ from the bereavement experienced following a natural death?

10 Influences of mental health, alcohol, and other drugs on behaviour

Mental health problems feature prominently in most social workers' practice, regardless of their specified area of expertise. From understanding the interplay between child protection and parental mental health and substance misuse, to the over-diagnosis of women with severe mental illness following trauma, to the role of co-existing depression and alcohol dependence across an array of lifelong problems, social workers must be informed and responsive to the complexities of mental health concerns that influence people's behaviours.

This chapter addresses some basic mental health concerns frequently found among social workers' case loads: mood disorders (depression and bipolar disorder), post-traumatic stress disorder (PTSD), schizophrenia, and issues of suicidality. It will also address some of the compounding implications of alcohol and drugs, and their mental health implications.

Relevance for social work

Social workers are in key positions to appreciate the complexities of mental health difficulties. A disproportionate number of children who are subjects of child protection conferences have at least one parent with mental health problems (Cleaver et al., 1999). From recognizing the debilitating effects of post-natal depression among new mothers, to working with teenagers with (often undiagnosed) post-traumatic stress disorder, to coordinating services for vulnerable adults with psychotic illnesses, to the potentially suicidal levels of depression noted among older adults, social workers are in crucial positions to observe, recognize, and respond to a daunting array of mental health conditions in their routine practice. Social workers must remember that mental health difficulties are not always a neutral subject; personal experiences and social history combine to make mental health concerns a source of fear, shame and exclusion for many.

Various labels, stereotypes and stigmas often preclude people with mental health difficulties from having access to the help they need, resulting in a great deal of unnecessary suffering. Social workers must challenge and address those barriers, as they represent an insidious form of oppression. One of the ways in which social workers can help do this is to be well informed about different mental health conditions, and what those conditions entail in terms of risks, characteristic symptoms, and effective treatment. Another way social workers can help is to be sufficiently well informed about various conditions in order to advocate for service users' needs being accurately met based on medical as well as psychosocial factors. Still another way social workers can resist the pervasive exclusion and stigmatization of vulnerable people is to be diligent in avoiding using conditions as labels. Again, social workers are urged to refer to people having various conditions (e.g. 'having schizophrenia'), rather than referring to people according to the conditions they have (e.g. 'schizophrenic', 'depressive', 'anorexic').

The use of labels has historical implications for mental health conditions. Terms such as 'madness', 'lunacy', and 'insanity' are often ill-defined, but powerful ways of describing and dismissing people in distress. Rosenhan's (1973) classic treatise 'On Being Sane in Insane Places' (Rosenhan, 1996) remains a cautionary tale of how easily labels are applied, especially when compared with removing them. Historically, women have been particularly vulnerable to assessments of so-called abnormality, where patriarchal medical and psychiatric traditions have institutionalized women ostensibly for mental health reasons, which in fact were more likely for reasons ranging from marital disputes to sexual, political, religious, and property-related factors (Chesler, 1996). Even the suffragettes were subjected to efforts to declare them 'insane' on the grounds of wanting votes for women.

People living in poverty and ethnic minorities worldwide appear subject to higher levels of diagnostic labels than their privileged and white counterparts. They are also less likely to have access to mental health services, and the services they receive are likely to be of a lower standard (Luthra et al., 2006; Wilkinson & Pickett, 2009). Social workers must be sensitive to issues of immigration, trauma, racism, the asylum-seeking process, and language barriers as they apply to vulnerable people needing mental health assessment and support.

In recent decades, many social workers in Britain have responded so strongly to the limitations of the medical model that they have effectively shunned it completely, opting instead for a 'social model' approach to understanding mental health. Through applying the social model, social workers often (rightly) emphasize the role society and the environment play in contributing to people's mental health difficulties, but without necessarily addressing some of the consistent diagnostic criteria of various conditions. A brief comparison of approaches follows (Table 10.1).

> Mrs B, age 60, has a history of depression. She has responded well to low doses of an antidepressant. She has fallen during the night twice in the past six months. The first time she broke her arm, and the second time she broke her leg. She now appears withdrawn and sad.

Table 10.1 Medical, social, and bio-psychosocial perspectives

Medical model	*Social model*	*Bio-psychosocial model*
X-ray Mrs B's limbs	Consider whether Mrs B's home is safe	Interview Mrs B to learn about her life
Apply casts to stabilize Mrs B's limbs	Remove scatter rugs on which she could trip	Learn that Mrs B was recently suddenly widowed
Remove casts when limbs are sufficiently healed	Improve lighting to improve visibility	Learn that since being widowed, Mrs B has been having several strong drinks at night to help her sleep
		Learn that Mrs B stopped taking her antidepressants three months ago
		Note that the drinks appear to contribute to her getting up during the night to use the bathroom, which was when she fell
		Consider whether bereavement work combined with reducing her alcohol use, plus medical treatment, resuming the antidepressants, and better lighting and fewer rugs would improve Mrs B's situation

From considering Mrs B's situation, the relevance of both the medical model and the social model can be appreciated. Both provide useful means of defining problems. Both are necessary, but not necessarily sufficient to address Mrs B's circumstances. From a bio-psychosocial perspective, social workers are more likely to combine both social and behavioural factors in their assessment process.

Despite its strengths, adhering solely to the social model can sometimes compromise social workers' effectiveness when working with chronically mentally ill populations. Especially when the medical model *misdiagnoses* people, social workers must be sufficiently familiar with diagnostic criteria to be able to advocate effectively for suitable treatment for vulnerable populations. Social workers are ideal advocates for service users who have mental health difficulties, but without some fluency in the diagnostic criteria associated with the medical model, it is difficult, if not impossible, to do so effectively.

Social workers' inherent appreciation of the role of context is vitally important to good practice with people with mental health difficulties. Environmental contributors to stress, substance misuse, and trauma are often key factors in complex mental health difficulties, including violence, homelessness, and recurrence of symptoms. Social workers must find constructive ways of linking social and contextual concerns with sound assessments (medical and social), in order to advocate for and serve the needs of mental health service users. When problems are defined solely according to medical or social dimensions, without the individual's psychological and personal factors also being addressed, service users' needs are unlikely to be adequately met.

Historical considerations

Understanding the *attribution* of causes for mental distress is important because it often determines what the subsequent response to and treatment of various conditions will be. Historic explanations of the causes of mental health difficulties have generally fallen into two main approaches: the supernatural and the organic. The supernatural approach brought us such beliefs as evil spirits or deities causing abnormalities. For example, the ancient Greeks attributed various psychiatric symptoms to 'divine madness', which was regarded with some favour, and seen as something to be interpreted, rather than eliminated.

During and after the Inquisition demonic possession was considered the cause of various abnormalities. Charges of witchcraft were based on the premise that people (mainly women) had been 'bewitched' by Satan, and should therefore be eliminated. 'Lunacy', resulting from the lunar influences (phases of the moon), was a popularly accepted explanation of mental distress for centuries.

From a supernatural approach, the logical response to abnormality may be prayer, or exorcism, or it may be interpretation (in such cases as 'divine madness', which could be considered a gift, rather than a curse). When supernatural explanations entail 'demonic possession', though, the response is more likely to entail interrogation, and possibly extinction (such as the historic burning at the stake or drownings for witchcraft) in order to protect the public from further contamination.

As for the organic approach, Hippocrates (c. 470–c. 370 BC) believed that abnormality was caused by imbalances in the various humours (bodily fluids); for example, an excess of black bile was linked with melancholia. He also proposed that a wandering uterus was the source of hysteria. So while he incorporated an organic causation of abnormality, Hippocrates also precluded the possibility of considering hysteria as being applicable to males.

From an organic approach, the historical responses have included some prospects that would now be considered barbaric, including trephining (drilling holes in the skull), bleedings, diets of milk and seeds, induced insulin comas, and shock treatments. Special asylums for the care of 'lunatics' or the 'insane' date from the eighteenth century, and were designed to segregate those considered abnormal from the general population. The introduction of major tranquilizers in the mid-twentieth century made the course of psychotic illnesses much more manageable for some, but also proved highly controversial as a means of chemically sedating people against their wishes for purposes of social control. Contemporary responses generally rely on the premise that many conditions are responsive to counselling and/or medication in order to alleviate painful symptoms.

The organic approach to explaining mental health conditions is linked with the belief that quite a few of the major categories of diagnoses are associated with genetic patterns. Some conditions (e.g. the mood disorders, schizophrenia, and alcohol dependence) tend to run in families. Genetic links for various conditions are supported by adoption studies and by twin studies, where concordance rates are as high as 70 per cent for both MZ twins having bipolar disorder when one has that condition (Passer et al., 2009). That does not mean that having a family member with a mental health condition necessarily predestines other family members to have that condition; it means that when we find family histories of a given condition, then there is a greater likelihood of finding it among other family members. These genetic patterns are similar to those noted among various medical conditions, such as diabetes and glaucoma.

Medical conditions, however, rarely carry the same degree of stigma as is found with mental health conditions.

Key concepts regarding mental health

The consideration of mental health difficulties is linked with concepts of 'abnormality' (meaning literally, 'away from the norm'). For most people, 'normality' falls somewhere along a continuum, and is rarely an absolute or fixed state. Most people experience a range of manageable emotional states and behavioural patterns as being 'normal' during any given day, without those variations posing a problem. Delineating 'abnormality' is a very inexact science. The main measures of 'abnormality' generally depend upon behavioural manifestations. Unlike medical conditions that can be determined through blood tests or X-rays, the recognition and categorization of mental health conditions rely primarily on observations of behaviour and upon people's ability to describe their own internal states (such as sadness, mania or anxiety). Ironically, the nature of some conditions (such as major depressive episodes and some psychotic conditions) often compromises people's ability to articulate what they are experiencing. The important capacity to elicit people's trust in the discussion of symptoms is sometimes more of an art than science.

The accurate use of terms and diagnoses is crucial when working with mental health concerns. Without careful and accurate use of terms, conditions become mere labels, and people's well-being can be jeopardized. This is particularly true for vulnerable populations, especially children. The two primary sources of diagnostic criteria used in Europe and the US are the World Health Organization's (1993) *International Classification of Diseases*, 10th edn (ICD-10), and the American Psychiatric Association's (2000) *Diagnostic and Statistical Manual IV-T-R* (DSM-IV-T-R). Despite their imperfections, the two sources of criteria provide a systematic means of categorizing symptoms associated with mental disorders.

Both the WHO and the APA acknowledge the inexact nature of defining abnormality in the framework of a 'disorder'. The WHO points out the imprecise meaning of the term disorder, but considers it preferable to such terms as 'disease' or 'illness' (WHO, 1992). The ICD-10 defines a mental disorder as:

> A clinically recognizable set of symptoms or behaviour associated in most cases with distress and with interference with personal functions. Social deviance or conflict alone, without personal dysfunction, should not be included in mental disorder as defined here.
>
> (WHO, 1992: 5)

The DSM-IV-T-R (APA, 2000: xxxi) defines a mental disorder as:

> A clinically significant behavioral or psychological syndrome or pattern associated with distress (e.g., a painful symptom), or with a significantly increased risk of suffering, death, pain, disability, or an important loss of

> freedom. In addition, the syndrome or pattern must not be merely an expected and culturally sanctioned response to a particular event, such as the death of a loved one.

When mental health problems occur, they often entail some basic distortions along the two important dimensions of *manageability* and being *maladaptive*. The concept of *manageability* refers to the varied emotions that most people routinely experience, but which remain functional and do not represent a problem. When emotional states (moods, anxiety, their perspectives on reality, etc.) or behaviours become unmanageable, then the ability to function is likely to become compromised. For example, if a mood state becomes manic, and is no longer manageable, then the risks of engaging in potentially self-destructive behaviours are high. In cases of psychotic episodes (such as are associated with schizophrenia), then hearing voices urging behaviours that are potentially dangerous, and which cannot be reliably anticipated by those around them may occur. Such experiences would entail emotional states and behaviours that are no longer effectively manageable by the individual.

The concept of being *maladaptive* refers to emotions, thoughts or behaviours that no longer serve the individual's best interests, and which compromise their ability to function. Most of the time, people can rely on having the capacity to adapt to various circumstances, events, or stressors that occur. Adaptive responses allow people to interact with others and cope effectively with new variables in their lives. When responses become maladaptive, people's thoughts, emotions, or behaviours are likely to become counterproductive and problematic. For example, if a person's response to having a hard day at work is to go home and become violent with their loved ones, then that is a maladaptive response to stress. If a university student's response to receiving a 'B' instead of the 'A' they expected on an assignment is to drown their sorrows with a bottle of gin and consider suicide, then that is a maladaptive response. Taken to extremes, maladaptive thoughts, emotions and behaviours may entail phobias, violence, high-risk behaviours, social withdrawal, and paranoid suspicions, to name a few. Such states represent maladaptive behaviours, thoughts and emotions that can prove counterproductive to the individual's overall level of functioning. An example of emotions and behaviours that have become unmanageable and maladaptive follows:

'Mandy' is 22 years old, with 5-year-old twin sons by her partner Jeff, who is 45. Mandy was a 16-year-old in care when she met Jeff; he was the TV repairman who came to her foster parents' home. Mandy had been in care for five years at the time. She had been neglected by her birth mother, and sexually abused throughout most of her childhood by her mother's partners. When they met, Jeff was recently divorced from his second wife. He paid Mandy a lot of attention, which she craved, where she was but one of five children in the home.

Mandy and Jeff saw each other secretly for some months. When her foster parents learned that she was seeing a man who was actually older than they were, they were concerned, and tried to convince Mandy to stop seeing Jeff. By that time, however, Mandy was pregnant. She moved out of her foster parents' home into Jeff's flat. She is still friendly with her former foster parents, although she knows they disapprove of Jeff, as they consider him something of a bully.

During the past two years, Mandy has gone to the casualty unit approximately thirty different times, complaining of chest pains, dizziness and shortness of breath. No organic cause of her symptoms has been found, and the hospital staff has come to see her as a 'frequent flyer', and do not take her complaints seriously. They have recommended that she seek counselling. Jeff usually accompanied Mandy to the hospital; he tends to ridicule her 'spells', and encourages their sons to see Mandy as a 'silly old cow'. They now join him in mocking her.

Mandy's episodes of chest pains and shortness of breath tend to follow verbal conflicts with Jeff. Mandy is very subservient to Jeff, who is quite demanding and dominant in their relationship. She avoids confrontations, and rarely challenges anything Jeff says, even when she disagrees. Jeff insists that he has never hurt her 'on purpose', although they both reluctantly acknowledge some 'accidental' injuries he has caused Mandy. Her dizziness has now reached a point where she is afraid of going outside their home unaccompanied for fear that she will collapse in public. Thus, she has simultaneously become increasingly isolated, and more dependent on Jeff for all driving, shopping and getting the boys to school, etc. Her most recent episode followed an incident in which she found Jeff berating one of the twins for a bed-wetting episode. Mandy began hyperventilating during the evening, and finally called an ambulance, as she was convinced she was having a heart attack. The (now familiar) ambulance drivers refused to take her to hospital, as her symptoms were inconsistent with cardiac arrest. Jeff and the twins now ridicule her even more than before.

While many of Mandy's presenting symptoms are congruent with what is known as a 'panic attack', they also provide examples of ways in which her emotions and behaviours are no longer within a manageable range, as they are not intentional on her part. She is not able to control or anticipate her episodes of dizziness, chest pains, or shortness of breath. Her symptoms have also become maladaptive, in that they have curtailed her autonomy, and are compromising her relationships with her partner and her children.

As yet, no single cause of mental health conditions has been identified, although various factors are linked with increased *vulnerability*. Children with insecure attachment patterns appear to be at heightened risk associated with subsequent symptoms of depression (Greenberg, 1999). Childhood trauma has been linked with depression and post-traumatic stress syndrome, among other conditions (Everett & Gallop, 2001; Ingram & Price, 2001; Widom, 1998). Experiencing the death of a parent during childhood (particularly before age 11) is associated with an increased risk of subsequent depression (Brown & Harris, 1978; Passer et al., 2009). Genetic linkages have been found in mood disorders, schizophrenia, and alcohol dependence (Friedberg et al., 2000; Ingham & Price, 2001; Sadock & Sadock, 2007). In and of themselves, however, neither life events nor genetics appear sufficient to explain mental health conditions, which do not occur in all survivors of trauma, or among all family members with the same genetic factors.

The *diathesis–stress model* of understanding causation helps to appreciate the role of context, and offers something of a balance between contributing biological and psychosocial factors (Brennan, 2006). For example, having depressed parents appears to predispose children to experience depression (Gladstone & Beardslee, 2000). Living in poverty, and being subjected to violence and abuse also appear to be predisposing factors (Everett & Gallop, 2001; Howe, 2005). Compounding stressors may entail biological factors, psychosocial factors, trauma, or life events, including illness, violence, war, bereavement, drug use, etc. If an individual's inherent level of predisposing risk is greater, then less stress will be necessitated to precipitate or trigger mental health problems. When predisposing risks are minimal, greater degrees of stress may be sustained without precipitating mental health difficulties. Various factors appear to support individuals' resilience, including having consistent, healthy attachments (Howe, 2005). The diathesis–stress relationship helps explain why some people appear more vulnerable to mental health problems than others who have experienced similar events. Congruent with systems theory, a diathesis–stress model provides a means of considering the combined and interactive effects of predisposing vulnerabilities as well as stressful precipitators that would not necessarily be sufficient independently to trigger mental disorders. Such factors remain in the category of risk, however. Social workers are encouraged always to distinguish between risk and destiny; they are quite distinct concepts.

Specific types of mental health conditions

A few of the mental health conditions that social workers are most likely to find among their case loads will now be discussed. Across the different conditions, close observation and listening skills are necessary in order to recognize symptomatic behaviours or difficulties. Mood disorders, schizophrenia and alcohol- and drug-related conditions are all associated with high rates of relapse or recurrence, making assessment and response to those conditions an ongoing and collaborative prospect, rather than a single event. Even acute episodes of most mental health conditions usually emerge gradually. The more gradual or insidious the onset of symptoms, the more difficult they are to detect. Sudden, drastic changes are more likely to be noticed. For that reason, continuity in case loads can play a crucial role in the role social workers can play in recognizing and responding to mental health problems among their cases.

Mood disorders

The mood disorders are among the mental health conditions social workers are most likely to encounter on a regular basis. Mood disorders involve an array of complex symptoms, which may be confused with medical conditions. They frequently co-occur alongside other conditions, including anxiety and substance-related conditions, which can complicate accurate assessment and response to symptoms (Craig, 2006).

Formerly referred to as 'affective disorders', the term 'mood disorders' refers to several conditions, including depression and bipolar disorder. Mood disorders have a long, complex history. Examples of depression ('melancholia') can be found throughout Greek and Roman histories, in the Bible, as well as in Shakespeare's works. King David, Martin Luther, Edvard Munch, William James, Winston Churchill, Cole Porter, Sylvia Plath, Virginia Woolfe, John Lennon, and Yves Saint Laurent are but a few of the more prominent examples of people who have experienced major depression. As you may realize, several of them also combined heavy alcohol intake with depression. Examples of prominent people believed to have bipolar disorder include Georg Frederic Handel, Vincent van Gogh, F. Scott Fitzgerald, Ernest Hemingway, Irving Berlin, Spike Milligan, and Stephen Fry, many of whom experienced hospitalizations for their conditions (Jamison, 1996). Histories of alcohol and drug misuse are also prominent in the lives of several of those noted.

For the purposes of this discussion, the four main examples of mood disorder that will be considered are major depression, dysthymia, cyclothymia, and bipolar disorder. Dysthymia and cyclothymia are considered 'persistent' mood disorders in the ICD-10. Conceptualizing the range of mood disorders is possibly simplified by thinking along a continuum (Figure 10.1).

Major depression ———— "Normality" ———— Bipolar disorder
(Dysthymia) (Cyclothymia)

Figure 10.1 A continuum of mood states.

Major depression affects multiple dimensions of a person's life. Considered from a bio-psychosocial perspective, it could be represented as overlapping areas that are defined by the depression. Figure 10.2 provides an example of how those overlapping influences could be portrayed.

The point at which all three spheres overlap can intensify the difficulties a person with depression experiences. In the biological dimension, the neurotransmitters serotonin and norepinephrine are consistently linked with depression, further supporting the biological nature of mood disorders (Pritchard, 2006; Sadock & Sadock, 2007). They appear to play a part both in the course and symptoms of depressive episodes as well as the effectiveness of antidepressant medication. Further, when someone with depression experiences sleep deprivation, they may also have difficulty concentrating on otherwise routine tasks, along with becoming irritable. Similarly, a person with depression who experiences fatigue associated with depression may also find it difficult to maintain basic responsibilities (such as parenting, attending classes, going to work, etc.). Such struggles may contribute to a sense of failure or hopelessness (thus exemplifying Beck's 'negative triad' discussed in Chapter 7). They may then see their entire life as having been pointless, their current situation as disastrous, and their future as an unbearably bleak prospect. Such interpretations raise risks of suicidality.

Depression can and does occur across the lifespan. Increased rates of clear symptoms of depression have been noted among children during recent decades (Hammen, 1997; Kaslow et al., 1999). Among children, emotionally clinging behaviours, school phobias, and withdrawal may be manifestations of mood disorders. Irritability and loss

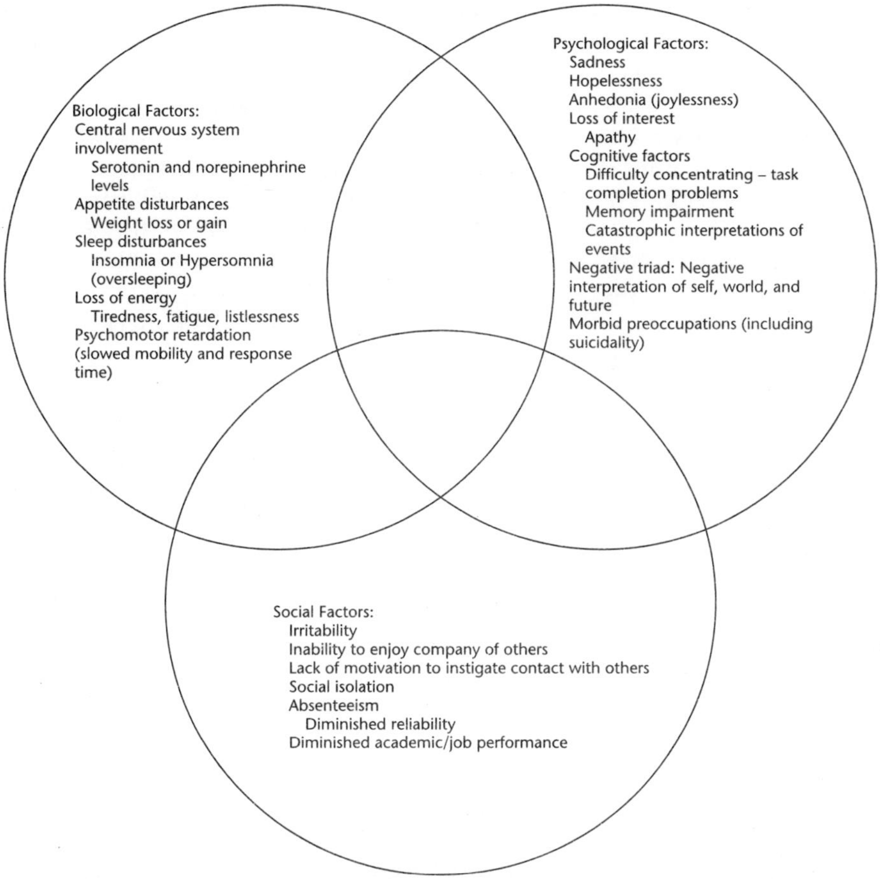

Figure 10.2 Biological, psychological and social factors relating to depression.

of appetite are noted features of depression among children and adolescents. Girls appear at greater risk of depression than boys, beginning at the transition from childhood to adolescence (Garber & Flynn, 2001; Taylor et al., 1995). Among adolescents, running away, substance misuse, and antisocial behaviour are often linked with depression. Family histories of depression appear particularly noteworthy when assessing children and adolescents for depression (Sadock & Sadock, 2007).

Depression is often under-diagnosed in later life, as it can be mistaken for a number of other conditions, including bereavement, memory loss, and physical decline. Various physical conditions, particularly diabetes and strokes are linked with a higher risk of depression (Dew, 1998). When older adults become socially isolated following retirement or being widowed, depression may easily go unrecognized because of the diminished opportunities to be observed by others.

Debates continue regarding whether women are more subject to depression, or whether women are more socialized to acknowledge their mood states and seek help with problems, and thus are over-represented in the statistics (Prior, 1999; Rogers & Pilgrim, 2005). Women have historically been more readily diagnosed with 'neuroses', which is no longer considered a valid diagnostic term, and which may have deflected attention from genuine depression (Appignanesi, 2008). Women worldwide consistently appear to have a higher incidence of depression than men, and with earlier onsets; women also appear to be at greater risk for anxiety disorders, which frequently co-occur with depression (Kohn et al., 1998; Hammen, 1997). In the UK, women are three times as likely as men to be diagnosed and hospitalized with depression (Cochrane, 1995; Gross, 2001). Women with physical illnesses appear particularly vulnerable to depression and anxiety (Dew, 1998). Despite women's higher rates of diagnosed and treated depression, however, men are at greater risk of dying from suicide across every age group (Pritchard, 2006).

Depressive episodes typically last two weeks or longer (APA, 2000). Children and adolescents tend to have prolonged and recurrent depressive episodes (Kaslow et al., 1999). While some depressive episodes are isolated events, they tend to be cyclical, meaning that they happen repeatedly. For most people, the periods of time between depressive episodes entail full remission, or a return to their previous level of functioning. Thus extended periods of wellness may well occur between depressive episodes (Sadock & Sadock, 2007). Some people experience seasonal patterns of depressive symptoms, particularly during the winter months (between September and April). 'Seasonal affective disorder' (SAD) is a type of depression that is associated with the seasonal changes in natural daylight that occur during the autumn and winter. Unlike other types of depression, SAD appears responsive to treatment with light boxes that replicate aspects of longer hours of sunlight (Kinsella & Kinsella, 2006).

Major depression has long been recognized as a debilitating condition, but the ways in which people have understood depression have changed considerably over the centuries. According to the DSM-IV-T-R criteria, major depression entails two or more depressive episodes, with at least a two-month interval between episodes. Depressive episodes represent a period of two weeks or more, in which the following symptoms represent a change from the person's previous level of functioning. The depressive symptoms are clearly distinct from medical conditions. The DSM-IV-T-R specifies that depressive symptoms must be distinct from bereavement. Regrettably, neither the DSM nor ICD criteria include distinct categories for childhood or adolescent mood disorders. Depressive symptoms are the source of 'clinically significant' distress or impairment in social, occupational, and other important areas of functioning for the individual. Five or more of the following symptoms characterize a major depressive episode:

A depressed mood most of the day, nearly every day, as indicated by either subjective report (feels sad or empty) or observation made by others (e.g., appears tearful). Note: In children and adolescents, can be irritable mood.

Markedly diminished interest or pleasure in all, or almost all, activities most of the day, nearly every day (as indicated by either subjective account or observations made by others).

Significant weight loss when not dieting or weight gain (e.g., a change of more than 5% of body weight in a month, or decrease or increase in appetite nearly every day). Note: In children, consider failure to make expected weight gains or growth.

Insomnia or hypersomnia (oversleeping) nearly every day.

Psychomotor agitation or retardation nearly every day (observable by others, not merely subjective feelings of restlessness or being slowed down).

Fatigue or loss of energy nearly every day.

Feelings of worthlessness, low self-esteem, or excessive or inappropriate guilt (which may be delusional) nearly every day (not merely self-reproach or guilt about being sick).

Diminished ability to think or concentrate, or indecisiveness, nearly every day (either by subjective account or as observed by others).

Recurrent thoughts of death (not just fear of dying), recurrent suicidal ideation without a specific plan, or a suicide attempt or a specific plan for committing suicide.

(APA, 2000: 356)

Dysthymia is a subtype of depression, involving a chronic pattern of depressed mood, and was only introduced into the diagnostic lexicon in 1980. Prior to 1980, people who met the criteria for what is now called dysthymia were relegated to the somewhat dismissive category of 'depressive neurosis' (Sadock & Sadock, 2007).

Dysthymia is less debilitating than a major depressive episode, but more enduring. Psychotic features (such as delusions or hallucinations) are not present with dysthymia. In some cases, however, people with dysthymia also experience a major depressive episode, superimposed upon the dysthymia, which is called 'double depression' (Maxmen & Ward, 1995).

Because of its early onset and chronicity, people with dysthymia often regard their low mood state as normal, or the only way they remember ever being. Thus, they are unlikely to see themselves as needing help, because of having no other frame of reference with which to compare their mood state. Dysthymic features may be more subtle than would be the case in major depression, including habitual gloominess, negativity, and humourlessness. Dysthymia is associated with considerable personal difficulties, including irritability, sarcasm, anger, poor relationships with others, and diminished productivity. Dysthymia is often associated with behaviours that others find annoying, including the 'help-rejecting complainer'. It often coexists with other mental health conditions, particularly major depression, substance misuse disorders, and personality disorders (Sadock & Sadock, 2007). The morose character of Eeyore and the television character Victor Meldrew might demonstrate several of the classic characteristics of dysthymia.

According to the DSM-IV-T-R (APA, 2000), dysthymia (meaning 'ill humoured') is primarily distinguished from a major depression by its onset, duration and its severity. Dysthymia usually entails a gradual but youthful onset (before age 20), and persists for at least two years (or one among children). While it is more chronic than a typical depressive episode, it is less acute (less severe). People with dysthymia often have extensive family histories of relations with mood disorders (depressive and bipolar) (Sadock & Sadock, 2007). Otherwise, the essential characteristic features of depression are also found among people with dysthymia (APA, 2000), which include two or more of the following (over a prolonged period over 2 years or more among adults):

Appetite disturbance (poor appetite or overeating)
Sleep disturbance (insomnia or hypersomnia)
Low energy, fatigue
Low self-esteem
Concentration difficulties, including indecisiveness
Feelings of hopelessness.

(APA, 2000)

Bipolar disorder, which was previously known as 'manic depression', is another mood disorder with which social workers often come in contact, although it is less prevalent than depression. Bipolar disorder represents a fluctuation between the extremes of depressed and manic moods (Passer et al., 2009).

The onset of bipolar disorder is generally young (during the late teens or early twenties), and it tends to occur at a younger age among men than women (Kinsella & Kinsella, 2006). Its course tends to be chronic, as it tends to involve cyclical or recurrent episodes of depression and mania (Ingram & Fortier, 2001). Bipolar disorder is even more strongly associated with family histories of mood disorders than is found with depression.

Mania involves euphoric and grandiose thoughts, in which people's perceptions of their capacities are often sufficiently distorted that they do not perceive realistic limitations to their abilities. Such distortions can impair judgement, and result in behaviour that may have significant repercussions for the self and others. Unlike depression, which can evolve very gradually and go unnoticed, a manic episode is generally not only quite noticeable, but virtually impossible to miss because of the individual's erratic behaviour. When manic episodes entail psychotic thinking, they are easily mistaken for schizophrenia (Craig, 2006).

Ironically, the onset of a manic episode may seem not only unremarkable, but even a desirable improvement from a depressive episode. The individual typically experiences an increased level of energy and creativity, which may not seem in need of any remedy. The lifting of the mood state may even precipitate a sense that alcohol seems a much better idea than prescribed medication. Bipolar disorder is often associated with profound levels of chaos and unpredictability. Erratic behaviours, spending sprees, sexual indiscretions, and sensation-seeking behaviours can make life difficult to manage, and take tremendous tolls on personal relationships.

Some people's cycles are relatively rapid, meaning that their episodes happen with greater frequency than those with slower cycles. When manic symptoms are severe and cycles are rapid (i.e. more than four times in a year), physical, social and cognitive functions are subject to considerable disruption (Kinsella & Kinsella, 2006).

According to the DSM-IV-T-R criteria, bipolar disorder involves the combination of depressive episodes and manic episodes, both of which can be debilitating. Manic episodes involve symptoms including an uncharacteristically and persistently elevated mood, lasting at least a week when untreated; they are not the result of substance use (although stimulant usage can mimic mania). Manic symptoms are sufficient to cause impairment in occupational, social, and personal functioning, and may necessitate hospitalization (APA, 2000). During a manic episode, at least three of the following symptoms are persistently present, and there should be four or more when irritability is the primary mood indicator:

- Inflated self-esteem (grandiosity)
- Diminished need for sleep (may actually go without sleep, or only sleep briefly)
- Increased talkativeness (speech may be pressured)
- Flight of ideas (racing thoughts)
- Easily distracted
- Psychomotor agitation, including increased goal-directed, purposeful activity (including social, sexual or work-related tasks)
- Excessive involvement in pleasure seeking activities (including high risks of painful or dangerous consequences such as sexual indiscretions, unwise decisions, poor assessment of danger, etc.).

(APA, 2000: 362)

Mania may involve severe symptoms, such as delusions (fixed, irrational beliefs) and hallucinations, which are generally considered psychotic features. When psychotic features are present in bipolar disorder, they are generally congruent with the predominant mood state (depression or mania). Untreated manic episodes may endure for up to three months (Sadock & Sadock, 2007).

Cyclothymia is related to bipolar disorder in similar ways to the relationship between dysthymia and major depression. Cyclothymia entails at least two years of chronically fluctuating mood disturbances that frequently meet the criteria for hypomania, but without meeting the full criteria for mania (APA, 2000). *Hypomania* involves a distinct period of 'persistently elevated, expansive, or irritable mood, lasting throughout at least four days, that is clearly different from the usual non-depressed mood' (APA, 2000: 365). Clear differences between hypomania and the individual's usual mood state are important considerations. Hypomania does not involve psychotic thinking, nor is it the result of substance use. It entails at least three of the following symptoms:

- Inflated self-esteem (grandiosity)
- Diminished need for sleep (e.g., sleeps for short periods and feels sufficiently rested)
- More talkative than usual
- Flight of ideas, or racing thoughts
- Shortened attention span (easily distracted)
- Psychomotor agitation (increased goal-directed, focused activity, including sexual energy)
- Excessive involvement in pleasure seeking activities (including high risks of painful or dangerous consequences such as sexual indiscretions, unwise decisions, poor assessment of danger, etc.).

(APA, 2000: 368)

Schizophrenia

The psychotic condition schizophrenia is often regarded as the most dreaded of mental disorders. Schizophrenia involves an array of cognitive and behavioural symptoms, and may actually represent several different conditions with different causes. The history of studying schizophrenia is linked with two names: Emil Kraepelin (1856–1926) and Eugen Bleuler (1857–1939). Kraeplin introduced the term 'dementia praecox' to classify the group of disorders that entailed a chronic and degenerative course that is now associated with schizophrenia. Bleuler actually introduced the term schizophrenia in 1911. When Bleuler used the term 'schizophrenia', he referred to a shattering of the mind, referring to disconnections between emotions, thoughts and behaviours. Subsequently, however, schizophrenia has commonly been confused with the term 'split personality', which is now referred to as dissociative identity disorder, and is a very distinct condition (Sadock & Sadock, 2007). Media representations of people manifesting extremely erratic behaviours have contributed to many people's misunderstanding of a very complex condition.

Careful attention to the features and characteristics of schizophrenia is essential to good practice. Misdiagnoses represent a sinister reflection of institutionalized racism, with disproportionate rates of schizophrenia being found among immigrant and ethnic minority groups (Singh & Burns, 2006). Some would also argue that schizophrenia is very much a reflection of cultural concepts and orientations, and may sometimes just reflect an intensified version of the human condition (Jenkins, 2004).

Various theories have been applied to explain the cause of schizophrenia. Psychoanalytic theorists have proposed that schizophrenia results from fixations resulting from early intrapsychic conflicts and inadequate object relations, with psychotic symptoms seen as a regression to oral or anal stages, involving impaired ego functions and the loss of reality testing. Symptoms are considered symbolic, and may represent unconscious wishes or urges. Family theorists Bateson and Jackson proposed that schizophrenia resulted from children receiving messages from parents that entailed a 'double bind', in which they were necessarily somehow going to fail. (Their premise was never replicated.) Family patterns of *pseudomutual and pseudohostile* expressions of emotions have been proposed as causes of schizophrenia. Likewise, families' levels of expressed emotional content, where children's schizophrenia has been attributed to more confrontational families' *high levels of expressed emotion* compared with more relaxed families' *low levels of expressed emotion* in their communication patterns (Passer et al., 2009).

The *social causation hypothesis* proposes that schizophrenia is caused by the high levels of stress experienced by people living in socio-economic deprivation. The social causation hypothesis is complicated by the *social drift hypothesis*, which proposes that having schizophrenia contributes to the deterioration of an individual's levels of personal and occupational functioning. With that deterioration, the individual is predisposed to a socio-economic decline into poverty, and thus to gravitating toward less desirable social environments (particularly urban poverty, substandard housing, unemployment, etc.). Questions abound as to whether the downward socio-economic drift is a cause or a consequence of schizophrenia (Passer et al., 2009).

Organic explanations for the occurrence of schizophrenia include genetic predispositions, as familial patterns are noteworthy. The more closely related a person is to a family member with schizophrenia, the greater the likelihood that they, too, will have schizophrenia. High concordance rates between monozygotic twins both having schizophrenia and evidence from adoption studies support a genetic component (Passer et al., 2009). The dopamine hypothesis involves the premise that schizophrenia results from excessive dopamine activity. Dopamine is a neurotransmitter linked with intellectual functioning, physical coordination, and the capacity to experience pleasure. Many of the acute symptoms associated with schizophrenia appear related to an over-production of dopamine (Kinsella & Kinsella, 2006). Other biological theories include maternal exposure to influenza epidemics during the second trimester of pregnancy, and schizophrenia functioning as an idiopathic autoimmune disease (Sadock & Sadock, 2007).

No single cause of schizophrenia appears sufficient to explain the cause of this complex condition. From a bio-psychosocial perspective, using a diathesis–stress model, schizophrenia is probably best understood to result from a combination of genetic or biological predispositions along with various psychosocial stressors that trigger its onset. While having a family history of schizophrenia is a risk factor for its development, it is not destiny. Likewise, while various events may precipitate psychoses in some individuals, those individuals may already be predisposed to develop schizophrenia. Importantly, poor parenting alone is insufficient to cause schizophrenia.

Part of what makes schizophrenia so complex and debilitating is its youthful onset. In most cases, symptoms of schizophrenia emerge during adolescence or early adulthood. Family members often describe people with schizophrenia as having always been 'a bit different', including consistent premorbid features such as shyness, social awkwardness, social withdrawal, or lack of curiosity (Kinsella & Kinsella, 2006). The onset of schizophrenia is generally gradual or insidious; an abrupt onset is uncommon. No single symptom is sufficient to assert that a person has schizophrenia. An array of symptoms, along with a history of problematic cognitive and behavioural disturbances is necessary in order to meet the criteria for schizophrenia.

The initial psychotic episode generally follows a 'prodromal' (or warning) period, which may be prolonged, in which assorted *negative symptoms* are prominent. Negative symptoms include blunted or flattened affect, social withdrawal, diminished functioning, neglected grooming, apathy, and diminished verbalization. Negative symptoms involve the absence of expected features such as facial expressiveness, verbal communication, and social interactions. Psychotic episodes generally entail evidence of *positive symptoms*, which include the presence of features that are present in addition to what would be expected or ideal (Passer et al., 2009). Positive symptoms include hallucinations, delusions, and other distinct manifestations of thought disorders, bizarre behaviours and speech, and distorted perceptions of reality (Kinsella & Kinsella, 2006). Positive symptoms are often compounded by the individual lacking insight into the implications of their behaviour, and a profound unawareness that they are communicating and behaving in ways that are not necessarily safe, appropriate or comprehensible to others.

The DSM-IV-T-R criteria for schizophrenia include the following:

> Two or more of the following 'characteristic symptoms' which are present for a significant portion of time during a one-month period (if left untreated):
>
> - Delusions
> - Hallucinations
> - Disorganized speech/expression (frequent derailment of incoherence)
> - Grossly disorganized or catatonic behaviour
> - Negative symptoms (flattened affect, alogia, or avolition)
>
> (Only one of the above symptoms is required when delusions are bizarre, or hallucinations include hearing a voice keeping up a running commentary on the individual's thoughts or behaviour, or two voices conversing.)
>
> Social/occupational dysfunction: One or more major area of functioning (e.g., work, study, relationships, grooming/self-care) show marked decline from the previous norm. When onset is during childhood or adolescence, then expected attainment of functions is not achieved.
>
> Duration: Continuous signs of disturbances persist for at least 6 months, including at least one month's duration for two or more of the 'characteristic symptoms' during the active phase.
>
> Symptoms are not better explained by schizoaffective or mood disorders, substance-related symptoms, medical conditions, or a pervasive developmental disorder.
>
> Longitudinal course may be one of the following:
>
> - Episodic with interspersed residual symptoms
> - Episodic with prominent negative symptoms
> - Continuous
> - Continuous with prominent negative symptoms
> - Single episode in partial remission
> - Single episode in full remission
> - Other/Unspecified pattern.
>
> (APA, 2000: 312)

The active phase of schizophrenia, or the psychotic episode, comprises some characteristic features associated with positive symptoms: delusions, hallucinations, thought disorders, and expressive disturbances. *Delusions* are fixed, irrational beliefs that do not respond to reality. Most delusions fall into one of four categories: religious, persecutory (paranoid), somatic (involving physical sensations), and grandiose (entailing special powers or knowledge). *Hallucinations* may be auditory (hearing voices), visual, tactile (physical sensations), olfactory (smell), or gustatory (taste). Auditory hallucinations are the most commonly noted type among people with schizophrenia. They may involve hearing very angry, dangerous voices berating the individual, or urging them to harm themselves or others. *Thought disorders* are often at the core of psychotic symptoms. They may entail distorted content (i.e. the capacity to distinguish reality from fantasy), or form. An important example may be the loss of a sense of ego boundaries experienced by the person with schizophrenia. This entails a bewildering loss of clarity of where the self starts and stops, which most people are fortunate enough to take for granted. Thought disorders also include such factors as racing thoughts, flights of ideas, tangential thinking, and looseness of associations. Such distortions are manifested through various types of expression, which may be spoken, written or drawn. Examples of spoken disturbances include word salad, in which actual words are spoken but in an incoherent order, echolalia, in which words, sounds, or phrases are repeated over and over again, and mutism, in which the person refrains from speaking at all (Kinsella & Kinsella, 2006; Sadock & Sadock, 2007). An example of written psychotic material is provided in Figure 10.3.

Schizophrenia is not a uniform condition; it varies enormously between individuals. There are several different types of schizophrenia which are both distinct from one another, and which have very different outcomes from one another. Three basic types distinguished in the DSM-IV-T-R are outlined below (APA, 2000).

Types of Schizophrenia

- Paranoid Type
  - Slightly later onset
  - Preoccupation with delusions and hallucinations (frequently 'command' hallucinations)
  - Delusions are persecutory
  - May be associated with violence
  - Less evidence of disorganized speech and behaviour than other types of schizophrenia
  - Less evidence of flat or inappropriate affect than other types of schizophrenia
- Disorganized Type ('Hebephrenic')
  - Young onset
  - Disorganized, chaotic behaviour and speech
  - Predominant, florid symptoms
  - Flat or inappropriate affect
- Catatonic Type
  - Characteristically distinct motor changes
    - Catalepsy (immobility, stupor)
    - Excessive, purposeless hyperactivity (potentially self-injuring)
    - Posturing (waxy flexibility, rigidity)
    - Prominent mannerisms (bizarre)
  - Extreme negativism (resistance to communications)
  - Echolalia or echopraxia
  - Comparatively rare compared with other types of schizophrenia

Other complicating factors associated with schizophrenia include post-psychotic depressions, as well as the likelihood of schizophrenia co-occurring with other mental health conditions. Some of those co-occurring conditions include mood disorders, anxiety, and substance-related conditions (particularly alcohol and nicotine).

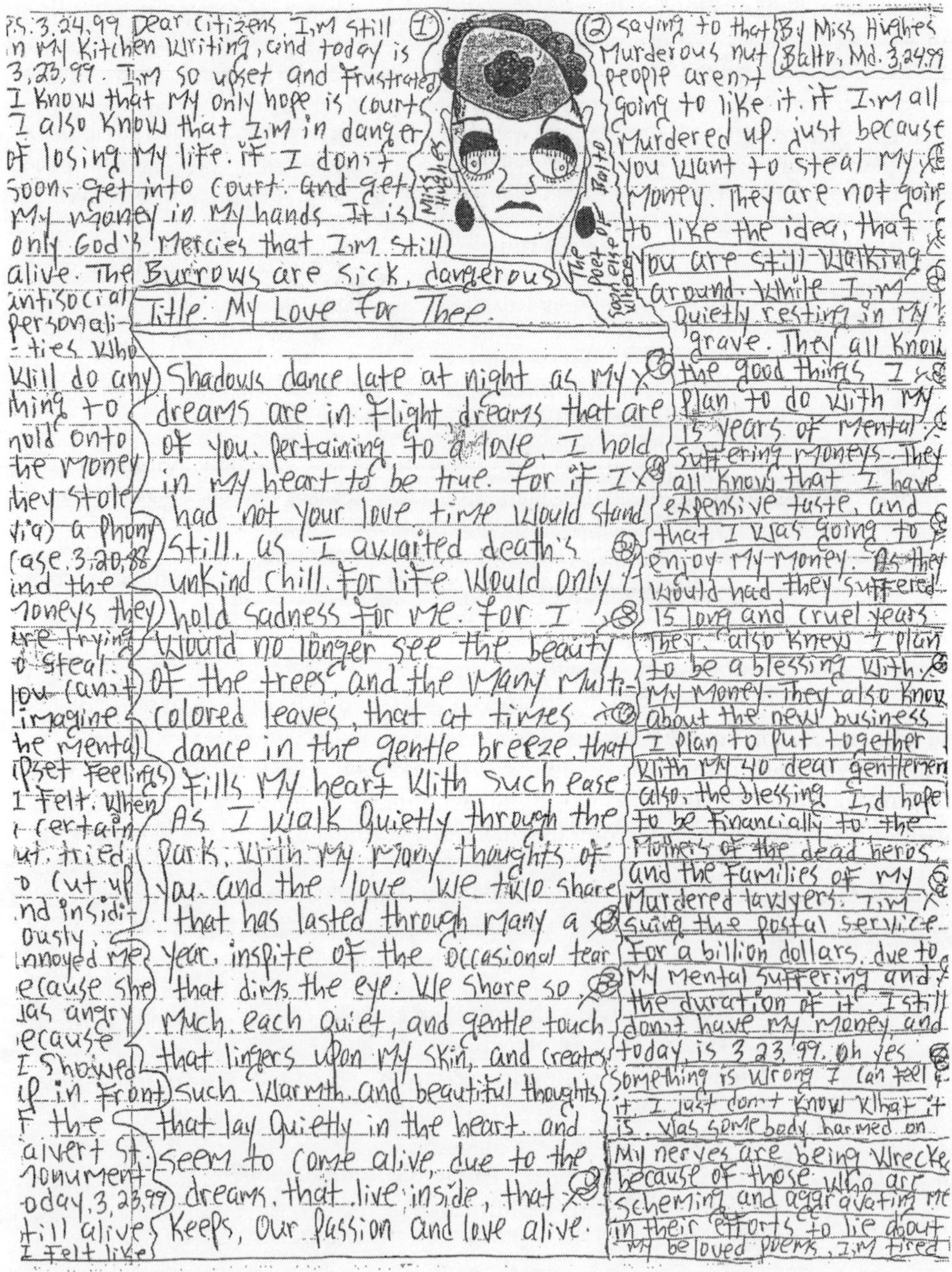

P.S. 3.24.99 Dear Citizens, I'm still in my Kitchen writing, and today is 3,23,99. I'm so upset and frustrated I know that my only hope is courts I also know that I'm in danger of losing my life. if I don't soon, get into court. and get my money in my hands It is only God's Mercies that I'm still alive. The Burrows are sick, dangerous antisocial personalities who will do anything to hold onto the money they stole via) a phony case. 3,20,88 and the moneys they are trying to steal. you can't imagine the mental upset feelings I felt. when a certain nut, tried to cut up and insidiously annoyed me because she was angry because I showed up in front of the Calvert St. monument today, 3,23,99 still alive. I felt like

(2) saying to that murderous nut people aren't going to like it. if I'm all murdered up. just because you want to steal my money. They are not going to like the idea, that you are still walking around. While I'm quietly resting in my grave. They all know the good things I plan to do with my 15 years of mental suffering moneys. They all know that I have expensive taste, and that I was going to enjoy my money. As they would had they suffered 15 long and cruel years They also knew I plan to be a blessing with my money. They also know about the new business I plan to put together with my 40 dear gentlemen also, the blessing I'd hope to be financially to the Mothers of the dead heros, and the Families of my murdered lawyers. I'm suing the postal service for a billion dollars. due to my mental suffering and the duration of it. I still don't have my money, and today, is 3.23.99. oh yes something is wrong I can feel it. I just don't know what it is. was somebody harmed on My nerves are being wrecked because of those who are scheming and aggravating me in their efforts to lie about my beloved poems, I'm tired

By Miss Highes Balto, Md. 3,24,99

Title: My Love For Thee.

Shadows dance late at night as my dreams are in flight, dreams that are of you, pertaining to a love. I hold in my heart to be true. For if I had not your love time would stand still, as I awaited death's unkind chill. For life would only hold sadness for me. for I would no longer see the beauty of the trees and the many multi-colored leaves, that at times dance in the gentle breeze. that fills my heart with such ease As I walk quietly through the park, with my many thoughts of you and the love, we two share that has lasted through many a year, inspite of the occasional tear that dims the eye. We share so much. each quiet, and gentle touch that lingers upon my skin, and creates such warmth and beautiful thoughts that lay quietly in the heart. and seem to come alive, due to the dreams. that live inside, that keeps, our passion and love alive.

Figure 10.3 An example of a letter written by a woman with paranoid schizophrenia, which she photocopied and distributed by the hundreds throughout a courthouse.

Post-psychotic depressions frequently follow acute psychotic episodes, and complicate an already complex condition, as well as heightening the risk of suicide, which is already high among people with schizophrenia (Wellman, 2006).

Post-traumatic stress disorder (PTSD)

The diagnosis of PTSD was only introduced in the DSM-III (1980), which followed the return of Viet Nam veterans manifesting an array of characteristic symptoms. Historical examples of PTSD long predate the introduction of the term, however, and can be found in such diverse cases as Pepys' diary following the Great Fire of London (1666), the American Civil War, Charles Dickens' reactions following a train crash, and the 'shell shock' that was prevalent among World War I veterans.

PTSD is a particularly relevant condition for social workers to understand, because of its linkages with childhood trauma and violence. Unlike other anxiety disorders, PTSD is explicitly linked with a precipitating trauma, and may occur at any age. Classic examples of stressors include war, rape, child abuse, kidnapping, torture, and serious accidents. Survivors of the concentration camps, the atomic bombings in Japan, survivors of the September 11 crashes and the July 7 London bombings have displayed PTSD-related symptoms. Symptoms persist for more than a month, and may be prolonged. In order to meet the DSM-IV-T-R criteria, symptoms must be sufficiently severe that they compromise basic aspects of functioning, such as relationships and work (Sadock & Sadock, 2007; Stewart & Israeli, 2002).

PTSD is often complicated by other factors, including survivor guilt, depression, and suicidality. Substance misuse often complicates the assessment and treatment of PTSD, which may relate to efforts to self-medicate as a means of managing intrusive memories and flashbacks. Comorbid substance use conditions appear closely linked with trauma experienced at a young age (Harrison & Abou-Saleh, 2002).

Not everyone who experiences the same trauma develops PTSD. The development of PTSD appears linked with the experience of utter helplessness at the time of the event. Sometimes people with PTSD experience genuine memory loss related to the actual event. In some cases, memories resurface later, which can be profoundly disturbing (Gross, 2001). PTSD symptoms are consistently linked with experiences involving overwhelming circumstances beyond the individual's control.

According to physiological studies, the autonomic nervous systems of people with PTSD appear more active and reactive than those of people without PTSD. The autonomic nervous system is involved in such responses as quickened heart rates, heightened blood pressure, and physical sensations of anxiety or fear (Sadock & Sadock, 2007). Some of the personal risk factors associated with heightened vulnerability to developing PTSD during adulthood are often found among social workers' case loads, and include the following:

- abusive childhood;
- being separated from parents during childhood;
- low levels of social support;
- pre-existing depression or anxiety;

- family histories of mood, anxiety, or substance misuse disorders (McNally, 2001).

Especially given the linkages with substance misuse disorders, social workers must be careful to distinguish between cause and effect with vulnerable people. Questions of whether someone is drinking to numb traumatic memories or whether their drinking places them at increased risk of being further traumatized are often relevant. Particularly when working with children and teenagers with PTSD, problematic behaviours may be easily misattributed to antisocial causes, rather than trauma-related reasons, meaning that social workers must be careful to know the difference.

The DSM-IV-T-R criteria for PTSD include the following:

- Exposure to a traumatic event in which the individual has experienced:
  - Actual or threatened with death or serious injury to the self or others and/or
  - Response to the event which involves intense fear, helplessness or horror (which in children may involve disorganized, agitated, or regressed behaviour)
- The traumatic event is persistently re-experienced in one or more of the following ways:
  - Recurrent, intrusive, distressing recollections of the event, including images, thoughts, or perceptions (Note: Among young children, this may entail repetitive symbolic play.)
  - Recurrent, distressing dreams of the event (Note: Among children, these may be frightening but unrecognized dreams.)
  - Sensations of re-experiencing the traumatic event, including illusions, hallucinations, and dissociative flashbacks, which may persist when awake
  - Intense psychological distress upon exposure to symbolic reminders/cues that resemble the traumatic event
  - Physical reactions to exposure to internal or external reminders of the traumatic event (e.g., tremors, choking, crouching)
- Persistent avoidance of stimuli associated with the trauma, and general emotional numbing compared with previous norms
  - Efforts to avoid thoughts, feelings, or discussions of the event
  - Efforts to avoid activities, places or people associated with the event
  - Inability to remember important aspect(s) of the event
  - Markedly lessened interest or participation in significant activities
  - Sense of a foreshortened future
- Persistent symptoms of increased arousal (distinct from pre-trauma norms) including two or more of the following:
  - Sleep disturbances
  - Irritability or angry outbursts
  - Diminished concentration
  - Hypervigilance
  - Exaggerated startle response.

(APA, 2000: 468)

Suicide

Derived from the Latin term for 'self-murder', suicide entails the wilful taking of one's own life. Suicide is strongly linked with the major mental health conditions, including alcohol and drug dependence. Severe depression, which often co-occurs with schizophrenia, PTSD, and alcohol and drug dependence, remains one of the strongest predictors of suicide across the lifespan. Approximately 15 per cent of people with clinical depression eventually kill themselves, which is over 20 times higher than is found in the general population (Passer et al., 2009). Among teenage girls, depression alone appears a risk factor for suicide, although teenage boys who die of suicide appear to have more complex symptoms, including mania, aggression, and substance misuse (Parrish & Tunkle, 2005). Suicide is the leading cause of untimely death among people with untreated schizophrenia (Wellman, 2006). Suicide risks are high among impulsive angry people who are also depressed (Maxmen & Ward, 1995).

Although more women attempt suicide, men are over four times as likely to die of suicide across all age groups (Pritchard, 2006). Suicide rates among adolescents have quadrupled since 1950, and suicide ranks among the leading causes of death for people aged 15–24 (Parrish & Tunkle, 2005). Older people attempt suicide less frequently than young people, but are more likely to employ more lethal methods, and after age 75 have three times the rate of suicides as younger people (Sadock & Sadock, 2007). Alcohol and drugs are consistent risk factors for suicide (Gibbins & Kipping, 2006). Statistical estimates of suicide represent an underestimate of their actual occurrence, because of the number of 'covert' suicides that are not recorded as suicides.

Crucial predictors of suicide are threats and previous attempts. Contrary to popular myth, threats are often quite genuine, and are sometimes subtle (such as an elderly person voicing an aversion to being a burden to their loved ones). Previous attempts are crucial predictors of suicide; the first three months after the first attempt appear crucial. Social isolation increases the risks of suicide among depressed people, as does alcohol dependence. Divorced men are three times more likely to die of suicide than divorced women. Being married and the presence of children in the home appear to lessen the risks of suicide (Sadock & Sadock, 2007).

One of the ironies of suicide is that it rarely occurs at the most severe stage of depression, but rather as the depression lifts, and the person experiences increased levels of energy with which to follow through with the suicidal urges (Passer et al., 2009). This pattern is particularly noteworthy when responses to anti-depressant medications may lift people's mood and energy levels sufficiently for their suicide risk actually to be heightened because of the intended benefits of the medication.

Social workers need to be able to differentiate between suicide attempts, gestures, and deliberate self-harm. Suicide attempts refer to unsuccessful efforts to kill oneself. Suicidal gestures may entail dramatically dangerous behaviour, which is not necessarily intended to be lethal. Deliberate self-harm (sometimes referred to as parasuicidality) is generally even more complex. Deliberate self-harm (DSH) is frequently noted among trauma survivors and among people with dissociative disorders, personality disorders, and substance dependence, and is not necessarily intended to be suicidal. Cutting is a common means of self-harming; wrists, arms, thighs and legs are the most frequent sites of cutting. For some people, self-harm reportedly relieves tension and provides a means of self-soothing, and is not intended to be lethal (Everett & Gallop, 2001; Sadock & Sadock, 2007). Given the overlap between DSH and potentially impaired judgement resulting from drinking or drugging, self-harm must always be taken seriously, regardless of intention.

Substance misuse and dependence

Social workers routinely work with cases involving either direct or indirect consequences of substance misuse or dependence. Given the complexities of different drugs' chemical properties, desired effects and consequences, social workers need to be familiar with the different drugs' properties.

While the DSM-IV-T-R regards substance use-related conditions as mental health disorders in and of themselves, the classification system used in the UK is somewhat different. The DSM criteria refer to 'abuse' rather than 'misuse'. Both the DSM and the ICD refer to 'dependence', rather than using the term 'addiction', which is generally regarded as unclearly defined and often used more to label than describe behaviours. Likewise, social workers are encouraged to refer to 'people with alcohol or drug dependence', as opposed to 'alcoholics' or 'addicts', which are often derogatory terms, and lacking in clarity.

Accurate use of terms to define substance-related problems is essential to good practice. The DSM-IV-T-R criteria for substance abuse (misuse) and dependence apply to any of the substances in question, although the physical and behavioural effects of different drugs vary according to their chemical properties. The DSM-IV-T-R criteria for substance abuse include the following:

- A maladaptive pattern of substance use leading to clinically significant impairment or distress, as manifested by one or more of the following during the same 12-month period:
    - Recurrent usage resulting in a failure to fulfil major role obligations at work, school, or home (e.g., absenteeism, expulsion from school, neglect of family or household responsibilities)
    - Recurrent usage in situations in which it is physically hazardous (e.g., while driving or operating machinery, or performing tasks requiring close attention)
    - Recurrent usage-related legal problems (e.g., arrests)
    - Continued use despite persistent or recurrent social or interpersonal problems caused or exacerbated by effects of usage (e.g., arguments, fights, inappropriate behaviours, etc.)
- The above symptoms have not met the criteria for substance dependence for this class of substance.

(APA, 2000: 199)

The DSM-IV criteria for substance dependence specify that it may involve physiological dependence (i.e. physical evidence of tolerance or withdrawal), or it may occur without physiological dependence). The DSM-IV-T-R criteria for substance dependence include the following:

- A maladaptive pattern of substance use, leading to clinically significant impairment or distress, as manifested by 3 (or more) of the following, occurring at any time in the same 12-month period:
    - Tolerance, as defined by either
        - A need for markedly increased amounts of the substance to achieve intoxication or desired effect, or
        - Markedly diminished effect with continued use of the same amount of the substance
    - Withdrawal, as manifested by either
        - Characteristic withdrawal syndrome for the specific substance, or
        - The same (or closely related) substance is used to relieve or avoid withdrawal symptoms
    - The substance is often taken in larger amounts or over a longer period than was intended
    - There is a persistent desire or unsuccessful efforts to cut down or control usage
    - A great deal of time is spent in activities necessary to obtain the substance (e.g., driving long distances, visiting different sources), use the substance (e.g., chain smoking), or recover from its effects
    - Important social, occupational, or recreational activities are given up or reduced because of usage
    - Usage is continued despite knowledge of having persistent or recurrent physical or psychological problems caused by or exacerbated by usage (e.g., usage-induced depressions, ulcers exacerbated by drinking, respiratory illness caused by smoking, etc.)

(APA, 2000: 197–8)

Substance-related conditions are strongly linked with many personal and family problems that predominate social workers' case loads, including child abuse and neglect, family violence, homelessness, violence, illness and death. Alcohol and nicotine are linked with more deaths in the US and the UK each year than all the illicit drugs combined.

Social workers must be familiar with some of the distinctions between different drug categories, because of the different effects (intended and otherwise) of usage. Sometimes the negative consequences of usage appear so obvious that the important role played by their *desired effects* may be overlooked. Desired effects are the intended benefits of usage; they may be sedation, sleep, wakefulness, or euphoria. Without understanding the desired effect of usage, the patterns of continued use and the challenges of abstinence may prove difficult to understand. A drug's desired effects play an important role in determining people's *drug of choice* (i.e. preferred substance). Many people will mix various substances (e.g. alcohol, cocaine, and heroin), which is sometimes called polydrug misuse/dependence, but when asked which would be their preferred drug if they could only use one, that will give an indication of their drug of choice. In some cases, *cross-tolerance* serves to complicate usage-related problems even further. Cross-tolerance refers to the chemical ability of one drug to produce the same (desired) physiological effect of another, allowing for effective substitution (Sadock & Sadock, 2007). For example, when benzodiazepines and alcohol are combined, elements of cross-tolerance may be observed, as they are both central nervous system depressants, and can replace or mutually enhance the desired benefits gained from usage. There can be undesired as well as desired consequences of cross-tolerance (Table 10.2).

Causes of substance-related conditions are often hotly debated by the helping professions. As with other conditions, there are arguments for biological or genetic causations, as well as psychosocial causes. Social workers are encouraged to consider a bio-psychosocial approach, involving a diathesis–stress model. Of the different substances, alcohol studies predominate in supporting a genetic component (Sadock & Sadock, 2007). People with alcohol dependence have family members with alcohol dependence about half the time, which is comparable to patterns found with family histories of diabetes and ulcers (Schuckit, 1995). Familial patterns for alcohol dependence are considerably higher than is found in genetic patterns with schizophrenia. Early onset alcohol dependence is strongly linked with a genetic risk factor (Rassool, 2002). Such patterns do not explain why approximately 50 per cent of people with alcohol dependence come from families without a relevant history, or why not all early onset patterns of alcohol dependence also entail family histories of alcohol dependence. Nor do the patterns necessarily address the environmental factors played by children's exposures to parental usage throughout childhood.

Age of onset of usage represents a relevant risk factor in assessing usage and problematic usage of substances. Earlier initiation to using alcohol and other drugs appears consistently linked with greater risks of dependence during adulthood. Usage beginning under age 14 appears particularly noteworthy (Grant & Dawkins, 1998; Adams et al., 2002).

People with substance-related problems are a very heterogeneous population. Factors involving *dual diagnoses* add further to that heterogeneity. The term dual diagnosis remains somewhat controversial in the UK, although it has been regarded as a major component of substance-related problems in the US for some time (DOH, 2002; Gibbins & Kipping, 2006). The term dual diagnosis refers to the co-occurrence (or comorbidity) of mental health disorders, and is often specifically used to understand the complex needs of people with comorbid substance-related conditions and other major mental health conditions (mood disorders, schizophrenia, etc.). Dual diagnoses typically represent an exponential rather than just additional intensification of mental health and socio-economic difficulties. Mental health symptoms are typically exacerbated by usage, and the usage patterns are generally exacerbated by the mental health symptoms.

From a bio-psychosocial perspective, dual diagnoses are associated with such complications as increased rates of HIV/AIDS, more difficulties adhering to medication

Table 10.2 Drugs, categories and consequences of usage

Drug	*Category*	*Desired effects and consequences*	*Undesired consequences*
Alcohol	Central nervous system (CNS) depressant	Enhanced sociability Relaxation Sexual disinhibition Sleep	Aggression Depression Sexual indiscretions Foetal alcohol effects/syndrome Dependence-related problems including medical complications
Amphetamines ('Speed')	CNS stimulants	Enhanced performance Alertness Wakefulness	Paranoia Aggression Impaired judgement Accelerated heart rate
Cannabis	Unspecified	Euphoria Relaxation, 'High'	Accelerated heart rate 'Amotivational syndrome' Cognitive impairment Distorted sensory perceptions Depression Weight gain Psychological dependence
Cocaine	CNS system stimulant	Enhanced performance Creativity Aphrodisiac properties (heightened stamina and pleasure) Wakefulness Increased sociability Appetite suppressant	Paranoia Insomnia Depression Psychotic episodes Mania Cardiac irregularities Psychological dependence Exchange of sexual favours for drug supply
Heroin	CNS depressant	Euphoria Relaxation Artistic creativity	Weight loss Constipation Infectious diseases associated with intravenous usage, including HIV/AIDS Flu-like withdrawal symptoms
Nicotine	CNS agonist (activates the dopamine reward system)	Relaxation Appetite suppressant Perceived sophistication Social affiliation	Physical withdrawal symptoms Lung and cardiovascular diseases Diabetes Hypertension Low-birthweight babies Death

Source: Adapted from APA (2000).

regimens, intensified mental health symptoms, increased rates of homelessness, and increased rates of violence (Gibbins & Kipping, 2006; Rassool, 2002). Assessment of dual diagnoses is further complicated by difficulties in establishing whether comorbid mood disturbances, anxiety, or psychoses are actually results of usage, or whether they are distinct from the usage (DOH, 2002; Harrison & Abou-Saleh, 2002).

When working with and understanding the complexities of alcohol- and drug-related problems, an understanding of the role of *denial* is an essential component of good assessments. Denial is the defence mechanism that allows people to disregard the implications of their behaviours. In the case of alcohol and other drugs, denial can serve to help avoid taking responsibility for the seriousness of the patterns of usage, as well as the consequences of usage. Sometimes the drinker/user is in denial about the consequences of their behaviour, and sometimes their family may be. In some cases, an entire household may be in denial, which makes interventions particularly difficult, as they are not likely to perceive linkages between usage and various problematic consequences. When denial is an active factor in the usage-related behaviour, it generally serves to protect the person from acknowledging or changing their usage patterns.

Social learning theory has been applied to the onset and continuation of substance usage, as it may help explain why people come to expect positive results from usage (Rassool, 2002). Especially in cases where problematic drinking and usage are associated with positive social/peer interactions, heavy intake is likely to be modelled and reinforced through credible role models. Usage may confer status and membership among a desired social group, thus reinforcing its perceived benefits, and minimizing its potential dangers.

The *self-medication hypothesis*, proposed by Khantzian (1997), refers to ways in which people use substances to control various negative feelings and experiences. Triggers to usage may include trauma, anxiety states (including panic attacks), mood disorders, loneliness, and bereavement, to name but a few. An example would be 'Mrs B's' use of alcohol following her husband's death mentioned earlier in this chapter. Unfortunately, the consequences of usage are rarely restricted solely to those intended or desired.

Based on a *diathesis–stress model*, substance-related conditions are understood as resulting from a combination of factors (Chassin et al., 2001; Rassool, 2002). Genetic predispositions, medical illnesses, availability, the drug's chemical properties, and various sociocultural factors (such as age at onset and role models) may serve to increase an individual's inherent vulnerability to problematic usage. Stressors or triggers may entail an array of factors, including trauma, impulsivity, peer influences, loneliness, boredom, and bereavement, which may serve to tilt the balance from use to misuse or dependence

Implications for practice

When working with people with mental health difficulties, social workers will often come across situations in which both the medical and social models of assessment and problem definition are necessary, but neither is sufficient to provide a comprehensive approach to practice. A bio-psychosocial approach may entail both medication and psychosocial interventions. The medical and psychosocial approaches need not be mutually exclusive. Combined (i.e. bio-psychosocial) approaches are increasingly supported by research findings (Pritchard, 2006; Rassool, 2002; Sadock & Sadock, 2007). Social workers are often in a crucial position to advocate for service users' benefits within both systems, but doing so entails being 'fluent' in the languages used in both systems.

Social workers are often in a position to influence ways in which people attribute responsibility for having mental health conditions, especially depression. When someone is reported to have depression, a commonly heard response is, 'What does he or she have to be depressed about?' Depression is not *about* anything, any more than having diabetes is about anything external. (When people learn that someone has diabetes, they rarely respond by asking 'What does he or she have to be diabetic about?') Social workers are often in a strong position to point out that mental health conditions are neither chosen, nor are they 'about' anything external. And, contrary to long-standing popular belief, they are not the result of weakness or moral failings!

Social workers working with ethnic minority and immigrant communities must remember that many cultures have no conceptual equivalent of 'depression' as it is understood in most western cultures. In other cultures, various physical or 'somatic' symptoms (such as headaches, breathing problems, sore throats) are more likely to represent the equivalent of depression among more western populations (Gross, 2001). Sometimes people from other cultures, accustomed to using other languages may use descriptions of physical symptoms associated with trauma that may be easily misinterpreted as psychoses. Social workers must be sensitive to racial and cultural factors when interpreting the ways in which symptoms are described using metaphors (Everett & Gallop, 2001). Social workers must also be mindful and resistant to the various ways in which institutionalized racism influences the assessment and services provided to people from ethnic minority and immigrant communities (Singh & Burns, 2006).

Whenever social workers are involved with mental health service users, they must be attuned to risks of suicide. Direct questions are necessary in order to assess the risk of suicide. Two basic questions are essential:

1. Do you ever feel that you would be better off dead, and that your death wouldn't matter? (This would be characteristic of passive suicidal ideation.)
2. Do you have thoughts about harming, or possibly killing yourself? (This would be indicative of more active suicidal ideation.)

Contrary to popular myth, asking questions to gauge a person's risks of suicidality are not sufficient to introduce the idea. Most people who are prone to considering suicide express relief when the subject is finally raised (Wellman, 2006). When there is reason to think a person is suicidal, they should not be left alone. Suicide is overwhelmingly associated with severe depression, which may entail cognitive distortions, but which is nonetheless imminently treatable for most people. Regardless of questions of manipulation or intent, when service users threaten suicide, social workers are professionally obligated to take those threats seriously (Everett & Gallop, 2001).

An important aspect of social workers' emphasis on contextual factors relates to working with people with mental disorders who resist taking their medications. While medications are often highly effective, they also come with side-effects and other aspects that can complicate adherence to prescribed dosages. As with most people who are prescribed medication of any sort, many mental health service users become ambivalent about continuing taking medications when they begin to feel better. Unfortunately, discontinuation of medications is often associated both with recurring symptoms (or relapse) as well as some professional frustration with people regarded as 'unmotivated' and 'uncooperative'. Social workers are in a strong position to establish levels of relationships with service users to develop the kind of rapport that is necessary to communicate about medication problems and issues of adherence in ways that can contribute to a better treatment outcome.

Social workers must appreciate the complex needs of people with dual diagnoses, as they often fall between different agencies, whose primary missions may not necessarily be well connected with each other. For example, when someone with schizophrenia and alcohol dependence is seeing one agency for their alcohol-related problems, another agency for management of their psychotic symptoms associated with schizophrenia, and still another provider is looking after housing and management of their diabetes, etc., it is essential that careful communication is established and maintained. Social workers are often in critically important positions to facilitate that level of communication on service users' behalf.

Social workers are often in key positions to recognize and respond to depression among older adults, and to advocate for assessments by GPs, who may have overlooked mood-related physical complaints. When older adults' depressive symptoms are dismissed as being normal for any age group, or 'just a grumpy old person', social workers must resist colluding with an insidious form of ageism. The disproportionate rates of suicide among people over age 65 attest to the seriousness with which depression among older people must be taken. Sadly, a generational norm of viewing depression as a weakness or even a moral failure often precludes older adults from acknowledging a need for help when there is a problem.

Ultimately, social workers seek to contribute to the enhancement of people's quality of life. For people with mental health disorders, this can be a very complex and challenging endeavour. Helping people with chronic mental health conditions to master practical, social and communications skills are crucial elements of good practice, as a means of enhancing the individual's autonomy and their access to resources, along with addressing the complex needs experienced by their loved ones. To achieve those goals, social workers must first earn the trust of people who have not always been treated respectfully, correctly, or caringly by society or the mental health system (Gamble, 2006). Considerable skill, combined with empathy and humility are necessary for good practice with this often-disregarded population.

Questions

1 What are some of the lay terms you associate with mental health conditions? How might some of these terms contribute to stigma and oppression?

2 What are the main differences between major depression and bipolar disorder?

3 What are some reasons that patterns of diagnosed depression among men and women vary so much? Which of the following factors do you consider relevant?
- Socialization
- Help-seeking norms
- Sex roles, e.g. 'macho' stereotypes deterring men from seeking help
- Use of alcohol to mask symptoms
- Fear of stigma
- Family roles and responsibilities

4 What are the key features of post-traumatic stress disorder (PTSD)?

5 In small groups, discuss the following:
(a) Do you find people with mental health difficulties frightening or intimidating?
(b) What are some ways in which you think social workers could make a difference in the ways in which people with mental health difficulties are regarded and treated?

6 Mental health service users who do not adhere to taking prescribed medication are sometimes seen as 'non-compliant', 'unmotivated', and 'self-destructive'. What are some of your thoughts about those labels?
(a) What are some factors that might deter people from taking psychotropic medications (anti-depressants, mood stabilizers, anti-psychotics)?
(b) Have you ever stopped taking a prescribed medication before completing the prescribed dosage? How might your reasons for doing so apply to someone taking psychotropic medications as well?

7 Consider the following scenario.

'Lydia's' older stepbrother (Tom) sexually abused her between ages 4 and 12. Tom consistently commented that she and her mother were financially dependent on his father's good will. So Lydia did not disclose the abuse throughout her childhood, even when it became violent.

She became a very compliant child, and was eager to please the adults around her. She never invited friends home with her for fear that Tom would also abuse them. Physically, Lydia developed prematurely, and by age 10 looked more like a teenager than a child. Tom used that fact to justify his continued abuse, stating that Lydia flaunted her physical maturity, and that she therefore 'wanted what she got'.

By age 8, Lydia had learned to imagine herself elsewhere (i.e. dissociate) when

Tom abused her. She began by imagining watching what was happening as if from the ceiling; she sometimes visualized herself in a different place and time altogether. At around age 10, she started hearing Tom's voice accusing her of 'wanting this', and being a 'slut', even when he was nowhere near. She would try to counteract the voices by becoming very busy, but it often proved useless. The accusatory voices continued.

When Lydia was 12, her mother was killed in a car crash, and her stepfather sent her to live with her maternal grandmother, where she continued to live for the next ten years. The sexual abuse stopped, and Lydia never disclosed it to her grandmother. Even after she considered herself safely away from Tom, though, she often had nightmares about the abuse, and often thought she saw him in crowds or in traffic.

When she was old enough to start dating, Lydia found herself very fearful of boys. They reminded her of Tom, and she generally found males intimidating. The only way she was able to relax enough to socialize with her peers was by being drunk. She found that by drinking, she could both tolerate boys' attention, as well as drown out the voices she heard when any sexual behaviour began. She also gained a reputation for being sexually available when drunk.

At 20, Lydia became involved with a very dominant man, who was also jealous. He routinely accused her of flirting with other men, and became violent in his attacks on her. Lydia would again hear Tom's voice calling her names. Lydia's partner was killed in a drunk-driving-related car crash three months after their daughter was born. Shortly after that, Lydia started hearing voices accusing her of being responsible for her mother's and her partner's deaths. She became very socially withdrawn, especially as when she went out, she kept thinking she was seeing her partner in the crowd, or in traffic. When her daughter was six months old, Lydia believed she heard voices telling her to jump from their apartment window. The health visitor arrived just in time to prevent Lydia from jumping, with her baby in her arms.

In hospital, Lydia was diagnosed with schizophrenia after disclosing that she had a history of hearing voices. She never disclosed her history of childhood abuse or domestic violence to the psychiatric staff. The psychiatrist was unaware of Lydia's mother's death in a car crash, and was not aware of how recently her partner had died. Neither bereavement nor trauma was considered in Lydia's assessment. She was prescribed anti-psychotic medications, which caused her to become lethargic and bloated. Her drinking increased, and she was generally regarded by the social services and psychiatric services as being chronically mentally ill, without any appreciation of her precipitating history.

In small groups, discuss the following questions:

(a) What are some of the inherent differences between a medical and a bio-psychosocial approach to understanding Lydia's behaviours?

(b) How are the differences in understanding Lydia's history likely to influence the way(s) in which she is probably going to be diagnosed and treated?

PART III

Social Dimensions of Behaviour

11 Systems theory, ecosystems and personal-cultural-social (PCS) perspectives

Unlike the theoretical perspectives presented in other chapters of this book, systems theory represents a very broad, abstract set of concepts that can be applied across an array of disciplines and fields of knowledge. Some argue that it is more of a model than a theoretical perspective. Systems theory provides a set of constructs that applies to understanding patterns of relationships and interactions between individuals, groups and the larger environment. While its basic constructs may seem deceptively simple, the application of systems theory across scientific and psychosocial practices represented a revolutionary move away from more traditional mechanistic frameworks. Systems theory and ecosystems perspectives emphasize the interrelatedness of the components of any system. Despite considerable overlap between systems and ecosystems concepts, the two are discussed separately in this chapter. The personal-cultural-social (PCS) model will also be discussed, as it provides a useful framework for the consideration of context, along with questions of nature vs. nurture. Systems, ecosystems and the PCS perspectives are all inherently congruent with a bio-psychosocial framework, as they provide ways of considering multiple dimensions of people's circumstances as complex wholes rather than isolated parts.

Relevance for social work

The relevance of systems theory for social workers is often found in the consideration of people in their environment, starting with their immediate relationships (partners and families), and extending into their community, society, the nation, etc. The ecosystems approach to social work practice evolved from general systems theory and the ecological theories in the environmental sciences (Hepworth, Rooney & Larsen, 2002). For social workers, systems theory and ecosystems perspectives provide frameworks with which to consider and explain such complex factors as inter-generational relationships, roles, gender identities and social affiliations in combination, rather than separate issues.

In order to assess people's problems, social workers must consider the reciprocal impacts of people and their environments. By approaching practice according to individuals' context, and their interrelatedness with the people and systems around them, social workers' perspectives on the focus of change are necessarily influenced in ways that differ from practice which focuses solely on the individual.

Systems theory has been applied across all levels of social work practice, including work with individuals, relationships, families, communities, organizations (such as schools, hospitals, protective services, etc.), as well as cultures. As one of the many theoretical approaches that evolved from practitioners' dissatisfaction with the psychoanalytic tradition, systems theory has traditionally appealed to the 'social' in social work (Payne, 1997). Because systems theory represents a value-free approach, it offers a means of defining problems and assessing needs in ways that incorporate personal and social systems' and subsystems' contributions and roles in people's circumstances (Greene, 1991b).

The *ecosystems perspective* provides an ecological metaphor that social workers have found useful in focusing on the interactions both within and between systems. Rather than focusing solely on an individual's psychological functioning, or just their family difficulties, the ecosystems perspective addresses the interactions between the person, their family, and the larger social environment, along with dissonance between any of those components (Germain & Gitterman, 1980).

One of the ways in which social work's perspectives are distinct from other helping professions is the emphasis placed on people's context as part of understanding their behaviour. The *personal-cultural-social (PCS)* model offers social workers an approach which takes a person's cultural and social contexts into consideration when defining and addressing their difficulties. By explicitly addressing context, the PCS model offers a means of considering environmental influences on people's behaviours, rather than presuming to label, pathologize or blame individuals for their difficulties.

Historical contributors to systems theory and ecosystems perspectives

Historically, *general systems theory* evolved from the writings of the Austrian-born biologist, **Ludwig von Bertalanffy** (1901–1972). Von Bertalanffy was a prolific author, who originally taught at the University of Vienna, then emigrated to Canada and then the US during the 1950s and 1960s. His basic proposal was that general systems theory represented a 'working hypothesis' contributing to a theoretical model to explain, predict, and control phenomena (Bertalanffy, 1962: 17). As such, general systems theory may be applied across all organizational levels, from molecular to social to global levels of organisms.

Systems are wholes comprising interrelated components or subsystems. Bertalanffy (1968: 37) proposed that general systems theory was applicable 'whatever the nature of their component elements and the relations of focus between them'. The components of systems represent an interactive and interdependent relationship. In order to remain adaptive, a system's components must necessarily remain dynamic in order to maintain an interactive exchange of ideas and energy. Thus systems and subsystems are not static units, but energized, interactive entities. There are times in which such energies may complicate social work assessment and interventions. Social workers must be mindful of the dynamic changeability of systems in order to anticipate and appreciate the nature of changes that occur.

Urie Bronfenbrenner (1917–2005) is among the better-known proponents of ecological theory. Born in Moscow, Bronfenbrenner's family immigrated to the US when he was aged 6. Educated at Cornell, Harvard, and the University of Michigan, Bronfenbrenner was inducted into the US Army the day after receiving his doctorate in 1942, and served in the US Army Medial Corps during World War II. A developmental psychologist, Bronfenbrenner (1979) proposed the concept of 'human ecology', which influenced subsequent concepts of the important role of a child's environment.

Bronfenbrenner was particularly well known for his cross-cultural studies on families and their support systems, as well as on child development. He was also a co-founder of the US Head Start programme, which is designed to provide a positive learning environment for under-privileged children prior to entering school. An often quoted remark is that before Bronfenbrenner, child psychologists studied the child, sociologists examined the family, anthropologists the society, economists the economic framework of the times, and political scientists the structure. Thanks to Bronfenbrenner's contributions to the ecological theory of human development and behaviour, these environments are viewed as a part of the life course and experience (Lang, 2005).

According to Bronfenbrenner's ecological concepts, five environmental systems interact to shape development and behaviour (Bronfenbrenner & Ceci, 1994). Individuals are thus understood as elements of a set of larger, nested systems, which often overlap. Metaphorically, it has been likened to a Russian doll, with the individual at the centre. The *microsystem* is the most immediate social setting in which human development occurs. The microsystem includes partners, spouses, families, peers, schools and employers. The individual generally has the most direct interaction with these elements of their environment. The *mesosystem* serves to link microsystems. The mesosystem entails the relationships between microsystems, such as the parent–teacher conference, or the doctor–patient relationship. The next level outward is the *exosystem*, which entails social settings or circumstances that influence the individual, but in which the individual is not necessarily a direct participant. Examples would include a partner's employer, government agencies, or a parent's own experiences of childhood. The next (and originally Bronfenbrenner's final) level is that of the *macrosystem*. The macrosystem comprises the cultural and social environments in which the other systems are embedded. Culture, ethnicity, religion, nationality, and the economy are examples of but a few of the macrosystems that define and organize the more institutional aspects of people's lives. Finally, in his later years, Bronfenbrenner proposed the *chronosystem* level to refer to the sociohistorical considerations that influence the human experience, which may be personal or historical (weddings, divorce during a child's schooling, economic recessions, wars, September 11, etc.). All of these systems function interactively to influence a person's development and behaviour across the lifespan.

While **Lev Vygotsky** (1896–1934) is generally included among the cognitive theorists, his sociocultural perspective on children's learning seems equally suited for consideration among the contributions to systems theories. Born in Russia the same year that Piaget was born in Switzerland, Vygotsky was very productive during the 1920s and 1930s, although much of his work was censored for political reasons in Soviet Russia. Sadly, scholars outside Russia lacked sufficient translations of his work to give it the attention it deserved until the 1970s (Ewen, 1998). Vygotsky died of tuberculosis at age 38, unaware of the prominence his work would eventually achieve long after his untimely death.

His social cognition model of learning, however, emphasized the role of culture as a prime influence on individual development. According to Vygotsky, children's learning necessarily occurs in the context of their culture, including their family environment. In some ways, Vygotsky's concepts were something of a precursor to systems theory and its influence on the context provided by the environment on individuals' behaviour.

Historically, social work's emphasis on appreciating the importance of context can be traced back to the pioneering work of **Mary Richmond** (1861–1928). A contemporary of Jane Addams, Richmond is credited with having transformed philanthropic charity efforts into a valid, organized profession based on specific values and methods (Agnew, 2003). Richmond's (1917) *Social Diagnosis* provided systematic views of social work practice, along with the relevance of law, medicine, psychology and logic in identifying and responding to people's difficulties. Richmond called upon schools and universities to train professional social workers in ways that would enhance the profession's practice.

Key concepts of systems theory

A *system* is understood as an organized whole; it is contained within boundaries that serve to distinguish that system from the external environment; within those boundaries, the system contains various interacting elements that serve to define its purpose. A system occurs whenever multiple elements interact, and when the characteristics of the system are distinct from those of its parts (Hepworth, Rooney & Larsen, 2002). Thus, on a biological level, each individual represents a complete system of interactive parts (organs, fluids, and energy) that interact with the larger system (partnerships, family members, etc.) within a larger social system (neighbourhoods, communities, cities, etc.). Likewise, social systems comprise individuals as parts, and are also components of larger systems. The metaphor of a Russian doll has often been applied to describing the ways in which systems are comprised of subsystems (Figure 11.1).

Systems are defined by the interactive or relational nature of their elements and with the greater environment. Systems entail a relational, rather than linear pattern of interactions and consequences. Unlike linear relationships, which entail one-directional flows of energy, in which one entity changes another, systems entail a transactional relationship, which is necessarily reciprocal. Thus, rather than a linear style of cause and effect, transactional relationships entail a more circular form of cause and effect (Germain, 1991). A key concept of systems theory is attributed to the Gestalt theorist

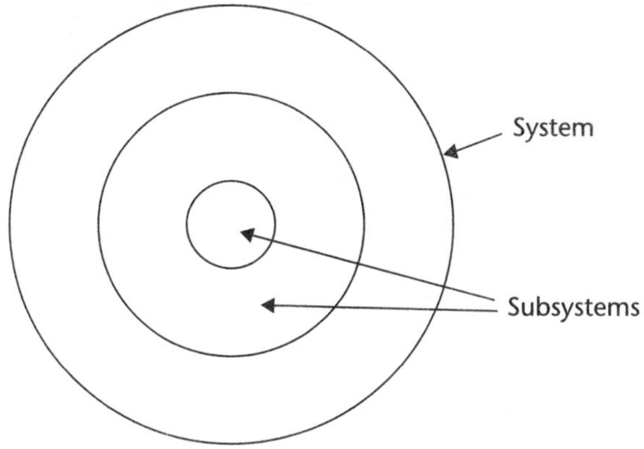

Figure 11.1 A diagram of systems and subsystems.

Max Wertheimer, which is that *the whole is greater than the sum of its parts* (King & Wertheimer, 2005).

Boundaries serve to define the parameters of systems and subsystems. Some boundaries are more obvious than others; skin, membranes, walls, national boundaries are but a few of the more obvious. Family membership, professional or social alliances, communities or language may also define various systems. Membership in those systems generally entails specific shared characteristics or abilities.

At each level, systems have their own *boundaries*, as do the interactive parts. Some boundaries are defined by role (parent vs. child). Others have to do with relationships (families vs. neighbours). Boundaries vary enormously in terms of firmness and looseness. The permeability of boundaries determines the level and degree of interaction between members of a given system, as well as with the external environment. Ideally, boundaries need to be sufficiently permeable to allow for growth and the exchange of information, goods and energy, as well as sufficiently firm to function protectively for purposes of integrity. Overly firm boundaries contribute to isolation and stagnation (characteristics of closed systems); overly permeable boundaries are associated with confused roles and chaos. If a system's boundaries are so firm as to characterize a closed system, then that is associated with *entropy*, or stagnation, which leads to disorganization and the inability to transform sufficient energy to continue functioning. Open systems are typically equipped to gather sufficient energy, matter and information to sustain functioning. *Synergy* entails the ability to use energy for purposes of regeneration including the creation of more energy.

According to general systems theory, biological and social systems are open, meaning that they interact with their environments and across boundaries. Those exchanges include sustenance, energy and information, and ensure development, growth and survival. Open systems are distinguished by the ongoing processes of input–transformation–output (Germain, 1991). The input entails information, matter and energy. The transformation process is dependent on the system's utilization of the information, matter and energy. And the subsequent output is the exchange that follows input, and entails the interaction between the system and the external environment. Using a family with children as an example of an open system, the input from the external environment could include material goods, housing, and education. The transformation would be the sustaining of growth and development of the family members. The output would include the parents' contributions to the community (taxes, jobs, etc.), children attending school, and the family's participation in the greater community environment; children being educated in ways that add to their subsequent capacity to contribute to the community would be another example of the system's output.

Within systems, there are subsystems. Considered as a system, the family mentioned could be looked on as comprising several subsystems: parents, children, and siblings. At the next level, the family is a subsystem of various other social systems (cultural, religious, educational, regional, national, etc.). Parents' employment serves as another environmental system (such as employers, stake holders, work-related affiliations, etc.).

Internal and external boundaries function at levels of openness or firmness that allow for the maximum functioning of the existing system. When either internal or external boundaries are overly rigid or overly permeable, however, the other is often found to be the reverse. The following case is used as an example of overly permeable internal boundaries and overly rigid external boundaries.

In 2008, a teenage girl in Texas reported a case of domestic violence that resulted in the removal of over 400 children from a polygamist sect's ranch. The children and their mothers were removed from a fundamentalist compound that was affiliated with a breakaway branch of Mormonism.

The 10,000-member sect followed the teachings of a 'prophet' who was a self-confessed polygamist, who was jailed on charges involving the rape of a 14-year-old girl who was forced to marry her cousin. Members of the sect believed that a man must marry at least three wives in order to be eligible to go to heaven. Women in the sect were taught that their eligibility to go to heaven depended on their being sufficiently subservient to their husbands. Investigators reported that girls as young as 13 were 'spiritually married' to older husbands in accordance with the sect's beliefs.

This example shows how internal boundaries between members of the sect appear to have been overly permeable, with children being placed in relationships for which they were not developmentally suited. Conversely, external boundaries between the sect and the surrounding environment were overly rigid, with outsiders being precluded from being aware of the sect's practices or the risks at which children were being placed. Because of the rigidity of those external boundaries, when children were removed from the sect, their adaptation to the external environment was predictably quite disturbing for them, because of their unfamiliarity with social norms other than those experienced in the confines of the sect's compound.

One of the results of such interactions is the dynamic 'ripple effects' of change within a given system. When change occurs in one part of the system, that change resounds or reverberates throughout the entire system, requiring adaptation on the part of other components of the system. Because of the interactive nature of systems, when change occurs with one component of a system, expecting the remaining components to continue unchanged is generally unrealistic. From a systems theory perspective, this is one reason why people experiencing marital difficulties would generally be discouraged from seeking individual counselling if they are seeking ways to sustain their marriage. Based on systems theory concepts, if they go into counselling seeking change, and the change occurs only on their part, then the system (i.e. their marriage) will necessarily need to change as well (Rooney, 2002b).

Metaphorically, systems operate similarly to the way in which harmony occurs in music. When multiple notes are played or sung simultaneously, they produce a particular sound or effect. When one of those notes is removed, then the sound necessarily changes. Likewise, in systems, when one element of the system is changed or removed, then the effect resonates throughout the entire system.

Just as melodies and harmonies depend on notes changing, systems also rely on growth and changes in the course of their functioning. Within systems, that necessitates *adaptation* on the part of those elements comprising the whole. An open system is not a static entity; it maintains a dynamic and changing *equilibrium* or balance (Germain, 1991). In that way an open system remains vital, by means of reciprocal interactions between its elements and with the environment, and thus avoids becoming stagnant.

Pincus and Minahan (1973) adapted systems models to social work practice in the US, with the idea of a *client system* comprising those persons seeking or receiving services. They proposed that people depend on an array of formal, informal and societal systems to help them meet their needs. Informal systems (family, friends, and neighbours) are generally the first port of call when seeking help, while formal systems (such as community resources, faith communities, etc.) may also be approached. Societal systems (government agencies, social services, hospitals, schools) are often sought as a matter of 'last resort'. While services provided in Britain comprise different levels of statutory levels, the concept remains applicable when considering the potential roles, hierarchies, and boundaries involved in service users' systems and their approach to and experiences with social services systems.

Systems theory is congruent with the concepts of the *diathesis–stress model*. Various types of vulnerability to difficulties need to be taken into consideration when making an assessment of risk. Vulnerabilities may include various personal, genetic, cultural or socio-economic factors. Stressors may include trauma, illness, abandonment, loneliness, poverty, or neighbourhood influences. Social workers need to be keenly aware of the interplay between such influences on a contextual level in order to appreciate the interactive role played by environmental stressors.

Key concepts of ecosystems

With the introduction of their 'life model' of social work practice, Germain and Gitterman (1980) significantly influenced the application of ecological systems theory in social work. Based on the premise that the application of ecological systems theory ('ecosystems') was conceptually congruent with ego psychology, Germain (1991) proposed that the emphasis on environment, action, self-management and identity were also congruent with good social work practice. Its emphasis on including physical (non-human) elements in its concepts of the environment distinguished the ecological perspective from general systems theory (Shriver, 1998). Ecosystems emphasize people's continual adaptation and interaction with the different aspects of their environment. That adaptation entails reciprocal change. Because of the inherent human need for an environment in which physical, psychological, and social needs are being met, social and environmental problems (poverty, crime, pollution) compromise the reciprocal adaptation process, and result in stress, illness and pathology.

Germain (1991) emphasized the ecological concept of *adaptation*. She focused on the active aspect of adaptation, distinct from the traditional connotation of a passive accommodation to the environment or the *status quo*. According to Germain, people strive for the best possible person–environment fit, in order that their needs, rights, abilities and aspirations may be met. Through that application of adaptation, people's efforts to bring about change in themselves, others, and their environment is more congruent with ecosystems concepts.

Homeostasis is the natural seeking of sameness or balance, which is found in nature, but also applies to human systems. Just as a person will seek to achieve homeostasis, or balance, upon tripping on an uneven pavement, systems also seek homeostasis in response to change or threats. Because most people resist change on a very primal level, homeostasis may be positive or negative. Ideally, it is a steady, balanced state in which an open system can function optimally to support the growth and development of all concerned.

When the environment contains sufficient nutrients and material goods for all concerned, its occupants can develop and thrive; when habitats contain insufficient resources, its occupants' physical, social, and emotional development is likely to be compromised. For example, when environments provide social support through such networks as family and friends, neighbours, faith communities, and pets, the impact of stressful life events appears to be potentially alleviated. By contrast, when environments provide insufficient social support, the interaction between the individual and the environment is likely to be more complex, with more risk of harm to the individual (Hepworth, Rooney & Larsen, 2002).

The environmental term 'niche' refers to the status or role occupied by a member of an organization. One of the developmental tasks facing people at various stages of the lifespan is to find one's niche in society, in order to achieve a stable sense of self and self-esteem. The capacity to establish that niche presumes that positive opportunities exist in the person's environment that are mutually congruent with needs and abilities. That premise may prove unrealistic for people who have been excluded from society on the basis of race, ethnicity, poverty, disability, or sexual orientation (Hepworth, Rooney & Larsen, 2002). Social work's inherent emphasis on social justice makes having an awareness of the implications of such concepts, which are components of systems theory, a fundamental aspect of assessment of people's circumstances.

Key PCS concepts

The 'personal-cultural-structural' or PCS framework provides a useful means of visualizing some of the interactions relevant to how individuals and their circumstances fit into a larger system. In the PCS framework, the three key levels are closely linked and mutually interactive as a context for one another.

In the PCS model, the 'P' refers to the *personal* or *psychological* elements involved; it refers to the individual's unique thoughts and feelings, or individual variables (genetic, developmental, or physical) that shape their understanding and behaviour. The 'C' refers to the *cultural* dimension of a person's circumstances. This would include those shared ways of experiencing the world around them that would be shaped by their cultural background and situation such as shared values, religion, ethnicity, and meanings attributed to events and views. The 'S' refers to the *social* or *structural* dimension of a person's circumstances, such as relevant networks of social hierarchies, power relations, authority and political influences that affect a person's circumstances. These influences may entail various levels of oppression, exclusion, and marginalization, or privilege and power over others (Thompson, 2006). Sometimes also referred to as the person-in-environment (PIE) model, the PCS model addresses the interactive aspects of coexisting dimensions between people and their environments (Hilarski et al., 2002).

While the three levels of the personal, cultural and social dimensions interface with one another, they also frequently overlap. For example, the cultural environment (C) in which mental health problems, sexism or homophobia are experienced often overlap with the personal (P) level of personal experiences of prejudice or biases. Similarly, an individual (P) who perceives themselves as being innately different from the expectations of their cultural group's norms (C) may internalize a sense of inadequacy or failure, thus leading to increased risks of social withdrawal or marginalized behaviours that generate social exclusion (S).

Ideally, *statis* evolves between the individual and their environment, in which their adaptation to the surrounding environment is nurtured through positive interactions between the individual (P) and those around themselves (C-S). Basic systems concepts (such as boundaries, hierarchies and subsystems) apply to the interaction and balance established between the individual and their immediate family and the social network in which they live.

From a traditional Marxist perspective, society's economic base provides an infrastructure that underpins the social or structural dimension of an individual's circumstances (Thompson, 2006). When individuals are denied access to adequate resources to meet their basic needs (food, housing, education, etc.), then their opportunities to succeed are necessarily compromised. The impact of such deprivation on the individual necessarily has both personal (P) and cultural (C) implications. Likewise, individuals (P) who experience oppression and exclusion on the grounds of race or gender in a racist society (S) will also be impacted by those experiences.

The PCS model can prove particularly useful to social work assessments as a means of considering the role of stress as it relates to people's behaviour. Derived from the Latin word meaning 'to draw together tightly', stress often overlaps between the individual (P), cultural (C), and social/structural levels of people's circumstances. Stress may function on any of the three levels, entailing such variables as illness, bereavement, or job loss on the personal (P) level, cultural oppression, forced migration, or racial discrimination on the cultural (C) level, and poverty, war, or natural disaster on the social/structural (S) level.

Beginning with the personal level, the role of stress may best be understood as a bio-psychosocial phenomenon. On a physical (bio-) level, stress may entail actual physical responses of fear or shock in response to a perceived threat. Selye's (1956) study of the human body's responses to stress contributed to the understanding of the physiology of people's response to stress. As part of what he called the *general adaptation syndrome*, Selye studied aspects of maintaining a steady temperature. When threats to that steady state of temperature (98.6°F/34.3°C) occur, the human body mobilizes an elaborate defence system to restore its homeostasis. Likewise, when challenges to safety or well-being occur, the resulting response often entails various physical components, including arousal of the central nervous system (CNS), and what is known as a *fight-or-flight* response (Lawrence & Zittel-Palamara, 2002).

In his model of stress, Selye (1956) emphasized that stress is not necessarily negative, and distinguished between stress and distress. (For example, the birth of a much-wanted infant may be an occasion of joy, but also heightened stress in the lives of new parents.) Selye outlined three phases of response to perceived threats associated with stress. The phases comprise: (1) an alarm reaction; (2) a stage of resistance, with adaptation being the intended outcome; and (3) a stage of exhaustion in which the previous level of adaptation or resistance may be sacrificed (Sadock & Sadock, 2007).

The following scenario depicts an example of various levels of stress experienced by an individual and his family.

'John', age 14, is the oldest of his parents' three children. They have lived in Britain since fleeing the violence in their native Zimbabwe. John and his younger sisters attend local schools, and are known as serious students. The family is active with the local church, which assisted them in seeking asylum from Zimbabwe. Although both trained as doctors in Zimbabwe, neither of John's parents is able to practise medicine in Britain. His father is employed as a laboratory assistant in the local hospital, and his mother works as a carer in a local nursing home. John's mother's only surviving brother and his family live nearby. The families are very close, as they are each other's only living relatives in Britain. John's younger cousins particularly admire him as their role model. The family's grandparents and other family members are believed to have died in the conflicts in their native country.

To help make ends meet, John delivered newspapers in the late afternoon on his bicycle. On his way home from his paper route on a winter's evening last year, John was attacked by a group of local youths who are known to be associated with the National Front. John suffered multiple broken bones and was unconscious for several days following the attack.

Since the attack, John is unable to maintain his balance properly. He walks with difficulty, and cannot resume riding his bicycle for fear of falling and injuring himself further.

Because John was unable to identify his assailants, the police were unable to make any arrests, even though they believe they know who was responsible.

Since the attack, John has struggled with school work, which is a drastic change for him. He has difficulty concentrating, and has angry outbursts at home. His sisters are increasingly anxious for John, and they avoid going outside unless they are with each other, for fear of being attacked by the same gang who attacked John.

John's parents feel increasingly isolated and afraid for their children. Several other Zimbabwean families in the district have reported similar types of attacks upon their teenage sons.

Several aspects of the stress experienced by John's family entail overlaps between the personal, cultural, and social dimensions. Focusing only on one dimension of stress is likely to prove inadequate for an effective grasp of the situation. Looking at the stress and anxiety experienced by John and his family, some of the concerns can be conceptualized as outlined in Table 11.1.

Table 11.1 Acute and chronic dimensions of stress across the PCS framework

	Acute	*Chronic*
Personal/family	• Physical trauma from assault • Days spent by John's bedside uncertain of his prospects for survival • Emotional consequences for John and his family of having been attacked • Academic implications of John's injury • Fear of retribution by assailants	• Poverty • Long-term implications of physical injuries • Financial implications of loss of John's income • Parents' concerns for John's long-term academic prospects • Ongoing sense of endangerment, vulnerability to attack experienced by John and his family
Cultural	• Minority status in time of crisis • Parents' experience of being trained doctors, yet excluded from their professions in Britain	• Immigrant status trying to navigate health system, schooling, police inquiries • Reliance on church-related support, rather than having extended family nearby
Social/structural	• Sense of being under attack by unknown enemies • Racial overtones of attack • Financial strain of John's parents being unable to take needed time off to be with him during his recuperation	• Loss of homeland • Immigrant status • Racial strain in neighbourhood • Financial strains • Lack of legal protection by police • Perpetrators of attack went unpunished

In the animal world, we can observe various examples of one creature perceiving danger from another, and being able to run away or attack. Using John's and his family's circumstances, the day-to-day realities of the fight-or-flight response to stress can be readily applied. While the actual physical actions of running away from or assaulting daily or symbolic reminders of his attack are unlikely, the negative emotional reactions (stress) remain very probable.

Implications for practice

While neither systems theory nor ecosystems perspectives propose methods for practice, both have contributed to the ways in which cases are defined and considered, as has the PCS model. Because systems theory provides support for considering people's behaviour in the context of the multiple systems in which they function, cases are no longer typically defined around an individual, but rather around the individual in the context of their various relevant social systems. By addressing individuals' circumstances as part of an assessment, social workers are likely to perceive and define problems very differently than they would if they concentrated solely on the individual.

An example would be the ecological systems concepts that make an important distinction between the role played by people's adaptation to and ways of coping with stress. According to Germain (1991), stressors are best understood as externally generated sources of disturbance. Coping or adaptation to those stressors is distinguished from the traditional psychoanalytic concepts of defences because defences are focused on internally generated anxieties. For social workers, this distinction can help empower service users to attribute responsibilities for stress and change in ways that are less pathologizing than some other theoretical models provide.

By using a PCS perspective to consider the situation of a person who has recently immigrated, a social worker would appreciate the complex overlapping of potential personal, cultural and social difficulties. Individually, someone who has immigrated may have experienced both a traumatic loss of their former lifestyle, and be facing numerous difficulties with employment and housing. Culturally, they may be isolated from familiar supports or aspects of language, religion, and diet that were previously taken for granted. Socially, they may be subjected to exclusion, discrimination, or living in substandard housing in which they feel vulnerable to harm. Thus their situation is influenced by the confluence of all these factors (among others) that in no way reflect any personal deficit so much as a very stressful combination of circumstances requiring careful attention and support.

General systems concepts and ecological systems concepts have contributed to the utilization of ecomaps as a tool used by social workers to provide a visual diagram depicting people's relationships and relevant systems in their lives. Initially developed by Hartmann (1978), ecomaps provide a means of demonstrating formal and informal supports as well as sources of conflict. Ecomaps provide social workers with a powerful assessment tool with which to help individuals and families visualize relationships, patterns, and sources of support and conflict in ways that are more effective than verbal

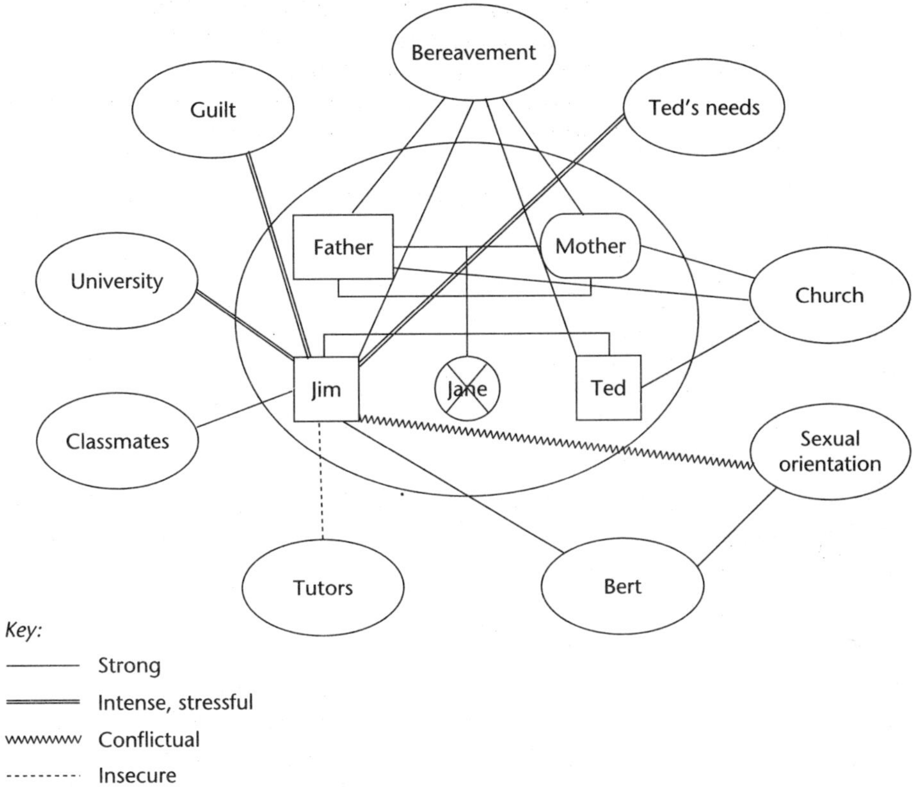

Figure 11.2 An ecomap for Jim.

discussions alone. The following hypothetical case is provided as an example of an ecomap's usefulness (Figure 11.2).

Jim is a 21-year-old second-year social work student. He is the oldest of his parents' three children, and spent his first year living in the halls of residence, because commuting from home was too time-consuming, and too expensive. He also wanted to immerse himself in university life, to get the most out of his degree programme. This year, however, he is commuting over 70 miles daily from home because of his family's needs.

During the summer after his first year at university, Jim's younger sister, Jane, died unexpectedly of heart disease. She had a congenital heart defect, and was on the waiting list for a transplant. She was 17 at the time of her death. His only remaining sibling is his 10-year-old brother, Ted. He felt that moving back home for the year was the only way for him to support his parents' and his brother's needs following Jane's death.

Although he did exceptionally well with his studies during his first year, Jim is struggling academically this year. He hasn't disclosed his sister's death to his classmates or his tutors, because he feels ashamed of not having discussed her before. He feels guilty for having spent last year having such a good time, and for devoting all his energy to his own needs and wishes, and wonders if he had been present at home last year, might his sister's condition not have deteriorated the way it did. He is finding it difficult to concentrate, and the hours spent driving also detract from time he would otherwise be able to study. His results have dropped noticeably.

Jim's parents are grief-stricken by Jane's death, and Jim is trying to compensate for their preoccupation by attending to Ted's needs, but it is a strain for him. Adding to Jim's concerns, he entered into his first sexual relationship last year, and is still very much involved. His partner (Bert) is another young man on the degree programme, but Jim has not disclosed his homosexuality to his family. He worries that they will notice that all of his phone calls are from the same person.

Criticisms and shortcomings of systems, ecosystems and PCS perspectives

While systems theory provides a wealth of concepts and metaphors for social work practice, it remains more descriptive and explanatory than prescriptive. It does not provide guidelines for practice *per se*, but rather provides a conceptual model with which to interpret and assess people's situations (Hepworth et al., 2002). Among the consistent criticisms of systems theory has been that, while it provides a useful conceptual framework, it is not research-friendly, as it defies empirical testing (Shriver, 1998).

Feminist critiques of systems theory entail objections to its traditional application of so-called 'nuclear families' (i.e. mother, father, and children) without sufficient attention to non-traditional household compositions (Jack & Jack, 2000). Other criticisms have been made of its emphasis on the whole, rather than its parts, potentially at the expense of attention being paid to individual circumstances and feelings of less verbal members (Wilson et al. 2008).

Questions

1 Match the following definitions and theorists with the concepts:

	Concept	Definition/theorist
____	Boundaries	(a) Lacking energy, resulting in stagnation
____	Homeostasis	(b) Ludwig von Bertalanffy
____	Statis	(c) Balance, stability
____	Entropy	(d) Urie Bronfenbrenner
____	Equilibrium	(e) Mary Richmond
____	General systems theory	(f) Ways in which parameters of systems and subsystems are defined
____	Microsystems and macrosystems	(g) The natural seeking of balance, familiarity, stability
____	Social diagnosis	(h) A state of balanced, nurturing adaptation

2 In small groups, discuss how the following may function as 'systems' within service user's perspectives:
   (a) The benefits system.
   (b) The foster care system.
   (c) The juvenile justice system.
   (d) The mental health system.

3 Consider the following case in relation to the systems in operation.

'Daisy' (age 35) is an Afro-Caribbean mother of four who is a new user of social services. She has recently separated from her long-term partner after the disclosure of his having sexually abused her 14-year old daughter. When you arrive for a home visit, Daisy appears tired and sad. She was widowed five years ago when her husband David died in a freak car crash, in which she was a passenger. Following the crash, she miscarried at five months into a pregnancy.

Daisy and her late husband David met at the local church in which they were both very active. David immigrated to England from Ethiopia, where his family had died from famine. He and Daisy fell in love, married, and had three children of their own: Matthew (16), Gloria (14), and Desmond (12). Daisy and David owned and operated a successful shop that specialized in Afro-Caribbean foods and spices. The entire family worked in the shop, which was very popular in their community. The family was also active in the local evangelical church, where Daisy and David sang in the choir.

During the past five years, Daisy has been less able to manage the shop. She has lost several suppliers because of her delayed payments. She has relied heavily on her sons to run the shop, and much of the responsibilities have been falling on Desmond during the past year. Daisy suspects that Matthew has stolen funds and goods from the shop, but has never confronted him. She is also vaguely aware that Matthew associates with a local gang. Sometimes gang members have been surrounding the shop's door, and she was aware that they intimidated customers, and cost her business. She has seen Matthew slipping merchandise to gang members without being paid.

Last year, Daisy entered into a relationship with a local man, 'Mr. X', who was a regular customer at the shop. Their parents had come from the same region, and they found they had much in common. During her involvement with Mr. X, he seemed to provide her sons with a positive role model. She hoped he would lead them away from gang-related activities. Unbeknown to Daisy, he was secretly abusing Gloria. Mr. X has been charged with sexual misconduct, and Daisy has been entirely cooperative in the investigation, and supportive of Gloria, but she says she is now ashamed to show her face in the community, much less at church.

Daisy describes feeling that she has failed as a mother, as a woman, and as a business person. She fears for her daughter's well-being, as well as for her sons. She fears losing her business, and considers having failed David's efforts and his memory. She also suspects that young Desmond is being lured into the gang-related activities he has witnessed his brother entering in recent years.

(a) What are some of the systems involved in Daisy's situation?
(b) How would you describe the boundaries of the various systems in this situation?
(c) What are some ways in which Daisy's personal, cultural, and social dimensions combine to intensify the stress she is experiencing? (Please consider such factors as gender, bereavement, and racism.)
(d) Please construct an ecomap for Daisy's family.

4 What are some of the ways in which attending university has created changes in your own PCS framework?

5 On which of the three levels of the PCS model do you think social workers need to focus more than the other two?

6 Using the PCS model, draw a representation of Rita's circumstances in the following case.

'Rita' (age 25) comes from a devoutly Muslim family. They emigrated from Pakistan to Bristol when Rita and her twin sister were infants. Rita's family run a successful business and both sisters attended prestigious schools where they excelled academically. Her twin ('Rima') observes strict Muslim practices, and has married a man chosen for her by their parents. She has a 2-year-old son, and is now expecting another baby. Rita, however, was singled out as being mathematically exceptional, and attended university in London. She has now completed her doctorate in economics, and lives in London, where she has gradually stopped observing traditional Muslim practices. Rita is employed as a market analyst by an international bank in London, and is considered highly capable in her job.

During her teens, Rita became aware of feelings of emotional and sexual attraction to other girls in her class. Although she never pursued any physical relations with her classmates, she describes having always been aware that she was attracted to females, rather than males. Her first same-sex relationship was with a fellow undergraduate when they were both 20. In the past two years, Rita has been in a monogamous relationship with 'Tess', of whom Rita's family is only aware as her flatmate. They have recently purchased a home together.

Only a few of Rita's closest associates are aware of her relationship with Tess, as she does not publicize her personal life among her professional colleagues. In recent months, Rita's family has become increasingly urgent about wanting her to 'settle down and get married'. They point out her sister's obvious happiness in the marriage they arranged for her. They have several prospective husbands in mind for Rita, and regularly urge her to arrange trips home in order to meet the men and their families.

(a) What would you consider the primary area of conflict within Rita's situation?
(b) How would issues of Islamophobia and/or homophobia apply to Rita's circumstances?

12 Families and family systems

The patterns of marriage, cohabitation, dual incomes, divorce, and remarriage have changed significantly during recent decades, making the stereotype of a traditional family (i.e. two married birth parents with children solely from their marriage) increasingly exceptional. Families are rarely perfect, and tend to be complex; they have apparently always been so. (Anyone doubting this may wish to consider the family history of Adam and Eve, and their two sons.)

This chapter addresses some of the aspects of families that shape people's behaviour, and ways in which social workers can apply an awareness of attachment issues, relationships, systems, and demographics to their understanding of the functions and challenges faced by families. Social workers are trained to appreciate the interaction between families and the larger society, and the ways in which families' diverse configurations, relationships, and values must be appreciated in order to inform sound practice.

Relevance for social work

Social work's historic emphasis on families and especially families experiencing adversity, dates back to the charitable organizations of the 1880s, and Mary Richmond's pioneering work in the US (Richmond, 1917). In the interim, both families and social work have undergone drastic changes, and the adversities experienced have possibly intensified. Much of social work practice remains concentrated on families' circumstances, functions, and difficulties. Protecting, preserving, strengthening and advocating for families remain core aspects of social work practice. Social workers are among the few professionals who routinely carry out their assessments in families' homes, which provides a uniquely contextual perspective on the importance and the functioning of the family.

Sometimes social work with families entails strictly practical services; much of social work entails assessment of complex families with multiple needs. From the complexities of working with families with children considered at risk, to the facilitation of the adoption of a new family member, to the coordination of families' roles in the rehabilitation process following a member's incarceration, to understanding the family's distress at the hospital bedside of a dying member, social workers are called upon to appreciate and respond to the complexities of family relationships.

Historic contributions to social work perspectives on working with families

The theories of families' functions and *family systems* that emerged in the US during the 1950s were influenced by many clinicians' dissatisfaction with both psychoanalytic and medical models' inadequacy to explain people's problems (Nichols & Schwartz, 1998). The concepts of group dynamics, especially those of **Kurt Lewin** (1890–1947), were very influential in the development of family theories. Levin's holistic *field theory* entailed concepts related to the role played by individuals' 'life space', and was influenced by *Gestalt theory*. Traditional psychoanalytic and medical concepts of causality tend to be linear, with people considered individually and apart from their families. The basic concepts proposed by family theorists were more circular and interactive. People's difficulties were seen as stemming from and being influenced and maintained by various family factors (Nichols & Schwartz, 1998).

While much of the social work literature addresses the nature of families either overtly or covertly, several authors' work has been particularly influential. Much of what became family theory stemmed from the pioneering work done by Jay Haley and Gregory Bateson. Salvador Minuchin's and Virginia Satir's work with families contributed further to the knowledge base. Originally considered quite radical when they were introducing their concepts during the 1950s, 1960s and 1970s, when psychodynamic approaches were still dominant, the Palo Alto Group's practical and systemic approaches to working with families remain congruent with social work practice.

Jay Haley (1923–2007) was among the founders of brief and family therapy techniques. Haley grew up in California, and originally planned to be a playwright. While studying for a master's degree in communication at Stanford University, Haley met Gregory Bateson, an anthropologist. Their collaborative efforts led to the founding of what became known as the 'Palo Alto Group' of family therapy (The Mental Research Institute), based in California (Ray, 2007). Their work introduced the concept of observing families as a group in order to understand people's behaviour. Their original publication (Bateson, Jackson, Haley, & Weakland, 1956) addressed their theories regarding the family roles when a member has schizophrenia, but has never been replicated. Haley subsequently collaborated with Minuchin while at the Philadelphia Child Guidance Clinic, and contributed to the evolution of Minuchin's structural family therapy during the 1970s. Haley combined a systemic framework to understanding people's problems, along with an appreciation of their strengths. His most influential book, *Problem Solving Therapy*, originally published in 1977, remains a classic.

Salvador Minuchin (1921–present) was born to Russian Jewish immigrant parents in

Argentina, and grew up in an anti-Semitic Argentinean culture. While studying medicine, Minuchin was jailed for three months for his opposition to the Peron government. He later served as a doctor in the Israeli army. From this unconventional background, Minuchin studied psychoanalysis in New York, but considered it an inadequate approach for the work he chose to do with poor urban youth (West & Bubenzer, 1993). While serving as the director of the Philadelphia Child Guidance Clinic, Minuchin collaborated with Haley and others in pioneering work with diverse families and problems in ways that defied psychoanalytic traditions. Minuchin proposed an approach that combined systems theory and communication theory with which to assess and work with troubled families. He also proposed that people achieve change through the power of relationships, rather than the psychoanalytic premise of analysis being necessary.

Through concepts he referred to as *structural family theory*, Minuchin proposed that families comprise subsystems with boundaries that influence their behaviour patterns. He introduced such terms as *functional* and *dysfunctional* families in relation to their capacity to adapt to various stressors (such as illness, infidelity, redundancy). Minuchin (1974) proposed that families' capacity to adapt depended primarily upon the clarity and appropriateness of their internal (subsystem) boundaries. Minuchin's (1974) text *Families and Family Therapy* is also a classic in the study of families.

Minuchin observed problematic patterns of boundaries involving *triangulation* among family members, which he described as resulting from two members of the family system consistently bringing in another (third party) family member when conflicts arise. An example would be when two parents are in conflict, and one parent consistently brings a child into the conflict to deflect or divert the conflict without actually resolving the problem. An example would be the following scenario, in which the husband had asked his wife to go by the cash machine on her way home from work, so that he would have cash for an early-morning taxi the following morning.

> *Husband:* Did you remember to go by the cash machine?
> *Wife:* Oh, no. I forgot.
> *Husband:* Great. You forgot *again.* (He turns to their teenage son.) Your mother is hopeless. Absolutely hopeless.

In such a scenario, one irritated partner not only globalizes the other's error, but also brings a third party (the son) into the discussion in a way that effectively precludes the other partner being able to respond constructively. Meanwhile, no matter what the son says, he is likely to alienate one or both parents. By their nature, triangles generate coalitions between different members of the family system, and often serve to exclude others from that coalition.

Triangulation may also take the form of distorted communication. An example would be (from the same family):

> *Wife:* Would you please tell your father that he's so late getting home tonight that he's missed supper? He'll have to find something he can cook for himself. I'm on my way to chair an important meeting at the town council.

In such an exchange, one irritated partner uses a third party (again, the son) to communicate with another. Conflict between the two parents remains unresolved, and the son is again placed in an unchosen coalition and an untenable position, in which he is likely to alienate one or both parents.

Virginia Satir (1916–1988) received her MA in Social Work from Northwestern University in Chicago in 1948. A prolific author and speaker, Satir also served as the director of training at the Mental Research Institute in Palo Alto, California, during the 1960s.

Satir built upon the concepts of family members' behaviour and communication by describing several family roles that can emerge and become consistent features of family difficulties and functioning. Satir proposed that communication patterns among troubled families are frequently vague and indirect. Examples include parents experiencing relationship problems who insist on discussing their children's difficulties instead. Sometimes parents speak to each other through their children, and avoid direct communication with one another. When such indirect communications become the norm, then children are often manoeuvred into the undesirable position of having to speak for one parent, and being manipulated into an alliance with one parent or the other, which often instils fear of alienating the other parent (Satir, 1983).

Key concepts about families, family functions, and family systems

While the family generally serves as the basic unit of human experience, not everyone defines the family in the same way. For social workers, a broad and flexible concept of family is essential, in order to approach practice in the most inclusive way possible. If social workers define families only according to the tradition of two (heterosexual) parents and their biological or adopted offspring, then many current (highly effective) families may be excluded from that definition.

Definitions of the family have generally focused either on their function or their structure, with *functional* definitions focusing more on those tasks performed, and with *structural* definitions focusing more on relationships. The traditional functionalist view of the family's purpose evolved from Durkheim's concepts of collective representations, and was summarized according to kinship and social expectations by Parsons and Bales (1955, cited in Abbott, Wallace, & Tyler, 2005: 146). While functional definitions often reflected somewhat dated post-World War II norms (i.e. two parents/one wage-earner), families in industrialized western societies typically continue to perform the following functions:

- Reproduction and replacement of the population

  Most societies consider the family unit as that setting in which children are produced.

- Care of the young

  Most societies view the family as the primary institution for raising children, and the source of key frameworks for patterns of attachment to specific individuals.

- Socialization of new members

  The family typically provides the setting in which children are provided with models of socially acceptable behaviours and norms, as well as coping skills.

- Regulation of sexual activity

  All societies have rules that apply to sexual behaviour in family units. Most serve to establish kinship and to preclude incest; most disapprove of extra-marital sex.

- Provision of material and emotional security

  Physical protection and nurturance and affection are primarily provided through the family unit, with particular emphasis on support during times of adversity (Zastrow, 2007).

Structural definitions generally focus more on relationships between members of the unit considered a family (Schriver, 1998). Those structural relationships include such premises as

- affection between spouses, partners, parents, and children;
- kinship (biological, adoptive, or through marriage) between members (siblings, multiple generations, extended family members);
- continuity of companionship and association (shared history and future);
- shared norms, values, ideals.

A family's structure provides a network of relationships and agreements that are essential for the family's functions. They are typically maintained through consistent communication, behaviours and memory in ways that provide continuity and permanence.

Families' contexts include factors such as their culture, ethnicity, family form, sexual orientation, access to basic resources, and their experience of oppression, discrimination, or exclusion, as well as their experience of power or privilege (Rooney, 2002a). Stressors experienced by the family also influence the context in which they are functioning. An appreciation of a family's context as well as the strengths they bring to the prospect of coping with adversity represents a crucial dimension of social work assessment.

Families are typically shaped according to various dimensions of the lifecycle. Starting with childbearing, the family provides the basis for their offspring's existence, and generally provides the context in which people form their earliest relationships, grow up and are socialized, and from which offspring eventually emerge in order to enter into other family relationships. From those relationships, the pattern continues with a further generation of offspring, and their development and eventual departure, following which parents may face an 'empty nest' experience, and later a decline in health that may necessitate some role reversals in which adult children become carers for their elderly parents (Carter & McGoldrick, 2005b).

Family systems

Social work practice has historically regarded individuals as members of interacting social systems, with the original system being the family of origin. Germain and Gitterman (1980) applied Bronfenbrenner's (1979) *ecological model* to studying families, as a useful means of conceptualizing the reciprocal causality and transactions between members of systems and their environments, which is readily applicable to understanding family systems. As noted in Chapter 11, family members comprise a family unit, entailing reciprocal relationships between members as well as relationships with the larger environment with which they interact as individuals and as a unit. The essence of applying systems theory entails seeing patterns (Wilson et al., 2008). Applying a systems approach to assessment also helps understand how family members perceive and define specific problems and their causes, either within or outside their family unit.

Understanding families as systems (microsystems), with interactive members (subsystems), and with transactions with the larger environment (the macrosystem) is generally congruent with social work practice. Using systems concepts, families are readily understandable in relation to the subsystems that exist. Those subsystems include the spouse–partner dyad, the parental dyad, the children subsystem, the sibling subsystem, the mother–daughter subsystem, the father–son subsystem, and so forth. Subsystems in the family are typically formed according to gender, generation, roles, and interests that serve the family's best interests and survival (Minuchin, 1974). Subsystems and roles may overlap and members may occupy more than one at a time (for example, simultaneously being a daughter, wife, sister and mother).

The ways in which boundaries (do or do not) function typically prove an essential element of family systems. *Boundaries* serve as abstract but crucial 'dividers' that distinguish members of the system from one another. They serve to define inclusion or exclusion within family operations. Internal boundaries determine the degree of closeness and distinctness between family members; external boundaries determine the degree to which outsiders are free to enter into the family system. In order to function healthily, boundaries need to be distinct, as well as sufficiently flexible yet permeable to allow for growth. The basic integrity of a family's subsystems usually depends on the rules observed by the family (Rooney, 2002a). As mentioned in Chapter 11, when internal boundaries are overly permeable, the external boundaries often prove overly rigid. In most western family configurations, boundaries are often exemplified by who sleeps with whom.

Boundaries are influenced by factors such as who is responsible for parenting, performing household chores, and behaviours that are or are not sanctioned by the family. When functional boundaries are violated, family members or others can be found intruding upon the functional domains of other family members. Examples may include grandparents counteracting parental instructions, or children assuming parental responsibilities for siblings.

Given the challenges inherent in families' functioning, the capacity to adapt to change and adversity is a crucial factor in such functioning. Minuchin (1974) referred to problematic family patterns of closeness and distance in terms of being either 'enmeshed' or 'disengaged'. Minuchin referred to enmeshed relationships as those in which boundaries between members were blurred, and thus precluded growth and autonomy. Enmeshment reflects relationships that have become unhealthily close, and which create imbalance within the family system. An example would be when a parent and a child are emotionally closer than the parental dyad. When family members were disengaged, Minuchin considered the relationship to have lost its cohesion and the capacity to maintain itself. An example of disengagement would be when parents no longer speak directly to each other, but only have messages relayed through their children.

According to Minuchin (1974), most families fall somewhere toward the centre of a continuum of extremes of internal boundary functions. The opposite extremes would represent *disengagement* (with overly rigid boundaries precluding closeness) and *enmeshment* (with overly permeable boundaries precluding distinctions between individual members). In disengaged families, the ripple effects experienced by members when change occurs with other members require extreme levels of stress in order to be appreciable. The following case is an example of a family demonstrating internal disengagement.

'Vera' (age 16) is enrolled in a local private school in an academically accelerated programme. She is the younger of two sisters. Her sister is away at university. Vera has always been a good student and her teachers expect that she will be offered places at a selection of prestigious universities.

During recent months, Vera has lost over a stone, and has appeared increasingly unwell. She is 5′8″ tall, and currently weighs just over five stone. Her teachers and classmates have expressed concern. Yesterday, she lost consciousness when she stood up to leave a classroom. The school phoned an ambulance, and Vera was taken to hospital, where she was placed on intravenous feeding and hydration. When her parents were contacted, they expressed surprise that anything was wrong, although Vera lives at home with them, and they were not aware of her drastically restricted food intake during the past year. Both parents are very involved in their careers, and are highly ambitious for their children. When informed that Vera was being admitted to hospital, her mother's first question was whether this would interfere with Vera's academic progression and her upcoming exams.

While 'Vera's' family relationships appear disengaged, her relationships with teachers and classmates appear to have remained strong. Indicators of the family's disengagement would include the parents' lack of awareness of Vera's health concerns, despite her noticeable weight loss, as well as her mother's perceived priorities being Vera's academic status more than her health.

Communication

Communication patterns are among the key concepts that stemmed from group work and have been applied to understanding families. How group members and family members communicate with one another is a crucial component of their functioning, especially in times of conflict or adversity. Distinctions between *content* and *process* are among the key aspects of group dynamics that have influenced family systems concepts. While content refers to what is said, process refers to how ideas are exchanged and communicated (Rooney, 2002b). Social workers are often in a position to observe how families experience conflict that is overtly about specific content, but the process of the communication can be far more complex, threatening and destructive than specific words. A familiar scenario described below is an example of distinctions between content and process.

Tina and Tony have been together three years; they are expecting their first child next month. Today is their anniversary. Tina has prepared Tony's favourite meal. As he returns home from work, Tony is speaking to his brother on his mobile phone. As he enters the door, Tina hears him arranging to meet at the pub in an hour, to watch a soccer game together.

Tina: I thought we would be staying home together tonight.
Tony: Yeah, but Terry and I want to watch the game together. You don't mind, do you? Hey, what's the problem?
Tina: Nothing.

Tony has clearly forgotten the anniversary. The content of Tina saying 'nothing' does not accurately reflect the emotions she is experiencing. The tone of how she says 'nothing' is likely to be far more informative than the word itself. If that tone is frosty, then Tony may not be paying sufficient attention to unspoken meanings. If the tone is resigned, then issues of sadness and hopelessness are going unspoken. In this case, content is not sufficient to interpret the process of what is being communicated between the two family members.

Left unaddressed and unresolved, the communication between Tina and Tony is likely to worsen. John Gottman (1999) refers to the 'Four Horsemen of the Apocalypse' to describe problematic communication patterns between partners. Those four patterns are criticism, defensiveness, contempt, and stonewalling.

Criticism entails negative messages that imply that the current conflict reflects a more global problem, and often involves some level of attack or blame. 'You *always* . . .' statements make a constructive response very difficult. 'I' messages that take some ownership for a complaint tend to be more constructive for purposes of communication. *Defensiveness* typically involves a posture of guardedness against a perceived attack. It often operates from a determination to avoid all criticism, but also precludes taking any ownership for the problem, or any constructive response to constructive criticism. Defensiveness makes communication that would repair problems very unlikely (Gottman, 1999). An example would be:

Tony: Hey! You just walked away while I was speaking!
Tina: Why not, you always do that to me.

Contempt reflects communication patterns that place one partner on a higher plane than the other. It often takes the form of mockery or disdain, and typically precludes positive communication. *Stonewalling* occurs when one partner withdraws from the interaction, and is unwilling or inaccessible to resume interactive communication (Gottman, 1999). Tina's 'nothing' would be an example of stonewalling, which makes positive communication very difficult to resume.

Satir (1983) particularly emphasized the importance of communication among family members. She argued that verbal and nonverbal communication could be *congruent* or *incongruent*. Incongruent communication, in which verbal and nonverbal messages do not match, is easily misinterpreted. Members of troubled families are often unsure of challenging such mixed messages, which may result in systemic communication difficulties. Satir also addressed the prospect of *double binds*, in which no matter how the message is interpreted, there will be a negative outcome. An example of a double bind would be a mother holding a plate of biscuits, asking 'Don't you like the biscuits I've made especially for you?' while saying 'If you eat too many biscuits, you'll become fat.'

Reciprocity, relationships and roles

Satir (1972) emphasized the reciprocity of relationships and the roles involved, and how their complementary nature makes such behaviours difficult to change. Complementary roles, such as 'rebel child' and 'good child', and 'rescuer' and 'peacemaker' are examples of roles that serve to maintain and constrain family relationships.

Ideally, family roles are complementary and reciprocal in ways that contribute to optimal functioning. They are generally learned in the course of social interactions within family systems, and reflect an individual's status. When applied to families, role theory suggests that each member of a family carries a variety of roles that are coherently integrated into the family's structure, and reflect various expectations, norms, and rules (Rooney, 2002a). Roles are generally reciprocal, and are subject to adaptation across developmental changes and changed circumstances. Interpersonal roles can be understood according to the degree to which they are 'harmonized', entailing degrees of complementarity and symmetry (Janzen & Harris, 1997).

Satir emphasized the role played by low self-esteem in relationships and family patterns of communication. She proposed that when partners with low self-esteem enter relationships, their emotional neediness creates a fear of expressing differences directly (1983). Such relationships often entail patterns of expecting one another to anticipate each other's thoughts as if through magic, which often results in tremendous frustration and disappointment, if not resentment. Satir (1972: 135) observed that some of the unrealistic demands that such levels of neediness can create include:

- If you love me, you won't do anything without me.
- If you love me, you'll do what I say.
- If you love me, you'll give me what I want.
- If you love me, you'll know what I want before I ask.

Family *rules* often govern mutual expectations and acceptable behaviours. They also entail issues of power distribution within the family. Power distribution relates to the decision-making processes practised by the family. Typically, the decision-making process is flexible and equitable, with members being able to rely on fairness and consistency. Strong alliances or collusion between family members may influence the distribution of power. In some cases, one family member may dominate the decision-making, thus skewing the balance within the family system. Ideally, the rules applied to decision-making are sufficiently flexible to respond to developmental and situational changes, with members being allowed increasing levels of autonomy and participation in decision-making as they mature. Family rules also pertain to patterns and norms of problem-solving among family members. One issue is how disagreements are settled, and how they are often governed by family rules, either overtly or covertly.

Another facet of family rules may involve what is sometimes known as *family myths*. Family myths entail an array of cognitive patterns, perceptions and expectations that typically come into the family's sayings and ways of responding to a variety of circumstances, or the world at large (Rooney, 2002a). The following case represents an example of a family myth.

> 'Howard' (age 14) is the youngest of five children. He has two sisters and two brothers. His sisters have been very academically successful. Both brothers struggled academically. Howard attends the same school that his siblings attended, where he has excelled at science and maths. His brothers and his father tease him at home, asking if he is sure he is really related to them, as 'Boys in this family aren't scholars', and 'Only girls in this family do well at school.'

Family myths can be positive or negative. While Howard's family's myths are relatively benign, some are less so. Some examples of potentially counterproductive family myths are listed in Box 12.1.

Satir also introduced such terms as 'the presenting problem' and 'the identified client' when working with troubled families. Her premise was that the problems identified as the starting point are not always the problems that are most relevant. Likewise, the family member who is the 'identified client' is sometimes the only one whose behaviour has been scrutinized, and who may be functioning as a 'symptom bearer' for

Box 12.1 Negative family myths

- Telling the truth is not important.
- Nothing ever changes in this family, so you had best learn to live with things as they are.
- Teachers don't like the children in our family, and that is why we never succeed academically.
- Double standards apply to behaviours expected of males and females in this family.
- Only weaklings apologize.
- Violence is an acceptable way of solving family disagreements.
- Social workers are paid to disrupt families, so never tell them anything that goes on in this family.
- Men in this family are expected to misuse alcohol and treat women badly.
- Women in this family are expected to tolerate abusive, demeaning treatment.
- Girls in this family are thick; all they're expected to do is get pregnant before leaving school.
- Everyone in this family is expected to live on benefits.
- If you are a member of this family, you keep our secrets, no matter what.
- The main way to get attention in this family is to be ill.

the troubled family as a whole. That individual may also be functioning as the family's *scapegoat*. The term scapegoat stems from its biblical usage, to refer to an individual who carries the blame of others. As it is used in the study of families, it often refers to a child whose behaviour is the focus of scrutiny in a family where (more serious) parental problems (such as alcohol and drugs, or infidelities) are being ignored.

The following case provides an example of 'scapegoating'.

'Anthony' (age 10) is a lively and attractive boy. His sister is 14. Both children have done well academically, but Anthony's behaviour at school has recently become problematic. He began clowning around in ways that disrupted class, and was not completing homework assignments. His teacher requested a meeting with Anthony's parents.

Anthony's mother teaches in a nearby town, and was embarrassed by Anthony's behaviour. Although Anthony's father was previously very involved in school-related concerns, he was 'at a business meeting', at the time of the meeting, and could not attend. His mother assured Anthony's teacher that she would do all she could to help Anthony improve his schoolwork.

When, two months later, Anthony's behaviour had not only not improved, but actually worsened, another meeting was called. Again, Anthony's father could not be present, but his mother informed his teacher that she would introduce restrictions on Anthony's extracurricular activities, until his schoolwork improved. His teacher and her supervisor requested that Anthony be evaluated for attention deficit disorder, to ascertain whether he should be medicated. His mother scheduled an assessment in two weeks' time. The next weekend, Anthony ran away from home, and was found three days later, walking to his grandfather's farm two hundred miles from his parents' home.

At that point, Anthony's parents acknowledged that their home situation 'might have contributed' to Anthony's behaviour. His father had been charged with embezzlement at his work, and was facing criminal charges. The parents were also having acrimonious rows about an extramarital affair Anthony's father was conducting with his assistant for over a year. This was not the first such affair, but it was the most public. Despite that, Anthony's parents insisted that Anthony and his sister remain unaware of their marital problems, and their father's work-related crisis.

'Anthony' and his behavioural problems at school provide an effective 'scapegoat' to distract both his family's and school's attention away from his parents' serious problems. Not only did his behaviour provide a focus of attention, but it also provided a subject about which his parents agreed.

From a family systems perspective, the interactive nature of the family necessitates attention to parental relationships as well as parent–child relationships. Because relationships are fundamental to children's cognitive, emotional and social development, family relationships are necessarily crucial to their well-being. Relationships are associated with assorted childhood competencies, including self-esteem, language skills, and general academic capacities, as well as social skills and their abilities to form and maintain attachments (Bowlby, 1982; Durkin, 1995). The context in which children's early experiences of relationships occur is a crucial factor for social workers to consider in appraising family relationships. Issues of attachment and trust are essential elements of children's emotional development within the family.

As noted in Chapter 5, any discussion of childhood attachment necessitates some reference to the work of John Bowlby. An important factor noted by Bowlby (1969) is that children often have multiple attachment figures, both simultaneously and sequentially. Their sense of emotional well-being evolves through connections and relationships with the people who care for them, including parents, siblings, grandparents, child-minders, aunts, uncles, and often a wide circle of friends and neighbours who provide a rich and varied source of emotional connections. From a bio-psychosocial perspective, attachment figures provide an array of protective and life-enhancing factors, including protection from harm, providing nourishment and nurturing, as well as emotional responsiveness to a child's needs. The traditional Euro-American emphasis on the mother–child dyad serving to define attachment has not always addressed the richness and variety of most children's emotional experiences.

Especially when one parent takes on the primary responsibilities of an infant's care, there is always a risk of the other parent feeling excluded. This also applies to cases in which a child's medical needs become the primary 'domain' of one parent, with the risk of the other parent feeling relegated to irrelevance.

The dynamic elements of parent–child relationships have been more widely examined than the relationships between siblings. Because sibling relationships entail both 'horizontal' elements between the children and the parent(s) as well as the 'vertical' relationship between the children, though, sibling relationships reflect both reciprocal and complementary characteristics (Hughes, 2003). Sibling relationships provide the context in which most children begin learning about competition (i.e. for parental attention as well as material resources), companionship, rivalry, negotiation skills, conflict resolution, and enduring relationships.

Sibling relationships often play a key role in children's physical and emotional environments. As the people with whom most people can expect to share the longest proportion of their lifespan, siblings also provide the most accessible means of experimenting with social learning, including competition, negotiation, and problem-solving skills. Relationships with siblings typically entail emotions that may be both strongly positive (loyalty, affiliation, shared secrets) and strongly negative (jealousy, rivalry, historic resentments). Siblings are also likely to provide the most enduring attachment in most people's lives. Sibling relationships appear to become closer during times of adversity, and may serve as a protective factor in subsequent stressful life events (Hughes, 2003).

Changing family demographic patterns

Until the 1970s, the typical pattern of relationships entailed heterosexual couples becoming formally engaged and marrying young without having previously lived together. Until the late twentieth century, living together before marriage was typically socially disapproved of and considered undesirable. Whereas in 1979 only 11 per cent of women in Britain between ages 18 and 49 were cohabiting, by 2002 it had risen to 29 per cent (General Household Survey, 2004). With the increase in rates of cohabitation, rates of marriage have simultaneously dropped. Within a generation, the patterns and rates of marriage and cohabitation in Britain have changed considerably. During that same generation, patterns of separation and divorce have also changed.

Historically, children born outside marriage were the exception, and society viewed their mothers with concern if not suspicion. Children of unmarried mothers were traditionally considered inherently disadvantaged, and social workers were frequently involved in assessments based primarily on the stigma associated with their mothers' marital status. Terms such as 'illegitimate' and 'bastard' were associated with considerable stigma. In recent generations the norms have changed, and in Britain today, approximately 40 per cent of children are born outside marriage (Abbott, Wallace, & Tyler, 2005). Those numbers, combined with the rising divorce rates, mean that many children will spend some if not most of their childhoods in families headed by a single parent.

Divorce and family disruption

While divorce was once considered a stigmatized exception to the rule, approximately 40 per cent of those marriages that occur each year will end in divorce (Allan, 2008). Ironically, perhaps, divorce rates rise during prosperous times, and drop during times of financial hardship (Ahrons, 2005). Most British divorces are granted to women, with the most common cause being the 'unreasonable behaviour' of the husband (Abbot, Wallace & Tyler, 2005). Because most mothers gain custody of their children following a divorce, and women typically earn less income than their husbands, the resulting arrangements for children typically presume fathers complying with court-ordered child-maintenance payments. In cases involving histories of 'unreasonable behaviour', continued financial dependence often entails complex ongoing arrangements.

Approximately 140,000 children under age 16 experience parental divorce in England and Wales each year (Boylan & Allan, 2008). Increasing numbers of children experience their parents' non-marital partnerships dissolve without formal recognition as a divorce, thus precluding informed estimates or evaluation. Whether the changes in patterns of marriage and divorce are good, bad, or indifferent aspects of society, social workers must understand the complex nature of families as they currently exist. They must also appreciate the resilience shown by the majority of children following disrupted parental relationships (Hughes, 2003).

Generalizing about the outcomes of divorce is difficult because divorce and family disruption are approximately as varied as families themselves. Recognizing individual families' differences is a crucial component of effective assessment. According to Block, Block and Gjerde (1986, cited in Hughes, 2003), boys from families that subsequently divorced displayed higher levels of aggression and impulsivity during childhood, while parents who subsequently divorced displayed higher rates of discord about child-rearing long before the divorce. Such findings raise questions of cause vs. effect (i.e. were the boys' levels of aggression reflective of ongoing parental tension that resolved following the divorce?). Extensive exposure to conflict appears to be more detrimental to children's long-term adjustment than parental divorce itself (Amato, 1995).

Concerns for children following parental separation/divorce include the likelihood of children having a poorer level of academic achievement, staying in full-time schooling for less time following parental divorce, and leaving home at a younger age (Pryor & Rodgers, 2001; Joseph Rowntree Foundation, 1998). Sexual activity at a younger age and higher levels of smoking and drinking also appear among children following separations and divorce, and males appear to be more prone to aggression, antisocial behaviour, and delinquency following parental separation/divorce than females. Pryor and Rodgers (2001) observe that daughters of divorced parents are more likely to have children outside marriage than those from intact families, and that children of divorced parents are more likely to have their first child at a younger age than their counterparts from intact families.

While a divorce represents a legal event, from a family's perspective it is much more likely to be experienced as a complex and multifaceted process, with roots in the past and implications for the future. For many people, divorce entails a process of bereavement, as relationships into which considerable energy and dedication have effectively died. With that loss, various expectations, identities and dreams are also ended. Carter and McGoldrick (2005a) address the complex experience of going through the 'emotional roller coaster' of a divorce, including some of the emotional transitions of the divorce process. Some of the predictably difficult emotional points identified by Carter and McGoldrick (2005a) are specified in Box 12.2.

Box 12.2 Emotionally difficult points during divorce and relationship disruption

- The times at which the decision to separate and divorce occur.
- The times at which the decision to separate and divorce are announced to the family and friends.
- Discussion and decisions regarding finances, custody and visitation arrangements.
- The actual physical separation, departure from the family home.
- The time at which the divorce becomes legally finalized.
- The times at which separated or former partners or spouses have contact related to finances or custody.
- Life events such as children's birthdays, graduations, weddings, the birth of grandchildren, grandparents' funerals, family members' accidents, illness, hospital stays.
- Former spouses' remarriages, relocations, health crises or death.

Following a divorce, continued contact with the non-custodial parent is often complex. Most of the available data focus on mothers having custody, as that is the more frequent arrangement. For many children, contact with non-custodial fathers ranges from disappointment to awkwardness to painful when ex-spouses/partners interrogate their children about each other's details. Relations between the ex-partners/spouses play a crucial part in the quality and quantity of visitations (Ahrons, 2005). Other variables that influence non-custodial fathers' likelihood of maintaining contact with their children include employment, housing, and children's gender. According to Bradshaw et al. (1999), employed fathers are twice as likely as unemployed fathers to maintain regular contact with their children following divorce. Not surprisingly, fathers who can afford housing with extra rooms following a divorce are more likely to maintain visitations from children following a divorce than fathers who are living with friends or in private-rented accommodations (Simpson, Jessop, & McCarthy, 2003). Fathers who embark on new relationships or partnerships before having resolved some of the remaining consequences of their previous relationship's disruption appear to have complex patterns of contact with their children (Simpson, Jessop, & McCarthy, 2003).

Sadly, many children are effectively deprived of contact with loving grandparents following divorce, for a number of reasons. Relocations, custody arrangements, and remarriage may all complicated grandparents' access to their grandchildren.

Most children, regardless of age, continue to wish their parents would reconcile and reunite (Joseph Rowntree Foundation, 1998). Most children continue to want to have contact and remain in relationships with both parents, regardless of the parents' relationship with each other. The loss of fathers in children's lives can reflect a profound, lifelong source of emotional pain. Mere presence, however, is not sufficient for a relationship. Genuine involvement and positive support are essential for any parent–child relationship.

Lone parenting

In the UK, the number of households headed by a lone parent has more than tripled in the past three decades; the increase involves both male and female lone parents, although the percentage of lone mothers is nearly seven times that of lone fathers (Abbott, Wallace, & Tyler, 2005). Following divorce or disrupted relationships, unless all contact with the non-custodial parent ceases, there are still two parents, albeit living in separate households. 'One-parent households' is perhaps a more accurate description of the resulting household compositions than 'lone parenting'.

Females head approximately 90 per cent of lone-parent households in Britain. Because of various economic, political, and social factors, lone mothers and their children are considerably more likely to experience poverty (Allan, 2008; Featherstone, 2003). Their vulnerability appears to be heightened if the woman became a mother at a young age (UNICEF, 2001). For women in Britain, financial hardship following divorce/disruption appears to have a significant effect on lone mothers' levels of distress. Factors associated with that hardship include the probability of lone-parent households living in rented accommodations, with less space, fewer amenities, and less access to social resources (including suitable play areas, libraries and cultural activities) than other families (Allan, 2008). For women from working-class backgrounds, being a lone mother is more likely to be a long-term prospect, and entail more enduring poverty than is the case for more priviledged women (Rowlingson & McKay, 2005).

Overall economic circumstances, including arrears with rental or mortgage payments, accumulated debts, living in rented accommodation, and having to share bathroom or laundry facilities appear as relevant as actual income regarding lone mothers' overall mental health (Pryor & Rodgers, 2001). According to Bradshaw (2002), nearly 60 per cent of children in lone-parent households were living in poverty. Social workers are called upon to appreciate some of the challenges faced by those children and their families in ways that avoid blaming the victims of poverty for their problems.

Overall, there is insufficient evidence to prove that either mothers or fathers are necessarily better suited to being lone parents solely on the basis of gender. Positive outcomes for children following parental divorce or household disruptions are associated with parenting that provides 'warmth, support, and monitoring; involvement in school activities and time spent with children' (Pryor & Rodgers, 2001: 219), none of which are determined by gender.

Much less is known about fathers as lone parents than is known about mothers. In one of the rare studies on lone fathers, DeMaris and Greif (1997) found noteworthy variables include the importance of having been involved as parents prior to the divorce or disruption. Fathers' experiences were less successful when the children were all the same sex, when there were three or more children, when conflict with the children's mother continued, and when the fathers were dating frequently (DeMaris & Greif, 1997). One of the variables that complicate assessing the outcome of children living with their fathers after a divorce is the incidence of troubled children being sent to live with their fathers because of disruptive behaviours at their mothers' homes

(Pryor & Rodgers, 2001). Such complications necessarily preclude clear interpretation of cause and effect of the roles of divorce, custody, and behaviour.

'Blended' families

Nearly one-fifth of all marriages that occurred in Britain during 2002 were remarriages for both parties (www.statistics.gov.uk in Abbott, Wallace & Tyler, 2005). Remarriages often result in the formation of a 'step-family', which comprises a household in which the child(ren) are biologically related only to one of the parents (Shriver, 1998). Some step-parents may proceed to become adoptive parents for their stepchildren. The resulting family configuration is sometimes called a *blended family* (Zastrow & Kirst-Ashman, 1994). In the UK, most blended families (approximately 90 per cent) comprise a couple with one or more children from the mother's previous partnership(s) alone (Abbott, Wallace & Tyler, 2005).

Despite the frequency with which step-family arrangements are encountered, various negative stereotypes persist. The term 'step-child' often denotes poor regard by those with authority, or having a second-class status. Stereotypes of the 'wicked step-mother' may have originated in the fairy tales, but are perpetuated by both the media and popular fiction. Most people who have experienced step-parents or step-parenting can attest to the complexities of the roles for all concerned.

The challenge of restructuring a family and its boundaries to include new step-parents and step-siblings necessitates various realignments and negotiations. Financial arrangements, including maintenance payments, require delicate and forthright discussions and agreements. Finding ways of maintaining relationships between children, parents, grandparents, and other significant extended family members are crucial elements of the restructuring process, as is the inclusion of new family members. Respecting and sharing memories of significant history remains an important part of the ongoing adaptation among blended families. Finding a healthy balance between past, present and future relationships is an ongoing challenge for blended families (Carter & McGoldrick, 2005a).

Fostering and adoptive families

Social workers have traditionally been at the forefront of working with families in the course of fostering and adopting children. *Foster care* entails varying lengths of time in which a child lives with a foster family, who are neither their birth parents nor their adoptive parents. *Adoption* entails the legal process by which a child becomes a permanent member of a family comprising parents other than the child's biological parents.

Foster care is generally intended as a temporary arrangement, and is contingent on the premise that the child's birth parents will be able to resume their parenting roles. Since that does not always occur, foster care sometimes becomes a 'permanent' solution to what was expected to be a temporary situation.

When foster care is entered into as a temporary arrangement, foster parents and children may be reluctant to invest themselves emotionally in a relationship that they expect to be short-term (Constable & Lee, 2004). Uncertain attachments often complicate foster care arrangements, and require considerable skills on the part of foster families and social workers to meet the needs of children who are emotionally and socially vulnerable (Fahlberg, 1991). Issues of previous emotional injuries, disappointments, breaches of trust, as well as unaddressed grief from repeated separations may all complicate the prospects of a successful experience in foster care. Frequent changes in environments, carers and relationships preclude children having the predictable environment that is crucial to the development of self-esteem and self-efficacy during childhood. For children who have been abused or neglected, the risks of emotional vulnerability are compounded (Schofield, 2008). Especially when children think it would be disloyal to their birth parents to establish attachments to foster families, the emotional situation can be particularly difficult for all concerned. Frequent changes of placements further compound children's experiences of foster care, especially when foster families find a child difficult, and request that they be placed elsewhere. Through such practices, children who are already likely to be emotionally fragile are subjected to further emotional challenges and distress.

A disproportionate number of children with disabilities are in foster care placements; once placed in foster care, those children are more likely to be in multiple placements, remain in the system longer, and are less likely to return to their birth parents than other children (Rosenberg & Robinson, 2004). For foster parents caring for children with disabilities, not only are sound parenting and stress management skills necessary, but strong advocacy, networking, and budgeting skills as well (Brown, 2007).

Foster care adoption occurs when a child has been placed initially into a foster family, and is subsequently placed for adoption. The adoptive parents are often the parents who previously fostered the child. The proportion of children adopted from foster care placement is rising in the UK, which generally entails children being older at the time of adoption, and more complex considerations regarding contact with birth families (Wolfgram, 2008).

Adoption entails an array of social and psychological factors. In some cases, adoption occurs in response to immediate family or community members' needs or crises; it may occur when a birth parent dies or is incapable of raising their own child. Adoption may also result from the courts determining that a child is suffering or at risk of suffering significant harm, in which case Care Orders or Child Protection Orders are issued to arrange for alternative care for the child (Kilpatrick, 2006).

Historically, many unmarried mothers were persuaded (or coerced) to place their child for adoption through various social and religious agencies. Many such adoptions also occurred privately or informally. The number of children available for adoption in western nations has dropped in recent decades for a variety of reasons, including the social acceptance of unmarried mothers raising their children, as well as the availability of contraceptives and abortions to prevent or terminate unwanted or unplanned pregnancies (Johnson, 2004).

Some adoptions occur in response to couple's inability to have their own biological offspring, or wanting more children than they already have. Some cases may reflect infertility or same-sex partnerships. Some adoptions occur when a lone parent marries a new spouse who wishes to become the legal parent (rather than a step-parent) to their spouse's child, including legally changing the child's name. Two inappropriate reasons for adoption are associated with subsequent difficulties: adoptions made in hopes of 'curing' infertility, and adoptions made solely to please one partner (Howe, 1995). When an adoption becomes legal or finalized, all parental responsibilities and rights are transferred to the adoptive parents, and there is no legal difference between a child born to those parents and one who is adopted by them. Adoptive parents are also responsible for informing a child of their adoption.

According to BAAF (2008), the average age of children adopted during 2007 was 4 years 2 months, with the majority (64 per cent) being between ages one and four years. The vast majority of children subject to Adoption Order applications by adoption agencies in the UK in recent years have been under age 10 (McSherry & Larkin, 2006). Regardless of the age at which a child is adopted, some issues appear consistently relevant following adoption. These include issues of attachment, trust and identity. As children's attachment behaviours are generally evident from around age 7 months for children in the adoptive and fostering systems, attention to their adaptations to changes in attachment figures is crucial (Aldgate, 2006). Especially when adoptions occur at a later age, or following traumatic events, children's concerns about their history, memories, the reasons for their adoption, and their not being responsible for what happened to them must be addressed with sensitivity and honesty (Edwards, 2008).

Some of the consistent issues that appear relevant to children who have been adopted relate to attachment and trust. Specifically, the question often arises about whether, having been 'rejected' by their birth parents, they are going to be rejected again by their adoptive parents. Especially when there are other children in the adoptive family, issues of rivalry and aggression are predictable (Miller, 2008).

During the 1970s, 'positive' or 'respectful' adoption language was introduced by Minneapolis social worker, Marietta Spencer, and continues to influence the preferred terms used to refer to adoptive families' relationships. Terms such as 'birth parents' or 'biological parents', rather than 'real' or 'natural' parents gained usage, as otherwise adoptive relationships were potentially referred to in ways that implied they were imaginary or unnatural (Johnson, 2004). Likewise, the use of terms such as 'real' children as opposed to 'adopted' children inferred that adoption entailed an inherent inferiority. Social workers are called upon to use terms very carefully when discussing adoption and adoptive relationships.

The key variables associated with positive experiences for adoptive parents apply across both heterosexual and same-sex couples (Martin, 1993; Carter, 2005). Those variables include:

- Good communication between partners.
- Both partners having the capacity to adapt to change.
- Both partners having realistic expectations of each other and the adoption.
- Having the capacity to tolerate frustration, chaos, sleep deprivation, and diminished privacy.

Diverse family forms

Although family forms vary widely, sociologists generally classify family systems according to whether they are *nuclear* or *extended* families. Nuclear families generally comprise parents and their children living in the same household. Extended families often include more than two generations, and members who are not necessarily immediately related by blood, such as aunts, uncles, cousins, and sometimes close family friends (Zastrow, 2007).

Some examples of diverse family forms include the following:

- childless heterosexual partners with long-term foster children;
- homosexual partners who have children from previous heterosexual relationships;
- childless partners who are the primary carers for one partner's parent, who has Alzheimer's and who lives in the couple's home;
- grandparents who are raising grandchildren because of illness, death, or imprisonment;
- nuclear family with one child living in a residential facility for children with severe learning disorders;
- partners who live apart because of military service, training, employment, or imprisonment.

Families headed by gay or lesbian couples are often subjected to levels of harassment, violence and exclusion that traditional heterosexual couples never experience. Access to benefits, and key entitlements and legal protection that heterosexual couples and their families take for granted can sometimes be compromised solely on the basis of sexual orientation (Rooney, 2002a). This may start with a lesbian's access to fertility treatment if she and her partner decide to go through *in vitro* fertilization in order to achieve pregnancy. Questions of whether sperm comes from a sperm bank or from a known donor may entail an array of medical, ethical and emotional dilemmas for the prospective parents, medical providers, and the families of origins of the prospective parents.

While the majority of children being raised by gay or lesbian couples were born in previous heterosexual partnerships, the Adoption and Children Act 2002 enabled same-sex couples in the UK to adopt children. The Civil Partnership Act 2004 provided the means for same-sex couples to register their partnerships legally, establishing their rights and responsibilities in accordance with those of other married people (Walker, 2008). Legislation alone, however, does not preclude discrimination and bias occurring. Gay and lesbian families consistently receive less social validation as family units than more traditional families take for granted. In some cases, gay and lesbian families refrain even from public acknowledgement of their relationships for fear of threats to their safety, employment, custody arrangements or housing status.

People from ethnic minorities who are also gay or lesbian face additional challenges of racial discrimination, and may find even less support and fewer resources within their communities because of cultural or social stigma associated with homosexuality. Such barriers may be subtle or overt, but social workers must be mindful of and responsive to the complex needs such social factors may entail for children and families of same-sex partners, and to stay current with relevant legislation.

Families with alcohol- and drug-related problems

Alcohol- and drug-related problems are among the most prevalent and complex problems families are likely to encounter. Substance-related problems feature prominently among families experiencing difficulties, including child abuse, neglect and violence (Cleaver et al., 1999; Forrester & Harwin, 2006; Howe, 2005). Particularly when working with neglectful families, social workers need to be mindful of some of the overlapping characteristics of systemic chaos and lack of cohesion that are sometimes features of both substance misuse and child neglect (Gaudin et al., 1996; Howe, 2005; Scannapieco & Connell-Carrick, 2005).

Social workers need to be familiar with the varied chemical properties and behavioural consequences of alcohol and other drugs in order to understand some of the implications for families. Most social workers are in positions where an informed familiarity with alcohol- and drug-related conditions and complications contributes to good practice.

Some basic concepts relevant to social workers' understanding of alcohol- and drug-related problems include the following:

- *Dependence:* Alcohol and drug dependence is associated with both increased tolerance and withdrawal symptoms upon the dosage being either diminished or stopped, along with the inability to use the substance in moderation.
- *Enabling:* The characteristic behaviours of loved ones, friends, or colleagues who protect the user/drinker from the consequences of their problematic usage. Examples include providing money with which to purchase substances, and making excuses for irresponsible behaviour (including parenting difficulties, or absences from work caused by usage). Enabling typically entails some redistribution of responsibilities within the family, to compensate for usage-related inadequacies.
- *Misuse/abuse:* Sometimes used interchangeably in the UK, misuse/abuse refers to problematic intake of a given substance, in which usage continues despite negative consequences. Such consequences may include alcohol-induced blackouts, or social or legal problems resulting from usage.
- *Self-medication hypothesis:* Self-medicating usage tends to be purposeful, particularly in managing anxiety or trauma-related difficulties. Self-medication is particularly relevant among survivors of abuse, rape, and violence.
- *Tolerance:* The necessity to consume an increased dosage in order to attain the same effect that was produced by a smaller dose in the past indicates the development of tolerance.
- *Withdrawal:* Symptoms of withdrawal occur when usage ceases or is drastically

> diminished. Symptoms range from headaches and hangovers to tremors and seizures. Withdrawal symptoms may be physical, psychological, or both, and vary according to the substance. An extreme example associated with alcohol dependence would be *delirium tremens*.

Alcohol- and drug-related conditions are no respecter of socio-economics, education, or gender; they occur across all social strata. Because alcohol is legal, its dangers are often underestimated. *Alcohol dependence* is not only easily complicated and camouflaged by other conditions (such as depression, anxiety, and gastric disorders), but it is also linked with more deaths each year than all the illicit drugs combined (Sadock & Sadock, 2007).

Many variables influence the roles alcohol and drugs play in family dynamics: whether the user is the mother or father, whether they are a lone parent, whether their usage is considered a 'secret', and whether their usage directly or indirectly endangers their children. An alarming number of children grow up without a sober parent to care for them, making expectations, rules, and consequences very variable concepts. Likewise, an alarming number of children are exposed to alcohol-related domestic violence. Alcohol is overwhelmingly linked with greater risks of violence in the home. More is known about male perpetrators of domestic violence and the role of alcohol in their behaviours than is known about the drinking patterns of women who have been injured. Women with alcohol- or drug-related conditions are often more vulnerable to violent partners than they would be otherwise (Barnett, Miller-Perrin, & Perrin, 1997).

Alcohol- and drug-related problems are increasingly linked with younger *onset of usage*. Social workers are urged to be attentive to young people manifesting problematic usage, especially when there is a family history of alcohol or drug problems. The onset of drinking or drug usage under age 14 is associated with four times the risk of subsequent dependence (Sadock & Sadock, 2007).

Foetal alcohol syndrome (FAS) occurs when the foetus is exposed to alcohol *in utero* through a pregnant woman's alcohol intake (Plant, 2000). Alcohol inhibits both intra-uterine and post-natal growth and development, and is associated with characteristic features, including microcephaly (a small head), facial malformations (including an absent or indistinct philtrum between the upper lip and the nose), and limb and heart defects. Children with FAS tend to be short in stature, and to have consistent behavioural problems (including impulsivity and learning difficulties) (Sadock & Sadock, 2007). Foetal alcohol syndrome typically involves children being both cognitively limited (and thus very vulnerable to exploitation as well as not learning from their mistakes), and very frustrating for their parents (Plant, 2000). For parents already struggling with alcohol-related problems, children with FAS may be profoundly vulnerable, as they may present greater behavioural and personal challenges than the parents are equipped to meet.

Bereavement

Grief and bereavement remain predictable complexities of family life. In a chronologically 'correct' world, parents die before their children, but not until those children are autonomous and emotionally prepared (which is rarely the case, under the best of circumstances.)

The death of a child remains among life's most profound sorrows. Adding to the emotional difficulties of mourning a child, parents' responses are often quite different, and not necessarily compatible or mutually supportive. Bereaved fathers are more likely to become emotionally withdrawn, to take refuge in their work, and to be discomforted by the child's mother's expressions of grief. Some bereaved fathers are fearful of losing control over their emotions, and feel uncomfortable responding to emotional outbursts. Their partner may perceive the man's lack of emotional expressiveness as emotional unavailability or even a form of abandonment when their emotional needs are the greatest, which may compound their sense of emotional loss. When both parents are able to be emotionally expressive and actively involved in a child's illness and death, the family bereavement process and the quality of the parents' relationship generally benefit (McGoldrick, 2005b).

The death of a child's parent involves a more absolute experience of loss than parental divorce entails. According to some, parental death may have a less negative impact on children than parental divorce (Amato, 1995, cited in Hughes, 2003). Children's response to bereavement varies greatly according to developmental age. Temperament, the circumstances of the death, family members' ability to communicate about the death, previous experiences with death, and the family's continued cohesion also influence how children respond to bereavement (Sadock & Sadock, 2007).

Children's grief reactions vary according to many factors, including developmental stages. Infants and toddlers who experience bereavement before being verbal typically respond to separation from an attachment figure with protest, which is followed by despair, and potentially by generalized emotional detachment. Young children may display some developmental regressions following bereavement, such as poor eating and sleeping habits, loss of speech, or bladder or bowel control problems. By around age 5, children are likely to be able to comprehend the permanence of death, as distinct from temporary separations. By the time children are school-aged, their response to bereavement is likely to entail both behavioural (over-activity, difficulties paying attention, impulsivity) and emotional (sadness, anxiety about the remaining parent's survival) aspects. Some children display strong feelings of anger or fears of abandonment; some become phobic or hypochondriacal (Sadock & Sadock, 2007). As with adults, school-age children often have near-hallucinatory experiences, in which they think they see the dead parent (Hughes, 2003).

Satir observed the difficulties children experience when adults either stop mentioning a deceased loved one, or virtually deify the deceased. As noted by Satir (1972: 189), children find it hard to relate to a ghost or a saint. The ability to express feelings, concerns and questions appears to be crucial for children's ability to cope effectively with bereavement. Rituals to commemorate the loved one's death also appear important; attending the funeral and participation in the family's mourning may prove beneficial (Sadock & Sadock, 2007).

From the findings of the Walthamstow Study, Harris and Bifulco (1991) observed correlations between maternal deaths during a girl's childhood and adequate parental care, and the girl's subsequent vulnerability to unsupportive relationships and marriages, along with higher risks of depression during adulthood. From the same study, Andrews and Brown (1988) considered maternal loss during childhood a potential 'provoking agent' for depression and lack of reliable social supports during times of crisis during adulthood.

Of all family bereavements, suicide is generally the most complex. Whether the suicide was that of a parent or child, the bereavement process is generally profoundly difficult, and further complicated by elements of anger, stigma, and remorse. (This is discussed further in Chapter 9.)

Consciously facing the loss, and expressing the emotions involved appear consistently linked with effective coping with bereavement. Weeping, reminiscing, and overt observances may prove beneficial. Unexpressed, unresolved grief is associated with risks of delayed grief reactions, which tend to be complex (Polansky, 1991).

Genograms

Genograms are among the more popular tools used by social workers when conducting family assessments. Attributed to Murray Bowen (1978), genograms provide a visual means of depicting family relationships and patterns through the use of an array of symbols. The commonly used symbols are provided in Figure 12.1. A genogram serves to depict a map of the family's structure, along with relevant information (dates, significant variables, etc.), as well as family relationships (McGoldrick & Gerson, 1985)

Ideally, genograms depict three generations. Readers are gently reminded of basic reproductive realities when constructing genograms: i.e., that two parents per offspring remain the norm. Despite some fathers' lack of involvement following conception, the child is still their offspring. Sometimes question marks go inside the figures, when the person's identity remains uncertain.

Using dates of birth and death often proves more useful than simply stating ages, which change. Also, noting dates of marriages or partnerships, as well as separations or divorces is often useful. When family histories include alcohol- or drug-related problems, those patterns may prove relevant. Sometimes different colours are useful to depict drugs of choice. Sometimes social workers find it useful to keep a box of different coloured pencils or crayons on hand when constructing genograms. A very useful tool with which to depict complex family arrangements, genograms may be constructed alongside service users in ways that utilize their expertise about their families.

Surely the Freud family remains one of the more fascinating families to consider for the purpose of constructing a genogram. A basic genogram of Sigmund Freud's family follows (Figure 12.2), along with some noteworthy points to consider (McGoldrick, 2005a; McGoldrick & Gerson, 1985).

Noteworthy points to ponder:

- The age difference between Jacob and Amalia Nathansohn Freud.
- Jacob's older sons' ages and their immigration to the UK in 1859, along with Sigmund's nephew and niece with whom he had been very close.
- Death of Sigmund's brother Julius (age 6 months) in 1858.
- Amalia's sequential pregnancies during Sigmund's first 10 years.
- Sigmund's four sisters' deaths in Nazi concentration camps.

Male	□
Female	○
Pregnancy	△
Stillbirth	⊠ or ⊗
Miscarriage	●
Abortion	*
Adoption	....
Death	⊠ or ⊗
Suicide	◧ or ◑
Marriage	————————
Non-marital partnership	---------------
Separation or divorce	------//------- ——//——
Conflictual relationship	/\/\/\/\/\/\
Very strong relationship	═════

Other possible variables:

Abuse (physical or sexual)
Alcohol- or drug-related problems
Genetic or medical conditions
Suicide
Violence
Pets

Figure 12.1 Commonly used genogram symbols.
Source: McGoldrick & Gershon (1985).

Implications for practice

Social work with families entails considerably more than just working with children. Good practice necessitates an understanding of family dynamics and the complex ways in which those dynamics influence people's behaviour. Some would argue that social work is more likely to entail working with families than solely with individuals, because of social work's emphasis on context. Working with families entails understanding that families are systems that are subject to change, operating within social systems (also subject to change) within an ever-changing world.

Just as social workers are called upon to respond to a diverse array of families, they are themselves also the products of a diverse array of family backgrounds. For that reason, while it is crucial for social workers to be aware of their own family's patterns and norms, it is equally important to avoid generalizing and projecting those norms onto others for whom they are not necessarily suitable. Social workers must be aware of

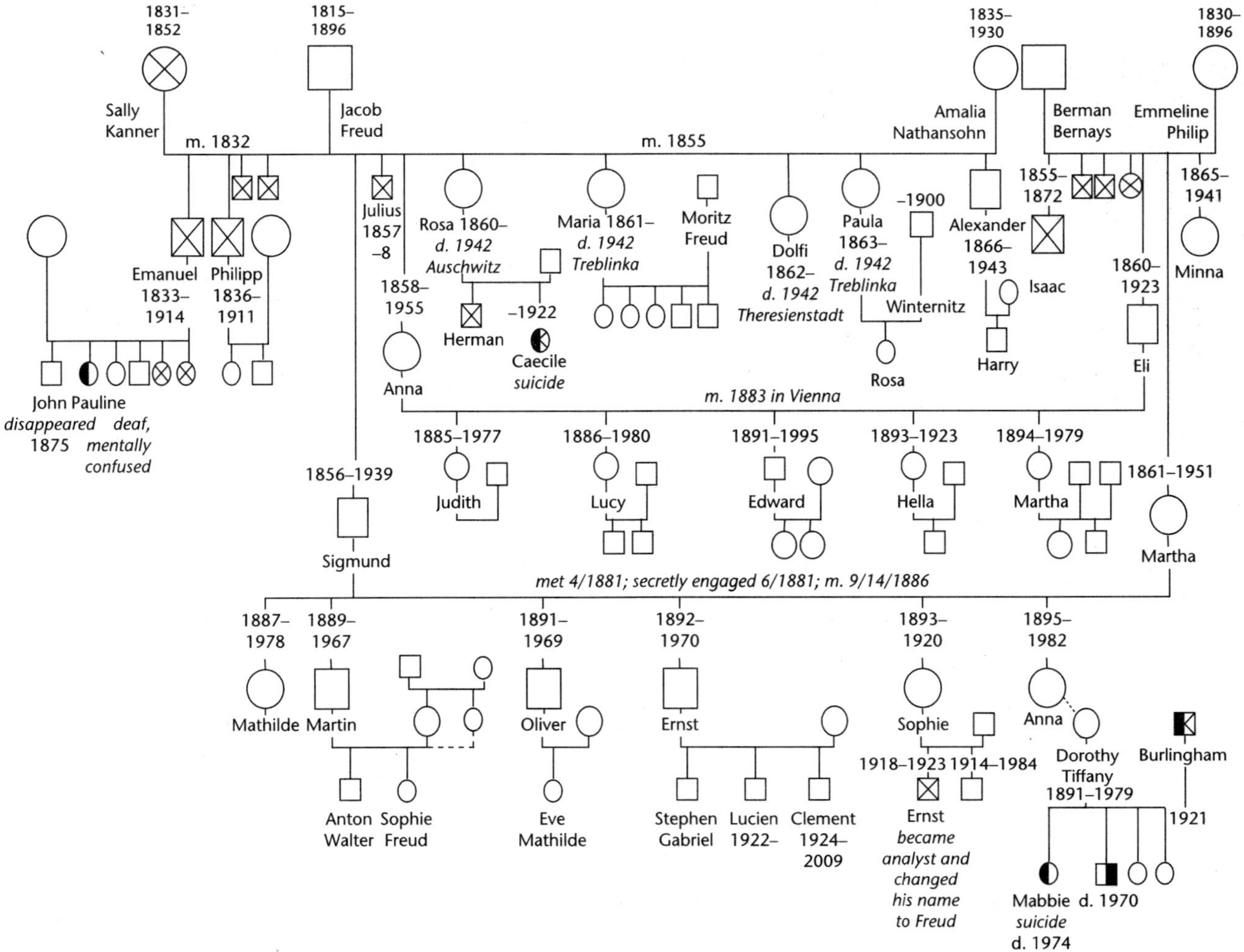

Figure 12.2 The Freud family genogram.

and respectful of the broad array of family structures that exist, and to appreciate the important functions they fulfil.

By using a systems approach when considering families, social workers have the means of incorporating a recognition of the family's strengths in their assessment. Especially when working with families experiencing adversity, using a strengths-based approach is a crucial component of social work assessments (Rooney, 2002a). From Minuchin's (1974) perspective, by helping families achieve restructuring of counter-productive roles and patterns, social workers can facilitate constructive changes that will enhance families' functioning.

Social workers must remember some key socio-economic elements about families most likely to receive social services. Most of the families receiving child protection services comprise 'non-traditional households' experiencing poverty and some degree of social exclusion. The estimated chance of a child (age 5–9) living in an owner-occupied home with two parents, with more rooms than people and no more than three siblings entering the care of British social services is approximately 1:7000 (Smale, Tuson, & Stratham, 2000: 18). In order to meet those children's needs and the needs of their families, social workers must maintain a clear perspective that incorporates strengths as well as risks to be assessed on an ongoing basis.

Families typically experience the highest levels of stress during points of transition (developmental, relocation, changed relationships, financial circumstances). Major transitions typically necessitate rebalancing, redefining, and realigning family members' internal relationships (Carter & McGoldrick, 2005b). When applying concepts of homeostasis to the understanding of family systems, understanding when some family members are either afraid of or opposed to the prospect of change can be crucial, as their resistance to change typically has a 'ripple effect' within the entire family.

Ultimately, social workers need to be especially mindful of the relationship between the family system and the macrosystem, particularly in cases involving social oppression or exclusion. Ethnic minority families, or families who experience the social system as punitive or dangerous may have different expectations, which shape different boundaries with the macrosystem, compared with families who enjoy social privileges.

Satir's work with families included an emphasis on enhanced communication, with the core element of honesty being considered fundamental. She focused on helping partners and family members take ownership of their statements, and emphasized the use of 'I-messages' as an element of building direct, clear patterns of communication (1983).

Coulshed and Orme (2006: 199) compare the prospect of understanding a family to 'jumping onto a moving bus', because of the social worker's temporary role in a dynamic, moving, changing entity. Satir (1983) also used *family sculpting* when working with troubled families. Sometimes used as both an assessment and therapeutic technique, family sculpting provides a way of physically arranging members of a family, with each person's place and posture determined by the member who is serving as the 'director'. The resulting positions produce a symbolic representation of the family's relationships and dynamics (Zastrow, 2007).

Thanks to higher levels of education, employment opportunities for women, and the contributions of the feminist movement, Western families are generally moving toward increasingly equitable arrangements for male–female roles and responsibilities within families. Many families continue to struggle with the ongoing disparities in expectations for women, including salary discrepancies and household expectations. As immigrant families adjust to Western norms, they too face similar challenges.

Parental substance misuse remains a common issue for many families with whom social workers are involved in child protective services. Social workers need to be knowledgeable about specific substances and the patterns and consequences of usage in order to conduct informed assessments. Especially when parents are not convinced that their usage is problematic, social workers need a sufficient knowledge base with which to contribute effectively to assessments and plans of intervention (Forrester & Harwin, 2006).

Poor parenting is consistently linked with children's lifelong difficulties. Ideally, parents are in a position to contribute to their children being prepared to fulfil their potential and to become contributing members of a larger social system. Social workers are called upon to help families achieve that goal to the best of their abilities. Most families continue to do the best they can do with what they have to offer. Most families still strive to 'get it right' to the best of their abilities. Social workers are called upon to validate and facilitate those efforts and aspirations.

Criticisms and shortcomings of family theory

Some would argue that much of the work represented in the literature about families stems primarily from middle-class Euro-American families. In their more recent publications, Carter and McGoldrick have addressed the changing demographics of family life to include such factors as lower birth rates and changing family configurations, thus moving away from the traditional child-centred focus (Carter & McGoldrick, 2005b; Schriver, 1998). That does not necessarily suffice to address some of the changing patterns of family configurations in the UK.

Feminists have challenged the premise that changes in family structures are increasingly egalitarian for women. According to feminist authors, women's positions in families remain subordinate and economically dependent on patriarchal systems, with the balance of power remaining primarily with men (Abbott, Wallace & Tyler, 2005). Such arguments necessitate a reconsideration of some of the implications of family systems.

Because motherhood is still regarded as being an essential and inherently female role, when families experience difficulties, and particularly when children have problems, the mother is often considered responsible. In many instances, this premise diminishes the role played by fathers, and is sometimes tantamount to blaming the victim. Because family theory does not necessarily address the social, economic, and political dimensions of women's circumstances, some consider it an inadequate approach to understanding the complexities experienced by women and their children.

Questions

1 Match the following concepts and analyst with the definitions:

	Concept	Definition
____	Double binds	(a) The individual who is blamed for others' problems
____	'Stonewalling'	(b) Congruent/incongruent communication
____	Alcohol dependence	(c) When one partner withdraws from interaction and communication in the midst of conflict
____	Scapegoat	(d) Evidence of tolerance and withdrawal symptoms
____	Microcephaly	(e) No matter how the message is interpreted, there will be a negative outcome
____	Foster care adoption	(f) Small head size associated with foetal alcohol syndrome
____	Virginia Satir	(g) Children being adopted resulting from a foster placement

2 How would you describe your family? Please write a description of your family of origin, including such factors as the following:

- Who are members?
- Ages, gender of members
- Religious or political affiliations
- Values shared by members
- Significant family activities
- Current stressors experienced
- Significant family strengths

3 In many parts of the world, arranged marriages remain the traditional practice. Parents determine their children's partners based on an array of characteristics and expectations. How would an arranged marriage differ from Western norms in relation to the following variables?
   (a) Family structure
   (b) Family roles
   (c) Domestic division of labour
   (d) Marital disruptions?

4 What are some of the implications of the declining rates of marriage for social work practice?

5 Read the following scenario and answer the questions that follow:

> 'Betty' (age 50) and 'Bob' (age 60) have been married for 25 years. Both are professionals who enjoy their careers. Their two daughters have recently finished university, and are preparing to move into a shared flat that Betty and Bob have helped them purchase. Bob plans to retire next year. They have been looking forward to having more

time together, and hope to enjoy some long-wished-for travel. Bob has been diagnosed with some early symptoms of Parkinson's disease, but they are hoping that the level of progression of his condition continues to develop slowly. At present, he is quite fit.

Betty's father died very young, and her mother remarried 'Tom', whom Betty has considered her father since childhood. Tom has been very close to Betty and Bob and their daughters. Last week, Tom had a massive stroke, and died in hospital at age 75.

Betty and her family have been aware of her mother's increasing forgetfulness during the past year. During the past week, the family has realized how much Tom compensated for Betty's mother, Ruth (age 73). Unbeknown to Betty, Ruth has not been driving for the past year, because she is prone to getting lost. Without Tom to help her in the mornings, Ruth became very confused and distressed on several occasions, and was not dressed when Betty arrived to drive her to the hospital. Following Tom's death, Ruth has repeatedly asked Betty 'Where is Tom? When is he coming home?'

How does Betty's family situation reflect the following?

(a) Step-family functioning
(b) Lifecycle issues
(c) Changing roles
(d) Inter-generational role reversals

6 Family myths can be positive or negative. What are some examples of positive family sayings and/or myths that have supported you in achieving your aspirations?

7 In pairs, please construct genograms for one another. When possible, try to gather information with which to include three generations. Please be mindful that this exercise is not intended to elicit any information about which students are uncomfortable disclosing.

13 Feminist perspectives on behaviour

Feminist perspectives are primarily defined by their approach to understanding problems in relation to women's experiences of disadvantages based on their sex, class and/or race. While feminism refers to a variety of thoughts and bodies of knowledge, it generally reflects some core concepts that are embodied in feminist theory. By its nature, feminist theory is anti-oppressive in its approach to problem definitions and solutions, and its focus is on challenging the traditional patriarchal norms and views of society and social problems.

Relevance for social work

Since gaining prominence during the 1970s, feminist perspectives have featured in the study and practice of social work, and have shaped perspectives on behaviour. Since the addition of 'women's' studies in the area of social work, sociology and psychology during the 1970s, feminist perspectives have increasingly influenced social work practice. Dominelli (2008: 111) defines feminist social work as practice that 'takes gendered inequality and its elimination as the starting point for working with women, whether as individuals, in groups, or within organizations, and seeks to promote women's well-being as women define it'. The explicit quest for social justice for women (and its implicit linkage with social justice for all) are core components of feminist perspectives.

Feminist perspectives are a vital element of social workers' regard for the parenting and caring roles often held by women at their own material expense. The often invisible and traditionally unappreciated roles of mothering and being a 'housewife' have often lacked recognition as legitimate 'work', because of not being financially rewarded in a capitalistic society. Distinctions between work (outside the home) that is socially and financially recognized and housework continue to be the topic of both social and governmental debates (Hockey & James, 2003). Social workers often work with families and households in which such inequities have taken tremendous tolls for generations of women.

As a profession whose female practitioners far outnumber the males, social work is in a unique position to incorporate feminist perspectives in both its curriculum and practice methods. That does not necessarily mean that social work practice fully reflects core feminist values, however, especially in statutory settings. Indeed, feminist theory points out the historically patriarchal premises and practices that have shaped welfare policy and practice (Stepney & Evans, 2000). Nonetheless, social workers are in powerful positions to incorporate pro-feminist practice in their work with women and families who have been subjected to oppressive social systems and practices that may be so insidious as to go unrecognized as oppression.

Historical background

Feminism's philosophical roots can be traced back to the Enlightenment and its ideals of the individual and social and economic change (Williams, 1996). As a social movement and doctrine, feminism dates back to eighteenth- and nineteenth-century efforts in England to advocate for legal and socio-economic equity for women (Barker, 2003). Along with opposing slavery and seeking voting rights ('suffrage') for women, many women's groups sought to challenge various deeply rooted societal problems. Several women's organizations, including the Women's Christian Temperance Union and the Women's Trade Union League, sought to provide services needed by women, and to advocate for women in ways that would influence legislation in the US and the UK (Agnew, 2003; Hyde, 2008). Philosophically, feminism has also challenged the Enlightenment ideal of reason as embodied by masculine models, and proposed that feminine knowledge and feminine ways of knowing are also coherent and valid (Williams, 1996).

The French philosopher and author **Simone de Beauvoir** (1908–1980) inspired generations of women with her (1949) book, *The Second Sex* (1988). In that work, she addressed various inequities experienced by women across society. Based on her own experiences and observations of mid-twentieth-century French norms, de Beauvoir described and analysed the ways in which women experienced subordination by men and by society in general. Her famous quote 'one is not born, but becomes, a woman' (1988: 295) eloquently challenged the premise that biology was destiny by distinguishing between social roles and anatomical functions. De Beauvoir contributed to the distinctions between sex and gender, pointing out that sex is biologically determined, while gender reflects socially constructed attributes. De Beauvoir effectively introduced the argument that motherhood served to subjugate women, and that social roles had been defined according to men's needs and objectives, at the expense of women's autonomy and fulfilment.

The origins of feminist theory are mainly from sociological studies of the inherent inequities embedded in culturally sanctioned oppression of women throughout history. *Radical feminism* has focused on the role played by patriarchy as a means of controlling women and their lives. From the radical feminist perspective, patriarchy is considered a central, primary problem needing solution (Abbott, Wallace & Tyler, 2005).

Radical feminist influences on sociological studies date from the early 1970s, and include **Anne Oakley**'s (1974) eloquent discussion of how gender roles are socially, rather than biologically, determined. In Britain, such arguments coincided with socially progressive legislation, including the Equal Pay Act (1970) and the Sex Discrimination Act (1975), which began to pave the way toward greater economic autonomy for women (Thompson, 2006). Oakley (1981) argued that industrialization had actually contributed to the oppression of women through influencing the systematic reduction in men's involvement in daily domestic routines, through women's increased financial dependence on men, and the isolation of women's housework and childcare from other forms of work or employment.

In her seminal book *Sexual Politics*, **Kate Millett** (1970) proposed that the inherently male-dominated power structures shaped the ways in which men subjugated women. Millett argued that patriarchy's pervasive influences on the lives of women outweigh economics or any other cultural ideology, through the dynamics of women's sense of powerlessness and male dominance. Occurrences such as the prolonged debate regarding the consecration of women bishops in the Church of England provide examples of ways in which women have been precluded from occupying roles for which only men (with identical training) were deemed eligible.

Shulamith Firestone (1970) argued powerfully on behalf of radical feminism, and proposed that sexual oppression functions as the primary and most fundamental form of oppression, superseding economic inequities. According to Firestone, basic reproductive roles and the biological family determined women's historic subjugation because of extended periods of physical and financial dependence upon men caused by pregnancy and the prolonged physical dependence of human infants. Examples include the pension differentials to which women are eligible at the age of retirement, based on years of paid employment that do not include maternity leave.

Black/post-colonial feminists have challenged Anglo-American feminism for being too simplistic and too Eurocentric. **Hazel Carby** (1987) used historical evidence to explore some of the discrepancies between the experiences of black women and the more Eurocentric feminist tradition. Carby questioned some fundamental feminist concepts such as the role played by the family in women's subjugation. She also questioned the premise that all males are necessarily patriarchal. **Patricia Collins** (2000) argued that differences between women, rather than between men and women demanded clearer consideration, particularly in light of the myriad ways in which ethnic minority women are systematically overlooked and minimized in society as well as research. Collins further explored the role played by class and heterosexism in the lives of black and minority ethnic women. Examples include health and fitness-related studies, especially those regarding variables such as stress- and diet-related conditions.

The American author **Alice Walker** introduced the term *womanist* in 1983 to refer to a black feminist or feminists of colour. According to Walker, womanism is defined by a quest for greater knowledge than has been traditionally considered necessary or even 'good' for women. Walker refers to a level of courage and wilfulness associated with womanism, likening womanism to feminism 'as purple is to lavender' (1983: xi–xii). As readers of her (1983) novel *The Color Purple* can attest, Walker's writing provides rich insights into black women's fortitude and endurance, as well as the capacity for triumph over oppression. Womanist perspectives emphasize the 'double jeopardy' of being both female and from an ethnic minority.

Key concepts of feminism

Feminism remains a broad array of perspectives. Challenging the traditional definitions and determinants of power and the use of power is a fundamental component of feminism (Hyde, 2008). Aspects of power include property ownership, the control and domination of others, the capacity to vote, reproductive choices, access to education and employment, and self-determination. Western feminism comprises a variety of approaches, including liberal, radical, humanist, Marxist, Black/post-colonial and postmodern perspectives. As varied as those perspectives may be, they share an emphasis on addressing the subordination experienced by women in an overwhelmingly male-dominated or patriarchal society.

A basic understanding of the term *patriarchy* is necessary in order to grasp the full implications of feminist perspectives. Literally translated as 'rule of the father' (Scott & Marshall, 2005), patriarchy refers to the traditional legal and social systems based on the authority of male heads of households. Patriarchy is broadly defined according to traditional male domination in domestic, social, economic, and political spheres, and refers to the historical disadvantages or oppression women have experienced both privately and publicly. Historically, the patriarchal traditions of most religions and their scriptures have been used (and abused) to justify women's subjugation. Because patriarchy is so often entrenched in cultures, histories and opportunities, various ways in which women are either subordinated or dominated by men often go unnoticed and unspoken because they are considered so routine.

Patriarchy is an intrinsic factor of gender inequality, and can be found in a variety of social structures that serve to subjugate women in ways that support the patriarchal *status quo* (Walby, 1990). Those structures include the following:

- paid work (which jobs are valued?);
- patriarchal domestic relations (household roles, responsibilities);
- patriarchal culture (social traditions);
- sexuality (including double standards of acceptability);
- male violence against women (including sanctioned violence);
- patriarchal arrangements endorsed by the state (laws, rights, opportunities).

The issue of paid employment is a key component of many feminist arguments. Because women have been excluded from many means of gainful employment, and because much of the domestic and child-raising work traditionally allocated to women has not been paid work, most women have been financially disadvantaged throughout history. Much of Western culture has been based on the premise that women (including those who are cleverer than their partners) have happily surrendered their ambitions in order to run a household and support the career of their (potentially less clever) partner. When women have chosen to remain in the workforce, they have traditionally found themselves victims of what is known as the 'glass ceiling', referring to the unspoken, invisible barriers that have precluded women from rising to the upper levels of corporate, academic and political authority.

The feminist term *malestream* has been used to denote the traditionally male-dominated perspective reflected in historic scientific and sociological studies. The male-based knowledge base has not only excluded female-based viewpoints, but has also excluded women from being in positions of intellectual authority or power in the construction of further knowledge. The feminist arguments against the sexist aspects of traditional scientific and sociological findings include the following points, summarized by Abbott, Wallace and Tyler (2005):

- Sociological research has often excluded women from studies, thus excluding data that would have reflected women's perspectives.
- Even when research conducted by sociologists has relied on all-male samples, the inference has been that the results can be generalized to apply to women as well.
- Sociological studies have rarely examined aspects of social life unique to women (e.g. household issues, childbirth, menopause, etc.).
- Topics of 'sex and gender' have historically been minimized among important explanatory variables in sociological studies, at the expense of women's experiences and perspectives being respected, or even considered relevant.

Women and poverty

Despite the nearly 40 years since the passage of the Equal Pay Act (1970), women are still more likely than men to experience poverty, defined as households receiving less than 50 per cent of the average household income after housing costs. Because social work is inherently devoted to the elimination of oppression and the alleviation of poverty, the feminist perspective is necessarily relevant to social workers' views on women's lives and circumstances.

A number of factors contribute to women's heightened risks of experiencing poverty (Maynard et al., 2008). The following are but a few of the factors that contribute to women's increased likelihood of living in poverty across the lifespan:

- Women receive lower wages (between 65 and 84 per cent) for the same work as men.
- Women are more likely than men to be lone parenthe or sheads of households (approximately 90 per cent of lone-parent households are female-headed).
- Women are more likely than men to be unpaid carers, providing care for family members on an informal basis.
- Women are more likely than men to be employed in part-time positions.

Women's access to benefits is routinely compromised because of being women. Not all women are entitled to maternity benefits, because of the intermittent patterns of their employment. Nor are all women entitled to unemployment and redundancy benefits, if their employment has been either part-time or sporadic. Such variables also influence pensions. Eligibility for partners' pensions following death or divorce also varies according to legal arrangements, which often preclude unmarried partnerships being acknowledged.

Given the risks of women living in poverty, some of the challenges associated with women parenting children while living in poverty are noteworthy. Despite improved national statistics on childhood mortality, low birth weight is still associated with infants born in poverty (Haralambos, Holborn, & Heald, 2004). Low birth weight is associated with an array of cognitive difficulties for children, influencing academic potential and lifelong achievement (Hack et al., 2002; Parrish, 2004). From a feminist perspective, the responsibilities of single mothers raising children with such complex needs are neither addressed nor supported by a patriarchal society, leaving both mothers and children unnecessarily vulnerable.

Women from working-class backgrounds appear more likely to become lone parents, and their experiences as lone parents vary widely from those of other women. Women from working-class backgrounds are more likely to remain lone parents longer and their poverty is more enduring in terms of its implications for them and their children (Rowlingson & McKay, 2005).

In both paid and unpaid settings, women occupy the majority of carers' roles in the UK (Mullender, 2008). In informal arrangements, which typically involve immediate family members, women are far more likely to be expected to forego paid employment in order to provide care for a loved one (parent, child, sibling). Across cultures, women have consistently been expected to care for sick, elderly and frail relatives without remuneration (Tanner & Harris, 2008). According to some estimates, carers are saving the government £57 billion yearly, through the informal arrangements made to look after disabled family members in the UK (Devo, 2007). While such arrangements are often best for those in need, they are not necessarily in women's best interests in terms of financial stability or pensions.

Feminism and the family

Women have traditionally been regarded as the primary determinants of their families' emotional well-being and social achievements. Even in the midst of domestic violence and paternal abandonment, women have historically shouldered the social and emotional responsibility for their family. From a feminist perspective, such expectations are neither realistic nor just.

Among the more prominent of the radical feminists, Germaine Greer (2000) argues that family life is effectively designed to women's disadvantage. Greer observes that while married men score consistently higher on all measures of psychological well-being than their unmarried counterparts, married women tend to be less content than unmarried women taking those same measures. She goes on to question the fulfilment available to women from motherhood, stating that,

> 'Mother' is not a career option; the woman who gave her all to mothering has to get in shape, find a job, and keep young and beautiful if she wants to be loved. 'Motherly' is a word for people who are frumpish and suffocating, people who wear cotton hose and shoes with a small heel.
>
> (Greer, 2000: 248)

If any occupation generates less status for women than 'housewife', then perhaps it would be that of 'retired', and some would argue that housewives have no means of retiring. Thus the challenges of women in later life demand attention from a feminist perspective. For many women now of retirement age, traditional gender roles determined their entire educational and occupational histories. Whether married, living with partners, unmarried or widowed, older women are often at a considerable economic disadvantage from their male counterparts. Older women are more than twice as likely to live in poverty as men their same age (Maynard et al., 2008). According to recent figures, 40 per cent of divorced women over age 65 qualify for income support, compared with 1 per cent of their married counterparts (Cochrane, 2008). From a feminist perspective, that disparity reflects a lifelong experience of patriarchy and oppression.

Women and crime

The study of female criminology is a specific area in which feminist empiricism argues that the existing body of knowledge is insufficient to understand crucial differences between men and women (Smart, 1995). An American saying, 'painting blue prison cells pink is not enough to make the system work for women', reflects some of the challenges inherent to feminist criminology.

While men commit the large majority of recorded crimes, when women commit violent crimes, they are often subject to a double standard imposed by society. As noted by Lloyd (1995), women who commit violent crimes are perceived to have violated two laws: the law of the land and the law of nature that relegates women to passive, caring roles that would preclude the capacity for violence.

Most women convicted of crimes come from economically disadvantaged backgrounds, with a large percentage having been brought up in care. Some researchers question whether middle-class or 'white-collar' female criminals may be more likely to be able to conceal their crimes, or whether women from lower socio-economic backgrounds are more vulnerable to committing crimes than their more affluent counterparts (Carlen, 1988). The combined influences of poverty and drug dependence consistently play noteworthy roles in women's criminal convictions. Drug dependence heightens women's risks of perpetrating and being victims of violent crimes (Bachar & Koss, 2001; Baty et al., 2008).

A crucial variable in the consideration of women and criminality is the high proportion of women offenders who have themselves been victims of earlier crimes. Childhood histories of abuse, trauma, running away, prostitution, and drug offences have all been correlated with subsequent imprisonment for women (Belknap, 1996; HM Chief Inspector of the Prisons, 1997). Women prisoners are also more likely than their male counterparts to have depression, engage in deliberate self-injury, to misuse alcohol or other drugs, and to rely on prescribed medications (Gross, 2001). From a feminist perspective, such behaviours must be considered in relation to the early influences of male perpetrators of violence and abuse and patriarchal dominance in female prisoners' lives.

In order to gather sufficient information with which to inform services that will meet women's needs, research must address the issue that women's histories and needs are often inherently different from those of their male counterparts. Feminist criminology argues that traditional methodological approaches to studying women's crimes are often inherently flawed, missing key factors (such as the roles played by childhood trauma and sexual violence), and will remain inadequate until the historical male bias is addressed.

Women and domestic violence

While strangers and acquaintances commit most of the violence perpetrated against men, intimate partners, spouses, or former spouses perpetrate most crimes against women (Mahoney, Williams & West, 2001). Unlike men, women are far more likely to be killed by an intimate partner (or former partner) than by a stranger; hence the use of the term *femicide* rather than 'homicide' to refer to women killed by their intimate partners (Campbell, 1992). While domestic violence (DV) is sometimes referred to as 'family violence' and 'intimate partner violence', for this discussion DV will be used to refer to violence that is perpetrated against a partner or spouse. While DV typically entails two direct participants, its implications for children, families, and households are immense.

Methodological differences complicate any accurate estimate of the prevalence of DV, which is likely to be under-reported in the first place. Domestic violence remains a crime that is often kept secret, and sometimes actually referred to as 'best kept behind closed doors'. Women experiencing DV often present their injuries to healthcare professionals as secondary to other symptoms or concerns (Baty et al., 2008). While the majority of reported cases reflect violence perpetrated by men against women, most statistical estimates fail to include violence by women against men, and violence between same-sex partners (Glicken & Sechrest, 2003).

Domestic violence is consistently correlated with substance misuse. Because alcohol often serves as a disinhibitor, it frequently contributes to violence both in and out of the home. Most studies address perpetrators' alcohol misuse. Fewer address the heightened vulnerability of women survivors of DV who also misuse alcohol (Humphreys et al., 2005). Women using crack cocaine appear particularly vulnerable to severe violence inflicted by their partners as well as their suppliers (Burry et al., 1999). Ironically, DV services for women with alcohol or drug dependence are often limited.

Questions abound as to whether the DV causes the alcohol/drug misuse, or vice versa (Baty et al., 2008). The end result, however, includes heightened vulnerability for women. From a feminist perspective, this vulnerability stems from patriarchal systems of dominance and control.

Many perpetrators of DV subscribe to stereotypical gender roles, including patriarchal dominance in the home. Along with traditional social roles, perpetrators also appear to subscribe to beliefs that alcohol is an acceptable dimension of masculinity, and alcohol-fuelled aggression is a male prerogative in the home (Humphreys et al., 2005). Many perpetrators also come from homes in which DV occurred, and often went unreported, thus raising questions of violence perpetrated against women being seen as acceptable, sanctioned male aggression (Mahoney et al., 2001). Social learning theory has been applied to understanding how witnessing DV during childhood can influence both partners' adult experiences of and regard for DV.

From a feminist perspective, DV reflects an array of societal ills, including overt and covert disregard for women who have been victimized. From a feminist perspective, the likelihood of a woman being financially dependent upon her male partner is an integral part of her vulnerability, as are pregnancy and new motherhood, which are also risk factors for DV (Baty et al., 2008). Particularly in cases in which women have either previously been in violent relationships, or when there have been previous violent episodes with a partner with whom she has remained, social and professional responses frequently amount to 'blaming the victim', somehow implying that the woman is responsible for her partner's violence. From a feminist perspective, the question is not so much a matter of 'why doesn't she leave him?' or 'why doesn't she move to another town?' so much as 'why isn't something being done about his violence?'.

Among women who have been assaulted, lesbian women have a particularly difficult time obtaining help. The limited data available are primarily based on small, non-representative studies, and only began to emerge during the 1980s. And while the patterns and prevalence of violence appear similar for women's homosexual and heterosexual relationships, several noteworthy differences arise. Among those distinctions, societal homophobia and discrimination combine to promote greater secrecy, along with the accumulated stressors and feelings of powerlessness that may contribute to the violence in the first place (Hart, 1986; Mahoney et al., 2001). Among the noteworthy distinctions in violent same-sex relationships is the threat of exposure to families or employers when the partnership is not publicly known, thus adding an additional psychological form of abuse and intimidation. Access to refuges may also be limited for lesbians, if they are made to feel unwelcome because of their sexual orientation (Renzetti, 1992).

Women from ethnic minority and immigrant communities face multiple barriers to disclosing and receiving support in response to DV. Black women report reluctance to disclose DV for fear of betraying their community's honour as well as issues of racism. Culture and language, along with fears of deportation, preclude many immigrant women from seeking or receiving the help they need in response to DV (Heath, 2008). Social workers are in crucial positions to address this inequity, and help ensure that all women are entitled to safety from violence.

Feminism and mental health concerns

Women have historically been over-represented in psychiatric statistics. Feminist arguments would address questions of traditional gender roles and inequities in explaining such findings, along with gender-based norms of help-seeking behaviours and acceptability of the sick role (Prior, 1999; Rogers & Pilgrim, 2005).

The occurrence of eating disorders, and their prevalence among teenage and young adult women are frequently associated with social and media emphasis on thinness and exercise. From a feminist perspective, the prospect of self-starvation could be seen as a reaction to patriarchal oppression.

The prevalence of depression among women has consistently been estimated as nearly twice that of men. Explanatory hypotheses have included hormonal differences, childbirth, and cognitive behavioural factors such as learned helplessness (Sadock & Sadock, 2007). Feminist approaches would emphasize the different psychosocial stressors experienced by women, and the socially accepted tradition of women internalizing distress. Social workers must be sensitive to the significantly higher rates of depression, heavy alcohol use, post-traumatic stress syndrome and suicidality among survivors of domestic violence (Howe, 2005; Baty et al., 2008). Psychiatry has a history of patriarchy that has served to pathologize, institutionalize and medicate women for such reasons as menopause, domestic violence, post-natal depression, being lesbian, and sexual disinterest (Appignanesi, 2008; Rogers & Pilgrim, 2005). Social workers need to be capable of advocating for accurate equitable assessments on behalf of vulnerable women.

Feminist perspectives on sexual violence

Sexual assault (rape) entails sexual contact that is unwanted by one of the participants, entailing physical and/or verbal force being applied. (See further discussion in Chapter 9.) Men perpetrate the overwhelming majority of reported rapes (Bachar & Koss, 2001; Parrish et al., 2001). Distinctions between sexual assault (rape) and sexual abuse are generally determined by the relationship between those involved. When there is a familial or caring relationship between the two parties (parent/child, siblings, step- or foster-parent/child, etc.), then sexual activity represents sexual abuse, although rape may still be a factor in that abuse. When consent for sexual contact is not mutual, then a crime is being committed. Rape is a violent crime in which sex is used as a weapon, not to be confused with a sexual act involving violence.

Two primary variables associated with women's vulnerability to being raped are past victimization (including abuse in childhood and adolescence) and alcohol. Because alcohol may already be a means of self-medicating following earlier trauma, the relationship between the two factors remains uncertain (Bachar & Koss, 2001). From a feminist perspective, both earlier trauma and the role played by alcohol are reflective of women trying to cope in a demeaning and dangerous environment, and reflect oppression.

Feminist perspectives on rape emphasize the role of men's inherent power differentials over women. From a feminist perspective, rape entails a societal problem as well as a personal crisis. This view holds society accountable for condoning or tolerating male views and behaviours that include sexual violence. From a feminist perspective, women's socialization to tolerate victimization is also a reflection of societal inequities (Zastrow & Kirst-Ashman, 1994). The feminist approach challenges such platitudes as 'boys will be boys', and 'forgive and forget', and seeks ways to hold perpetrators of sexual violence accountable for their behaviour.

Most rapes are planned, and while stranger rapes can and do occur, rapists are usually known to the woman (Parrish et al., 2001). In part because of knowing the perpetrator, rape remains among the least reported crimes. By not reporting the rape, many women come to regard themselves as being somehow responsible for it having happened. From a feminist perspective, this reflects a patriarchal and sexist society.

Feminist approaches to practice

When using a feminist approach to practice, problems are typically approached from a gendered, socio-political and multi-systemic perspective. Power differences between women and men are generally considered crucial to defining needs and problems as well as solutions in ways that promote an egalitarian outcome (Orme, 2002).

A feminist perspective includes awareness of ways in which social institutions have helped maintain traditional, stereotypical gender roles; helplessness, passivity, and dependence on unhealthy relationships are among the results of those traditions (Jasinski, 2001). Supporting women to assert their inherent authority and values in which their own 'voice' is validated is a key aspect of feminist practice, which emphasizes empowering women to achieve desired changes in their lives, especially in resisting bureaucratic oppression (Orme, 2002).

Ultimately, feminist approaches endeavour to support women in the assertion of genuine authority on their own behalf in order to actualize their inherent potential and strengths. Sometimes this is enhanced through working with other women, and seeing other women in roles of genuine authority and power. As noted by Orme (2002), most social work is practised by women and with women, across the array of services provided. Especially in cases involving female social workers working with female service users, several shared frames of reference can provide a powerful means of effective intervention. Mutual familiarity with shared experiences such as living and working in a male-dominated society, double workloads (paid and domestic), and caring familial roles can prove useful means of establishing rapport and enhanced communication (Milner & O'Byrne, 2002).

Dominelli (2008: 111) summarizes some of the shared characteristics of feminist social work, which include the following:

- upholding women's right to be free from oppression;
- having women speak for themselves in their own voices;

- listening to what women have to say;
- creating alternative lifestyles in the here and now;
- integrating our theories and practice;
- seeking collectivist solutions that respect women's individuality and uniqueness;
- valuing women's contributions; and
- using women's individual experiences to make sense of social realities.

Criticisms and shortcomings of feminist perspectives

Feminism's varied array of perspectives and priorities can be argued as a lack of unified intellectual focus (Dominelli, 2008). From a *postfeminist* perspective, the possibility of defining a single feminist viewpoint appears increasingly unlikely, in part because of an array of competing interests and identities that are also associated with inequality and dominance. Various subgroups of feminist thinkers emphasize their identities in conjunction with other factors, including black feminists, Muslim feminists, lesbian feminists, and eco-feminists (Faludi, 1992). Some would argue that feminism's job is effectively accomplished, and that women no longer need to consider issues of oppression and dominance as they relate to gender differences. Rates of poverty, violence, lone parenting, mental health, and continued differences in pay for women and men, however, make that viewpoint difficult for social workers to sustain.

Radical feminism has been criticized for its emphasis on blaming men, and for its emphatic focus on negative aspects of male/female relations. According to some critics, this view contributes to an adversarial dynamic, and does not necessarily provide a way forward (Bryson, 1999). Some argue that feminism neglects to address some of the emotional privileges and personal rewards associated with motherhood. Other arguments include the role played by financial privilege, and the role played by capitalism rather than patriarchy as a means of dominating the lives of women. According to some critics, while feminist theory has articulated the inadequacy of the existing (malestream) framework, it has been less articulate about what could function as an alternative (Abbott, Wallace, & Tyler, 2005).

Some of the research associated with feminist theory has been questioned on the grounds of empirical rigour (Sheldon, 2000). For example, particularly in feminist studies of violence against women, critics have argued that the feminist focus on gender is too narrow, and that the single-variable explanation is insufficient to explain the complexities of the subject. Feminist studies have also been criticized for their failure to explain the small percentage of women who are violent against men in a culture so dominated by patriarchy (Jasinski, 2001).

Sadly, one of the most pervasive and insidiously patronizing criticisms of feminism has to do with various stereotypes of shrill, humourless women who don't like men. As noted by the humorous writer Marian Keyes (2005), 'You can be a feminist and a. wear pink, b. have sex with men, and c. enjoy a good laugh.'

Questions

1 Match the following concepts and definitions:

	Concept	Definition
____	Patriarchy	(a) Feminist alternative to 'mainstream', denoting male-dominated perspectives
____	'Malestream'	(b) Rape
____	Sexual assault	(c) Feminist alternative to 'homicide', referring to women killed by violent partners
____	'Femicide'	(d) 'Rule of the father'

2 How are/were household and caring duties distributed in your family? Are/were those duties and roles equally shared between genders? How would you explain those distributions of roles and duties?

3 Some argue that an array of patriarchal structures support the gender inequities that oppress women. Which of the following structures (paid work, divisions of household chores, child care responsibilities, a patriarchal culture, sexuality, male violence, and the state) would you associate with the following points?:

- Traditionally low salaries paid to teachers.
- Women are more likely than men to work part-time.
- The negative effect of motherhood on private pension eligibility.
- Women's patterns of paid and unpaid work.
- Rape survivors being interrogated following the report of a rape having been perpetrated against them.
- Women's pay remains 73–82 per cent of that of their male counterparts in Britain.
- Women are at greater risk of poverty later in life than men.

4 Read the following scenario:

> Joan (age 20) was walking home from the station after dark. She became increasingly aware of footsteps behind her in the car park. The man who was walking behind her came up and asked for directions to the station. She stopped to point out that he was walking in the opposite direction from the station, when he grabbed her arms, and forced her into a nearby car. He gagged her, to prevent her cries for help being heard, then drove to a secluded area and raped Joan. Afterward, he drove her back to the station and shoved her out of the car and drove away. When two women found Joan on the pavement, with the gag still around her face, they phoned the police. When the police arrived, they first questioned whether Joan knew her assailant, and whether she had been drinking. Only after ascertaining that she did not know her rapist did the police begin asking questions to determine how they might find him.

From a feminist perspective, discuss the implications of the consequences of the events described.

(a) What are some of the inherently sexist or ageist components of the responses to Joan?

(b) What does the interrogation of a rape victim imply about the responsibility for the crime?

(c) Would imagining Joan being Asian or African-Caribbean change your perspective? Discuss.

5 Read the following scenario:

'May' (age 70) immigrated to England from Trinidad in the 1950s. She worked most of her life as a cleaner in the private home of two wealthy families. Her husband 'Will' was also from Trinidad. He worked in construction until an injury resulted in his being physically disabled when he was 50. Will died last year, following a long struggle with heart disease and diabetes. May was his primary carer for over ten years.

May lives in the home where she and Will raised their two children. The neighbourhood has deteriorated, and she no longer feels safe to go out after dark. May's pension is limited, as it is mainly based on Will's declared income, which ceased when he became disabled.

May and her long-time neighbour and close friend Sally met for coffee and cake in each other's homes most days. They enjoyed sharing stories of their children growing up, and their mutual memories. Both were avid readers, but May's sight is now very poor, and Sally used to read her post for May. Sally recently had a stroke, however, and was moved to a nursing home. May no longer has a neighbour whom she knows well enough to contact or visit.

Sally's son tried to visit May one evening last week when he was in Sally's home cleaning it in order to put it up for sale. May did not recognize him when he knocked on her door, and became very agitated. She thought he was a drug dealer, or a possible intruder. She phoned the police, who responded very slowly. They found Sally weeping in her sitting room, frightened and alone. They wondered if she was paranoid or senile.

From a feminist viewpoint, consider the following concerns in relation to May's situation, including your views on which would present the greatest barrier to her receiving the support needed:

- gender;
- age;
- economic hardship vs. economic privilege (of May's employers);
- paid vs. unpaid work;
- social isolation and vulnerability.

14 Theories of sociological and socio-economic influences on behaviour

Various perspectives on sociology and socio-economics have influenced social work. Because of social work's emphasis on understanding the role of access to resources as that relates to social justice and serving people in need, sociological or socio-economic concepts are important dimensions of social work's approach to understanding people's behaviour. This chapter provides an overview of some of the theories and theorists who have influenced our understanding of society in general, and socio-economic influences relevant to people's behaviour.

Relevance for social work

Social work's inherent appreciation of the context in which people function necessarily entails an awareness of such environmental influences as family, community, education, religion, cultural norms, and socio-economic status. It also entails awareness of the impact that socio-economic status has upon all the other influences mentioned, as well as physical and mental health. The dichotomy between those with privileges and those who live in poverty has traditionally been defined as 'the haves and the have-nots'. Because social work frequently functions on behalf of people facing needs created by living in poverty, or without adequate support, an understanding of some of the implications of poverty is essential to good practice.

Social workers are required to apply particular sensitivity when distinguishing between the roles played by poverty and issues of intentional neglect when assessing families in crisis because poverty and deprivation play critical roles in families' capacities to achieve and to provide for children's needs. These distinctions begin with how problems are defined. Rather than perceiving people's difficulties as necessarily reflecting some innate personal or family deficit, Marxist thinking has influenced the social work perspective on defining problems in relation to social and structural inequities.

Contemporary authors often distinguish between the principles of the individual ('microsystems') and other larger groups ('macrosystems') in order to understand the influences of culture and society on people's behaviour and the ways in which people change and grow. Social workers need to understand the microsystems (individual needs), macrosystems (larger groups or organizations) as well as the interface between them in order to influence positive changes across systems (Lyons et al., 1998).

Historical background

With its very name coming from the Latin *socius* (companion) and the Greek *ology* (the study of), the field of sociology shares an academically 'crossbred' status with social work. Both are among the relatively newer areas of study to be included among fields of academic degrees taught at traditional universities, with sociology having only achieved degree status during the 1960s in Britain. At its core, sociology is that social science most focused on understanding society in general, and the dimensions and implications of change and conflict in the broader society. Historically, sociology has been closely linked with efforts to reform society in ways that benefit the greatest number of its members.

The French writer **August Comte** (1798–1857) is credited with having introduced the term 'sociology' as a distinct area of scientific study. Comte argued for the legitimacy of sociology's knowledge base, equating the intellectual validity of the laws related to the social world with the validity of laws of nature. Comte introduced the idea of 'positive philosophy', referring to the ability to collect information about society that could be objectively observed and classified. The sociological concepts Comte considered crucial were relatively neutral: they did not infer internal meanings, morals, or emotions. Rather, they related strictly to sociological facts, and were confined to observable or measurable elements for objective interpretation.

Largely unappreciated during his lifetime, the work of German-born philosopher, economist and social scientist **Karl Marx** (1818–1883) has influenced sociological thinking for over a century. The son of an intellectual family, Marx's education included studying literature, law, economics and history. He edited several influential newspapers during his thirties, but eventually fled to England because of his radical political views. His philosophies of economics and politics were shaped by living through the turbulent socio-political upheavals that accompanied the Industrial Revolution, and his observations of the socio-economic inequities that occurred.

Marx envisioned an ideal (utopian) society as one in which exploitation of the least powerful members would no longer be the norm. By making ownership of property and resources communal, all would be brought together to strive toward the greatest common good. Thus, Marx envisioned members of society achieving both personal and collective fulfilment, without the need for religion, which he considered irrelevant.

Marx challenged traditional thinking regarding the distribution of resources and the value of work in ways that changed history. A prolific thinker and author, Marx's writings were produced over more than 40 years. He died in his armchair, and is buried at Highgate Cemetery in London. He left numerous unfinished manuscripts, which were subsequently interpreted and finished by others.

Subsequent views on what have come to be considered 'class struggles' have been strongly influenced by the works of Marx and his contemporaries Friedrich Engels (1820–1895) and Max Weber. Their lives covered a period of vast political and economic upheaval, including industrialization and wars.

Marx's contemporary **Max Weber** (1864–1920) also influenced sociological thinking, particularly ideas regarding social class differences. Unlike Marx, Weber focused more on the role of 'relations of exchange' (i.e. the capacity to purchase or possess goods) as defining class distinctions (Giddens, 1997). Weber's analysis emphasized the role of supply and demand as they influenced people's capacity to own property or other assets they needed. Weber's view of social divisions comprised three key factors: (1) *class*, related to the stratification of the economic order; (2) *status*, related to the stratification of the social order; and (3) *party*, related to the stratification of the political order (Best, 2005). Weber famously linked what came to be known as the 'Protestant work ethic' with economic productivity free of the hierarchical structure of the Catholic Church. He is considered by some to have founded the sociology of religion (Weber, 1905/2001). Ironically, Weber was subsequently a consultant at the Treaty of Versailles.

Because of his attention to the characteristics of groups of individuals as well as social structures (or systems), the French author **Emile Durkheim** (1858–1917) is sometimes considered both a sociologist and an anthropologist. Durkheim focused attention both on the characteristics and structures of groups, more than the individual characteristics of their members. Because of his attention to people's beliefs, customs, and values as being 'social facts' to be considered, Durkheim's views distinguish him from the traditional views of Auguste Comte. His rigorous efforts to employ quantitative methods of data collection also distinguished him from his scientific predecessors. His *macro-level functionalism* is regarded as one of the key sociological theories (Hilarski et al., 2002).

Building upon Durkheim's work, **Robert Merton** (1910–2003) delineated five different ways in which members of society could respond to the need for goals that is associated with anomie (see p. 270). Writing in the 1930s, Merton's proposed ways include *conformity*, or acceptance of approved channels; *innovation*, or rejecting conventional means of success in favour of deviant means, including crime; *ritualism*, or a scaling down of expectations and resignation to bureaucratically rule-governed behaviours lacking innovation or creativity; *retreatism*, which Merton applied to 'psychotics, outcasts, and chronic drunkards' among others; and *rebellion*, which entails rejection of goals and the conventional means of attaining them, in favour of alternative goals and means.

Historically, the work of **Seebohm Rowntree** (1871–1954) makes him one of the pioneers among those seeking to define and measure poverty in Britain. Beginning with his study of poor families in York in 1899, Rowntree went on to provide a conceptual definition of poverty. He conceptualized poverty around a minimum sum that would suffice to provide for a family's subsistence (shelter, fuel, light, food, clothing, etc.). He adjusted his sums according to family size. Rowntree's subsequent work expanded into aspects of life that were more reflective of relative poverty, by including such things as newspapers, books, holidays and presents in family needs (Rowntree & Lavers, 1951).

One of the key influential functionalists following World War II, **Talcott Parsons** (1902–1979) proposed that societies achieve order and stability through *value consensus*, or a general agreement about what is valued or accepted. Parsons proposed that stratification systems result from societies' shared values. Thus, those whose performance is valued by their society will be likely to be rewarded, or regarded with prestige because of the perceived merit of their achievements. Conversely, those whose contributions are not valued will not attain power or prestige because of the lack of merit ascribed to their functions. Thus, they are more likely to occupy positions of lower social status.

In contrast to more traditional Marxist and Weberian theories, French sociologist **Pierre Bourdieu** (1930–2002) ascribed importance to the role of culture in addition to economic aspects of social stratification. According to Bourdieu, both culture and lifestyle serve to influence individuals' chances of upward social mobility. He argued that four main sources of capital applied to chances of upward mobility. Those types are: *economic capital*, or material wealth; *cultural capital*, which includes education as well as artistic or creative capabilities; *social capital*, referring to social affiliations, trustworthiness, or contributions; and *symbolic capital*, referring to the concept of status resulting from a reputation for competence, respectability or honour.

Key concepts

Briefly summarized, Marx viewed society as being necessarily stratified into two major groups, a ruling class and a subject (or working) class. He viewed the ruling class as having power to exploit and oppress the subject class through ownership and control of the means of production on which the working class depended for employment, housing, and necessary purchases (i.e. land, factories, shops, etc.). The result of such inherent imbalances necessarily entailed social conflict, in which the ruling class could be expected to protect its privilege and dominance. Historically, Marx likened the conflict between classes to the tradition of land-owning feudal lords and the landless serfs who worked the land. Likewise, Marx identified the basic class conflict as that between the *bourgeoisie*, or capitalist/land-owning class, and the *proletariat*, or working class, who work for wages paid by the bourgeoisie.

Among his more renowned statements, Marx referred to religion as 'the opiate of the people' (Marx, cited in Bottomore and Rubel, 1963). Seeing religion as both an instrument of social control and an insidious means of oppression, Marx argued that it functioned primarily to maintain the *status quo*, or existing social order. Although the verse was eventually dropped from the English Hymnal (see Williams, 1933), such sentiments as those from the popular Victorian hymn 'All Things Bright and Beautiful' demonstrate the relevance of Marx's arguments:

> The rich man in his castle,
> The poor man at his gate,
> God made them high and lowly,
> And ordered their estate.

Marxist arguments against religion include the ways in which some religions extol the virtues of suffering (including slavery), and thus justify oppression, by promising rewards in the afterlife. Such an arrangement sanctioned and perpetuated the *status quo* by implying that a creator of such injustices must implicitly condone them. More contemporary examples to support Marxist arguments against religion's influences on society may be found in the relationship between the US Republican Party and the 'religious right' in the early twenty-first century in America.

Marx argued that religion was used to keep the lower classes in a subservient position, along with maintaining the legitimacy of the oppressive ruling classes. The phrase, 'the parson has ever gone hand in hand with the landlord', was used by Marx and Engel to denote the system whereby the lord of the manor received support from the legitimacy bestowed upon him from the local pulpit, and reciprocated by endowing the church with financial support (Haralambos, Holborn, & Heald 2004: 410). Conversely, the lord of the manor was sometimes known to withhold financial support when messages from the pulpit were not to his liking. Thus, the *status quo*, or existing social order, was perpetuated, and change remained unlikely.

Marx's view of society reflected a composite of interconnected factors, including religious, economic, political, legal, and educational institutions. He believed that such institutions could only be understood in the context of their reciprocal influences. Of those influences, however, he regarded economic factors as having the most primary influence over the others.

Marx asserted that people's primary concerns have to do with the social relationships of economic production, which do not necessarily entail a source of social change. According to Marx, however, social change is most likely the result of the contradictions and conflict inherent in the economic system. That change reflects the mutual influences of social influences, of which he emphasized the role of economics as the primary source of energy.

Emile Durkheim and the macro-functional model

The macro-functional model maintains that the broader community serves as an interconnected *system*, of which individuals are the components. Unlike the medical model's primary focus on the problem presented by the individual, the macro-functional model, which is congruent with much of social work's perspective, focuses on ways in which social systems' deficits influence the problems experienced by individuals. For example, with medical science having reduced childhood mortality, greater numbers of children live into adulthood. With that advance, however, prolonged life expectancies have increased the population, and thus contributed to an array of housing, political, economic, environmental, and moral dilemmas.

From a macro-functionalist perspective, while poverty is caused by a damaged economy, there are potentially positive outcomes from sustaining poverty, and thus poverty serves a *functional* purpose. For example, as long as people live in poverty, they are more likely to be available to perform the less desirable tasks at lower wages than they would receive if they had other options. The eradication of poverty would, in fact, necessitate a drastic redistribution of resources (Zastrow & Kirst-Ashman, 1994).

From Durkheim's functionalist perspective, all social change begins with some form of deviance. Since the absence of change would entail atrophy, or stagnation, Durkheim proposed that society itself generates deviance for its own well-being. Thus, deviance from the norm is not necessarily a negative factor. In fact, Durkheim observed the necessity of originality both for the process of positive change and criminality. Durkheim's concern with such factors as comparative rates of occurrence of specific phenomena among different groups led to his influential studies of crime and suicide. From his perspective, crime is not only inevitable, but it can also be functional. By that, Durkheim sought to link those aspects of crime that were simply deviant from the existing social norm with the potential for positive social change. Acts of civil disobedience, such as protesting war, or opposition to institutionalized oppression would be examples of such functions of crime. According to Durkheim, crime only becomes dysfunctional, or detrimental to society, when its rates go outside the normal ranges. Thus he considered excessively high crime rates suggestive of something having gone inherently wrong with society (Haralambos, Holborn, & Heald 2004).

His famous study on social and cultural influences on suicide demonstrates Durkheim's distinct approach to understanding society as well as his views on scientific methods for collecting data. Durkheim attempted to explain relevant statistical patterns by dividing suicides into three social categories: *egoistic, altruistic,* and *anomic.* He proposed that egoistic suicide refers to those lacking strong integration into any social group (e.g. 'loners', perpetrators of violence, etc.); altruistic suicide refers to those who are susceptible to excessive involvement or integration with a social group (e.g., suicide pacts, etc.); and anomic suicide refers to those who have experienced a fragmentation of their social integration or affiliation (e.g. retirement, social exclusion, etc.).

In his study of suicides, Durkheim sought to establish correlations between the occurrence of suicide and various social factors, such as religion, education, and national culture. He proceeded to correlate suicide rates and the degree to which individuals were integrated into their various social affiliations, and the degree to which society regulated individuals' behaviours across different groups. From this, Durkheim proposed different suicide types (*altruistic, fatalistic, egoistic,* and *anomic*). Of these types, he considered the anomic type most prevalent in industrial societies. In such industrial settings, traditional norms and values had ceased to have relevance, and he regarded the resulting suicides as resulting from rapid social change and its subsequent uncertainty among its individual members. Durkheim noted increased rates of suicide during periods of economic depression as well as during periods of prosperity. He attributed the anomic suicides to society's insufficient regulation of or indifference to the individual during both booms and slumps, as both economic extremes are associated with the uncertainty of anomie (Haralambos, Holborn, & Heald 2002; Zastrow & Kirst-Ashman, 1994).

Durkheim also used the concept of *anomie* to reflect a pervasive dissolution of social cohesion and stability. He proposed that 'anomie' results from situations in which rules and norms have become meaningless. In that state, when rules lack relevance, a level of normlessness or social anarchy emerges. Individuals as well as society may respond to such anomie in different ways. Among those ways of responding, Durkheim regarded criminality as a potential response to a sense of meaningless and despair. A sense of being detached or socially marginalized from a positive affiliation with the larger society would therefore precede the criminality. Because deprivation and unemployment are often linked with that social exclusion, the role of anomie in the manifestation of criminality is a key concept for social workers to grasp.

Durkheim considered the achievement of the right balance of social integration and regulation to be essential for any healthy society, and argued that primitive societies tended to have excesses of both, while industrial societies had insufficient amounts of either. From this perspective, Durkheim sought to understand rates of suicides in different societies in order to understand the roles played by various social factors that shape human behaviour.

The distribution of resources

While egalitarianism (i.e. a world in which wealth is distributed equally among all members of society) remains a long-cherished dream for many, the realities of the distribution of material goods remain inequitable for most. Wealth, power, and prestige remain key markers of those inequities. The term *social stratification* refers to the ways in which distinct social groups are ascribed different status according to wealth, power, and prestige. Such strata involve various *hierarchies*, in which people occupying the same strata share or suffer similar positions and options. For example, in Indian traditions, people were divided into different castes of varying levels of privilege or status. In modern Britain, people's status may be distinguished by whether they have or have not attended university or are employed.

Social strata may be described as either open or closed. In closed systems, few opportunities exist through which individuals can enhance their social status. The caste system provides an example of a traditionally closed social system, in which people's status is determined by their parents' status. In open systems, an individual may have access to other strata through *social mobility*. Such mobility entails the achievement of class position through personal characteristics and abilities rather than ascribed features such as their parents' status. Capitalistic societies typically provide examples of open systems.

The role of poverty related to access to resources

In order to understand the role poverty plays in people's behaviour, a shared definition of what is being meant by the term 'poverty' is necessary. A distinction between 'absolute' and 'relative' poverty is also relevant to most discussions. Poverty refers to a state in which essential resources are lacking. The term 'absolute poverty' usually refers to the absence of necessary resources to support existence. 'Relative poverty', however, typically refers to the standards of society at a given time. Thus relative poverty is determined in accordance with the standards of material wealth of the surrounding society.

Efforts to define and measure absolute and relative poverty remain controversial. The United Nations' efforts to define the concepts of poverty at the 1995 Copenhagen World Summit on Development resulted in a two-tier definition. In that effort, absolute poverty was defined as:

> A condition characterized by severe deprivation of basic human needs, including food, safe drinking water, sanitation facilities, health, shelter, education and information. It depends not only on income but also access to services.
>
> (United Nations, 1995)

Instances in which material needs are unmet often entail other facets of life in which there is deprivation. The term *multiple deprivation* is used to refer to the combined influences of material poverty coexisting with undesirable working conditions, undesirable schooling opportunities, and an overarching sense of powerlessness to change things for the better. According to the 1995 UN Summit, this relates to *overall poverty*, which broadly represents '[a] lack of participation in decision-making and in civil, social and cultural life' (United Nations, 1995).

During the 1960s and 1970s, the work of **Peter Townsend** (1928–present) and **W.G. (Garry) Runciman** (1934–present) contributed to the understanding of poverty in Britain. Townsend conducted a social survey, employing questionnaires to gather data from over 2,000 households, and over 6,000 individuals. Townsend's focus was on what he referred to as *relative deprivation*, in which poverty is defined by its extension far beyond material deficits. Arguing that any objective and consistent measurement of poverty necessitates factoring in relative deprivation, Townsend pointed out the relevance of such variables as access to social participation and inclusion. According to Townsend, a comprehensive definition of poverty entails:

> When they lack the resources to obtain the types of diet, participate in the activities and have the living conditions and amenities which are customary, or at least widely encouraged or approved, in the societies to which they belong. Their resources are so seriously below those commanded by the average individual or family that they are, in effect, excluded from the ordinary living patterns, customs and activities.
>
> (Townsend, 1979)

In his important work, *Relative Deprivation and Social Justice*, Runciman (1966) focused on people's subjective perceptions of being disadvantaged in comparison to those having similar attributes. He explored institutionalized inequalities experienced by those living in poverty, and people's perceptions of the resulting injustices. Runciman emphasized the importance of subjective perceptions of deprivation and injustice, as distinct from the historical emphasis on compromised physical health resulting from absolute poverty.

Although it still lacks a commonly agreed definition, the term *social exclusion* has gained popularity as a descriptor of circumstances in which people's access to positive participation in society is precluded through multiple deprivation. The concept of exclusion bears some parallels to Townsend's and Runciman's ideas of relative deprivation. The term social exclusion typically carries a considerably less negative connotation than the more historical usage of the term 'underclass'.

The American, **Charles Murray**'s term *underclass* has gained common usage among contemporary sociologists. Rather than being defined solely by income or lack thereof, Murray introduced the term 'underclass' to refer to a strata of society that he saw as being perpetually dependent on government benefits, and thus unlikely to aspire to or be empowered to achieve economic stability or self-sufficiency (Murray, 1996). Defined more by behaviours and values, the underclass is often blamed by others for representing a potential threat to social and economic stability through criminal activity, drug use, illegitimacy, and the resulting consumption of taxpayers' money.

Especially in capitalistic societies such as Britain, poverty typically entails a complex array of social realities. These realities consistently include low social status, undesirable housing, poorer health status, compromised access to education that would support employable skills and relative social and political powerlessness in comparison with those with privileges (Kempson, 1996; Wilkinson, 1996).

Social workers are called upon to distinguish between the role played by poverty and any inherent personal or family weaknesses among those people in need of their services. For social workers, the challenge remains how to understand the role played by poverty, and how various types of deprivation influence people's circumstances and opportunities. Understanding the contextual roles of poverty include such considerations as access to basic needs as well as distinctions between poverty and intentional neglect, unemployability, or juvenile delinquency. Unlike other aspects of state welfare services, social work brings with it a perspective from which to appreciate the complexities of people's environments, rather than simply viewing their difficulties as reflecting personal failings or inadequacies.

Criticisms and shortcomings of Marxist theory

While Marx's arguments have had profound social and political consequences, twentieth-century Soviet and Eastern European history has provided examples of failures to attain his utopian goals. Historically, communal property ownership has not proven well implemented. The crucial role played by a steadily expanding middle class was not addressed in Marx's theories.

Similarly, economics and religion have been used by various institutions to sanction the subservient position of women to men throughout history. Despite the historical role played by various institutions to determine women's economic subjugation to men, Marx did not address gender issues among his arguments about domination.

While Marxist arguments against the manipulative role played by religion in the sanctioning of oppression are quite powerful, his discourses on religion do not address the existence of religion in settings where it does not contribute to oppression. For example, the early Christian Church often served to oppose Roman rule in ways that were politically radical for their time. In the United States, the abolition movement was also associated with various church-based efforts to end slavery on religious and moral grounds. Contemporary examples of Liberation Theology, especially in Latin America, are clear evidence of ways in which the church not only has not supported oppression, but challenged it in politically and socially relevant ways.

Implications for practice

While sociology and economics do not purport to apply directly to practice, social work's inherent values of social justice necessarily make sociological ideas relevant. The challenges of understanding and confronting poverty and various forms of deprivation and exclusion are part of the fabric of good social work practice. Understanding the contextual roles of poverty and deprivation necessitates an awareness of how people's basic needs may not be met because of socio-economic forces that reflect inherent injustices (Wilkinson & Pickett, 2009). Social work in the UK is faced with the paradoxical dilemma of balancing its functions on behalf of a state that may actually sanction some forms of social oppression, against its value base of advocating for social change and the empowerment of vulnerable populations. Today's social work students are entering a society in which the disparities between privilege and poverty are possibly greater than they have been in the past century. Sadly, the solutions are not as readily obvious as the questions relating to achieving an equitable and just society. But then if it were easy, it would presumably be called 'social play' instead of 'social work'.

Questions

1 Match the following concepts, theorists and definitions:

____	Sociology	(a) August Comte
____	The proletariat	(b) Max Weber
____	The bourgeoise	(c) The working class
____	Anomie	(d) *(Gr)* Study of companions
____	Protestant work ethic	(e) The capitalist/land-owning class
____	Positive philosophy	(f) A state of normlessness, social detachment

2 Challenging injustice and inequality to targeted groups in society is a key aspect of social action. How would you describe the contribution of Marxist theory to your ideas of social justice?
   (a) How would you define wealth?
   (b) How would you define power?
   (c) How would you define prestige?

3 What are some examples of the ways in which wealth, power, and prestige are inequitably distributed in your day-to-day life?

4 What are some examples of ways in which socio-economic inequities could be lessened?

5 How would you describe the role of religion in current examples of social conflict?

6 What are some ways in which terrorists citing religiously based extremism may be demonstrating what Durkheim described as anomie?

7 Of the following items, which would you consider a home without them to be indicative of absolute poverty? Multiple deprivation? Neither?

Mobile phone	Personal computer	Washing machine
Internet access	Alcohol	Clock
Indoor plumbing	News broadcasts	Microwave oven

8 Karl Marx envisioned an equitable society in which people shared their resources in order that all needs could be met. How does that vision reflect social work values today?

Bibliography

Abbott, P., Wallace, C. & Tyler, M. (2005) *An Introduction to Sociology: Feminist Perspectives*, 3rd edn. London: Routledge.

Adams, G., Cantwell, A.-M. & Matheis, S. (2002) Substance use and adolescence. In C. Essau (ed.) *Substance Abuse and Dependence in Adolescence: Epidemiology, Risk Factors and Treatment*. Hove: Brunner-Routledge, pp. 1–20.

Adler, A. (1924) *The Practice and Theory of Individual Psychology*. New York: Hartcourt, Brace.

Agnew, E. (2003) *From Charity to Social Work: Mary E. Richmond and the Creation of an American Profession*. Champaign, IL: University of Illinois Press.

Ahrons, C. (2005) Divorce: an unscheduled family transition. In B. Carter & M. McGoldrick (eds) *The Expanded Family Life Cycle: Individual, Family and Social Perspectives*, 3rd edn. Boston: Allyn and Bacon, pp. 381–398.

Ainsworth, M.D.S. (1973) The development of infant–mother attachment. In B. Caldwell & H. Ricciuti (eds) *Review of Child Development Research*, vol. 3. Chicago, IL: University of Chicago Press, pp. 1–94.

Ainsworth, M.D.S. (1991) Attachments and other affectional bonds across the life cycle. In R. Hinde, J. Stevenson-Hinde & P. Marris (eds) *Attachment Across the Life Cycle*. London: Routledge.

Ainsworth, M.D.S., Blehar, M., Waters, E. & Wahl, S. (1978) *Patterns of Attachment: A Psychological Study of the Strange Situation*. Hillsdale, NJ: Lawrence Erlbaum Associates.

Ainsworth, M.D.S. & Bowlby, J. (1991) An ethological approach to personality development. *American Psychologist*, 46(4): 333–341.

Aldgate, J. (2006) Ordinary children in extraordinary circumstances. In D. Iwaniec (ed.) *The Child's Journey Through Care: Placement Stability, Care Planning, and Achieving Permanency*. Chichester: Wiley, pp. 17–39.

Allan, G. (2008) Families. In M. Davies (ed.) *The Blackwell Companion to Social Work*, 3rd edn. Oxford: Blackwell, pp. 326–332.

Allport, G. (1937) *Personality*. New York: Holt.

Allport, G. (1963) *Pattern and Growth in Personality*. New York: Holt Rinehart & Winston.

Allport, G. & Odbert, H. (1936) Trait names: a psycho-lexical study. *Psychological Monographs*, 47.

Amato, P. (1995) Children's adjustment to divorce: theories, hypotheses and empirical support. *Journal of Marriage and Family*, 55: 628.

American Humane Association (2002) The next step: exploring the link between violence to people and animals. In *AHA, Protecting Children and Animals: Celebrating 125 Years*. Edgewood, CO: AHA, pp. 60–64.

American Psychiatric Association (2000) *Diagnostic and Statistical Manual of Mental Disorders*, 4th edn. Text Rev. Washington, DC: APA.

Andrews, B. & Brown, G. (1988) Social support, onset of depression and personality: an exploratory analysis. *Social Psychiatry and Psychiatric Epidemiology*, 23(2): 98–108.

Appignanesi, L. (2008) *Mad, Bad and Sad: A History of Women and the Mind Doctors from 1800 to the Present*. London: Virago.

Arnold, R. (1997) *Raising Levels of Achievement in Boys*. London: National Foundation for Research.

BABCP *Code of Ethics*. British Association of Behavioural and Cognitive Psychotherapies. Cambridge: Cambridge University Press.

Bachar, K. & Koss, M. (2001) From prevalence to prevention: closing the gap between what we know about rape and what we do. In C. Renzetti, J. Edleson & R.K. Bergen (eds) *Sourcebook on Violence Against Women*. Thousand Oaks, CA: Sage, pp. 117–142.

Bagley, C. & Tremblay, P. (2000) Elevated rates of suicidal behavior in gay, lesbian, and bisexual youth. *Crisis*, 21: 111–117.

Baldry, A. (2007) 'It does affect me': Disruptive behaviors in preadolescents directly and indirectly abused at home. *European Psychologist*, 12(1): 29–35.

Balint, M. (1965) *Primary Love and Psycho-analytic Technique*. London: Tavistock.

Bandura, A. (1969) *Principles of Behavior Modification*. New York: Holt, Rinehart and Winston.

Bandura, A. (1977) Self-efficacy: Toward a unifying theory of behavior change. *Psychological Review*, 84: 191–215.

Bandura, A. (1986) *Social Foundations of Thought and Action*. Englewood Cliffs, NJ: Prentice-Hall.

Bandura, A., Ross, D. & Ross, S. (1961) Transmission of aggression through aggressive models. *Journal of Abnormal and Social Psychology*, 63(3): 575–582.

Bandura, A. & Walters, R. (1959) *Adolescent Aggression*. New York: Ronald Press.

Barker, R. (2003) *The Social Work Dictionary*, 5th edn. Washington, DC: National Association of Social Workers.

Barlow, D., Raffa, S. & Cohen, E. (2002) Psychosocial treatments for panic disorders, phobias, and generalized anxiety disorder. In P. Nathan & J. Gorman (eds) *A Guide to Treatments That Work*, 2nd edn. New York: Oxford University Press, pp. 301–335.

Barnett, O., Miller-Perrin, C. & Perrin, R. (1997) *Family Violence across the Lifespan*. Thousand Oaks, CA: Sage.

Bateson, G., Jackson, D., Haley, J. & Weakland, J. (1956) Toward a theory of schizophrenia. *Behavioral Science*, 1(4): 251–264.

Baty, M., Alhusen, J., Campbell, J. & Sharps, P. (2008) Female victims of violence. In J. Keeling & T. Mason (eds) *Domestic Violence: A Multi-Professional Approach for Healthcare Practitioners*. Maidenhead: Open University Press, pp. 37–45.

Beck, A. (1963) Thinking and depression. *Archives of General Psychiatry*, 9: 324–333.

Beck, A. & Weishaar, M. (1989) Cognitive therapy. In R.J. Corsini & D. Wedding (eds) *Current Psychotherapies*. Itasca, IL: Peacock.

Beckett, C. (2002) *Human Growth and Development*. London: Sage.

Beers, M., Porter, R., Jones, T., Kaplan, J. & Berkwits, M. (eds) (2006) *The Merck Manual of Diagnosis and Therapy*, 18th edn. Whitehouse Station, NJ: Merck.

Belknap, J. (1996) *The Invisible Woman: Gender, Crime and Justice*. Belmont, CA: Wadsworth.

Bem, S. (1989) Genital knowledge and gender constancy in preschool children. *Child Development*, 60: 649–662.

Berne, E. ([1961] 1978) *Transactional Analysis in Psychotherapy*. New York: Ballantine Books.

Berne, E. (1973) *The Games People Play: The Psychology of Human Relationships*. Harmondsworth: Penguin.

Bertalanffy, L. von (1951) General systems theory: a new approach to unity of science. *Human Biology*, 23(4): 346–361.

Bertalanffy, L. von (1962) General systems theory: a critical review. *General Systems Yearbook*, 7: 1–20.

Bertalanffy, L. von (1968) *General Systems Theory, Human Relations*. New York: Braziller.

Best, S. (2005) *Understanding Social Divisions*. London: Sage.

Bianchi, S. (2000) Maternal employment and time with children: dramatic change or surprising continuity? *Demography*, 37: 401–414.

Blank, G. & Blank, R. (1994) *Ego Psychology: Theory and Practice*, 2nd Rev. edn. New York: Columbia University Press.

Boeree, G. (2006) Personality theories: Viktor Frankl. http://webspace.ship.edu/cboer/frankl.html (accessed 15 February 2008).

Bosma, H., Peter, R., Siegrist, L. & Marmot, M. (1998) Two alternative job stress models and the risk of coronary heart disease. *American Journal of Public Health*, 88(1): 68–74.

Bottomore, T. et al. (eds) (1992) *The Dictionary of Marxist Thought*. Oxford: Blackwell Publishers.

Bottomore, T.B. & Rubel, M. (eds) (1963) *Karl Marx: Selected Writings in Sociology and Social Philosophy*. Harmondsworth: Penguin.

Bowlby, J. (1951) *Maternal Care and Mental Health*. Geneva: World Health Organization.

Bowlby, J. (1969) *Attachment and Loss*, vol. 1 *Attachment*. New York: Basic Books.

Bowlby, J. (1979) *The Making and Breaking of Affectional Bonds*. London: Tavistock.

Bowlby, J. (1982) Attachment and loss: retrospect and prospect. *American Journal of Psychoanalysis*, 52: 664.

Bowlby, J. (1988) *A Secure Base: Clinical Applications of Attachment Theory*. London: Routledge.

Boylan, J. & Allan, G. (2008) Family disruption and relationship breakdown. In M. Davies (ed.) *The Blackwell Companion to Social Work*, 3rd edn. Oxford: Blackwell, pp. 11–17.

Bradshaw, J. (2002) Child poverty and child outcomes. *Children and Society*, 16: 131–140.

Bradshaw, J., Stimson, C., Skinner, C. & Williams, J. (1999) *Absent Fathers?* London: Routledge.

Brennan, G. (2006) Stress vulnerability model of serious mental illness. In C. Gamble & G. Brennan (eds) *Working with Serious Mental Illness: A Manual for Clinical Practice*. London: Elsevier, pp. 43–53.

Briere, J. (1992) *Child Abuse Trauma: Theory and Treatment of the Lasting Effects*. Newbury Park, CA: Sage.

British Association for Adoption and Fostering (BAAF) (2008) *Summary Statistics on Children in Care and Children Adopted from Care, and Searching for Birth Relatives in England*. Available at: http://www.baaf.org.uk/info/stats/England (accessed April 2008).

Bronfenbrenner, U. (1979) *The Ecology of Human Development: Experiments by Nature and Design*. Cambridge, MA: Harvard University Press.

Bronfenbrenner, U. & Ceci, S. (1994) Nature–nurture reconceptualized in developmental perspective: a bioecological model. *Psychological Review*, 101: 568–586.

Brown, D. (1994) An ordinary sexual life? A review of the normalisation principle as it applies to the sexual options of people with learning disabilities. *Disability and Society*, 9(2): 122–144.

Brown, G. & Harris, T. (1978) *Social Origins of Depression: A Study of Psychiatric Disorder in Women*. London: Tavistock.

Brown, J. (2007) Fostering children with disabilities: a concept map of parent needs. *Children and Youth Services Review*, 29(9): 1235–1248.

Brown, L. (2007) Empathy, genuineness – And the dynamics of power: a feminist responds to Rogers. *Psychotherapy: Theory, Research, Practice, Training*, 44(3): 257–259.

Brown, L. & Gilligan, C. (1993) *Meeting at the Crossroads: The Landmark Book About the Turning Points in Girls' and Women's Lives*. New York: Ballantine.

Browne, A. & Finklehor, D. (1986) Initial long-term effects: a review of the research. In D. Finklehor, S. Araji, A. Browne, S. Peters & G. Wyett (eds) *A Sourcebook on Child Sexual Abuse*. Beverly Hills, CA: Sage.

Bryson, V. (1999) *Feminist Debates: Issues of Theory and Political Practice*. Basingstoke: Palgrave.

Burman, E. (1994) *Deconstructing Developmental Psychology*. London: Routledge.

Bury, C., Powis, B., Ofori-Wilson, F., Downer, L. & Griffiths, P. (1999) *An Examination of the Needs of Women Crack Users with Attention to the Role of Domestic Violence and Housing*. London: Lambeth, Southark and Lewisham Health Authority in collaboration with the National Addiction Centre and the Brixton Drug Project.

Cambridge, P. & Mellan, B. (2000) Reconstructing the sexuality of men with learning disabilities: Empirical and theoretical interpretations, *Disability and Society*, 15(2): 293–311.

Campbell, J. (1992) 'If I can't have you, nobody can': power and control in homicide of female partners. In J. Radford & D. Russell (eds) *Femicide: The Politics of Woman Killing*. New York: Twayne, pp. 99–113.

Cancer Research UK (2003) Press release archives. http://info.cancerresearchuk.org (accessed: 27 August 2007).

Carby, H. (1987) *Reconstructing Womanhood: The Emergence of the African-American Woman Novelist*. Oxford: Oxford University Press.

Carter, B. (2005) Becoming parents. In B. Carter & M. McGoldrick (eds) *The Expanded Family Life Cycle: Individual, Family and Social Perspectives*, 3rd edn. Boston: Allyn and Bacon, pp. 249–273.

Carter, B. & McGoldrick, M. (2005a) The divorce cycle. In B. Carter, M. McGoldrick (eds) *The Expanded Family Life Cycle: Individual, Family and Social Perspectives*, 3rd edn. Boston: Allyn and Bacon, pp. 373–380.

Carter, B. & McGoldrick, M. (2005b) Overview: the expanded family life cycle. In B. Carter & M. McGoldrick (eds) *The Expanded Family Life Cycle: Individual, Family and Social Perspectives*, 3rd edn. Boston: Allyn and Bacon, pp. 1–26.

Cassidy, J. (1999) The nature of the child's ties. In J. Cassidy & P. Shaver (eds) *The Handbook of Attachment: Theory, Research, and Clinical Applications*. New York: Guilford, pp. 3–20.

Charlesworth, L., Viggiani, P. & Wood, J. (2003) Middle childhood. In E. Hutchison (ed.) *Dimensions of Human Behavior: The Changing Life Course*, 2nd edn. Thousand Oaks, CA: Sage, pp. 199–245.

Chassin, L., Collins, R., Ritter, J. & Shirley, M. (2001) Vulnerability to substance use disorders across the lifespan. In R. Ingram & J. Price (eds) *Vulnerability to Psychopathology: Risk Across the Lifespan*. New York: Guilford, pp. 165–172.

Chen, J.-Q. & Gardner, H. (2005). Assessment based on multiple-intelligences theory. In D. Flanagan, J. Genshaft & P. Harrison (eds) *Contemporary Intellectual Assessment: Theories, Tests, and Issues*, 2nd edn. New York: Guilford, pp. 77–102.

Chesler, P. (1996) Women and madness: the mental asylum. In T. Heller, J. Reynolds, R. Gomm, R. Muston & S. Pattison (eds) *Mental Health Matters: A Reader*. Basingstoke: Palgrave, pp. 46–53.

Clark, C. (1995) Competencies and discipline in professional formation. *British Journal of Social Work*, 25(5): 563–580.

Cleaver, H., Unell, I. & Aldgate, J. (1999) *Children's Needs – Parenting Capacity: The Impact of Parental Mental Illness, Problem Alcohol and Drug Use, and Domestic Violence on Children's Development*. London: The Stationery Office.

Clewell, T. (2004) Mourning beyond melancholia: Freud's psychoanalysis of loss. *Journal of the American Psychoanalytic Association*, 52(1): 43–67.

Coates, S. (2004) John Bowlgy and Margaret S. Mahler: their lives and theories. *Journal of the American Psychoanalytic Association*, 52: 571–601.

Cochrane, K. (2008) Divorce costs women. *Guardian (G2)* 19 March, p. 19.

Cochrane, R. (1995) Women and depression. *Psychology Review*, 2: 20–24.

Collins, P. (2000) *Black Feminist Thought*. London: Routledge.

Compassionate Friends (2000) *Surviving Your Child's Suicide*. Oak Brook, IL: Author.

Constable, R. & Lee, D. (2004) *Social Work with Families: Content and Process*. Chicago: Lyceum Books. Inc.

Cooper, D. & Denner, J. (1998) Theories linking culture and psychopathology: universal and community-specific processes. *Annual Review of Psychology*, 49: 559–584.

Coulshed, V. (1991) *Social Work Practice: An Introduction*, 2nd edn. Basingstoke: Macmillan.

Coulshed, V. & Orme, J. (2006) *Social Work Practice: An Introduction*, 4th edn. Basingstoke: Palgrave.

Craig, T. (2006) Severe mental illness: symptoms, signs and diagnosis. In C. Gamble & G. Brennan (eds) *Working with Serious Mental Illness: A Manual for Clinical Practice*. London: Elsevier, pp. 85–109.

Cree, V. (2000) *Sociology for Social Workers and Probation Officers*. London: Routledge.

Day, N., Zuo, Y., Richardson, G., Goldschmidt, L., Larkby, C. & Cornelius, M. (1999) Prenatal alcohol use and offspring size at 10 years of age. *Alcoholism: Clinical & Experimental Research*, 23: 863–869.

De Beauvoir, S. ([1949] 1988) *The Second Sex*. London: Jonathan Cape.

DeMaris, A. & Greif, G. (1997) Single custodial fathers and their children. In A. Hawkins & D. Dollahite (eds) *Generative Fathering: Beyond Deficit Perspectives*. Thousand Oaks, CA: Sage, pp. 134–146.

Denney, J. & Davis, E. (2006) Integrated approaches to relapse prevention. In C. Gamble & G. Brennan (eds) *Working with Serious Mental Illness: A Manual for Clinical Practice*. London: Elsevier, pp. 341–358.

Department of Health (2000) *Assessing Children in Need and Their Families: Practice Guidance*. London: The Stationery Office.

Department of Health (2002) *The Mental Health Policy Implementation Guide: Dual Diagnosis Good Practice Guide*. London: DOH.

Department of Health (2006) *Working Together to Safeguard and Promote the Welfare of Children*. London: The Stationery Office.

Department of Health and Human Services, Substance Abuse and Mental Health Admin. (2001) *Mental Health: Culture, Race, and Ethnicity: A Supplement to Mental Health: A Report of the Surgeon General*. Bethesda, MD: US Public Health Service.

Devo, J. (2007) The carers saving the UK £57 billion a year. *Professional Social Work*, July: 8–9.

Dew, M. (1998) Psychiatric disorder in the context of physical illness. In B. Dohrenwend (ed) *Adversity, Stress, and Psychopathology*. New York: Oxford University Press, pp. 177–218.

Dominelli, L. (2008) Feminist theory. In M. Davies (ed.) *The Blackwell Companion to Social Work*. Oxford: Blackwell, pp 110–120.

Doolittle, P. (1997) Vygotsky's zone of proximal development as a theoretical foundation for cooperation learning. *Journal on Excellence in College Teaching*, 8(1): 83–103.

Durkin, K. (1995) *Developmental Social Psychology*. Oxford: Blackwell.

Edwards, J. (2008) On being dropped and picked up: the plight of some late-adopted children. In D. Hindle & G. Shulman (eds) *The Emotional Experience of Adoption: A Psychodynamic Perspective*. London: Routledge, pp. 136–147.

Elkind, D. (1967) Egocentrism in adolescence. *Child Development*, 38: 1025–1034.

Elkind, D. & Bowen, R. (1979) Imaginary audience behavior in children and adolescents. *Developmental Psychology*, 15: 38–44.

Ellis, A. (1962) *Reason and Emotion in Psychotherapy*. New York: Lyle Stuart.

Eriksen, T.H. (2002) *Ethnicity and Nationalism: Anthropological Perspectives*, 2nd edn, London: Pluto Books.

Erikson, E. (1950) *Childhood and Society*. New York: W.W. Norton.

Erikson, E. (1959) *Identity and the Life Cycle*. New York: Norton.

Erikson, E. (1964) *Insight and Responsibility*. Toronto: McLeod.

Erikson, E. (1968) *Identity: Youth and Crisis*. New York: W.W. Norton.

Erikson, E. (1982) *The Lifecycle Completed*. New York: Norton.

Erooga, M. & Print, B. (2001) Assessing parental capacity when intrafamilial sexual abuse is a concern. In J. Howarth (ed) *The Child's World: Assessing Children in Need*. London: Jessica Kingsley, pp. 303–320.

Evans, F.B. (1996) *Harry Stack Sullivan: Interpersonal Theory and Psychotherapy*. London: Routledge.

Everett, B. & Gallop, R. (2001) *The Link Between Childhood Trauma and Mental Illness: Effective Interventions for Mental Health Professionals*. London: Sage.

Ewen, R. (1998) *An Introduction to Theories of Personality*, 5th edn. London: Lawrence Erlbaum Associates.

Fahlberg, V. (1991) *A Child's Journey Through Placement*. Indianapolis: Perspectives Press.

Fairbairn, R. (1952) *Psychological Studies of the Personality*. London: Tavistock.

Faludi, S. (1992) *Backlash: The Undeclared War Against Women*. London: Chatto & Windus.

Featherstone, B. (2003) Taking fathers seriously. *British Journal of Social Work*, 33: 239–254.

Fenichel, M. (2000) New concepts in practice: on therapy – a dialogue with Aaron T. Beck and Albert Ellis. American Psychological Association 108th Convention. Current Topics in Psychology. Available at: www.fenichel.com/Beck-Ellis.shtml (accessed 12 January 2008).

Finkelhor, D. & Brown, A. (1986) Initial and long-term effects: a conceptual framework. In D. Finkelhor (ed) *A Sourcebook on Child Sexual Abuse*. Newbury Park, CA: Sage, pp. 180–198.

Firestone, S. (1970) *The Dialectics of Sex*. London: Paladin.

Firth, H. (1995) *Children First: A Framework for Action*. Basingstoke: Hampshire County Council.

Fonagy, P. (1999) Psychoanalytic theory from the viewpoint of attachment theory and research. In J. Cassidy & P. Shaver (eds) *Handbook of Attachment: Theory, Research, and Clinical Applications*. New York: Guilford Press, pp. 595–624.

Forrester, D. & Harwin, J. (2006) Parental substance misuse and child care social work: findings from the first stage of a study of 100 families. *Child and Family Social Work*, 11: 325–335.

Fox, N., Kimmerly, N. & Shafer, W. (1991) Attachment to mother/attachment to father: a meta-analysis. *Child Development*, 62: 210–225.

Francis, B. (2000) *Boys, Girls, and Achievement: Addressing the Classroom Issues*. London: Routledge/Farmer.

Frankl, V. (1992) *Man's Search for Meaning*, trans. I. Lasch. London: Rider.

Franklin, P. (2005) Dreaming by the book: Freud's 'The Interpretation of Dreams' and the history of the psychoanalytic movement. *Journal of Nervous and Mental Disorders*, 193(1): 74–75.

Freud, S. (1900) *The Interpretation of Dreams*. In J. Strachey (ed.) (1953–1966) *The Standard Edition of the Complete Psychological Works of Sigmund Freud*, Vols. 4–5. London: Hogarth Press.

Freud, S. (1905) Three essays on sexuality. In J. Strachey (ed. and trans.) (1953) *The Standard Edition of the Complete Works of Sigmund Freud*, Vol. 7, London: Hogarth, pp. 135–245. Freud, S. (1917) *Mourning and Melancholia*. In J. Strachey (ed.) (1953–1966) *The Standard Edition of the Complete Psychological Works of Sigmund Freud*, Vol. 14. London: Hogarth Press.

Freud, S. (1923) *The Ego and the Id*. In J. Strachey (ed.) (1953–1966) *The Standard Edition of the Complete Psychological Works of Sigmund Freud*, Vol. 14. London: Hogarth Press.

Friedberg, R., Crosby, L. & Friedberg, G. (2000) Ward, I'm worried about the Beaver: issues in early identification and intervention with children experiencing depression and anxiety. *Journal of Cognitive Psychotherapy*, 14(1): 25–35.

Gamble, C. (2006) Building relationships: lessons to be learnt. In C. Gamble & B. Brennan (eds) *Working with Serious Mental Illness: A Manual for Clinical Practice*. London: Elsevier, pp. 73–83.

Garber, J. & Flynn, C. (2001) Vulnerability to depression in childhood and adolescence. In R. Ingram & J. Price (eds) *Vulnerability to Psychopathology: Risk Across the Lifespan*. New York: Guilford, pp. 175–225.

Gardner, H. (1983) *Frames of Mind: The Theory of Multiple Intelligence*. New York: Basic Books.

Garvin, C. (1991) Social learning and role theories. In R. Greene & P. Ephross (eds) *Human Behavior Theory and Social Work Practice*. New York: Aldine de Gruyter, pp. 151–176.

Gaudin, J., Polansky, N., Kilpatrick, A. & Shilton, P. (1996) Family functioning in neglectful families. *Child Abuse and Neglect*, 20(4): 363–377.

Gelardi, J. (2004) *Born to Rule: Granddaughters of Victoria, Queens of Europe*. London: Headline.

General Household Survey (2004) *Living in Britain: The General Household Survey*. London: HMSO.

George, C. (1996) A representational perspective of child abuse and prevention: internal working models of attachment and caregiving. *Child Abuse and Neglect*, 20(5): 411–424.

Gerhardt, S. (2004) *Why Love Matters: How Affection Shapes a Baby's Brain*. London: Routledge.

Germain, C. (1991) *Human Behavior in the Social Environment: An Ecological View*. New York: Columbia.

Germain, C. & Gitterman, A. (1980) *The Life Model of Social Work Practice*. New York: Columbia University Press.

Gibbins, J. & Kipping, C. (2006) Coexistent substance use and psychiatric disorders. In C. Gamble & G. Brennan (eds) *Working with Serious Mental Illness: A Manual for Clinical Practice*. London: Elsevier, pp. 249–272.

Giddens, A. (1997) *Sociology*, 3rd edn. Cambridge: Polity Press.

Gilbert, W., Nesbitt, T. & Danielsen, B. (1999) Childbearing beyond age 40: pregnancy outcomes in 24,302 cases. *Obstetrics and Gynecology*, 93: 9–14.

Gill, J. (2002) Reported levels of alcohol consumption: binge drinking within the UK undergraduate population over the last 25 years. *Alcohol and Alcoholism*, 37(2): 109–120.

Gilligan, C. (1993) *In a Different Voice: Psychological theory and Women's Development*. Cambridge, MA: Harvard University Press.

Ginsberg, L., Nakerud, L. & Larrison, C. (2004) *Human Biology for Social Workers: Development, Ecology, Genetics, and Health*. Boston: Pearson.

Gladstone, T. & Beardslee, W. (2000) The prevention of depression in at-risk adolescents: current and future directions. *Journal of Cognitive Psychotherapy*, 14(1): 9–23.

Glassman, W. & Hadad, M. (2004) *Approaches to Psychology*, 4th edn. Maidenhead: Open University Press.

Glicken, M. & Sechrest, D. (2003) *The Role of the Helping Professions in Treating the Victims and Perpetrators of Violence*. Boston: Allyn and Bacon.

Goddard, E., Plant, M., Plant, M., Davidson, I. & Garretsen, H. (2000) Drinking patterns. In M. Plant & D. Cameron (eds) *The Alcohol Report*. London: Free Association, pp. 56–78.

Good, M. (1995) Karl Abraham, Sigmund Freud, and the fate of the seduction theory. *Journal of the American Psychoanalytic Association*, 43(4): 1137–1167.

Goffman, E. (1963) *Stigma: Notes on the Management of Spoiled Identity*. Englewood Cliffs, NJ: Prentice Hall.

Gottman, J. (1999) *The Marriage Clinic*. New York: Norton.

Grant, B. & Dawson, D. (1998) Age of onset of drug use and its association with DSM-IV drug abuse and dependence: results from the National Longitudinal Alcohol Epidemiological Survey. *Journal of Substance Abuse*, 10: 163–173.

Greer, G. (2000) *The Whole Woman*. London: Anchor.

Greenberg, M. (1999) Attachment and psychopathology in childhood. In J. Cassidy & P. Shaver (eds) *Handbook of Attachment: Theory, Research, and Clinical Applications*. New York: Guilford Press, pp. 469–496.

Greene, R. (1991a) The ecological perspective: an eclectic theoretical framework for social work practice. In R. Greene & P. Ephross (eds) *Human Behavior Theory and Social Work Practice*. New York: Aldine de Gruyter, pp. 261–296.

Greene, R. (1991b) General systems theory. In R. Greene & P. Ephross (eds) *Human Behavior Theory and Social Work Practice*. New York: Aldine de Gruyter, pp. 227–260.

Greene, R. (1991c) Person-in-environment, human behavior theory, and social work method. In R. Greene & P. Ephross (eds) *Human Behavior Theory and Social Work Practice*. New York: Aldine de Gruyter, pp. 1–18.

Greene, R. & Ephross, P. (1991) Classical psychoanalytic thought, contemporary developments, and clinical social work. In R. Greene & P. Ephross (eds). *Human Behavior Theory and Social Work Practice*. New York: Aldine de Gruyter, pp. 39–78.

Gross, R. (2001) *Psychology: The Science of Mind and Behaviour*, 4th edn. London: Hodder and Stoughton.

Guntrip, H. (1973) *Psychoanalytic Theory, Therapy, and the Self: A Basic Guide to the Human Personality in Freud, Erikson, Klein, Sullivan, Fairbairn, Hartmann, Jacobson & Winnicott*. New York: Basic Books.

Hack, M. & Fanaroff, A. (1999) Outcomes of children of extremely low birthweight and gestational age in the 1990s. *Early Human Development*, 53: 193–218.

Hack, M., Flannery, D., Schluchter, M., Carter, L., Borawski, E. & Klein, N. (2002) Outcomes in young adulthood for very low birth weight infants. *New England Journal of Medicine*, 346: 149–157.

Hall, G.S. (1904) *Adolescence: Its Psychology and its Relation to Physiology, Anthropology, Sociology, Sex, Crime, Religion and Education*, 2 vols. New York: Appleton.

Hammen, C. (1997) *Depression*. Hove: Psychology Press.

Haralambos, M., Holborn, M. & Heald, R. (2004) *Sociology: Themes and Perspectives*, 6th edn. London: Collins.

Harne, L. & Radford, J. (2008) *Tackling Domestic Violence*. Maidenhead: Open University Press.

Harrigan, M. & Baldwin, S. (2003) Conception, pregnancy, and childbirth. In E. Hutchinson (ed.) *Dimensions of Human Behavior: The Changing Life Course*, 2nd edn. Thousand Oaks, CA: Sage.

Harris, C. (2005) Central Asia. In S. Joseph & A. Najmabadi (eds) *Encyclopedia of Women and Islamic Cultures: Family, Law, and Politics*, vol. 2. Boston: Brill, pp. 141–142.

Harris, T. & Bifulco, A. (1991) Loss of a parent in childhood, attachment style, and depression in adulthood. In C. Parkes & J. Stevenson-Hinde (eds) *Attachment Across the Life Cycle*. London: Routledge, pp. 234–267.

Harrison, C. & Abou-Saleh, M. (2002) Psychiatric disorders and substance misuse: psychopathology. In G. Hussein Rassool (ed.) *Dual Diagnosis: Substance Misuse and Psychiatric Disorders*. Oxford: Blackwell Science, pp. 43–57.

Hart, B. (1986) Lesbian battering: an examination. In K. Lobel (ed.) *Naming the Violence*. Seattle, WA: Seal, pp. 173–189.

Hartmann, H. ([1939] 1978) *Ego Psychology and the Problem of Adaptation*. New York: International Universities Press.

Haug, K., Irgens, L., Skjaerven, R., Markestad, T., Baste, V. & Schreuder, P. (2000) Maternal smoking and birthweight: effect modification of period, maternal age and paternal smoking. *Acta Obstetric Gynecology Scandinavia*, 79: 485–489.

Haley, J. (1987) *Problem Solving Therapy*, 2nd edn. San Francisco: Jossey-Bass.

Heath, I. (2008) Domestic violence: a family health perspective. In J. Keeling & T. Mason (eds) *Domestic Violence: A Multi-professional Approach for Healthcare Workers*. Maidenhead: Open University Press, pp. 167–175.

Hepworth, D., Rooney, R. & Larsen, J. (2002) *Direct Social Work Practice: Theory and Skills*, 6th edn. Pacific Grove, CA: Brooks/Cole.

Herrera, V. & McCloskey, L. (2001) Gender differences in the risk for delinquency among youth exposed to family violence. *Child Abuse and Neglect*, 25: 1037–1051.

Hester, M. (2006) Asking about domestic violence: implications for practice. In D. Humphreys & N. Stanley (eds) *Domestic Violence and Child Protection: Directions for Good Practice*. London: Jessica Kinsley, pp. 97–109.

Hilarski, C., Dziegielewski, S. & Wodarski, J. (2002) Mezzo and macro perspectives: group variables in human growth and development. In J. Wodarski & S. Dziegielewski (eds) *Human Behaviour and the Social Environment: Integrating Theory and Evidence-Based Practice*. New York: Springer, pp. 141–156.

Hinde, R. & Stevenson-Hinde, J. (1991) Perspectives on attachment. In C. Parker & J. Stevenson-Hinde (eds) *Attachment Across the Lifecycle*. London: Routledge, pp. 52–65.

HM Inspector of Prisons (1997) *Women in Prison: A Thematic Review*. London: Home Office.

Hockey, J. & James, A. (2003) *Social Identities Across the Lifespan*. Basingstoke: Palgrave.

Holmes, T. & Rahe, R. (1967) The social adjustment rating scale. *Journal of Psychosomatic Research*, 11: 213–218.

Horney, K. (1950) *Neurosis and Human Growth: The Struggle Toward Self-Realization*. New York: Norton.

Horney, K. (1967) *Feminine Psychology*. New York: Norton.

Howe, D. (1995) Assessing adoptions in difficulty. In F. Turner (ed.) *Differential Diagnosis and Treatment in Social Work*, 4th edn. New York: Free Press, pp. 806–817.

Howe, D. (2005) *Child Abuse and Neglect: Attachment, Development and Intervention*. Basingstoke: Palgrave.

Howe, D., Brandon, M., Hinings, D. & Schofield, G. (1999) *Attachment Theory, Child Maltreatment and Family Support*. Basingstoke: Palgrave.

Hughes, C. (2003) Making and breaking relationships: children and their families. In A. Bainham, B. Lindley, M. Richards & L. Trinder (eds) *Children and Their Families: Contact, Rights and Welfare*. Oxford: Hart, pp. 33–46.

Humphreys, C. (2008) Domestic violence. In M. Davies (ed.) *The Blackwell Companion to Social Work*, 3rd edn. Oxford: Blackwell, pp. 27–33.

Humphreys, C., Regan, L., River, D. & Thiara, R. (2005) Domestic violence and substance use: tackling complexity. *British Journal of Social Work*, 35: 1303–1320.

Hunter, I. (2004) William James. In R. Gregory (ed.) *The Oxford Companion to the Mind*, 2nd edn. Oxford: Oxford University Press.

Huth-Bock, A., Levendosky, A. & Semel, M. (2001) The direct and indirect effects of domestic violence on young children's intellectual functioning. *Journal of Family Violence*, 16(3): 269–290.

Hyde, C. (2008) Feminist social work practice. In T. Mizrahi & L. Davis (eds) *Encyclopedia of Social Work*, 20th edn. New York: Oxford University Press, pp. 216–221.

Ingram, R. & Fortier, M. (2001) The nature of adult vulnerability: history and definitions. In R. Ingram & J. Price (eds) *Vulnerability to Psychopathology: Risk across the lifespan*. New York: Guilford, pp. 39–54.

Ingram, R. & Price, J. (2001) The role of vulnerability in understanding psychopathology. In R. Ingram & J. Price (eds) *Vulnerability to Psychopathology: Risk Across the Lifespan*. New York: Guilford, pp. 3–19.

Jack, G. & Jack, D. (2000) Ecological social work: the application of a systems model of development in context. In P. Stepney & D. Ford (eds) *Social Work Models, Methods*. Lyme Regis: Russell House Publishing.

James, W. (1890) *The Principles of Psychology*. New York: Henry Holt.

Jamison, K.R. (1996) *Touched with Fire: Manic-Depressive Illness and the Artistic Temperament*. New York: Simon & Schuster.

Janson-Bjerklie, S., Ferkeitch, S. & Benner, P. (1993) Predicting the outcomes of living with asthma. *Research in Nursing and Health*, 16(4): 241–250.

Janzen, C. & Harris, O. (1997) *Family Treatment in Social Work Practice*, 3rd edn. Itasca, IL: Peacock.

Jasinski, J. (2001) Theoretical explanations for violence against women. In C. Renzetti, J. Edleson & R.K. Bergen (eds) *Sourcebook on Violence Against Women*. Thousand Oaks, CA: Sage, pp. 5–21.

Jenkins, J. (2004) Schizophrenia as a paradigm case for understanding fundamental human processes. In J.H. Jenkins & R. Barrett (eds) *Schizophrenia, Culture, and Subjectivity*. Cambridge: Cambridge University Press, pp. 29–61.

Johnson, P. (2004) *Speaking Positively: Using Respectful Adoption Language*. Indianapolis, IN: Perspectives Press.

Joseph Rowntree Foundation. (1998) *Divorce and Separation: The Outcomes for Children*. Available at: www.jrf.org.uk/knowledge/findings/foundation/spr6108.asp (accessed 11 April 2008).

Jung, C. (1933) *Modern Man in Search of a Soul*. New York: Harcourt, Brace & World.

Jung, C. & Hull, R. (trans.) (1991) *The Archetypes and the Collective Unconscious*. London: Routledge.

Jung, C. & De Laszlo, V. (eds) ([1938] 1993) *The Basic Writings of C.G. Jung*. New York: Modern Library.

Kaslow, N., Croft, S. & Hatcher, C. (1999) Depression and bipolar disorder in children and adolescents. In *Child and Adolescent Psychological Disorders: A Comprehensive Textbook*. New York: Oxford University Press, pp. 264–281.

Kelley, H. (1971) *Attribution in Social Interaction*. Morristown, NJ: General Learning Press.

Kelley, H. (1992) Common-sense psychology and scientific psychology. In M. Rosenzweig & L. Porter (eds) *Annual Review of Psychology*, Vol. 43. Palo Alto, CA: Annual Reviews, pp. 1–23.

Kempson, E. (1996) *Life on a Low Income*. York: Joseph Rowntree Foundation.

Kenny, L. & Kenny, B. (2000) Psychodynamic theory in social work: a view from practice. In P. Stepney & D. Ford (eds) *Social Work Models, Methods and Theories: A Framework for Practice*. London: Russell House.

Kernsmith, P. (2008) Sexual coercion and domestic violence. In J. Keeling & T. Mason (eds)

Domestic Violence: A Multi-professional approach for Healthcare Practitioners. Maidenhead: Open University Press, pp. 57–61.

Keyes, M. (2005) *Further Under the Duvet*. London: Penguin.

Khantzian, E. (1997) The self-medication hypothesis of addictive disorders: a reconsideration and recent applications. *Harvard Review of Psychiatry*, 4: 231–244.

Kilpatrick, R. (2006) Children in alternative care: are their needs being met? In D. Iwaniec (edn.) *The Child's Journey Through Care*. Chichester: Wiley, pp. 61–77.

Kimmel, S. (2008) Gender symmetry in domestic violence: a falsely framed issue. In J. Keeling & T. Mason (eds) *Domestic Violence: A Multi-professional Approach for Healthcare Practitioners*. Maidenhead: Open University Press, pp. 21–35.

King, D.B. & Wertheimer, M. (2005) *Max Wertheimer and Gestalt Theory*. London: Transaction Publishers.

Kinsella, C. & Kinsella, C. (2006) *Introducing Mental Health: A Practical Guide*. London: Jessica Kingsley.

Kirst-Ashman, K. & Hull, G. (1999) *Understanding Generalist Practice*, 2nd edn. Chicago: Nelson-Hall.

Klein, M. ([1957] 2002) *Envy and Gratitude (1946–1963)*. New York: Free Press.

Kohlberg, L. (1963) The development of children's orientation toward a moral order: I. Sequence in the development of moral thought. *Vita Humana*, 6: 11–33.

Kohlberg, L. (1976) Moral stages and moralization: the cognitive-developmental approach. In T. Lickona (ed.) *Moral Development and Behavior: Theory, Research, and Social Issues*. New York: Holt, pp. 31–53.

Kohn, R., Dohrenwend, B. & Mirotznik, J. (1998) Epidemiological findings on selected psychiatric disorders in the general population. In B. Dohrenwend (ed.) *Adversity, Stress, and Psychopathology*. New York: Oxford University Press, pp. 235–284.

Kopp, S. (1976) *If You Meet the Buddha on the Road, Kill Him!* New York: Bantam.

Kroger, J. (1996) *Identity in Adolescence: The Balance Between Self and Other*, 2nd edn. London: Routledge.

Lang, S. (2005) Urie Bronfenbrenner: in appreciation. *Association for Psychological Science Observer*, 18(11).

Lawrence, S. & Zittel-Palamara, K. (2002) The interplay between biology, genetics, and human behavior. In J. Wodarski & S. Dziegielewski (eds) *Human Behavior and the Social Environment: Integrating Theory and Evidence-Based Practice*. New York: Springer, pp. 39–63.

Levinson, D. (1986) A conception of adult development. *American Psychologist*, 41: 3–13.

Lloyd, A. (1995) *Doubly Deviant, Doubly Damned: Society's Treatment of Violent Women*. Harmondsworth: Penguin.

Lorenz, K. (1935) The companion in the bird's world. *Auk*, 54: 245–273.

Loretto, W., Duncan, C. & White, P. (2000) 'Ageism and employment: controversies, ambiguities, and younger people's perceptions', *Age and Society*, 20(3): 279–302.

Lundy, B., Jones, N., Field, T., Nearing, G., Davalos, M., Pietro, P., Schanberg, S. & Kuhn, C. (1999) Prenatal depression effects on neonates. *Infant Behavior and Development*, 22: 119–129.

Luria, A. (2004) Vygotsky, Lev. In R. Gregory (ed.) *The Oxford Companion to the Mind*, 2nd edn. Oxford: Oxford University Press.

Luthra, A., Bhugra, D. & Bhintade, R. (2006) Cultural issues. In C. Gamble & B. Brennan (eds) *Working with Serious Mental Illness: A Manual for Clinical Practice*. London: Elsevier, pp. 359–373.

Lyons, P., Wodarski, J. & Feit, M. (1998) Human behavior theory: emerging trends and issues. *Journal of Human Behavior in the Social Environment*, 1(1): 1–21.

Mahler, M. & LaPerriere, K. (1965) Mother–child interaction during separation–individuation. *Psychoanalytic Quarterly*, 34: 483–498.

Mahler, M., Pine, F. & Bergman, A. (1975) *The Psychological Birth of the Human Infant*. New York: Basic Books.

Mahoney, P., Williams, L. & West, C. (2001) Violence against women by intimate relationship partners. In C. Renzetti, J. Edleson & R.K. Bergen (eds) *Sourcebook on Violence Against Women*. Thousand Oaks, CA: Sage, pp. 143–178.

Manktelow, R. (2008) Mental health social work. In M. Davies (ed.) *The Blackwell Companion to Social Work*, 3rd edn. Oxford: Blackwell, pp. 260–268.

Marinelli, L. & Mayer, A. (2003) *Dreaming by the Book: Freud's Interpretation of Dreams and the History of the Psychoanalytic Movement*, trans. S. Fairfield. New York: Other Press.

Marshall, M. & Rowlings, C. (1998) Facing our futures: discrimination in later life. In B. Lesnik (ed.) *Countering Discrimination in Social Work*. Aldershot: Arena.

Martin, A. (1993) *The Lesbian and Gay Parenting Handbook*. New York: HarperCollins.

Maslow, A. (1943) A theory of human motivation. *Psychological Review*, 50: 370–396.

Maslow, A. (1971) *The Farther Reaches of Human Nature*. New York: Viking.

Masten, A., Burt, K. & Coatsworth, D. (2006) Competence and psychopathology. In P. Cicchetti & D. Cohen (eds) *Developmental Psychopathology: Risk, Disorder, and Adaptation*, vol. 3, 2nd edn. New Jersey: Wiley, pp. 696–738.

Matto, H. (2003) Young adulthood. In E. Hutchison (ed.) *Dimensions of Human Behavior: The Changing Life Course*, 2nd edn. Thousand Oaks, CA: Sage, pp. 305–340.

May, R. (1969) *Love and Will*. New York: Norton.

May, R. (1983) *The Discovery of Being: Writings in Existential Psychology*. New York: Norton.

May, R. (1991) *The Cry for Myth*. New York: Norton.

Maynard, M., Afshar, H., Franks, M. & Wray, S. (2008) *Women in Later Life: Exploring Race and Ethnicity*. Maidenhead: Open University Press.

Maxmen, J. & Ward, N. (1995) *Essential Psychopathology and Its Treatment*, 2nd edn. New York: Norton.

McCarter, S. (2003) Adolescence. In E. Hutchison (ed.) *Dimensions of Human Behavior: The Changing Life Course*, 2nd edn. Thousand Oaks, CA: Sage, pp. 247–302.

McGoldrick, M. (2005a) History, genograms, and the family life cycle: Freud in context, In B. Carter & M. McGoldrick (eds) *The Expanded Family Life Cycle: Individual, Family and Social Perspectives*, 3rd edn. Boston: Allyn and Bacon, pp. 47–68.

McGoldrick, M. (2005b) Women through the family life cycle. In B. Carter & M. McGoldrick (eds) *The Expanded Family Life Cycle: Individual, Family and Social Perspectives*, 3rd edn. Boston: Allyn and Bacon, pp. 106–123.

McGoldrick, M. & Gerson, R. (1985) *Genograms in Family Assessment*. New York: Norton.

McGoldrick, M. & Walsh, F. (2005) Death and the family life cycle. In B. Carter & M. McGoldrick (eds) *The Expanded Family Life Cycle: Individual, Family, and Social Perspectives*, 3rd edn. Boston: Allyn & Bacon, pp. 185–201.

McLellan, D. (1973) *Karl Marx: His Life and Thought*. Basingstoke: Palgrave Macmillan.

McManiman, J. (2001) The invisibility of men's pain. In B. Everett & R. Gallop. *The Link Between Childhood Trauma and Mental Illness: Effective Interventions for Mental Health Professionals*. Thousand Oaks, CA: Sage, pp. 253–270.

McNally, R. (2001) Vulnerability to anxiety disorders in adulthood. In R. Ingram & J. Price (eds) *Vulnerability to Psychopathology: Risk Across the Lifespan*. New York: Guilford, pp. 304–321.

McSherry, D. & Larkin, E. (2006) Exploring regional trends in pathways to permanency. In D. Iwaniec (ed.) *The Child's Journey Through Care*. Chichester: Wiley, pp. 113–130.

Miller, [illegible]. (2008) Understanding an adopted child: a child psychotherapist's perspective. In D. Hindle & G. Shulman (eds) *The Emotional Experience of Adoption: A Psychodynamic Perspective*. London: Routledge, pp. 57–69.

Millett, K. (1970) *Sexual Politics*. New York: Doubleday.

Milner, J. & Myers, S. (2007) *Working with Violence: Policies and Practices in Risk Assessment and Management*. Basingstoke: Palgrave.

Milner, J. & O'Byrne, P. (2002) *Assessment in Social Work*, 2nd edn. Basingstoke: Palgrave.

Minuchin, S. (1974) *Families and Family Therapy*. Cambridge, MA: Harvard University Press.

Mooney, C.G. (2000) *Theories of Childhood: An Introduction to Dewey, Montessori, Erikson, Piaget and Vygotsky*. St Paul, MN: Red Leaf Press.

Mullender, A. (1996) *Rethinking Domestic Violence: The Social Work and Probation Response*. London: Routledge.

Mullender, A. (2008) Gendering the social work agenda. In M. Davies (ed.) *The Blackwell Companion to Social Work*. Oxford: Blackwell, pp. 313–317.

Mullender, A. & Humphreys, C. (1998) *Domestic Violence and Child Abuse: Policy and Practice Issues for Local Authorities and Other Agencies*. London: Local Government Association.

Murray, C. (1996) *Charles Murray and the Underclass: The Developing Debate*, London: IEA Health and Welfare Unit.

Murphy, S. (2000) Deaths: final data for 1998. *National Vital Statistics Report*, 48: 1–105.

Myers, I., McCaulley, M., Quenk, N. & Hammer, A. (1998) *MBTI Manual: A Guide to the Development and Use of the Myers Briggs Type Indicator*, 3rd edn. Washington, DC: Consulting Psychologists Press.

Myhill, A. & Allen, J. (2002) *Rape and Sexual Assault of Women: The Extent and Nature of the Problem. Findings from the British Crime Survey. Home Office Research Study 237*. London: TSO.

Najman, J., Williams, G., Nikles, J., Spence, S., Bor, W., O'Callaghan, M., Le Brocque, R. & Anderson, M. (2000) Mothers' mental illness and child behavior problems: cause-effect association or observation bias? *Journal of Child & Adolescent Psychiatry*, 39: 592–602.

National Health Services (2006) *Infant Mortality and Low Birth Weight*. Directorate of Public Health, Tower Hamlets PCT 2007. www.publichealth.thpct.nhs.uk/PublicHealth Report (accessed 16 Sept. 2007).

Nichols, M. & Schwartz, R. (1998) *Family Therapy: Concepts and Methods*, 4th edn. Boston: Allyn and Bacon.

Oakley, A. (1974) *The Sociology of Housework*. Oxford: Martin Robinson.

Oakley, A. (1981) *Subject Women*. Oxford: Martin Robinson.

Office of National Statistics (2004) www.statistics.gov.uk.

Oliver, M. (1983) *Social Work with Disabled People*. London: Macmillan.

Orme, J. (2002) Feminist social work. In R. Adams, L. Dominelli & M. Payne (eds) *Social Work: Themes, Issues and Critical Debates*, 2nd edn. Basingstoke: Palgrave, pp. 218–226.

Osofsky, J. (1999) The impact of violence on children. *The Future of Children*, 9(3): 33–49.

Owusu-Bempah, K. (2008) Culture, ethnicity and identity. In M. Davies (ed.) *The Blackwell Companion to Social Work*, 3rd edn. Oxford: Blackwell, pp. 318–325.

Paabo, S. (2001) Genomics and society: the Human Genome and our view of ourselves. *Science*, 291: 1219–1220.

Parents, Families and Friends of Lesbians and Gays (PFLAG) (2001) *Read This Before Coming Out to Your Parents*. Washington, DC: Sauerman.

Parrish, M. (2004) Urban poverty and homelessness as hidden demographic variables relevant to academic achievement. In D. Boothe & J. Stanley (eds) *In the Eyes of the Beholder: Critical Issues for Diversity in Gifted Education*. Texas: Proofrock Publishers, pp. 203–211.

Parrish, M., Felice, M. & Feroli, K. (2001) Rape. In R.A. Hoekleman, S. Friedman, et al. (eds) *Primary Pediatric Care*, 4th edn. St Louis, MO: Mosby.

Parrish, M. & Tunkle, J. (2003) Working with family members following their child's suicide. *Family Therapy*, 30(2): 63–76.

Parrish, M. & Tunkle, J. (2005) Clinical challenges following an adolescent's death by suicide: bereavement issues faced by family, friends, schools, and clinicians. *Clinical Social Work*, 33(1): 81–102.

Parsons, T. (1951) *The Social System*. New York: Free Press.

Parsons, T. (1965) The normal American family. In S. Farber, P. Mustacchi & R. Wilson (eds) *Man and Civilization: The Family's Search for Survival*. New York: McGraw-Hill.

Parsons, T. & Bales, R. (eds) (1955) *Family, Socialization and the Interaction Process*. New York: Free Press.

Passer, M., Smith, R., Holt, N., Bremmer, A. Sutherland, K. & Vliek, M. (2009) *Psychology: The Science of Mind and Behavior*, 3rd edn. Boston: McGraw-Hill International.

Payne, M. (1997) *Modern Social Work Theory*, 2nd edn. Basingstoke: Palgrave.

Payne, M. (2002) On being critical in social work. In R. Adams, L. Dominelli & M. Payne (eds) *Critical Practice in Social Work*, Basingstoke: Palgrave.

Phinney, J. & Kohatsu, E. (1997) Ethnic and racial identity development and mental health. In J. Schulenberg, J. Maggs, and K. Hurrelman (eds) *Health Risks and Developmental Transitions in Adolescence*. New York: Cambridge University Press.

Piaget, J. (1932) *The Moral Development of the Child*. Harmondsworth: Penguin.

Piaget, J. (1970) *Biology and Knowledge*, 2nd edn. Edinburgh: Edinburgh University Press.

Pincus, A., Minahan, A. (1973) *Social Work Practice: Model and Method*. Itasca, IL: Peacock.

Pittman, A.-L. & Wolfe, D. (2002) Bridging the gap: prevention of adolescent risk behaviors and development of healthy nonviolent dating relationships. In C. Wekerle & A.-M. Wall (eds) *The Violence and Addiction Equation: Theoretical and Relationship Violence*. Hove: Brunner-Routledge, pp. 304–323.

Plant, M. (2000) Drinking during pregnancy. In M. Plant & D. Cameron (eds) *The Alcohol Report*. London: Free Association Books, pp. 34–38.

Polan, H. & Hofer, M. (1999) Psychobiological origins of infant attachment and separation responses. In J. Cassidy & P. Shaver (eds) *Handbook of Attachment: Theory, Research, and Clinical Applications*. New York: Guilford, pp. 162–180.

Polansky, N. (1991) *Integrated Ego Psychology*, 2nd edn. New York: Aldine de Gruyter.

Popple, K. (2002) Community work. In R. Adams, L. Dominelli & M. Payne (eds) *Critical Practice in Social Work*. Basingstoke: Palgrave, pp. 149–158.

Preto, N. (2005) Transformation of the family system during adolescence. In B. Carter & M. McGoldrick (eds) *The Expanded Family Life Cycle: Individual, Family, and Social Perspectives*, 3rd edn. Boston: Allyn & Bacon, pp. 274–286.

Prior, P. (1999) *Gender and Mental Health*. New York: New York University Press.

Pritchard, C. (2006) *Mental Health Social Work: Evidence-Based Practice*. London: Routledge.

Pryor, J. & Rodgers, B. (2001) *Children in Changing Families: Life After Parental Separation*. Oxford: Blackwell.

Quinn, P. (1998) *Understanding Disability: A Lifespan Approach*. Thousand Oaks, CA: Sage.

Rassool, G. (2002) Substance use and dual diagnosis: concepts, theories and models. In G. Rassool (ed.) *Dual Diagnosis: Substance Misuse and Psychiatric Disorders*. Oxford: Blackwell Science, pp. 12–32.

Ray, W. (2007) Jay Haley – a memorial. *Journal of Marital and Family Therapy*, 33(3): 291–292.

Reiss, D., Hetherington, E., Plomin, R., Howe, G., Simmens, S., Henderson, S., O'Connor, T., Bussell, D., Anderson, E. & Law, T. (1995) Genetic questions for environmental studies: differential parenting and psychopathology in adolescence. *Archives of General Psychiatry*, 52: 925–936.

Renzetti, C. (1992) *Violent Betrayal: Partner Abuse in Lesbian Relationships*. Newbury Park, CA: Sage.

Richmond, M. (1917) *Social Diagnosis*. New York: Russell Sage Foundation.

Robbins, B. (1999) Rollo May. www.mythsandlogos.com.May.html (accessed February 2008).

Roberts, J. (1988) Why are some families more vulnerable to child abuse? In K. Browne, C. Davies & P. Stratton (eds) *Early Prediction and Prevention of Child Abuse*. Chichester: Wiley, pp. 58–78.

Robertson, J. & Bowlby, J. (1952) Responses of young children to separation from their mothers. *Courier of the International Children's Centre*, 2: 131–142.

Robinson, L. (2007) *Cross-cultural Child Development for Social Workers: An Introduction*. Basingstoke: Palgrave.

Rodgers, B. & Pryor, J. (1998) *Divorce and Separation: The Outcomes for Children* York: Joseph Rowntree Foundation.

Rogers, A. & Pilgrim, D. (2005) *A Sociology of Mental Health and Illness*, 3rd edn. Maidenhead: Open University Press.

Rogers, C. (1951) *Client-Centered Therapy*. Boston: Houghton-Mifflin.

Rogers, C. (1985) Toward a more human science of the person. *Journal of Humanistic Psychology*, 25: 7–24.

Roland, A. (1988) *In Search of the Self in India and Japan*. Princeton, NJ: Princeton University Press.

Rooney, G. (2002a) Assessing family functioning in diverse family and cultural contexts. In D. Hepworth, R. Rooney & J. Larsen (eds) *Direct Social Work Practice: Theory and Skills*, 6th edn. Pacific Grove, CA: Brooks/Cole, pp. 259–298.

Rooney, G. (2002b) Enhancing family relationships. In D. Hepworth, R. Rooney & J. Larsen, (eds) *Direct Social Work Practice: Theory and Skills*, 6th edn. Pacific Grove, CA: Brooks/Cole, pp. 477–518.

Rosenberg, S. & Robinson, C. (2004) Out-of-home placement for young children with developmental and medical conditions. *Children and Youth Services Review*, 26(8): 711–723.

Rosenhan, D. (1996) On being sane in insane places. In T. Heller, J. Reynolds, R. Gomm, R. Muston & S. Pattison (eds) *Mental Health Matters: A Reader*. Basingstoke: Palgrave, pp. 70–78.

Rossman, B. (2001) Longer term effects of children's exposure to domestic violence. In S. Graham-Bermann & J. Edleson (eds) *Domestic Violence in the Lives of Children: The Future of Research, Intervention and Social Policy*. Washington, DC: American Psychological Association.

Rowlingson, K. & McKay, S. (2005) Lone motherhood and socio-economic disadvantage: Insights from quantitative and qualitative evidence. *The Sociological Review*, 53: 30–49.

Rowntree, S. & Lavers, G. (1951) *Poverty and the Welfare State*, Longman: London.

Rowsell, C. (2003) Domestic violence and children: making a difference in a meaningful way for women and children. In M. Calder & S. Hackett (eds) *Assessment in Child Care: Using and Developing Frameworks for Practice*. Lyme Regis: Russell House, pp. 282–301.

Runciman, W.G. (1966) *Relative Deprivation and Social Injustice: A Study of Attitudes to Social Inequalities in 20th Century Britain*. London: Routledge.

Rutter, M. & Hersov, L. (eds) (1985) *Child and Adolescent Psychiatry*. London: Blackwell.

Rutter, M. & O'Connor, T. (1999) Implications of attachment theory for child care policies. In J. Cassidy & P. Shaver (eds) *Handbook of Attachment: Theory, Research, and Clinical Applications*. New York: Guilford, pp. 823–844.

Ryan, C. & Futterman, D. (1998) *Lesbian and Gay Youth: Care and Counseling*. New York: Columbia University Press.

Sadock, B. & Sadock, V. (2007) *Kaplan and Sadock's Synopsis of Psychiatry: Behavioral Sciences/Clinical Psychiatry*, 10th edn. Philadelphia, PA: Lippincott, Williams and Wilkins.

Saleebey, D. (1992) *The Strengths Perspective in Social Work Practice*. New York: Longman.

Saleebey, D. (1996) The strengths perspective in social work practice: extensions and cautions. *Social Work*, 41: 296–305.

Sartre, J-P. (1948) *Existentialism and Humanism* (trans. P. Marlet). London: Methuen.

Satir, V. (1972) *Peoplemaking*. Palo Alto, CA: Science and Behavior Books.

Satir, V. (1983) *Conjoint Family Therapy*, 3rd edn. Palo Alto, CA: Science and Behavior Books.

Scannapieco, M. & Connell-Carrick, K. (2005) *Understanding Child Maltreatment: An Ecological and Developmental Perspective*. New York: Oxford University Press.

Schaffer, R. (1996) *Social Development*. Oxford: Blackwell Publishing.

Schofield, G. (2008). Childhood. In M. Davies (ed.) *The Blackwell Companion to Social Work*, 3rd edn. Oxford: Blackwell, pp 361–367.

Schön, D. (1983) *The Reflective Practitioner: How Professionals Think in Action*. New York: Basic Books.

Schuckit, M. (1995) *Drug and Alcohol Abuse: A Clinical Guide to Diagnosis and Treatment*, 4th edn. New York: Plenum.

Schumacher, J. (2008) Treatment and alcohol. In J. Keeling & T. Mason (eds). *Domestic*

Violence: A Multi-professional Approach for Healthcare Practitioners. Maidenhead: Open University Press, pp. 129–137.

Scott, J. & Marshall, G. (2005) *Oxford Dictionary of Sociology*. Oxford: Oxford University Press.

Segal, J. (2004) *Melanie Klein*, 2nd edn. London: Sage.

Segall, M., Dasen, P., Berry, J. & Poortinga, Y. (1999) *Human Behavior in Global Perspective: An Introduction to Cross-cultural Psychology*, 2nd edn. Boston, MA: Allyn and Bacon.

Seligman, M.E.P. (1979) *Helplessness: On Depression, Development and Death*. San Francisco: Freeman.

Selye, H. (1956) *The Stress of Life*. Highstown, NJ: McGraw-Hill.

Sgroi, S. (1988) *Handbook of Clinical Intervention in Child Sexual Abuse*. Lexington, MA: D.C. Heath.

Shaffer, H.R. (1996) *Social Development*. Oxford: Blackwell.

Sheldon, B. (2000) Cognitive behavioural methods in social care: a look at the evidence. In P. Stepney & D. Ford (eds) *Social Work Models, Methods and Theories: A Framework for Practice*. Lyme Regis: Russell House, pp. 65–83.

Shriver, J. (1998) *Human Behavior and the Social Environment: Shifting Paradigms in Essential Knowledge for Social Work Practice*, 2nd edn. Needham Heights, MA: Allyn & Bacon.

Sigelman, C. & Rider, E. (2003) *Lifespan Human Development*, 4th edn. Belmont, CA: Wadsworth/Thompson.

Simpson, B., Jessop, J. & McCarthy, P. (2003) Fathers after divorce. In A. Bainham, B. Lindley, M. Richards & L. Trinder (eds) *Children and Their Families: Contact, Rights and Welfare*. Oxford: Hart, pp. 201–219.

Singh, S. & Burns, T. (2006) Race and mental health: there is more to race than racism. *British Medical Journal*, 333: 648–651.

Skinner, B.F. (1965) *Science and Human Behavior*. New York: Free Press.

Skinner, B.F. (1972) *Beyond Freedom and Dignity*. New York: Bantam.

Skinner, B.F. (1987) Skinner on behaviourism. In R.L Gregory (ed.) *The Oxford Companion to the Mind*. Oxford: Oxford University Press, pp. 90–92.

Smale, G., Tuson, G. & Stratham, D. (2000) *Social Work and Social Problems: Working Towards Social Inclusion and Social Change*. Basingstoke: Palgrave.

Smart, C. (1995) *Law, Crime, and Sexuality: Essays in Feminism*. London: Sage.

Smith, M. (2002) Howard Gardner and multiple intelligences. *The Encyclopedia of Informal Education*. Available at: http://www.infedn.org/thinkers/gardner.htm.

Spitz, R. (1945) Hospitalism: an inquiry into the genesis of psychiatric conditions in early childhood. *Psychoanalytic Study of the Child*, vol. 1. New York: International Universities Press.

Spitz, R. (1946) Analytic depression. *Psychoanalytic Study of the Child*, Vol. 2. New York: International Universities Press.

Stepansky, P. (ed.) (1988) *The Memoirs of Margaret S. Mahler*. New York: Free Press.

Stepney, P. (2000) The theory to practice debate revisited. In P. Stepney & D. Ford (eds). *Social Work Models, Methods and Theories: A Framework for Practice*. Lyme Regis: Russell House, pp. 20–29.

Stepney, P. & Evans, D. (2000) Community social work: towards an integrative model of practice. In P. Stepney & D. Ford (eds) *Social Work Models, Methods and Theories: A Framework for Practice*. Lyme Regis: Russell House pp. 105–115.

Streissguth, A. (1991) Neonatal effects of alcohol use. In J. Kinney (ed.) *Clinical Manual of Substance Abuse*. St Louis, MO: Mosby, pp. 202–206.

Streissguth, A., Randals, S. & Smith, D. (1991) A test–retest study of intelligence in patients with fetal alcohol syndrome: implications for care. *Journal of the American Academy of Child and Adolescent*, 30: 584–587.

Streissguth, A.P., Sampson, P., Barr, H., Bookstein, F.L. & Olson, H. (1994) The effects of prenatal exposure to alcohol and tobacco: contributions from the Seattle Longitudinal Prospective Study and implications for public policy. In H.L. Needlebaum & D. Bellinger (eds) *Prenatal Exposure to Toxicants*. Baltimore, MD: Johns Hopkins University Press.

Stewart, S. & Israeli, A. (2002) Substance abuse and co-occurring psychiatric disorders in victims of intimate violence. In C. Wekerle & A.-M. Wall (eds) *The Violence and Addiction Equation: Theoretical and Clinical Issues in Substance Abuse and Relationship Violence*. Hove: Brunner-Routledge, pp. 98–122.

Sullivan, H.S. (1953) *The Interpersonal Theory of Psychiatry*. New York: Norton.

Tanner, D. & Harris, J. (2008) *Working with Older People*. London: Routledge.

Taylor, J., Gilligan, C. & Sullivan, A. (1995) *Between Voice and Silence: Women and Girls, Race and Relationship*. Cambridge, MA: Harvard University Press.

Teicher, M. (2000) Wounds that time won't heal: the neurobiology of child abuse. *Cerebrum*, 2(4): 50–67.

Teicher, M., Tomoda, A. & Anderson, S. (2006) Neurobiological consequences of early stress and childhood maltreatment: are results from human and animal studies comparable? *Annals NY Academy of Science*, 1071: 313.

Thomas, A. & Chess, S. (1986) The New York Longitudinal Study: from infancy to early adult Life. In R. Plomin & J. Dunn (eds) *The Study of Temperament: Changes, Continuities, and Challenges*. Hillside, NJ: Lawrence Erlhaum, pp. 39–52.

Thomas, R.M. (1999) *Human Development Theories: Windows on Culture*. Thousand Oaks, CA: Sage.

Thompson, N. (2000) Existentialist practice. In P. Stepney & D. Ford (eds) *Social Work Models, Methods and Theories: A Framework for Practice*. Lyme Regis: Russell House, pp. 116–124.

Thompson, N. (2005) *Understanding Social Work: Preparing for Practice*. Basingstoke: Palgrave.

Thompson, N. (2006) *Anti-Discriminatory Practice*, 4th edn. Basingstoke: Palgrave.

Thorndike, E.L. (1911) *Animal Intelligence*. New York: Macmillan.

Townsend, Peter (1979) *Poverty in the United Kingdom*. Harmondsworth: Penguin.

United Nations (1995) *The Copenhagen Declaration and Programme of Action: World Summit for Social Development*. New York: United Nations.

United Nations (2001) *Early Marriages, Child Spouses*. Florence: UNICEF.

U.S. Department of Health and Human Services (DHHS) (1999) *Mental Health: A Report of the Surgeon General*. Rockville, MD: DHHS.

U.S. Department of Health and Human Services (DHHS) (2001) *Mental Health: Culture, Race, and Ethnicity: A Supplement to Mental Health: A Report of the Surgeon General*. Rockville, MD: DHHS.

U.S. National Library of Medicine (2007) Medline Plus. Available at: http://ghr.nlm.nih.gov/condition=hemophilia (accessed: 26 August 2007).

Vaillant, G. (1977) *Adaptation to Life*. Boston: Little, Brown.

Vaillant, G. & Milofsky, E. (1980) Natural history of male psychological health: IX. Empirical evidence for Erikson's model of the life cycle. *American Journal of Psychiatry*, 137: 1348–1359.

van der Kolk, B. (1994) The body keeps the score: memory and the evolving psychobiology of posttraumatic stress. *Harvard Review of Psychiatry*, 1: 253–265.

Vaughn, B. & Bost, K. (1999) Attachment and temperament: redundant, independent, or interacting influences on interpersonal adaptation and personality development? In J. Cassidy & P. Shaver (eds) *Handbook of Attachment: Theory, Research, and Clinical Applications*. New York: Guilford, pp. 198–225.

Venes, D. (ed.) (2005) *Taber's Cyclopedic Medical Dictionary*, 20th edn. Philadelphia: F.A. Davis.

Vesely, F. (2008) Viktor-Frankl-Institut. Available at: http://logotherapy.univie.ac.at/e/bibE.html (accessed April 2008).

Vourlekis, B. (1991) Cognitive theory for social work practice. In R. Greene & P. Ephross (eds) *Human Behavior Theory and Social Work Practice*. New York: Aldine de Gruyter, pp. 123–150.

Walby, S. (1990) *Theorizing Patriarchy*. Oxford: Blackwell.

Walker, A. (1983) *In Search of Our Mothers' Gardens: Womanist Prose*. San Diego, CA: Harcourt Brace.

Walker, J. (2008) Partnership and parenting. In M. Davies (ed.) *The Blackwell Companion to Social Work*, 3rd edn. Oxford: Blackwell.

Waterhouse, L. (2008) Child abuse. In M. Davies (ed.) *The Blackwell Companion to Social Work*, 3rd edn. Oxford: Blackwell, pp. 18–26.

Watson, D. & West, J. (2006) *Social Work Process and Practice: Approaches, Knowledge and Skills*. Basingstoke: Palgrave

Watson, J. (2007) Reassessing Rogers' necessary and sufficient conditions of change. *Psychotherapy: Theory, Research, Practice, Training*, 44 (3): 268–273.

Watson, J.B. (1913) Psychology as the behaviorist views it. *Psychological Review*, 20: 158–177.

Watson, J.B. (1925) *Behaviorism*. New York: Peoples' Institute Publishing Co.

Weber, M. ([1905] 2001) *The Protestant Ethic and the Spirit of Capitalism*, London: Routledge.

Weber, W. (2001) Young people's alcohol consumption reaches alarming levels in Europe. *The Lancet*, 357 (9256): 617–618.

Weiner, B. (1986) *An Attributional Theory of Motivation and Emotion*. New York: Springer.

Wellman, N. (2006) Assessing risk. In C. Gamble & B. Brennan (eds) *Working with Serious Mental Illness: A Manual for Clinical Practice*. London: Elsevier, pp. 145–164.

West, J. & Bubenzer, D. (1993) Salvador Minuchin: practitioner and theoretician. *The Family Journal*, 1(3): 277–282.

Widom, C. (1998) Childhood victimization: early adversity and subsequent psychopathology. In B. Dohrenwend (ed.) *Adversity, Stress, and Psychopathology*. New York: Oxford University Press, pp. 81–95.

Wieland, S. (1997) *Hearing the Internal Trauma: Working with Children and Adolescents Who Have Been Sexually Abused*. Thousand Oaks, CA: Sage.

Wilkinson, R. (1996) *Unhealthy Societies*. London: Routledge.

Wilkinson, R. & Pickett, K. (2009) *The Spirit Level: Why More Equal Societies Almost Always Do Better*. London: Penguin.

Williams, F. (1996) Postmodernism, feminism and difference. In N. Parton (ed.) *Social Theory, Social Change and Social Work*. London: Routledge, pp. 61–76.

Williams, R. Vaughn (ed.) (1933) *The English Hymnal*, London: Oxford University Press, No. 587.

Wilson, K., Ruch, G., Lymberty, M. & Cooper, A. (2008) *Social Work: An Introduction to Contemporary Practice*. Harlow: Pearson.

Winborg, K., Kesmodel, U., Henriksen, T., Olsen, S. & Secher, N. (2000) A Prospective study of smoking during pregnancy and SIDS. *Archives of Disease in Childhood*, 83: 203–206.

Winnicott, D. (1958) *Collected Papers: Through Pediatrics to Psychoanalysis*. New York: Basic Books.

Winnicott, D. (1964) *The Child, the Family, and the Outside World*. London: Penguin.

Winnicott, D. (1965) *The Maturational Processes and the Facilitating Environment*. London: Hogarth Press.

Winnicott, D. (1968) Playing: its theoretical status in the clinical situation. *International Journal of Psychoanalysis*, 49: 591–599.

Wolfgram, S. (2008) Openness in adoption: What we know so far – a critical review of the literature. *Social Work*, 53(2): 133–142.

Wood, M. & Sher, K. (2002) Sexual assault and relationship violence among college students: examining the role of alcohol and other drugs. In C. Wekerle & A.-M. Wall (eds) *The Violence and Addiction Equation: Theoretical and Clinical Issues in Relationship Violence*. Hove: Brunner-Routledge, pp. 169–193.

Woodward, K. (1995) 'Tribute to the older woman: psychoanalysis, feminism and ageism'. In M. Featherstone & A. Wernick (eds.) *Images of Ageing*. London: Routledge.

Woody, D. (2003a) Early childhood. In E. Hutchison (ed.) *Dimensions of Human Behavior: The Changing Life Course*, 2nd edn. Thousand Oaks, CA: Sage, pp. 157–195.

Woody, D. (2003b) Infancy and toddlerhood. In E. Hutchison (ed.) *Dimensions of Human Behavior: The Changing Life Course*, 2nd edn. Thousand Oaks, CA: Sage, pp. 111–155.

World Health Organization (1946) Preamble to the Constitution of the World Health Organization as adopted by the International Health Conference, New York, 19–22 June, 1946; signed on 22 July 1946 by representatives of 61 states (Official Records of the WHO, no. 2, p. 100) and entered into force on 7 April 1948. Available at: http://www.who.int (accessed on 22 August 2007).

World Health Organization (1993) *International Classification of Diseases*, 10th edn. Geneva: WHO.

World Health Organization (2001) *International Classification of Functioning, Disability and Health (ICF)*. Geneva: WHO.

Yalom, I. (1985) *The Theory and Practice of Group Psychotherapy*, 3rd edn. New York: Basic Books.

Zangwill, O. (2004) Anna Freud. In R. Gregory, (ed.) *The Oxford Companion to the Mind*, 2nd edn. Oxford: Oxford University Press.

Zastrow, C. (2007) *The Practice of Social Work: A Comprehensive Worktext*, 8th edn. Belmont, CA: Thomson Brooks/Cole.

Zastrow, C. & Kirst-Ashman, K. (1994) *Understanding Human Behavior and the Social Environment*, 3rd edn. Chicago: Nelson-Hall.

Index

A-B-C Principle, cognition/cognitive development, 128–129
abuse, child *see* child maltreatment
accommodation, cognition/cognitive development, 114–115
adaptation
  ecosystems perspective, 210
  theory, 7
Adler, Alfred, 83–84
adolescence
  alcohol/drug-related problems, 44
  cognitive development, 43–44
  developmental models, 42–44
  imaginary audience phenomenon, 43
  personal fable, 43
  sexual orientation, 44–45
  social development, 44
adoptive families, 236–238
adulthood, 80–81, 86–87, 95
aggression, learning, 121–122
Ainsworth, Mary, 84–86
alcohol/drug-related problems
  adolescence, 44
  families, 240–241
  FAS, 32, 241
  middle/late adulthood, 46–47
  pregnancy, 32
  young adulthood, 46
Allport, Gordon
  humanism, 135, 136–138
  trait theory, 135, 136–138
anal stage, psychosexual stages, 60–61
analytic psychology, 88–89
ante-natal factors, developmental models, 31
anxiety, 88
Apgar Scale, newborns, 35
assimilation, cognition/cognitive development, 114–115
attachment, 84–86, 94
  Ego Psychology perspectives, 77–79
  Internal Working Models, 80–82
  Neo-Freudian perspectives, 77–79
  responses, 81–82
  stages, 80
attachment difficulties, 153
attachment theory, 80–81, 86–87, 95
attribution theory
  learning, 124–126
  mental health problems, 172–173

Bandura, Albert, 113, 121–122
Bandura's social learning theory
  cognition/cognitive development, 120–121
  learning, 120–121
Beck, Aaron
  cognition/cognitive development, 113, 129–130
  cognitive triad of depression, 129–130
  depression inventory, 130
behaviour, 1–2
  bio-psychosocial perspective, 2
  biological influences, 15–29
  medical influences, 15–29
  relevance for social work, 1–2
  socio-economic influences, 264–274
  sociological influences, 264–274
  theory, 4–12
  trauma influences, 150–169
  understanding, 4–12
behaviourism, 98–109
  biofeedback, 107
  classical conditioning, 99, 103
  criticisms, 107
  debates, 107
  historical background, 99–102
  implications for practice, 106–107
  key concepts, 102–103
  law of effect, 100
  operant conditioning, 102, 103–106
  Pavlov, Ivan, 99
  relevance for social work, 98
  Skinner, B. F., 102
  'Skinner Box', 102, 107
  systematic desensitization, 106–107
  Thorndike, Edwin, 100
  Watson, John Broadus, 100–102
bereavement
  families, 241–243
  traumatic, 162–163
Berne, Dr Eric, 83
bio-psychosocial approach, illness/disease/disability, 23–24

bio-psychosocial model, 16–17
mental health problems, 171–172
bio-psychosocial perspective, 16–17
behaviour, 2
biofeedback, behaviourism, 107
biological influences
behaviour, 15–29
relevance for social work, 15–16
bipolar disorder, 182–183
birth weight, developmental models, 34–35
'blended' families, 236
boundaries
families, 225–226
systems theory, 207
Bourdieu, Pierre, 267
Bowlby, John, 86–87
Bronfenbrenner, Urie, 205

Carby, Hazel, 252
CBT *see* cognitive-behavioural therapy
child maltreatment
physical abuse, 151–153
sexual abuse, 153–157
trauma influences on behaviour, 151–157
childhood, developmental models, 40–42
chum period, 93
classical conditioning
behaviourism, 99, 103
Pavlov, Ivan, 99
cognition/cognitive development, 110–133
see also learning
accommodation, 114–115
adolescence, 43–44
assimilation, 114–115
A-B-C Principle, 128–129
Bandura, Albert, 113
Bandura's social learning theory, 120–121
Beck, Aaron, 113, 129–130
CBT, 131
cognitive-behavioural perspective, 128–130
cognitive triad of depression, 129–130
concrete operations stage (approximately 7–11 years), 116–117
criticisms, 131–132
depression inventory, 130
Ellis, Albert, 113, 128–129
equilibrium, 114–115
factors influencing, 114
formal operations stage (approximately age 11 onward), 117–118
historical background, 111–113
implications for practice, 130–131
James, William, 111
key concepts, 113–121
Kohlberg, Lawrence, 112–113
Kohlberg's stages of moral reasoning, 119–120
Piaget, Jean, 111–112
Piaget's theory of cognitive development, 113–118
preoperational stage (approximately 2–6 or 7 years), 116
relevance for social work, 110–111
role theory, 123–124, 130–131
self-efficacy, 122
sensorimotor stage (birth to 2 years), 115
shortcomings, 131–132
social learning theory, 120–121
Vygotsky, Lev, 112, 205–206
Vygotsky's social cognition learning model, 118–119
cognitive-behavioural therapy (CBT), 131
cognitive triad of depression, Beck, Aaron, 129–130
Collins, Patricia, 252
commonly encountered conditions, overview, 28–29
communication, families, 227–228
comprehensive theory, 8
Comte, Auguste, 265
concise theory, 8
concrete operations stage (approximately 7–11 years), cognition/cognitive development, 116–117
conditioning
classical conditioning, 99, 103
operant conditioning, 102, 103–106
conscious, Topographical Conception, 55
constructs, theory, 7–8
continuous reinforcement, operant conditioning, 105–106
crime, women, 256–257
cyclothymia, 183

Darwin, Charles, 19
de Beauvoir, Simone, 251
deduction, theory, 8
defence mechanisms
personality theory, 57–58
psychoanalytic, 57–58
demographic patterns, families, 232
depression, 178–182
cognitive triad of depression, 129–130
depression inventory, 130
dysthymia, 181–182
post-natal depression, 35–36
developmental constructs, Freud, Sigmund, 58–62

developmental models, 30–48
  adolescence, 42–44
  ante-natal factors, 31
  birth weight, 34–35
  childhood, 40–42
  early childhood, 40–41
  Failure to Thrive (FTT), 38
  fears, 39
  foetal period, 33–34
  implications for practice, 47
  infancy, 36–38
  middle childhood, 41–42
  middle/late adulthood, 46–47
  newborns, 35
  post-natal depression, 35–36
  pregnancy, 31–33
  prematurity, 34
  relevance for social work, 30–31
  sexual orientation, 44–45
  temperament, 38–39
  toddlers, 39–40
  young adulthood, 46
developmental theories, Erikson, Erik H., 64–71
diathesis-stress model, 26–27
  mental health problems, 177
  systems theory, 209
  substance-related, 196
disability, bio-psychosocial approach, 23–24
disease, bio-psychosocial approach, 23–24
divorce, families, 232–234
domestic violence
  see also child maltreatment
  influences on behaviour, 157–159
  power and control wheel, 158–159
  women, 257–258
drugs, substance misuse/dependence, 192–196
Durkheim, Emile, 266, 268–270
dynamic theory, 8
dysthymia, 181–182

early childhood, developmental models, 40–41
eclampsia, pregnancy, 34
ecosystems perspective
  adaptation, 210
  criticisms, 216
  historical contributors, 204–206
  homeostasis, 210
  implications for practice, 214–216
  key concepts, 209–210
  relevance for social work, 204
  shortcomings, 216
ego functions, 77–79
Ego Psychology perspectives, 76–97
  attachment, 77–79
  criticisms, 95–96
  debates, 95–96
  ego functions, 77–79
  historical background, 77
  historical contributors, 83–93
  implications for practice, 94–95
  key concepts, 77–82
  object relations theory, 82
  relevance for social work, 76
  Transactional Analysis (TA), 83
Ellis, Albert
  A-B-C Principle, 128–129
  cognition/cognitive development, 113, 128–129
empirical support, theory, 11
entropy, systems theory, 207
equilibrium, cognition/cognitive development, 114–115
Erikson, Erik H.
  developmental theories, 64–71
  historical background, 62–63
  life stages of development, 64–71
  psychosocial theory, 63–64
  relevance for social work, 52
Eriksonian perspectives
  criticisms, 71–72
  debates, 71–72
  implications for practice, 72–73
ethical issues, theory, 11–12
evolution, genetic concepts, 19–20
existentialism, 134–149
  criticisms, 147–148
  debates, 147–148
  Frankl, Victor, 142–143, 144–145
  historical contributors, 141–143
  implications for practice, 146–147
  key concepts, 143–145
  Kopp, Sheldon, 143
  May, Rollo, 143, 145
  relevance for social work, 134–135
  Sartre, Jean-Paul, 141–142
explanatory theories, 7
extinction, operant conditioning, 106

Failure to Thrive (FTT), developmental models, 38
families, 220–249
  adoptive families, 236–238
  alcohol/drug-related problems, 240–241
  bereavement, 241–243
  'blended' families, 236
  boundaries, 225–226
  communication, 227–228
  criticisms, 247–248

demographic patterns, 232
diverse family forms, 239–240
divorce, 232–234
family disruption, 232–234
family myths, 229–230
family systems, 225–226
feminism, 255–256
fostering, 236–238
genograms, 243–244, 245
historic contributions, 221–223
implications for practice, 244–247
key concepts, 223–225
lone parenting, 235–236
reciprocity, 228–232
relationships, 228–232
relevance for social work, 220–221
roles, 228–232
scapegoating, 230–231
shortcomings, 247–248
triangulation, 222–223
FAS *see* foetal alcohol syndrome
fears, developmental models, 39
feminism, 250–263
see also women
approaches to practice, 260–261
criticisms, 261
families, 255–256
historical background, 251–253
key concepts, 253–254
'malestream', 254
mental health problems, 259
patriarchy, 253–254
radical feminism, 251–252
relevance for social work, 250–251
sexual assault (rape), 259–260
sexual violence, 259–260
shortcomings, 261
fight-or-flight response, 152
Firestone, Shulamith, 252
foetal alcohol syndrome (FAS), 32, 241
foetal period, developmental models, 33–34
formal operations stage (approximately age 11 onward), cognition/cognitive development, 117–118
fostering, families, 236–238
Frankl, Victor, existentialism, 142–143, 144–145
Freud, Anna, 62, 87
Freud, Sigmund, 51–62
see also psychoanalytic concepts
developmental constructs, 58–62
historical background, 52
The Interpretation of Dreams, 54
personality theory, 56–58
psychoanalytic concepts, 52–56
psychosexual stages, 59–62
relevance for social work, 51
FTT *see* Failure to Thrive

Gardner, Howard, Theory of Multiple Intelligences, 126–128
gender identity, toddlers, 40
genetic concepts, 18–22
conditions linked with genetic transmission, 20–21
Darwin, Charles, 19
evolution, 19–20
haemophilia, 21
Human Genome Project, 20
interactionist view, 22
Mendel, Gregor, 18–19
nature vs. nurture, 22
predisposition, 22
Romanov dynasty, 21
twin studies, 21–22
genital stage, psychosexual stages, 62
genograms, families, 243–244, 245

haemophilia
genetic concepts, 21
Romanov dynasty, 21
Haley, Jay, 221
Hartmann, Heinz, 87
health
defining, 17
non-medical influences, 16
hierarchy of needs
humanism, 139–141
Maslow, Abraham, 139–141
historical background
behaviourism, 99–102
cognition/cognitive development, 111–113
Ego Psychology perspectives, 77
Erikson, Erik H., 62–63
Freud, Sigmund, 52
humanism, 135–136
learning, 111–113
Neo-Freudian perspectives, 77
historical considerations, mental health problems, 172–174
historical contributors
ecosystems perspective, 204–206
Ego Psychology perspectives, 83–93
existentialism, 141–143
Neo-Freudian perspectives, 83–93
systems theory, 204–206
holding environment, 93, 94
homeostasis, ecosystems perspective, 210
Horney, Karen, 87–88

Human Genome Project, genetic concepts, 20
humanism, 134–149
  Allport, Gordon, 135, 136–138
  hierarchy of needs, 139–141
  historical background, 135–136
  key concepts, 136–141
  Maslow, Abraham, 136, 139–141
  person-centred theory, 138–139
  phenomenological perspective, 136–138
  relevance for social work, 134–135
  Rogers, Carl, 135–136
  self-actualization, 139–141
  self theory, 138–139
  trait theory, 135, 136–138
hypomania, 183
hypothesis
  self-medication hypothesis, 6, 10
  theory, 8, 10

ICF *see* International Classification of Functioning, Disability and Health
illness, bio-psychosocial approach, 23–24
imaginary audience phenomenon, adolescence, 43
imprinting, 90–91
in vitro fertilization (IVF), 31
induction, theory, 8
infancy, developmental models, 36–38
inferiority, 83–84
information sources, health-related conditions, 29
intelligence
  basic ideas, 126
  Theory of Multiple Intelligences, 126–128
  types, 126–128
interactionist view, genetic concepts, 22
Internal Working Models, attachment, 80–82
International Classification of Functioning, Disability and Health (ICF), 18
interpersonal psychiatry, 91–93
The Interpretation of Dreams, Freud, Sigmund, 54
IVF *see in vitro* fertilization

James, William, cognition/cognitive development, 111
Jung, Karl, 88–90

Klein, Melanie, 90
Kohlberg, Lawrence, cognition/cognitive development, 112–113
Kohlberg's stages of moral reasoning, cognition/cognitive development, 119–120
Kopp, Sheldon, existentialism, 143

labels, mental health problems, 170–171
latency stage, psychosexual stages, 62
law of effect
  behaviourism, 100
  Thorndike, Edwin, 100
learned helplessness theory, 10–11, 122–123
learning, 110–133
  see also cognition/cognitive development
  aggression, 121–122
  attribution theory, 124–126
  Bandura, Albert, 113
  Bandura's social learning theory, 120–121
  historical background, 111–113
  key concepts, 113–121
  observational learning, 121–122
  relevance for social work, 110–111
  social learning theory, 120–121
life-altering conditions, bio-psychosocial approach, 23–24
life cycle, psychosocial theory, 63–64
life stages of development, Erikson, Erik H., 64–71
locus of control, 125
lone parenting, 235–236
Lorenz, Konrad, 90–91

macrosystems, theory, 9
Mahler, Margaret, 91
maladaptivity, mental health problems, 175–176
'malestream', feminism, 254
maltreatment, child *see* child maltreatment
manageability, mental health problems, 175–176
Marx, Karl, 265–266
Marxist theory
  criticisms, 272–273
  shortcomings, 272–273
Maslow, Abraham
  hierarchy of needs, 139–141
  humanism, 136–138, 139–141
  self-actualization, 139–141
maternal rejection, 38
May, Rollo, existentialism, 143, 145
medical influences
  behaviour, 15–29
  non-medical influences on health, 16
  relevance for social work, 15–16
medical model
  criticisms, 27–28
  mental health problems, 171–172
  self-determination, 28
  shortcomings, 27–28
  social model of disability, 28
  cf strengths perspective, 25–26
  theory, 9–10
  understanding illness, disease and disability, 18

Mendel, Gregor, genetic concepts, 18–19
mental disorder, defining, 174–175
mental health problems, 170–200
  attribution theory, 172–173
  bio-psychosocial model, 171–172
  diathesis-stress model, 26–27, 177
  feminism, 259
  historical considerations, 172–174
  implications for practice, 196–198
  influences on behaviour, 170–200
  key concepts, 174–177
  labels, 170–171
  maladaptivity, 175–176
  manageability, 175–176
  medical model, 171–172
  mood disorders, 177–183
  organic approach, 173–174
  PTSD, 189–190
  relevance for social work, 170–172
  schizophrenia, 184–189
  social model, 171–172
  substance misuse/dependence, 192–196
  suicide, 191–192
  vulnerability, 176–177
Merton, Robert, 266
microsystems, theory, 9
middle childhood, developmental models, 41–42
middle/late adulthood
  alcohol/drug-related problems, 46–47
  developmental models, 46–47
Millett, Kate, 252
Minuchin, Salvador, 221–223
mood disorders, 177–183
  bipolar disorder, 182–183
  cyclothymia, 183
  depression, 35–36, 129–130, 178–182
  dysthymia, 181–182
  hypomania, 183
Murray, Charles, 272
Myers-Briggs Type Indicator, 94

nature vs. nurture, genetic concepts, 22
negative reinforcement, operant conditioning, 104
Neo-Freudian perspectives, 76–97
  attachment, 77–79
  criticisms, 95–96
  debates, 95–96
  ego functions, 77–79
  historical background, 77
  historical contributors, 83–93
  implications for practice, 94–95
  key concepts, 77–82
  object relations theory, 82
  relevance for social work, 76
  Transactional Analysis (TA), 83
neuroses, 88
newborns
  Apgar Scale, 35
  developmental models, 35
non-medical influences on health, 16
nutrition, pregnancy, 32

Oakley, Anne, 252
object relations theory
  Ego Psychology perspectives, 82
  Neo-Freudian perspectives, 82
observational learning, 121–122
Occam's razor, theory, 8
operant conditioning
  behaviourism, 102, 103–106
  continuous reinforcement, 105–106
  extinction, 106
  negative reinforcement, 104
  punishment, 104–105
  reinforcement, 104
  schedules of reinforcement, 105–106
  shaping, 105
oral stage, psychosexual stages, 59–60
organic approach, mental health problems, 173–174
organization, this book, 3
overview
  commonly encountered conditions, 28–29
  specific conditions, 28–29
  this book, 3

parenting, lone, 235–236
parents, impact on, 23
parsimony, theory, 8
Parsons, Talcott, 267
patriarchy, feminism, 253–254
Pavlov, Ivan
  behaviourism, 99
  classical conditioning, 99
PCS model *see* personal-cultural-social (PCS) model
person-centred theory
  humanism, 138–139
  Rogers, Carl, 138–139
personal-cultural-social (PCS) model
  criticisms, 216
  key concepts, 211–214
  relevance for social work, 204
  shortcomings, 216
  stress, 213–214
personal fable, adolescence, 43

personality theory
defence mechanisms, 57–58
Freud, Sigmund, 56–58
personality typology, 89–90
phallic stage, psychosexual stages, 61–62
physical abuse, influences on behaviour 151–153
see also child maltreatment
Piaget, Jean, cognition/cognitive development, 111–112
Piaget's theory of cognitive development, 113–118
post-natal depression, developmental models, 35–36
post-traumatic stress disorder (PTSD), 189–190
sexual abuse, 154
sexual assault (rape), 160
poverty
resources distribution, 271–272
women, 254–255
power and control wheel, domestic violence, 158–159
practice, and theory, 7
preconscious, Topographical Conception, 55
predictive theory, 8
predisposing factors, mental health problems, 26–27
predisposition, genetic concepts, 22
pregnancy
alcohol/drug-related problems, 32
birth weight, 34–35
developmental models, 31–33
eclampsia, 34
FAS, 32
foetal period, 33–34
newborns, 35
nutrition, 32
prematurity, 34
stress, 31–32
teratogens, 32
prematurity, pregnancy, 34
preoperational stage (approximately 2–6 or 7 years), cognition/cognitive development, 116
protective factors, mental health problems, 26–27
psychoanalytic concepts, 52–56
see also Freud, Sigmund
criticisms, 71–72
debates, 71–72
defence mechanisms, 57–58
implications for practice, 72–73
Structural Conception, 54–55, 56–57
Topographical Conception, 54–56
psychoanalytic theory, 11
psychosexual stages
anal stage, 60–61
Freud, Sigmund, 59–62
genital stage, 62
latency stage, 62
oral stage, 59–60
phallic stage, 61–62
psychosocial theory
Erikson, Erik H., 63–64
life cycle, 63–64
PTSD *see* post-traumatic stress disorder
puberty, developmental models, 42–43
punishment, operant conditioning, 104–105

radical behaviourism, Skinner, B. F., 102
radical feminism, 251–252
rape, influences on behaviour, 160–161
reciprocity, families, 228–232
reinforcement, operant conditioning, 104
rejection, maternal rejection, 38
relationships, families, 228–232
relevance for social work
behaviour, 1–2
behaviourism, 98
biological influences, 15–16
cognition/cognitive development, 110–111
developmental models, 30–31
ecosystems perspective, 204
Ego Psychology perspectives, 76
Erikson, Erik H., 52
existentialism, 134–135
families, 220–221
feminism, 250–251
Freud, Sigmund, 51
humanism, 134–135
learning, 110–111
medical influences, 15–16
mental health problems, 170–172
Neo-Freudian perspectives, 76
personal-cultural-social (PCS) model, 204
socio-economic influences, 264–265
sociological influences, 264–265
systems theory, 203–204
theory, 4–7
trauma influences on behaviour, 150–151
resources distribution
poverty, 271–272
socio-economic influences, 270–272
sociological influences, 270–272
Richmond, Mary, 16, 206
Rogers, Carl
humanism, 135–136
person-centred theory, 138–139

self theory, 138–139
role theory, cognition/cognitive development, 123–124, 130–131
roles, families, 228–232
Romanov dynasty
genetic concepts, 21
haemophilia, 21
Rowntree, Seebohm, 266–267
Runciman, W. G. (Garry), 271–272

Sartre, Jean-Paul, existentialism, 141–142
Satir, Virginia, 223, 228–230
scapegoating, families, 230–231
scenario, theory, 5–7
schedules of reinforcement, operant conditioning, 105–106
schizophrenia, 184–189
types, 187
variability, 187
school, middle childhood, 41–42
self-actualization, humanism, 139–141
self-determination, medical model, 28
self-efficacy, cognition/cognitive development, 122
self-medication hypothesis, theory, 10
self theory
humanism, 138–139
Rogers, Carl, 138–139
sensorimotor stage (birth to 2 years), cognition/cognitive development, 115
separation-individuation theory, 91, 92, 94
sexual abuse
see also child maltreatment
influences on behaviour, 153–157
sexual assault (rape)
feminism, 259–260
influences on behaviour, 160–161
sexual orientation
adolescence, 44–45
developmental models, 44–45
sexual violence, feminism, 259–260
shaping, operant conditioning, 105
sibling rivalry, 84
Skinner, B. F.
behaviourism, 102
radical behaviourism, 102
'Skinner Box', behaviourism, 102, 107
social development, adolescence, 44
social learning theory, 10, 110–111
cognition/cognitive development, 120–121
learning, 120–121
social model, mental health problems, 171–172
social model of disability, medical model, 28
social workers, stress management, 165–166
socio-economic influences
behaviour, 264–274
historical background, 265–267
implications for practice, 273
key concepts, 267–270
macro-functional model, 268–270
relevance for social work, 264–265
resources distribution, 270–272
sociological influences
behaviour, 264–274
historical background, 265–267
implications for practice, 273
key concepts, 267–270
macro-functional model, 268–270
relevance for social work, 264–265
resources distribution, 270–272
sources of information, health-related conditions, 29
Spitz, Rene, 38
strengths perspective, 24–26
cf medical model, 25–26
stress
diathesis-stress model, 26–27, 177
PCS model, 213–214
pregnancy, 31–32
social workers, 165–166
stress management, 165–166
variables, 26
Structural Conception, psychoanalytic concepts, 54–55, 56–57
substance misuse/dependence, 192–196
suicide, 191–192
Sullivan, Harry Stack, 91–93
synergy, systems theory, 207
systematic desensitization, behaviourism, 106–107
systems theory, 7, 10, 203–209
boundaries, 207
criticisms, 216
diathesis-stress model, 209
entropy, 207
historical contributors, 204–206
implications for practice, 214–216
key concepts, 206–209
relevance for social work, 203–204
shortcomings, 216
synergy, 207

TA *see* Transactional Analysis
temperament, developmental models, 38–39
teratogens, pregnancy, 32
theory
adaptation, 7

approaches, 9
behaviour, 4–12
components, 7–8
comprehensive, 8
concise, 8
constructs, 7–8
criticisms, theoretical framework, 12
deduction, 8
dynamic, 8
empirical support, 11
ethical issues, 11–12
evaluating, 10–12
explanatory theories, 7
functions, 8–9
hypothesis, 8, 10
implications for practice, 9–12
induction, 8
learned helplessness theory, 10–11
macrosystems, 9
medical model, 9–10
microsystems, 9
models, 9
Occam's razor, 8
parsimony, 8
perspectives, 9
and practice, 7
practice, implications for, 9–12
predictive, 8
psychoanalytic theory, 11
relevance for social work, 4–7
scenario, 5–7
self-medication hypothesis, 6, 10
social learning theory, 10
systems theory, 7, 10
Theory of Multiple Intelligences, 126–128
Thompson, N., 7
Thorndike, Edwin
behaviourism, 100
law of effect, 100
toddlers
developmental models, 39–40
gender identity, 40
Topographical Conception
conscious, 55
preconscious, 55
psychoanalytic concepts, 54–56
unconscious, 55–56
Townsend, Peter, 271
trait theory, humanism, 135, 136–138
Transactional Analysis (TA), 94
Ego Psychology perspectives, 83
Neo-Freudian perspectives, 83
trauma influences on behaviour, 150–169
bereavement, traumatic, 162–163
child maltreatment, 151–157
domestic violence, 157–159
implications for practice, 163–166
relevance for social work, 150–151
sexual assault (rape), 160–161
stress management, 165–166
triangulation, families, 222–223
twin studies, genetic concepts, 21–22

unconscious, Topographical Conception, 55–56

violence, 164–165
von Bertalanffy, Ludwig, 204–205
vulnerability, mental health problems, 176–177
Vygotsky, Lev, cognition/cognitive development, 112, 205–206
Vygotsky's social cognition learning model, 118–119

Walker, Alice, 252–253
Watson, John Broadus, behaviourism, 100–102
Weber, Max, 266
WHO *see* World Health Organization
Winnicott, Donald, 93
women
see also feminism
crime, 256–257
domestic violence, 257–258
poverty, 254–255
World Health Organization (WHO)
health definition, 17
ICF, 18

young adulthood
developmental models, 46